Praise for *The Idea of Australia*

'A penetrating analysis, and a valuable contribution to the debate over what Australia is, once was, and might yet become.' **Melissa Lucashenko, Miles Franklin Award–winning author of** *Too Much Lip*

'Inevitably, *The Idea of Australia* will draw comparisons with *The Lucky Country*—a similarly timely, urgent and skilful reading of an Australian moment. Julianne Schultz brings a lifetime as scholar, editor, academic and arts leader to her analysis. The result is subtle, powerful and compelling—a book which demands attention, and rewards with a singular vision of the people we have become.' **Professor Glyn Davis AC, author of** *On Life's Lottery*

'As Australia lurches into a deeply uncertain and ill-defined future retarded by leaders who've forgotten how to lead, Julianne Schultz reflects on how we might shake off our fears, our mediocrity and our moral torpor, and rediscover the country we once promised to be.' **Kerry O'Brien, author of** *Keating*

'An unflinching look at the contradictory myths and realities that make up the idea of this country. Schultz has written a book that is timely, bracing, and ultimately hopeful.' **Yassmin Abdel-Magied, author of** *Yassmin's Story*

'*The Idea of Australia* is a triumph of art, politics, literature, history, and the deepest scholarship. Grand themes of dispossession, exclusion, equality, fairness, culture, media and "the incurable flaw" at the heart of our nation, interspersed with vignettes of personal reflection spring-boarding through a formidable sweep of history.

This is a book that sparkles with curiosity, self-reflection, and sophistication, a riveting journey through the uncertain terrain of the idea of a nation.

Julianne Schultz takes us into the darkest corners of a history we would rather forget and a history we thought we knew, always with hope for the better place we can become. History as a way of imagining the future. A towering achievement.' **Professor Jenny Hocking, author of** *The Palace Letters*

'Disruptive, bold and brilliant, *The Idea of Australia* is a work of masterful synthesis, intimate reflection and stunning vision. Schultz sees not what she wants to see, but what was there all along: a nation full of promise and heartache, ambition and self-defeat. The germ of truth and reason is there, if only we can find the courage to grow it.' **Professor Clare Wright OAM, Stella Prize–winning author of** *The Forgotten Rebels of Eureka*

'A cerebral *Who Do You Think You Are?* for a nation, inviting reflection and inciting action. A contemporary classic in the making.' **Associate Professor Christine Wallace, author of** *How to Win an Election*

'This vast and generous book shows the full beauty and possibility of the practice of paying attention—across all levels of life from the personal to the political. It's the result of asking how and why, of exploration and navigation, of connecting dots, and of insisting that the place that's now called Australia can—and must—be more than it has yet become.

The magnificent achievement of a magnificent and curious mind, this is a call—made with warmth, urgency and sparkling erudition—for what Julianne herself describes as "a response richer with courage and imagination than we have become accustomed to".

It's a demonstration of the best kind of imaginative leadership, the broadest understanding of this nation's mental, emotional and mythological ecosystems—and their extraordinary potential—and the mighty scope of critical thinking available to someone who's stood at the centre of national conversations and thought-leadership throughout a unique and impressive career.

Julianne both thinks and cares about this country: she's passionate about justice, equality, democracy, creativity, integrity and change; the ways that these things intersect; the ways they can be transformative and transformed. She is one of this country's most nuanced thinkers, not only dealing in but demanding complexity, lateral thinking, and always with an eye to the biggest of big pictures. The depth and breadth of her knowledge and inquiry has always felt two steps ahead of almost anyone else's as she has tackled—and lived—the ongoing work of understanding how and why we have the Australia we have now; its betrayals, its blindsides, its opportunities.

Above all, this is a personal and passionate account that does its readers the courtesy of trusting their intelligence and curiosity through the richness of both on the page.' **Dr Ashley Hay, author of** *A Hundred Small Lessons*

'Schultz, using the metaphor of the COVID X-ray, distils many occasions in our history from opaque to light revealing the good, bad and ugly of who we are as a nation. As we struggle through a global pandemic, we have choices and decisions to make to ensure a healthier, more equitable and peaceful world. *The Idea of Australia* is both inspirational and aspirational, guiding a light on a path of a journey we need to travel—that of truth-telling and reconciliation.' **Professor Patricia Davidson, Vice Chancellor and President, University of Wollongong**

'A wonderfully enthralling read. Julianne Schultz writes a powerful book which weaves together her personal stories and therefore lived experience with the great ideas that could and should enliven the notion and nation of Australia.

She starts from the deep truth embedded in Australia that it is unique as it is the home the oldest living cultures in the world. The silence that remains at the heart of our national debate means that we have failed to embrace the strength and beauty and shame at the heart of our nation. However she sees many signs for optimism: the exclusion that defined us a nation has been and is being broken down by examples such as the generosity of First Nations people found in the *Uluru Statement from the Heart* and the strength and courage of the four women who were the Australians of the Year in 2021.

Julianne Schultz's professional career taught her the value of listening—deep and respectful listening. If we listen carefully enough then we might just know our past well enough to be able to foster, if not utopia, then at least an enduring open, innovative and generous society.

Julianne Schultz's deep knowledge of and genuine love of Australia and Australians with all our virtues and faults has animated spirited insights in the idea of Australia that we turn away from at our peril.' **The Honourable Roslyn Atkinson AO**

'In pandemic times, Julianne Schultz takes the pulse of the nation. The result is an exhilarating personal journey through the landscape of ideas that shape Australia, written with a fierce belief in the power of culture, creativity and the arts to reinvent our politics. At once anecdotal and analytical, conversational and critical, Schultz's book is a response to the degradation of Australian public culture in the twenty-first century. It is a discerning distillation of a lifetime of "earwigging" the Australian people and a heartfelt cry of both frustration and hope. A brilliant successor to Donald Horne's *The Lucky Country*.' **Professor Tom Griffiths AO, Ernest Scott Prize–winning author of *The Art of Time Travel***

'*The Idea of Australia* seamlessly joins memoir, history, commentary and vision in an invigorating meditation on a "somewhere", Australia, whose stories have been Julianne Schultz's life work. It will be essential reading for anyone interested what is abiding about this country—both the good and the bad—as well as what it might become if we have the courage, will and imagination to renew it.' **Professor Frank Bongiorno AM, author of** *The Eighties*

'*The Idea of Australia* is a stunning book—thought-provoking, ambitious in scope, insightful, deeply personal, highly original, and thoroughly well-researched. With a fast-moving narrative and incisive commentary, it is above all enjoyable to read. It is a masterclass in using personal and family stories to explore and illuminate the larger and longer stories that affect us all.

In her search for the soul of the nation she calls home, Julianne Schultz deploys the investigative and storytelling skills of the experienced journalist, writer, and editor to produce a work that expertly and seamlessly combines history, memoir, political analysis, and cultural reflection. It is a remarkable history of the present.

The Idea of Australia expresses both love of a country the author feels fortunate to call home, and a deep anger at its failings and shortcomings, often along the fault lines of race, class, gender, and inequality. From this combination of deep attachment and trenchant critique comes an impassioned plea for a more confident, open, and compassionate society.

This book will surely stand as one of the most exciting and influential products of the COVID-19 pandemic, reverberating through public life long after the pandemic has ended.' **Professor Ann Curthoys AM, author of** *Taking Liberty*

'*The Idea of Australia* is a thoroughly researched view of this nation which draws on a lifetime's experiences and observations of the author, Professor Julianne Schultz.

Most notable is Julianne's deft sidestep of the common fault of journalists or academics who take to print. Almost invariably these classifications of author make the horrid error or writing for their peers, not for the general public.

The depth of her knowledge of Indigenous history and progression is astounding, as is her understanding of the intricacies of government and party politics.

A brand-new citizen arriving in Australia would need only to read this book to have a serious grip on where we as a nation and a people have come from, and what, in Julianne's studied view, the future holds.

It may have taken just a year or two to collate, but is truly representative of a lifetime spent with one's eyes and ears open—and the outstanding ability to explain it to us all. A marvellous read.

My one regret is not being aware when we worked together in the newsroom of the nickname she had earned as a schoolchild. Pure gold.' **Tony Koch, journalist**

'In a significant contribution to the never-finished project of forging a national identity, Julianne Schultz combines memoir, history and acute observation to dissect Australia's soul. Schultz cuts to the heart of the matter, identifying the structures of forgetting that prevent an honest reckoning with our past and invoking an idea of Australia that is braver and more generous.' **Peter Mares, author of** *Not Quite Australian*

'*The Idea of Australia* unmasks the tragic gap between the promise and realities of our nation. Applying a clear-eyed lens to our past, present and possibilities, Schultz's book should be compulsory reading—for every curious visitor, hopeful migrant and more securely embedded Australian.' **Dr Natasha Cica, author of** *Pedder Dreaming*

'In this beautifully written work Julianne Schultz searches astutely and bravely for the soul of our nation. Schultz rightly identifies in Australia a prevailing "Terra Nullius of the mind" which arises "by rarely going back to first principles and examining the past". She draws on a lifetime of rich experience as a senior journalist, academic, woman and mother. This book is no mere academic treatise. It engages the reader with clear, bold propositions backed up by evidence and argument.

The author confronts contemporary issues affecting First Nations people who "have experienced and continue to experience the bristles of exclusion" and forcefully contends that "this makes the offer from the delegates to the Uluru Constitutional Convention of a way to contribute to a fuller expression of Australian nationhood even more extraordinarily generous".

Schultz does not refrain from critique. In this respect her work reminds one of A.D. Hope's famous poem "Australia" written in 1939 describing our country as "a vast parasite robber-state/Where second-hand Europeans pullulate/Timidly on the edge of alien shores".

Schultz's work is not only a searingly honest look at the past but also a stirring call for "unusual urgency" on the pandemic and climate change in order to develop "a different industrial architecture" to "provide meaning and sustain lives and values that put respect and integrity first". After all, the search for our nation's soul demands not merely reflection but action.'
The Honourable Matt Foley

'Countries don't just happen—they need to be designed. Julianne Schultz mixes personal anecdote with deeply grounded research to show that it is not too late—we can still salvage an equitable and progressive country from where we are.' **Tone Wheeler, architect**

'Vivid and rich in historical detail, *The Idea of Australia* is an immersion in the characters, landscapes, ideas, stories and myths that have shaped our nation from deep time to the present. Julianne Schultz, one of Australia's foremost public intellectuals, blends memoir and personal experience with the forensic, insightful analysis for which she is renowned. She offers an object lesson in how the Humanities disciplines deepen and enrich our understanding of Australia's complex history, its promise, potential and foundational flaws. *The Idea of Australia* is a timely and urgent call for Australians to chart a shared path towards a bolder, more imaginative and inclusive idea of their country. At this critical juncture, our futures depend on it. Utterly compelling, engrossing and extraordinary.' **Professor Anne Tiernan, co-author of** *The Gatekeepers*

'*The Idea of Australia* is as unflinchingly personal as it is political. Her analysis winds back and forward through time like a fever-dream, weaving together events, facts and memories to the hope and ambition that we could do much, much better.' **Professor Pat Hoffie AM, editor of** *Place Matters*

'With skill and prescience, Julianne Schultz takes us on an intrepid expedition into the interior of the Australian mind, from the fault lines of its secretive, "Duck and Cover" past into a "She'll Be Trite" kind of present, with its "readiness to punish, shame and belittle". In the process, she reveals a society still trying to fashion its debatable future upon shaky foundations of insupportable myths, bruised hopes and the evasion of inconvenient truths: "Lost dreams and found dreams" in Australia . . . dancing together here in a mesmeric and highly digestible narrative.' **Dr Raymond Evans, author of** *A History of Queensland*

JULIANNE SCHULTZ

The Idea of Australia

A search for the soul of the nation

ALLEN&UNWIN
SYDNEY・MELBOURNE・AUCKLAND・LONDON

First published in 2022

Copyright © Julianne Schultz 2022

All rights reserved. No part of this book may be reproduced or transmitted in any form or by any means, electronic or mechanical, including photocopying, recording or by any information storage and retrieval system, without prior permission in writing from the publisher. The Australian *Copyright Act 1968* (the Act) allows a maximum of one chapter or 10 per cent of this book, whichever is the greater, to be photocopied by any educational institution for its educational purposes provided that the educational institution (or body that administers it) has given a remuneration notice to the Copyright Agency (Australia) under the Act.

Allen & Unwin
83 Alexander Street
Crows Nest NSW 2065
Australia
Phone: (61 2) 8425 0100
Email: info@allenandunwin.com
Web: www.allenandunwin.com

 A catalogue record for this book is available from the National Library of Australia

ISBN 978 1 76087 930 3

Author photograph by Nikki Short
Index by Garry Cousins
Set in 12/17 pt Adobe Garamond Pro by Midland Typesetters, Australia
Printed and bound in Australia by Griffin Press, part of Ovato

10 9 8 7 6 5 4 3 2 1

 The paper in this book is FSC® certified. FSC® promotes environmentally responsible, socially beneficial and economically viable management of the world's forests.

For my remarkable parents, Noel and Cynthia, my loving husband Ian and our brilliant children Isabelle and Carl. Your courage, imagination and generosity are my inspiration.

and

In memory of Anne Coombs, one of the fearless women who made Australia better. She dreamed big, achieved much, but died much too young.

To Miguel —
I hope you enjoy & find some insights into us odd Aussies!
Regards
Julia

'Attention is the rarest and purest form of generosity.'

Simone Weil

'Membership of the nation is defined in civic, not ethnic terms . . . an open, positive, warm-hearted nation is capable of appealing not just to dry reason, but the deep human need for belonging and the moral imperative of solidarity.'

Timothy Garton-Ash

'We raise questions about our individual or national identity as part of the process of deciding what we will do next, what we will try to become.'

Richard Rorty

'Be bold, be bold, be bold. How else are reforms won?'

Rose Scott

CONTENTS

1. Terra Nullius of the Mind — 1
2. Slightly Better Than Average, Again — 14
3. From Somewhere — 31
4. Stories We Tell Ourselves — 51
5. Architecture of Silence — 71
6. Hidden in Plain Sight — 93
7. A Fair Go — 116
8. Lucky, Not So Smart — 137
9. Utopian Dreaming — 154
10. Gliding Forward — 172
11. The Incurable Flaw — 198
12. Making the Nation — 213
13. Small Brown Bird — 233
14. The More Things Change . . . — 253
15. Personal Becomes Political — 272
16. Soul Destroying — 295
17. Remaking the Nation — 315
18. People Like Us — 339

| **19.** Power Players | 365 |
| **20.** From Little Things . . . | 391 |

Acknowledgements	417
Notes	420
Index	442

1
Terra Nullius of the Mind

AUSTRALIA REMAINS AN oddly amorphous idea. *What idea?* some ask. *No idea*, others respond. The continent is solid, physically distinctive and vast. But the idea of its essence, and what it might be, has been contested ever since British ships 'first rose like a cloud out of the sea'.[1] The definition of a nation that is more than a place is still a work in progress, denied by those who consider it 'the settler state known as Australia' but celebrated by those whose lives have been transformed by life in a relatively safe, rich and ordered society.

The paradox is that Australia is both solid and provisional. An island continent with thin soils, underground seas, rainforests, deserts, serpentine rivers, endless beaches and minerals accreted over millions of years. A derivative nation, ready to absorb and transform ideas carried on the wind like migratory birds from afar. A place where forgetting is essential, making a mockery of the most celebrated epigram, 'Lest we forget'. *Best we forget* would be more honest.

Describing Australia's defining nature beyond the physical—her spirit, her essence—rarely gets beyond worthy but anodyne statements of universal values, pride in democratic institutions, and boastful backslapping about being the most successful multicultural nation in the world. It has taken a long time for the inconvenient truth to penetrate that, for all the many and real achievements of the past two centuries, Australia is only truly unique as home for 65 millennia to the world's oldest continuing civilisation. The numbers drip off the pen, but the reality of what they mean—of how people lived, survived and thrived—forces a pause. Until that truth is fully embraced, the paradox will prevail, erode the soul of the nation and leave Australia half-formed.

For nearly 250 years, waves of new arrivals have landed, their minds packed with expectations shaped by images absorbed elsewhere. Even before the eleven ships in the First Fleet edged their way through Sydney Harbour's towering sandstone gateposts in 1788, ideas of Australia had taken root in other hemispheres. For millennia, philosophers, explorers, artists and novelists had conjured a Great South Land. For those who had always been here, the place and its spirit did not need conjuring; it was real, living and rich with meaning.

Relocation to the other side of the globe was, and often still is, traumatic and gruelling. It is scarcely surprising that the journey, the bureaucratic hurdles it demands and its settlement legacy, often dent curiosity about what came before. Instead, those setting foot on the vast, mysteriously inviting continent project new visions and dreams. These notions have over the centuries taken different forms: prison, frontier, colony, model society, experiment, deputy sheriff, utopia, wasteland. Or—prosaically, and with a sigh of relief—a country that works, most of the time.

New arrivals squint into the fierce sun to better focus their dreams and imagine a future. Those dreams are generally personal, sometimes opportunistic and often relieved, but they are seldom informed by knowledge of what came before, whether 10, 50, 200 or (heaven forbid) 65,000 years ago. By rarely going back to first principles and examining the past, a terra nullius of the mind has prevailed. Unchallenged tendrils of memory are easily twisted to gird myths.

Terra Nullius of the Mind

For English speakers who have a nodding acquaintance with other places touched by the British Empire, Australia seems reassuringly recognisable. With familiar institutions, language and place names, and the detritus of global popular culture. But even the most privileged stumble on the invisible trip-wires beneath the surface. Networks, history, custom, class and race make the seemingly familiar more complicated, at times confounding. Change, ambition and doing things differently are surprisingly hard in a place that is at once cosmopolitan and provincially deferential, young and ancient, in Asia but not of it, without much history yet brimming with it.

Generations of settlers, old and new, have generally preferred to think of Australia, literally and figuratively, as a blank slate on which their dreams could be etched. As the Sydney journalist Gavin Souter once observed, the 'child of 1788 is no father to the man of today'. Writing about his city in 1965, he found 'the echoes of the past too faint to hear', sensing that they had been 'shouted down by the present'.[2] This was plausible as the bustle of post-war growth obliterated the sandstone buildings of another era to make way for shimmering modernist towers of steel, concrete and glass. Entire inner-city neighbourhoods were bulldozed and their poor residents moved to new, distant suburbs. The complacency of British provincial life in the Southern Hemisphere unsettled by the arrival of millions of unconvincingly assimilated 'New Australians'.

Still, the elegant stylist wondered if 'the past still frets our subconscious like a wind at the door.' *But, does it really?* Gavin Souter asked. At the time, he thought not.[3] More than half a century on, the answer is yes. Forgetting is not as easy, or shamefully essential, as it once was. Close study has revealed much more about the place, her people and mores that gives reason to fret. The knowledge that trauma, like privilege, passes across generations forces a profound recalibration.

This may not matter much in the ebb and flow of daily life, although the appearance of First Nations place names in public spaces and the explosion of interest in family history suggest that tide is turning. Curiosity about things unspoken demands attention. Hidden tales emerge from chance encounters and the records of lives that have been stripped, by time and digitisation, of the fear and shame that once enveloped them. Even those intrigued by the words and stories that add a lot, and sometimes confound, are so busy juggling the demands of family, work and *esse* that there is little time to reflect on how these twigs of the past litter big-picture, public sense-making. That is left to those who seem to have the most to gain: leaders who prefer to burnish the surface. For all the millions of dollars spent on national branding campaigns, co-opting even Aboriginal mythology and superstars,[4] it has proved impossible to come up with a defining idea beyond the banal clichés and mythic half-truths that were once sufficient—brash, relaxed, sunburnt, vast, ancient, practical—and a joyously sentimental song that says simply 'we are one'.

IN THE 576 pages of *My Country*, the collection of 'a few' of the stories, essays and speeches he wrote over 45 years, journalist David Marr declared with characteristic passion:

> My country is the subject that interests me most, and I have spent my career trying to untangle its mysteries . . . Wanting to understand my country came, right from the start, with wanting it to change. I had a naïve notion that change would come simply by setting out the facts with clarity and goodwill. I had a lot to learn . . . Why, I wonder, is a secular, educated, prosperous and decent country so prey to fear and capable of such cruelty? Why are we ruled from the edges?[5]

These and similar questions have also shaped my career as a journalist and academic. My life as a woman and a mother formed another

Terra Nullius of the Mind

set of questions, and a perspective generally overlooked by the men who held sway. My search for the soul of the nation gathered new urgency as the dangers of being 'ruled from the edges' challenged the ethos I absorbed growing up. Australians have generally opted, often by very narrow margins, for conservative governments. The politics were not always immutable. The prevailing ethos was increasingly inclusive, tolerant, egalitarian, independent, ambitious, and engaged with the region. Ideas are fragile and need to be nurtured, but these produced such a prosperous and decent society, it was tempting to think they were robust. Then, in the early years of a new century, they came under serious challenge. The movement that emerged after Pauline Hanson was elected to federal parliament in 1996 seemed to defy logic and widespread support. The ideas of a generation, which had been displaced, were revived. Instincts that grew from feelings not thought bloomed on the coat tails of 'freedom' loving populist grievance, racism and lazy insularity. Before long, the parameters of a new/old ethos were being set from the edges. It was a voice of Old Australia and touched a nerve that easily spooked the mainstream parties. The electoral system means that the most disaffected 2 or 3 per cent can determine winners. Those 'on the edges' have power. Momentum built for years, with media amplification and little official challenge. It was marked by increasingly angry attacks on the First Nations peoples, women, immigrants, refugees, Muslims, lesbians, gays and others who had been welcomed into the mainstream. Abuse was normalised. In October 2018, One Nation's Pauline Hanson almost bluffed the Senate into supporting a motion declaring 'It's alright to be white.' She convinced 28 senators, including 23 from the Coalition, to vote with her. In the slippery language that has been used to excuse otherwise unconscionable actions in the past—protecting Aboriginal people by putting them in reserves, preventing drowning by stopping the boats and incarcerating refugees—Senator Hanson argued that not supporting the bill would prove 'anti-white racism is well and truly rife in our society'.[6] Senior and even self-described moderate members of the Liberal–National Coalition government, and sections of the Murdoch media, agreed.[7] Only three votes separated the ayes from the nos. It was not a joke. The Australian Senate very nearly endorsed the language of white supremacy. Reports flew around the world suggesting that the discredited White Australia policy was still alive. Personal and national shame was unavoidable—the ABC's Australia Talks survey showed that three-quarters of Australians know that racism is real and not directed at the white majority.

I have spent a lifetime travelling around Australia, earwigging and interviewing, attending meetings and conferences, reading and analysing. I have seen these racist sentiments, and their angry siblings—keeping women in the kitchen, refugees in detention and First Nations peoples out of sight or in jail—flow and ebb. They were once close to the surface but receded as the benefits of living in a more equal and diverse society were shared. And then, with a puff of wind from populist movements across the seas, they were back. The tail again wagging the dog.

Like David Marr and many others, I have sought to understand the impulses that allow some changes to happen, stall others and allow yet others to be wound back. Maybe it was simply a matter of time, demographics and education. As the eminent historian Linda Colley has observed, without catastrophe, most change takes three score years and ten to move from idea to reality. A lifetime. Whether the COVID-19 pandemic will prove to be a sufficient catastrophe to provoke a speedier, more profound transformation will only be judged when the history is written. In the meantime, this plague has provided a powerful X-ray of the strengths and weaknesses in the body politic. X-rays are diagnostic tools; they hint at what happened before, reveal fault lines and, when interpreted with expertise, suggest treatments that will mend the broken bone.

Terra Nullius of the Mind

My inquiry into the soul of this land began well before the pandemic revealed long-ignored or overlooked elements about the place and her people. Journalism was the ideal platform. Being an educated outsider is useful; it helps to see the whole fishbowl, not just the next fish. My starting point, growing up in country manses, was distinctive. For years I listened to sermons which explored questions raised in the Gospels. *What good will it be to gain the whole world, yet forfeit their soul? What can anyone give in exchange for their soul?*[8] It would have been nice not to be so poor, but the answer went beyond the material, to an inner life shaped by values. That was where the soul resided. As a child, hypersensitive to hints of hypocrisy, I tried to make sense of how a conscience influenced the way people lived and behaved. I watched and listened as parishioners chatted after church, at card nights and at other social functions. But I remained aloof in the way that the children of pastors have always learned to be. My interest was less in passing judgement, more in trying to understand the complications of life and what happened when conscience bumped into reality.

Over the decades since the 1960s, as my country and I grew up, I witnessed remarkable changes in social relations and understanding. Values stretched to embrace equality and justice, and acceptable behaviour changed. But still we cling to myths that help us live with contradictions, and lull us into not analysing so we don't have to take responsibility.[9] There is a persistent reluctance to grasp the knowledge needed to create new narratives and opportunities that might displace fear and allow a dynamic hybrid reality to flower. And there are enduring questions. Why are those who preach conservatism prepared to trash valuable institutions and the most humane values in pursuit of power? Why are our leaders so unambitious? Why do old fears and threats lie dormant for decades only to bubble to the surface, like groundwater from the vast Artesian Basin? What does it take to acknowledge the past, make amends and forge a new future?

In searching for answers, I had to dig further into the history I thought I knew: to reconsider the legacies of invasion, settlement and Federation, the timidity and ambition of the twentieth century. I have sought to see more sharply the patterns of periods of dynamism and openness, caution and censoriousness. I wanted to better understand the tension between labour and capital, men and women, black and white, immigrants and native born, conservationists and developers. I have endeavoured to make sense of the repeated, almost childish, reluctance to go to first principles, and the readiness to punish, shame and belittle.

This book distils my journey to plumb these questions, to braid narratives of my experience into the arc of history and contemporary issues, and to try to understand why some foundational flaws seem indelible.

Writing *The Idea of Australia* has provided me with a reason and opportunity to read scores of books that illuminate stories and debates that were once hidden. The silencing, during what has become known as the culture wars of the past 25 years, sent many scholars and family historians back to the archives. There they discovered stories that had been long forgotten or deliberately obscured. It is no longer an excuse to say, 'We didn't know', or to ask 'Why weren't we told?'

I wanted to understand how, for all her material success, and with more natural and institutional advantages than almost any other nation, many feel Australia has lost her moorings, morally and strategically. How we forgot our ambition to show the world what an inclusive, compassionate and humane society might achieve. How it *is* possible to embrace both collective good and individual achievement. Why we chose to allow many to live in poverty and without secure housing. Why our First Nations peoples are the most incarcerated in the world. Why we persistently resist learning about the past, let alone fully atoning for it. Why this essential step, to imagine and create a genuinely inclusive and robust future for all, is so hard.

Terra Nullius of the Mind

I have looked for stories that help explain why Australians repeatedly respond the way we do—both generously and churlishly, defensively and confidently. Stories that honour those who dreamed big and those whose smaller lives were a gift to those they touched. Stories that reflect on why we are so unwilling to reckon with the admittedly unedifying elements of history or explore in more detail the underpinnings of the great achievements and near misses. Stories that may even offer some insights to inspire new confidence.

Many suffered terribly, but for some these plague years have provided an unplanned opportunity for hibernation and reflection. For those of us unencumbered by the extra burdens of job insecurity, caring and home schooling, with good health, loving partners and comfortable homes, it was almost a gift. A time to read and write; to cook, garden and tidy; to think; and to find new ways of connecting with neighbours who were once invisible. As the lockdowns dragged on, they tested the resilience of even the most privileged. Domestic abuse, job loss, business collapse, hunger, anxiety and mental illness spiked and the pain in many people's lives could not be ignored.

Within weeks of the novel coronavirus making its way from bat to human and into our then-crowded airports in January 2020, it became clear that the oldest unresolved tropes in Australia's foundation story were set to be replayed. All around the world, commentators talked about the COVID X-ray revealing the broken bones of societies and institutions. And so it was here. Resilience, compassion, adaptation and readiness to cooperate for the common good came from one X-ray plate; longstanding fault lines of race, class, inequality and the legacy of underinvestment in public services came from another. Bitter, sometimes ideological harshness that could be papered over in the good times became vast cracks. The poor, many of whom were redefined as essential workers, were, as always, the most vulnerable.

People of Chinese and, later, Indian heritage again became targets. The freedom of association trumpeted in the Australian Values

Statement[10] had to be tested in the courts to allow the truth that black lives matter to be demonstrated in the streets. Women, recent arrivals and visa holders were again treated as second class. The drawbridge to what was once called the Hermit Democracy was pulled up. For months planes with thousands of empty seats arrived at Sydney Airport every day. The ability to come and go was determined by nameless officials behind computer screens. Refugees, marooned international students and the undocumented languished, depending on charities supported by the kind hearted. Citizens living abroad felt abandoned and betrayed, some were even threatened with jail and fines if they sought to return home. Safety prevailed; fear was the greatest distraction, and it sapped imaginative empathy. It was better than mass deaths and collapsing systems, but a far-from-perfect skeleton for a nation.

What made the pandemic a unique global and domestic crisis was that it arrived in the sails of a vast ship of change. It is always hard to identify a catastrophe as it is unfolding, but this was one that had been brewing for a long time. It had many ingredients: climate change, globalisation, geopolitics, inequality, crumbling faith in democracy and institutions, and the digitisation that at once makes the world smaller and more threatening.

When what became known as the Spanish flu swept the world in 1918–19, the population was just under two billion people. A century later, the new coronavirus had nearly eight billion potential hosts. Epidemiologists had been warning for decades that the incursions into the natural world from this population growth, and the land clearing and climate change that necessarily accompanied it, would inevitably provide a ready pathway for viruses to move across species. The ease of transmission was unimaginable a century before. Never had so many people been so mobile: jumping on and off planes, and moving from densely populated cities to remote regions all over the globe. Human beings on the move were the perfect vectors for a virus to achieve its ambition of spread. Until it hit the hurdle of human genius in the form of genetic science, vaccines, public health and global supply chains.

Terra Nullius of the Mind

Crises always provoke a reaction. Those that are recognised early provide an inflection point, a moment when the shortcomings of the past might be tackled. As the Australian response swung into action in March 2020, it was clear that the immediate problem of a rampant virus and limited hospital capacity would be addressed. Medical advice would prevail. A once unimaginable direction to close schools and businesses, stay at home and stop working was eased by more money than had ever before been despatched from the public purse.

In the time-honoured Australian way, systems swung into action, announcements were made and made again, interest groups were accommodated, but big underlying issues were ignored. Dollars flooded into bank accounts, reports of corruption reached new levels, and institutions weakened by faith in the market failed. The notion of grabbing the crisis to imagine the future languished. As Sean Kelly wrote in *The Game*, 'we have all become incredibly skilled at finding ways not to look at what is in front of us'. There were many projects, some that had struggled for support for years, but the single biggest idea—a gas pipeline to connect supplies on one side of the nation, tied to the $1.5 billion Modern Manufacturing Strategy on the other side of the country—was mocked as uneconomic, and untimely as climate change recalibrated, and economies seemed to stall. The decision to scrap a $90 billion contract with the French for submarines and a new strategic alliance, and to rely once again on the United Kingdom and United States, was condemned by former prime ministers on both sides as a strategic mistake for an independent nation.[11]

The curious mix of arrogance, insularity and lack of ambition was manifest in 'the plan' Prime Minister Scott Morrison prepared for the United Nation's COP 26 summit in Glasgow in November 2021. The policy was showered with ignominy. Lord Deben, chair of the UK Climate Change Committee, spoke with (imperial) paternal distress when he described it as 'disappointing' and 'sad'. The prime minister had called it 'The Australian Way' but failed to define what that might mean. His critics suggested political paralysis, rather than the sunny uplands of a pragmatic, future-focused, well-resourced nation. Maybe, Peter Lewis, *The Guardian*'s pollster, argued, it meant to 'play friends off against each other, lurching into complex relationships like a drunk on a bender, upending tables and demanding someone buy you your next drink . . . to rat on your mates when you have a blue . . . deflecting blame when you get called out, using others as a human shield rather than taking responsibility yourself'.

Australia shrank after the enormous losses of the First World War. Despite the boastfulness of political leaders that war made the nation, it became more insular and provincial. The lesson of this became clear during the Great Depression, which was made worse for Australians by bad policy decisions. Those who lived through it were determined those mistakes would not be repeated. The next war provided the impetus they needed to fundamentally change the inward-looking society that had evolved. Even before the bombs of the Second World War devastated Darwin, planning and urgent discussions had begun about how to use the crisis to construct a modern, well-educated, more independent, industrial nation.

A pandemic is not a war. But COVID-19, moving as it did across species in one of the epicentres of 21st century global power, is an early warning that climate change may be as profound as war. It will need all the brains and perspectives possible. Like the pandemic, it cannot be solved by economics and science alone, or together. Solutions will need the insight into the human condition that comes from philosophy, psychology, anthropology and history—approaches that make provincial politicians nervous. Ways of seeing they have encouraged us to forget or ignore and branded as dangerous. The pandemic is best thought of as the canary in the mine of the enormous transformation of climate change that will reshape the world. Putting the domestic COVID X-ray into this context demands a response richer with courage and imagination than we have become accustomed to.

Terra Nullius of the Mind

People of my generation—late baby boomers—have in many ways been blessed. We have spent our lives in an increasingly open era, wars touched most of us lightly, education granted us the means to experience a world that was more accessibly connected than ever before in human history. Our values were shaped in a time when expanding ideas of human rights were progressively recognised and supported by a society with enough resources to make them real. This unlikely legacy of the conflagration and human sacrifice in the wars before we were born was a gift. The Universal Declaration of Human Rights has still not been adopted in Australia, but over a lifetime its impact has transformed and shaped expectations of collective rights and responsibilities. The increasingly noisy mantra of libertarian freedom misses this core point.

Many of us have been able to pass these blessings to our children, who are more open minded, worldly and informed than any previous generation. Our ideas have become their instincts, just as D.H. Lawrence predicted. It is confronting to realise that they now face a more challenging and constrained future than we could have imagined as we nursed them as babies and watched them as they grew. Climate change, inequality and environmental degradation have all been exacerbated by neoliberal economics. The gaps between generations, and between the haves and have-nots, have increased.

This book explores some of these tensions, unpicking the unexamined myths, the nature of power and the way it is exercised, and pointing to the reasons why this cannot be a crisis that we shamelessly squander. By exploring different ideas of Australia, I hope to trigger conversations that will help us find a pathway to a future that learns from the best (and worst) of the past and suggests a way of imagining a new outward-looking, expansive, inclusive and innovative society—one that will make us, to borrow the slogan of a northern New South Wales political party, 'slightly better than average, again'.

2

Slightly Better Than Average, Again

As CAPTAIN ARTHUR Phillip's little flotilla made landfall after nine months at sea, the old men and women of the Gweagal and Bediagal clans on the low-lying shores of Botany Bay sang songs of expulsion and the young men repaired their spears. Phillip had prepared his 'Noah's Ark of small-time criminality' with meticulous attention to detail, double checking the refit of merchant ships for human cargo and counting supplies. He was driven by duty and Enlightenment ambition, with a vision of a different sort of penal settlement on communal land, without slaves or arbitrary punishment. His brief was filled with misinformation so his vision was soon found wanting. Before long, skirmishes with the Gadigal people began, and transported thieves 'walked the streets in irons, pulled ploughs like oxen, and nursed their hatreds'.[1] In this punishing environment, far away from the centre of authority in London, greed, fear and personal ambition prevailed. First Nations peoples died in battle and from disease as the penal settlements grew, convicts laboured and escaped, settlers cleared the land, created families and built. Within decades the settlement gave way to colonies, colonies to states, states to Federation, Federation to independent nationhood.

Slightly Better Than Average, Again

Ever since this makeshift settlement was established in 1788 on the angophora-fringed fingers of Sydney Harbour, there have been contests. Between people and ideas. Between individualism and collective good. This runs like a motif through politics and public life. It was there in the debates in the colonial parliaments, and in the newspapers that reported and challenged the powers that be; in the conferences that shaped Federation; in later decisions about minimum wages, education, migration and industry; and in repeated disputes about conscription, sovereignty and geopolitics.

These arguments have a long history with well-known protagonists. Jeremy Bentham, the English social reformer, was one. The polymath philosopher, democrat and prison designer was an advocate for government that ensured the greatest good for the greatest number. He thought and wrote a lot about the settlement that became Australia. Today Bentham's 'auto-icon'—his skeleton, dressed in clothes and topped with a replica wax head, with his favourite walking stick, Dapple, in hand—sits in the middle of the student atrium at University College London. It is on display, just as Bentham requested in his will. His prolific writings were widely read in the colonies and provided a counterweight to the prevailing authorities. He opposed transportation, favoured self-government, and urged that land should be sold, not taken.[2] He considered the failure to come to a legal agreement with traditional owners a flaw and predicted it would be 'incurable'.[3] On the other side of the argument, those who grew rich from this failure could see no flaw. Ever since, their successors have prevaricated, denied, co-opted and made minor concessions to maintain the status quo—so comfortable for them—that grew from it. It has, so far, proved to be incurable, just as Jeremy Bentham foretold.

This vast land, that First Nations peoples consider 'unceded and sovereign', has a life of its own. Elyne Mitchell wrote the Silver Brumby books from her home near the Snowy Mountains—Ngarigo and Walgal country—and observed that anyone who paid attention knew the land 'held dreams far, far older than history'. Land was, and still is, the key to power and wealth. People, institutions and culture followed.

The governors despatched from Britain to create a new outpost were first captivated and then enraged by the million people living on the continent. Joseph Banks, the gentleman scientist who did more than anyone else to shape this imperial project, was certain it was 'thinly inhabited' and there would be little resistance. When this proved wrong, he added human heads to his shopping list of flora and fauna. Pemulwuy, the 'brave independent' Eora warrior, his name derived from the Dharug word for 'earth', waged a twelve-year guerrilla war against the new arrivals in his domain of what they called Sydney. Rather than being captured and tried, he was assassinated with official sanction in 1802, his head preserved in a jar and sent as a trophy to Banks in England—one that, unlike many of his other antipodean artefacts, he did not share with his collaborators in other museums.[4] The failure to negotiate treaties and provide a legally robust basis for settlement was unusual at the time and is inexcusable now, a failure that demonstrates that the foundation of the nation is unresolved.

At heart, the core challenge remains how to synthesise ancient and modern ways of being, both temporal and physical. Even before the anticipated ravages of climate change began to take their toll, Australia had established herself as a world leader in extinction—of flora, fauna, languages. For First Nations peoples, the gifts of nature are essential, not commodities to trade. The earth is as alive as any mother sharing her DNA. Everything flows from this simple but confounding fact. Reverence of the land is shared by many ancient systems of sense making, grounding law, religion and morals to inform and shape everything. On this continent it produced a system of knowledge and belief that makes the Christian idea of the Holy Trinity seem simple.

The founding principle of modern Australia could not be more different. It depends on land. Land that is for taking, buying, selling, clearing, developing, farming, digging up and profiting from. Debates over how to allocate the land that had been claimed in the name of King George III prefigured later disputes about who owned the gold and other minerals just under the surface. Official patronage was the key. Thus, the ongoing political tension between landowners and the rest was set. Centuries later decisions about land use are still most likely triggers of corruption inquiries. Most jurisdictions, excluding the Commonwealth, ban donations by property developers.[5]

Property ownership and the use of the nation's 7.6 million square kilometres of earth for mining, agriculture and development continue to be the bedrock of wealth and influence. Native title has, after protracted legal action, returned more than one-third of the country to its traditional owners, but their rights are limited.[6] In aggregate, each square kilometre is shared by just three people, enough to make everyone rich. But not everyone gets a share. Some, like the legendary and ill-fated Greek King Croesus, became unimaginably wealthy through the fruits of the land. The richest individuals enjoy a time-honoured status that tracks through two centuries of pastoralists, miners and developers. Australia's national wealth still, primitively, derives from this lopsided dependence on land, minerals and global trade.

Patrick Wolfe was an iconoclastic scholar of settler colonialism who came to believe that the quest for land more than anything else shaped societies like Australia. At heart was a brutal 'logic of elimination': killing, removing, jailing, neglecting, assimilating and culturally absorbing traditional owners to seize the land.[7] If ever proof were needed that this mentality, which had sat unchallenged at the core of the national psyche, was no longer unassailable, it was displayed with remarkable clarity in the early months of the pandemic. Rio Tinto, the world's second-largest minerals corporation, deliberately and knowingly blew up the Juukan Gorge caves and their 46,000-year-old treasures for another $135 million of Pilbara iron ore. When the traditional owners, the Puutu Kunti Kurrama and Pinikura peoples, objected, the response in global financial centres to condemn the action took the company by surprise. The rules of engagement had changed; respecting traditional owners was no longer an optional extra. The laws still worked to favour miners, but three senior executives lost their lucrative jobs. This was unprecedented in the land Down Under, 'where men plunder'. The oldest contest was revived; but there could no longer be just one winner who took it all.

―――

ON THE NIGHT of 2 January 1788, not long before *Scarborough* made landfall in what was to become Botany Bay, her relieved convict passengers put on a play for their fellow travellers. Their spirit of make-believe had survived the arduous journey. Eight years later the colony's baker Robert Sidaway supervised the building of a Georgian theatre, with a pit, gallery and boxes, and became its first impresario.[8] Audiences of former convicts, soldiers and settlers paid as they would in London, according to class and means. A seat in a box cost five shillings, two and six in the pit, and those in the gallery paid a shilling. Others were let in to be entertained by convict actors whose 'emigration . . . proved most useful to the British nation' if they had meat, flour or spirits to trade.[9] Four years later, when Philip Gidley King became governor of New South Wales, he closed the theatre in a fit of pique. For five months this unlikely audience had laughed as the Lord Chief Justice in Shakespeare's *Henry IV Part One* was mocked and insulted. It must have felt deliciously familiar, risky and dangerous. Governor King took it personally and razed the playhouse. There would be no more performances for three decades. A tradition of censorship was born, and a creation story that put power and culture at odds.

As this suggests, many of those who started to make their futures in the Great South Land were neither passive nor ignorant. It was a motley crew and an ethos evolved over time informed by contest.

Slightly Better Than Average, Again

Administrators influenced by the liberalism of the age jockeyed for support; those exiled because of their politics found new followers; humanitarians who considered transportation a form of slavery lobbied London and challenged those who feared losing free labour; missionaries keen to spread the word of their god were recruited; scientists and explorers sought the new and exotic; and refugees from poverty and failed European revolutions pursued democratic visions that tempered the ambitions of the land grabbers, slave traders and craven administrators. They all hungrily consumed news that arrived by ship and later by telegraph—the quarterly journals of ideas produced in Britain, American literary magazines, and local newspapers.[10]

By the 1880s, some of the most important writers of the age made the long journey and described a most unlikely place. It was 'the land of newspapers',[11] one writer observed; newspapers flourished in cities and new townships, delivered free and stuffed with government advertising. Some were radical, most were not. All enjoyed more freedom than the press in Britain but were almost always ready to acquiesce to official demands and the interests of the powerful. The promise and responsibility of the fourth estate was carefully and persuasively argued in the journals that travelled across the oceans to the new settlement.[12] By the turn of the century, Australians were the most literate people in the world, voracious readers, and the most lucrative market in the empire for British book publishers.[13] Newspapers were the essential source of news and the home of advertising. They soon became a proxy for power that spooked politicians.

The idea that newspapers could hold government to account and detach their owner's economic interests was fragile in the nineteenth century, but increasingly found wanting in the next. Ever since William Charles Wentworth launched *The Australian* in 1824, in opposition to the government-sanctioned *Sydney Gazette*, owning a newspaper has been a passport to political influence. It is one of Australia's most enduring features, a breeding ground for oligarchs and reformers, those currying favour and exercising influence. A century after Wentworth tested authority with his paper, Keith Murdoch took political influence to a new level. He dispensed favours, sought rewards and shaped the society with his papers. He was a manager, not an owner, and his son Rupert learned the difference. Keith Murdoch made no secret of his desire for power. As another child of the manse, he had seen the advantages that were bestowed on the well connected. He assiduously sought entry to this select club through his journalism and used it shamelessly to advance the interests of his patrons and those he favoured. It was an approach to life and work that sowed the seed of his son's unprecedented global media empire, and one of the enduring characteristics of the nation. Rupert Murdoch unapologetically flaunts his influence: *what is the point of owning a media empire if you don't use it?*[14]

Over a century, the 'land of newspapers' gave way to the most concentrated media system in the developed world. Even conservative prime ministers conceded they didn't 'have the guts' to challenge the proprietors.[15] Keith Murdoch's practice of acquisition, merger and closure marked the beginning of a trend that led inexorably to his son's company owning three-quarters of the nation's newspapers. The steps towards this outcome were shaped by governments. The Menzies government enabled the newspaper companies to also own television stations and deliver flickery black-and-white images to living rooms. By the time these images were fleshed out in full colour, three families—Fairfax, Packer, Murdoch and The Herald and Weekly Times (the company once led by Keith Murdoch)—were beneficiaries of one of the most concentrated, and profitable, media systems in the world. They were ubiquitous, promoting programs and stars across their newspapers, magazines, television and radio channels. When in 1986 the Labor government gave them the choice to become queens of screen or princes of print the system blew up, but within two decades the media was as concentrated as ever. Cities that once had competing morning and evening newspapers had just one. Monopolies became normal, newspapers literally shrank, television morphed into a carefully crafted distraction pretending to be reality, and radio became a platform for hectoring. By the time the internet remade the information world, and another government relaxed media ownership rules and regulation, the space for informed public discussion was hard to find amid the noisy churn of constant news, with its carefully managed claims and counterclaims designed to obfuscate and distract.

———

WHEN I WAS offered the job of creating and editing *Griffith Review* in 2003, the only thing that was not negotiable was the name. Glyn Davis, the recently appointed vice-chancellor of Griffith University, and I had been discussing the diminishing space for public-interest journalism for years. From his vantage point at 100 George Street, Brisbane, as the director-general of the Queensland state premier's department, he had watched with disquiet as the city's monopoly newspaper grew thinner and more strident. The ABC had become more cautious and less local as it reeled from ever more cuts, while serious people of ideas—writers, academics, journalists—found it harder to find platforms for ideas that needed more than 600 words to be expressed.

Griffith Review was designed to address this by fostering and informing public debate. As I wrote at the time, it sought 'to provide a bridge between the expertise of specialists and the curiosity of readers, to explore issues at greater length and with more time for reflection than is possible under the relentless pressure of daily events, to provide opportunities for established and emerging writers, thinkers and artists to tease our complexity and contradiction and propose new ways of thinking and seeing'.[16] Each issue would be organised around a topical theme, aiming to amplify the big issues, add critical perspectives and personal insights, and be both creative and analytic. It was to be a 21st-century reinvention of the quarterly journals that had long informed public life in Australia.

The scope was vast, but I worried that using the word 'Griffith' in the title would suggest it was just another branch of the university's public relations machine. We agreed it would range beyond the university, beyond Brisbane and Queensland; draw in writers and readers from around the nation; and become an independent showcase of quality writing, serious thinking and new ideas—a national publication with a Queensland accent.

There was a solution to the issue of the name: tying the 'Griffith' in the title back to the university's then overlooked namesake, Sir Samuel Griffith. He had been an important figure in colonial Queensland and in Federation, a key author of the Australian Constitution, a former Queensland premier and attorney-general, the author of its Criminal Code, and the first chief justice of the High Court of Australia. His nickname was 'Slippery Sam'. There were few biographies of the man to flesh out his story, and his name had been appropriated by groups associated with libertarian think tanks. We settled on describing him as 'iconoclastic and non-partisan'. Over time, we learned that his legacy was more complicated. This did not really capture the fraught complexity of his contribution in a brutal colony.

The rhythm of my life for the next two decades was set: six months before publication, choose a theme; commission and edit the 30 or so contributions; work through unsolicited manuscripts; write an intro that tied it together; and push it out to bookshops and subscribers into the media and scores of public events. My mentors advised me to trust my judgement when deciding on themes and choosing writers. *You'll know what's right*, they said. As each edition landed and touched a topical nerve, it seemed they were correct. It looked uncanny as the themes coincided with the most urgent subjects of public debate by the time the book was published. I was often asked how I chose, how they managed to be so on topic. I would generally brush the question aside. I said anyone who paid attention and had worked in the media learned to anticipate. That the best writers are artists attuned to the undercurrents of public life.

This was too self-deprecating. In truth, understanding and anticipating the ebb and flow of national conversation comes from my deep and somewhat disgruntled immersion in the underlying threads and stories that bind this *somewhere*. The silences and the noise, the forgotten histories and the people who made them, the deep tendrils of trauma and shame, and the celebration of joy and good fortune. With variations, and with remarkable, often unwarranted resilience, they return time and again like an incoming tide.

DESPITE THE LACK of resolution between history and myth, I feel fortunate that Australia is the *somewhere* I call home. I imagine how dull it would be to come from a country whose stories have been publicly picked over and known for centuries, where there is little new to uncover, few opportunities for discovery. Over my lifetime, Australia has mystified, disappointed, delighted and challenged me. She has slowly revealed more of herself, peeling back layers that were once invisible or impenetrable. As the veils have lifted, I, like many others who were paying attention, recalibrated ideas of the place and her people. This made it possible to better imagine her potential, to experience the joy she offers, and to learn from her deeply embedded, multifaceted trauma and shame as much as from her successes.

The Australia I know today is much more complex and interesting than I could have imagined in the parochial community where I spent my childhood, or the frustrating insularity of country-town Brisbane under a punishing but 'slap dash, she'll be right kind of autocracy'.[17] The population has since doubled and become more diverse, better educated, more aware of the world, richer—but meaner at the edges, thanks to a churlish, cynical public domain.

The society that has grown on this continent and its islands is, at its best, generous, open minded, curious, respectful, ready to adapt and accommodate. At its worst, it is puffed up with hubris, complacent, lazy, judgemental and angry. We have built enduring institutions, a strong economy, rich cultures and respectful values. Too often, though, the default response is grounded in fear rather than the generosity that should amplify the gifts we have been given, and those we have taken without asking.

In seeking to articulate an idea of Australia that is now fit for purpose, there is a need to tease out the tendrils of the past that have been absorbed without thought, to isolate and cauterise the unexamined and unlovely DNA that will otherwise pass epigenetically from one generation to the next. Transformation is at the heart of the Australian story, though rarely celebrated as a guide for the future. In 1836, decades before he published his epoch-defining book *On the Origin of Species*, Charles Darwin observed the colony with the same critical eye that would later inform the theory that bears his name. He considered the convicts shameless, inclined to cowardice, unable to exercise a plan that required cool assessment or courage, and susceptible to government bribes. '[As a] place of punishment . . . as a real system of reform it has failed but . . . as a means of making men outwardly honest—of converting vagabonds, most useless in one hemisphere, into active citizens of another, and thus giving birth to a new and splendid country—a grand centre of civilisation—it has succeeded to a degree perhaps unparalleled in history.'[18]

David Marr wrote that he was no longer sure that change could come by setting out the facts with clarity and goodwill. I too am no longer sure where these transformative conversations will happen. There is more knowledge than ever, but institutions have been deliberately weakened. Policy changes are held captive by political gridlock. Politics so professionalised that it is detached from values. Political party membership has shrunk to a couple of hundred thousand people. The boundaries around communities of interest are ring-fenced by social media opprobrium. The news media that was once a relatively dispassionate clearing-house has become a noisy shadow. The public broadcasters that provided the bedrock and springboard for so many conversations, educating generations in the process, have been weakened almost to breaking point by political and commercial attacks. The internet, which once promised a new openness, has delivered access to more information than was once imagined possible. It also gave the megaphone to the loudest voices and pushed many into ghettos of like-minded people to prevent being overwhelmed.

The gap between what polls show people want and what political leaders offer has rarely been greater or more skilfully manipulated. It is encapsulated in three competing television programs broadcast every evening. *The Drum* on the ABC is led by two spirited, highly intelligent women and a line-up of smart, thoughtful, often unlikely participants from all corners of the land—people who look like those you see every day—who have considered what they want to say. *The Project* on Network 10 is exercised by similar issues but with more glitz, its savvy hosts well aware that their younger audience is also preoccupied with big social issues. At the same time, regional commercial television broadcasts programs fronted by a handful of Sky News commentators once restricted to the tiny audience on Foxtel. They shout their opinions at the camera, puffed up with angry certainty, ready to harangue and belittle those who do not share their views. The difference between these programs could not be greater, and embodies the tension between public life as it is done and how it might be.

In this noisy, opinionated world, where people are readily and powerfully bullied, where the swirl of events makes it hard to get your moorings, the new silence is more censorious than any social media pile-on. In a lifetime in journalism, I have never witnessed political leaders so quick to refuse to be interviewed, but happy to play favourites behind the scenes with leaks and text messages. Not being available for an interview was once a matter of some moment, the last tactic of a politician who wanted to punish or hide. Now it is routine. Day after day, presenters say: *We sought an interview, but they were unavailable.* The shamelessness that makes it possible for leaders to tough out crisis after crisis while waiting for focus to shift is extraordinary. A refuge of professional cynics exploiting short attention spans.

Whether this refusal to engage will satisfy those impatient for a richer, more diverse and more nuanced conversation about who we are—and, more importantly, who we might be—remains to be seen. Transformative public discussions have forced previous changes, and the big sweep of history suggests they will again. The do-nothing compromises, lack of imagination and courage, and short-term solutions favoured by those who are happy to live with broken principles to maintain power and the status quo, are at the heart of the problem. As the world shifts around us, adjusting to the changing climate and geopolitics, it will soon be clear that standing still is not a luxury we can afford.

―――――

COVID-19 MADE LANDFALL in Australia immediately after the summer fires that for weeks had turned the sky orange and thickened the air with ash, and left people exhausted and fearful about the future. Thirty-four people and at least a billion animals had been killed, more than 3000 homes incinerated, and seventeen million hectares destroyed. The fires came at the end of the hottest year on record; the environmental forces unleashed by climate change were unpredictable but could no longer be wished away. The COVID X-ray revealed in sharp relief what was broken in country after country. The fissures broke along the old lines. Deep race memories inflected the earliest response, and then the X-ray became even more revealing.

We were surprised by people's willingness to go home and stay there, their growing trust in expertise and leaders, the speedy revival of the states as real centres of power, the ease with which international borders shut, and migration—the bedrock of the economy for decades—stopped. We were stunned by the real costs and limits of the privatised public services, the ease with which women were treated as second-class citizens, the hypocrisy of calling underpaid essential workers 'heroes', the cavalier treatment of visa holders. We were taken aback by a renewed focus on inequity, mental health and domestic abuse, but not surprised by the continuing prevarication about the value of Black lives. We were disappointed by the ease with which education and culture, the sectors that help us make meaning, were sidelined. Each of these responses can be traced back to debates that have remained unresolved throughout the life of the nation.

Heeding the well-worn adage, *Never let a crisis go to waste*, Australians did not take long to amplify the simmering but unresolved discussion about what sort of nation this is and might be. Some preferred to use the disasters as a propaganda tool to entrench the status quo. But in the early months of the first lockdowns, there was a sense of urgency and collective readiness to do things differently. No one would wish for disaster to force difficult conversations and changes that would otherwise be unwelcome. But a global pandemic that was, initially at least, relatively well managed by a nation that is also an island continent, suggested that Australia could demonstrate what an inclusive, fair and smart group of people might achieve. Not by luck, but by design. Australians behaved well and reaped the rewards. People around the world gazed with admiration and envy upon an apparent nirvana unencumbered by the past, safe and free.

That was until they looked more closely. In the second year, the fault lines became more obvious and invited international criticism. Even the liberal American magazine *The Atlantic* asked, 'How long can a country maintain emergency restrictions on its citizens' lives while still calling itself a liberal democracy?'[19] Libertarian politicians and commentators who take their cues from American think tanks were happy to amplify this message, encouraging distrust and hinting at the need for civil insurrection. The front pages of the Murdoch papers in states with Labor premiers were relentless in their condemnation. It was scarcely surprising that some saw an uncanny similarity between the angry mob that stormed the United States Capitol in January 2021, and the one that pissed on the Shrine of Remembrance in Melbourne nine months later.[20]

The anger that was so readily stoked was a reminder that behind the promise of the land of a fair go is a complex society that has increasingly advantaged the few; that is cavalier about its unique natural environment; that is wilfully, stubbornly reluctant to change; and that is unwilling to examine founding principles and make tough decisions. As always, the gap between expectations and delivery spoke volumes. This was not another *Aussie, Aussie, Aussie! oi! oi! oi!* moment, but a time to recalibrate and consider anew what a robust idea of Australia might look like in a century that is likely to be beset by disasters beyond our control, even when we pull up the drawbridge.

The moment that many had been looking for to drive change seemed to have arrived. Civil society and interest groups with well-developed agendas for a more sustainable, equitable, inclusive, respectful and innovative society sprang into virtual action. There were more webinars and Zoom chats on offer than it was possible to find time for in even the most sophisticated electronic diary. Hundreds of thousands signed up to hear experts, ask questions, make suggestions, and discuss how to reset the economic and social levers to ensure that the country could continue to flourish in an unexpectedly uncertain future. They discussed new ideas, built community networks, tried to reach beyond the clichés, published books, distilled and adapted the best thinking from around the world.

Slightly Better Than Average, Again

The year before the pandemic, the ABC's huge Australia Talks survey had shown that the population was receptive to social and economic change, but had no expectations of the political leadership needed to make it possible. Two crises in a few months was a genuinely unprecedented situation, a reminder from the gods of the duty of stewardship of people and place[21]—maybe this would be the moment for a serious conversation about what a future Australia might be like. As the bellwether sign outside the Gosford Anglican Church declared in late May 2020: 'Let's not get back to normal. Normal wasn't working.' This view was widely but far from universally shared.

But those with the controlling hand on Australian politics and public life were not keen on informed and nuanced discussion that might require action or disrupt the status quo. Rather than forming a brains trust to boldly imagine and advocate a better future, official advice shrunk. Political language was stripped of meaning in well-rehearsed talking points that revealed much by saying little. The discussion that civil society engaged with so actively barely made it onto the public agenda. Power is never happily ceded by those who hold it.

There were lessons to be learned from the initial response to the fires and the lockdown—about a generosity of spirit, and a willingness to act collectively, listen to experts and take responsibility. Imagine a better future. These lessons had been tucked away in the national memory cabinet while the good times rolled—from exporting finite resources and importing cheap products and eager people. For decades, any debate that required a moral core—climate change, population, refugees, diversity, human rights, First Nations recognition—had been shut down by hectoring bullies. Coming to terms with Australia's past, actively, visibly and institutionally, is the first crucial step before we can imagine ourselves as a nation fit for the profound challenges that a world disrupted by climate change, globalisation and digitisation will demand.

What are the elements that define the idea of Australia? What, if anything, makes us unique, fair, lucky or smart? How has change happened in the past? What were the points of resistance and transformation? What do our rather prosaic values actually mean? Are we able to have robust discussions? What are the chances that we can make Australia 'slightly better than average, again'? Can we actually make our own future and aim high, or are we more comfortable just pretending to be fair as we fail to invest in being smart, all the while crossing our fingers and hoping that our luck does not run out?

3

From Somewhere

EVERYONE COMES FROM somewhere. Even if you like to think you are your own creation, a citizen of the world following your own whims and dreams, there is always a *somewhere*, or several, that provide the bedrock of your being. Places put a sensory stamp on you, even if you don't realise it at the time. It is often physical and always emotional. The memory can mug you when you least expect it, and reduce jet-lagged travellers to tears. It may be triggered by the way the light falls at a certain time of day, the mist rising over a valley, the sun glinting on surf, a shimmering mirage on a country road, or by the sound of a magpie, the roar of a football crowd, a howling wind, a song, or the intonation in a voice. Maybe it is the smell of summer rain steaming in tropical air, the crush of gum leaves, choking bushfire smoke, stale beer tramped into sticky carpets; or the taste of salty water at the back of your throat when you dive into a wave, or the melting ice-cream you ate to take away that bitter taste.

For years I tried to find the peppery smell of the summer wallum on Minjerribah (North Stradbroke Island) in the dunes that guarded other beaches. I would embarrass my children as I reached into the bush to crush a leaf to see if it would release *that* smell. I did this up and down the east coast, crunching banksia and tea tree leaves, bits of pandanus, she-oak and casuarina before I gave up. It is a unique aroma of just one place, 'Straddie'—the distillation of its unique flora, fauna, water, sand and wind, rain and sun. It is more distinctive than any spray puffed by the perfume ladies in David Jones as you make your way across its marble floors. And much more evocative. Even recalling the hunt for that peppery aroma immediately conjures memories from almost every phase of my life.

Long before it became the preferred holiday destination of Brisbane's professional class, Straddie was a place rich with joy but laden with trauma and shame. For the Quandamooka peoples, it is a part of their being. I first travelled across the waters of Moreton Bay, rich with jellyfish, turtles, dugongs and dolphins, on a school biology trip, passing islands that had once been prisons, leper colonies and places of exile. We were to stay in the former asylum. Maybe it was because I hadn't lived in Queensland long, but there was something about the lightness of the air and welling water that told me this was a special place. We were there to learn about marine ecosystems, carefully picking our way through mangroves to collect samples of murky water, mucking about on boats to gather seaweeds and scoop ladles of invisible plankton from the warm waters. It was a lesson in the links that sustain and nourish a complex network of life. The astonished joy of finding countless tiny creatures swimming in a drop of water under a microscope made me think I should become a marine biologist. It was an ambition that didn't last the year.

In the early 1970s, the notion of an ecosystem was purely an ecological concept, explaining the complex connection between living creatures and their environment. But the bigger lesson I took from that trip was about the interconnectedness of human life and the cruel world in which it played out. Incidentally, because it was a science trip, it became an opportunity to begin to learn about the people who had

From Somewhere

lived on the island for tens of thousands of years. This signalled more than curiosity about scientific inquiry. It was a sensory experience in a place alive with human beings and their stories.

Over the next decade, tens of thousands of school children met the great poet and advocate Oodgeroo Noonuccal, whom we then called Mrs Kath Walker, and learned more about Minjerribah. Through her, middle-class Brisbane kids learned that Aboriginal connections with their city were alive, deep and close by. And beautiful. This marked the beginning of a very different way of seeing and being. It was completely at odds with the prevailing images of Aboriginality: segregation, impoverished settlements, foreboding missions or boomerangs, ashtrays and tourist shop kitsch. Her patient, impassioned and persistent storytelling shook these preconceptions to their core.

After years of measured and effective political activism at home and abroad, the well-connected and influential poet had a new mission. She had felt the pressure from a younger generation of activists to step aside. She retreated to the island of her childhood, and established a *gunyah* at One Mile where she and the other six children in the Ruska family grew up.[1] The bayside settlement had once been an Aboriginal mission, close enough to the asylum that accommodated ageing, destitute and mentally ill men to walk to work but far enough away to be invisible. The Ruska family had ties to the island that went back generations, but by the time Oodgeroo returned she was worried that the island was dying, the birds and animals disappearing. The shy nautiluses that emerged from the ocean had been chased away; cars belched fumes; tourists scattered cans, cigarettes and even the hulks of their vehicles; and sand mining drowned out the sounds of natural life. She was determined to preserve and share the deeper drumbeat of a more complex sense of belonging. In 1972, the year after she returned and I first visited, *Stradbroke Dreamtime*, her poetic recollections and stories, was published. It has been in print ever since and took root in my being.

The transformative insight from that school trip, into the ancient human ecosystem, was an unintended outcome of my first journey across the bay my Prussian forebears had crossed five score years and twelve before. In the manner of Queensland school camps in that rough-and-ready time, we stayed in the ramshackle timber building where peeling paint revealed some of the scars of its past. At night the boys pretended to be the ghosts of the ill and destitute who had once lived there, carelessly reminding us to be afraid of what had come before. The place reeked of history, but, as was always the way, no one talked about it. It just was.

By the time I returned to the island as a university student, I knew that the building we had stayed in was the remnant of the dwelling that had given the island its purpose for many decades. Straddie had long been one of the many islands where colonial administrators deposited the sick, frail and criminal. First a manned lookout, then a prison in one of the most brutal convict settlements. Then, in 1850, a quarantine station where dozens of would-be settlers who had travelled to Queensland from Plymouth on the *Emigrant* were left to die of typhus. Soon it would become home to a Spanish Catholic mission. A lazaret where those suffering from that debilitating disease would not embarrass or infect the able-bodied followers, and then an asylum where the residents were confined to wards or housed in tents. Those sent to the island were left largely to see out their days with little support. The beauty and abundance of the place, the spectacular sunsets back across the bay, must have provided some comfort for the destitute and ill exiles, but as far as the officials and polite society were concerned, they were out of sight and mind.

This was not the first time I learned that places can carry an imprint of trauma and shame as well as joy. The frisson of embarrassment, the scar of a deep hurt, or the dimly perceived sense that something once happened there and left its imprint. Oodgeroo Noonuccal was always ready to share the stories. She spoke about the island as it was before

From Somewhere

Lieutenant James Cook called the rocky outcrop on the north-east tip Point Lookout. Before Matthew Flinders and NSW surveyor-general John Oxley recorded it as an island. Before the Quandamooka peoples gave refuge to escaped convicts, affording them a status as returning spirits that they did not deserve. Before the cruel Captain Patrick Logan sent troops to clear the Nunukul, Ngugi and Goenpul peoples' bora rings and fish traps to create another island prison. Before Governor Darling named it for the Earl of Stradbroke, and the port of the western edge Dunwich for an English viscount. She told of times before the battles between soldiers and locals left dozens dead. Before a matron beat a child to death and the Myora mission school closed.[2] Before it became a human dumping ground. Before massive dredges began to rip millions of tonnes of sand off the dunes, and out of the spine, of the second largest sand island in the world.

Oodgeroo was a beautiful woman, her graceful presence more imposing than her size, a fierce advocate and storyteller. She had grown up on the island; her father Ted Ruska had satisfied the Controller of Aborigines that his blood line was sufficiently diluted to allow him to work outside the control of Queensland's *Aboriginals Protection and Restriction of Opium Act 1897*, the law that terrorised the First Nations people and whose provisions would prevail (with amendments) for three score years and fourteen. Permission was granted annually, but the threat that at any moment his status could be revoked and the family sent to a reserve was real—even more so because he successfully campaigned to be paid as much as the white men.

Oodgeroo's mother, Lucy, came from western Queensland, and experienced the brutality of separation from her Aboriginal mother and Scottish father when she fell pregnant two years before Federation. By the time Lucy's daughter turned six she was classified as 'quadroon' and sent to an orphanage, never again to meet. The ever-present threat that officials could take children away has stamped generations of families with an enduring adrenal fight-or-flight response. Young

Kath Ruska's island childhood, learning the ancient stories, language and dances from the old grannies as they chopped tobacco, peeled vegetables and collected firewood, along with newer stories from the *Queensland Reader* at Dunwich School, came to an end when she turned thirteen and boarded the ageing steamer S.S. *Otter* to travel across the bay for a job as a housekeeper and 2/6 a week.[3] Her life as a political activist and writer began a decade later.

Seven years before my school visit to Straddie, Kath Walker's first collection of poems, *We Are Going*, was published and went on to sell 10,000 copies, more than any Australian poet since C.J. Dennis. The great poet Judith Wright was then a reader at Jacaranda Press and spotted her talent. Judith Wright became her close friend, and fierce advocate. *We Are Going* was followed two years later by *The Dawn is at Hand*. Critics in southern newspapers dismissed her writing as protest poems, but she found a ready audience in those who shared her outrage. Kath Walker was proud that her poetry had, in her words, stimulated awareness 'about the plight of the aborigines', and helped set the scene for the 1967 referendum that Australians overwhelmingly supported. The constitutional amendment allowed First Nations people to be counted in the census, and gave people the confidence to vote and the Commonwealth power to make laws.[4] It did not ban racial discrimination, offer constitutional recognition or even require First Nations people to vote.[5] Kath Walker was a worldly woman who had seen politics up close, and suspected her sales were a '*succès de curiosité*' as 'the work of an Aboriginal'. There were limits, as she wrote in the preface to *The Dawn is at Hand*: 'even atrocities were never to be mentioned by nice people'. Her poems were described by the grand dame of political letters, Mary Gilmore, as works that 'belong to the world'. This was just one phase of Oodgeroo's life as an activist who believed change was possible, but in her poems she captured the enduring loss and grief: 'This site was ours, you may recall,/ Ages before you came at all'.[6]

From Somewhere

I HAD ALWAYS sensed this. I didn't know why or how I had absorbed this essential knowledge. Australian history in our schoolbooks didn't get much beyond explorers, bushrangers and goldminers, and geography lessons that required us to delineate the state boundaries and memorise the names of towns, mountains and rivers. Before our move to Brisbane, I had spent most of my life in a remote Lutheran settlement deep in the Western District of Victoria. There, my imagination had been my best friend. The one-church, one-school, one-hall, one-oval, one-cemetery, two-tennis-court settlement was ringed by giant pine trees. There were plenty of mysteries to try to imagine my way out of. A cemetery with graves going back a century held the remains of those who sought to create a religious utopia, farmers who made a living from the rich windswept plains, victims of the Spanish flu and tiny babies who did not survive infancy.

In the 1960s it was one of the wealthiest parts of Australia; the wool boom meant that the farmers with the biggest spreads and fleeciest merinos would get huge cheques for their produce—at their peak these cheques could be up to a million pounds, tens of millions of dollars in today's coin. My father, Noel, was a Lutheran minister, and the farmers in his congregation had been there for a long time. They were not the descendants of the squatters with the massive spreads. Still, they had enough land to ensure that throughout the 1960s the churchyard car park was full of lairy, brightly coloured cars with big fins, gorgeous petrol-guzzling monsters that they parked under the cypress trees every Sunday.

The area, which at the time we lived there radiated from the town of Hamilton, was rich for a very simple reason: the volcanic plains had produced extraordinarily fertile soils that provided sustenance for countless sheep and cattle. Seven thousand years ago, millions of years after the first volcanoes erupted, some were still active, providing enduring creation stories for those who had lived there since time immemorial. The physical residue of lava rocks, pockmarked like Aero chocolate bars, still littered the countryside. Many had been reshaped into fences and foundations. Long-extinct volcanoes popped out of the plains. It was windy, wet, hilly and lush with lakes, streams and waterfalls—we called the rugged sandstone Gariwerd mountains that loomed on the horizon the Grampians.

The descendants of the squatters who had taken the land for free had substantial houses, while survivors of more recent wars eked out an existence on soldier-settlers plots that were too small, except in the very best of times, to produce enough to support a family. These farms were dotted all over the country, on land that had been acquired or reallocated from Crown land and Aboriginal reserves, to provide a home and job for the shattered soldiers returning from the Great War. Returning First Nations soldiers who had previously lived on these same reserves were told they could not apply. A gift of land was a time-honoured practice in this imperial project. Distributing it to soldiers who returned from the European war was the big *land idea* in this post-war moment of crisis. Australia's economy was still primarily agricultural. It was not a success. Peasant-sized farms might have been sufficient in another age, but the end of the First World War marked the beginning of another era that gathered speed after the second global conflagration. By the 1960s, few soldier-settlers remained. Agriculture was being consolidated and industrialised.

I was a curious child who was free to roam the country roads and lanes on my bike; to take the chance of riding on railway tracks and bridges that were rarely used by trains; to explore; to pick mushrooms, fruit and wildflowers; to watch shearers and harvesters at work; and to wonder about what had happened before. Our pine-enclosed hamlet was dominated by two bluestone buildings—the new church and the old, which had since become a schoolroom—its perimeter was defined by soaring pine trees and the cemetery.

I probably spent more time than would be recommended for children today in that graveyard, wondering about the lives of those who found their final resting place there. Here were the shared plots of extended families. Many of the old men and women had the excessive consonants of Central European surnames, born in faraway places and buried in this untended plot. Ours was a community grounded in the nineteenth-century immigration from the Northern Hemisphere, which effectively ensured there was little chance of return for the Gunditjmara who had been forcibly removed decades earlier and later hustled into reserves. Prussians, Danes, Hungarians and Dutch had been coming to the Australian colonies for decades; by that century's close, German speakers were the fourth-largest group of settlers. They were a more than usually mixed bunch: religious exiles who became farmers and winemakers, intellectuals who had despaired of change in their homelands and left to help shape colonial debates, missionaries who sought to convert, goldminers seeking a fortune, peddlers who became businessmen, scientists who documented the mysteries of the land and its creatures, artists and land-hungry farmers who responded to the offer to clear what they were assured was unsettled land. They considered themselves culturally German, were loyal to England, but dreamt of an Australian nation.[7]

Twentieth-century German warmongering made many of these people, and their descendants, feel like enemy aliens. Settlements they had long lived in were given bucolic names better suited to the English countryside, schools were closed, speaking German was unacceptable. During the First World War years, 6890 people of German heritage were interned in an improvised and capricious system of detention camps dotted around the country during the war that killed 20 million and injured another 21 million, decimated a generation and destroyed families. Victory was not sufficient for Australian Prime Minister Billy Hughes, who was determined that Germany should suffer and was instrumental in the decisions that made the next world war even more horrifying than the first. After the Great War, 6150 of the internees and their families were deported to a devastated Germany, a country that the Australian-born had never set foot in before.[8]

The pattern was repeated 21 years later when Germany again launched another even more catastrophic war, and another generation became enemy aliens in Australia, their names anglicised, and those under suspicion interned alongside those of Italian and Japanese heritage. People with German names had learned to be cautious, make themselves invisible, live quietly, engaging as little as possible with public life, change their names, speak softly.

In our little community, everyone had a German surname or one that hinted at its origins, but they felt safe. Those with English or Scottish names were our betters, sitting at the top of the district's hierarchy, living in once-grand houses, exuding certainty that they were of finer stock than the rest of us. If there was an '*other*' in those still bitterly sectarian days, they were Catholic, people who also had their own schools and tribal alliances. Little had been forgiven since Martin Luther had nailed his *Ninety-five Theses* on the door of a church in Wittenberg in 1517. Class and religion were a potent cocktail, the gulf unbridgeable enough to split a family or kill a relationship.

So, armed with my imagination, I cycled along the roads and disused railway tracks, ducked under barbed-wire fences and walked across paddocks to find the remnant sites of disused farms and houses, pace out the stone foundations, pick what would now be heritage plums and apples from the gnarled fruit trees in long-forgotten orchards, pull the weeds from rusty fences around headstones, and imagine life for the settlers and the religious obsessives who set up intentional communities, scrapping tribes whose different theological interpretations of the same text meant they could hardly bring themselves to talk to each other. A lingering sense of loss and trauma was never far from the surface, ready to be gleaned from a grimace, a raised eyebrow, snatches of conversation or a silent response.

From Somewhere

WHAT WAS MISSING was any sense of anyone being there between the time the volcanoes erupted and the 1830s when the squatters descended. I had a feeling for the country, for the native plants and wildlife that hung on despite the crops and livestock. I was vaguely aware there had been reserves for Aboriginal people at Lake Condah and Framlingham, closer to the coastal towns of Portland and Warrnambool. My sister, brother and I played 'cowboys and Indians', re-enacting the American frontier battles we watched on television. When we were the Indians, we hid in the reeds, sloshed across muddy creek beds, crouched behind trees as we pulled arrows from our homemade bows. When it was time to be cowboys, we marched across the bridge above the creek and into the paddocks, cap guns at the ready. Cowboys always won.

I don't recall if we even dimly wondered if other similar battles had happened in these green, lava-strewn hills and valleys. As a daughter of the Lutheran Church, I knew about Aboriginal missions in Hermannsburg and elsewhere in Central Australia, in the segregated outer reaches of New South Wales and even in the far north of Queensland. It took years before I learned that these fertile lands known as Gariwerd had been the home of the Gunditjmara peoples for tens of thousands of years; that it carried their creation story, which was no more fanciful than the one we learned about the world being created in seven days; that they had built sustainable settlements, trapped fish, husbanded the land; caught kangaroo, yabbies and eels, and made cloaks from possum skins to protect from the fierce winter chill.

We now know much more. The richness of the First Nations cultural heritage in this part of Victoria is what you would expect for such fertile lands. The Budj Bim Cultural Landscape is now a national park registered on the UNESCO World Heritage List exclusively for its Aboriginal cultural values. As Bill Gammage and Bruce Pascoe reminded us in their respective books *The Biggest Estate on Earth* and *Dark Emu*, much of this had been known since earliest

European settlement. Some of the uniqueness of the local civilisation was captured by the artists, the explorers, the anthropologists—those who asked the First Australians and those who looked, curious people whose humanity drove them. Of course, many others just saw an enemy standing in the way of something they wanted. To paraphrase Henry Reynolds, the historian who has done so much to make the frontier past visible, *why wasn't I told*?

I well recall as a child of about ten going to the South Australian Museum on North Terrace in Adelaide with my grandparents, who were conscientious members of the Lutheran community in the church's heartland. Their connection to the church's Central Australian missions was made tangible by the Albert Namatjira watercolour of a ghost gum in a creek bed on the wall of my grandfather's den, a boomerang on the sideboard. On this day, we looked at the Aboriginal collections that the museum had, and still has, including an extraordinarily chilling collection of brutal settlement artefacts.[9] I recall seeing human skulls and not knowing how to make sense of them. On the way out of the museum we passed an old Aboriginal man. He moved, and whether I jumped, took a step sideways or had some other reaction, I don't recall. I can feel my shame and his humiliation like it was yesterday. I remember thinking: *How can he be alive? We have just seen the exhibition. They are all dead.*

They weren't, of course. A fact that came into sharp relief the next year as the campaign to recognise Aboriginal and Torres Strait Islander people as citizens reached even these most insular rural communities. By the end of my first year of high school, the great anthropologist W.E.H. Stanner delivered the ABC's Boyer Lectures. His sonorous voice crackled through the transistor radio that accompanied me everywhere: 'What may well have begun as a simple forgetting . . . turned into habit and over time into something like a cult of forgetfulness practised on a national scale. We have been able for so long to disremember the Aborigines that we are now hard put to keep them in mind even when we most want to do so.' At the time, Stanner thought optimistically that the 'great Australian silence' could not survive the research that was revealing the depth of complex cultures, research that he was confident would 'renovate . . . categories of understanding', along with community interest and goodwill. His unspoken fear was that 1968 might be another year when recognition seemed within reach, and become 'just another year on the old plateau of complacency'.[10]

He was right to temper his optimism. Old habits of wilful ignorance die hard and can be easily revived when trying to decipher conflicting information. Especially when it is charged with politics. Bruce Pascoe's book *Dark Emu* broke the silence as it made its way from the tiny Magabala Books offices in Broome to hundreds of thousands of bookshelves. He had unapologetically drawn on the records of settlers and explorers to explain how First Nations peoples husbanded their resources, kept themselves fed and clothed for millennia, and suggested the lessons that might be learned in a climate-challenged world. It was, on one level, an unremarkable explanation, but it found an audience hungry for information, sensing there was more to the story than they had heard. It inflamed critics, who disputed interpretations, questioned footnotes, pointed to more recent and sophisticated sources and understandings of knowledge systems, noted vast regional differences, and argued the danger of imposing the limits of one knowledge system on another. In 2021, when a fresh debate erupted about *Dark Emu* and its author, the process of silencing that Stanner described again came into focus. #GreatAustralianSilence briefly trended on Twitter. As if to prove the point of the power of silence to render us ignorant, many young people commented that they had never heard the phrase before but would use it in future.

To some degree, Stanner was right: 'mythologising and disremembering are part and parcel of each other'.[11] On 27 May 1967, the year before he delivered his lectures, an overwhelming majority of people in all the states had voted to recognise First Nations peoples and enable the Australian government to exercise authority and usurp the brutality of the protectionist and assimilationist state regimes. Over the next few years after his lectures there was more talk that land rights, possibly even a *Makarrata* treaty and way of coming together after conflict, might follow. It was becoming clear, even to a teenager in the backblocks of the Western District, that the self-justifying notion of a doomed race that had so tangibly been exhibited in the display cases of the South Australian Museum was nonsense, despite the brutal efforts of the true believers and the complacency of the rest. The legacy of researchers—anthropologists, theologians, linguists, archaeologists, historians who listened—and the increasingly important work of Indigenous writers, activists and scholars began to build. The once blank slate of Australian history was again filled with the stories of human beings doing the things that human beings do—making meaning, families, societies; living with the land in a deep spiritual connection. It was another 29 years before the knowledge of traditional owners collected by anthropologists became publicly accessible. The colourful map of First Nations crafted by David Hoxton and published by the Australian Institute of Aboriginal and Torres Strait Islander Studies was revealing. Unlike the arbitrary straight lines of state boundaries, which only occasionally twist to follow a river or mountain range, this map of language groups mirrors the land. Rachel Perkins, the filmmaker who grew up steeped in this knowledge, galvanised the nation when she said years later at the 2020 Summit in Parliament House, Canberra: 'If you are looking for the one thing that makes Australia unique, it is that it is home to the oldest living cultures in the world.' When you absorb the enormity of that fact, the way you see changes and what you see cannot be unseen.

From Somewhere

The silence that Stanner described is deeply ingrained and perpetually reinforced. He described it as 'a structural matter, a view from a window which has been carefully placed to exclude a whole quadrant of the landscape'.[12] Silence is active as well as passive, a powerful way to 'shun'. Maybe that was why the school trip to Straddie had made such a deep impression. My childhood had been marked by endless road trips, noting the two-faced white roadside markers that counted the distance from Adelaide to Melbourne, Sydney to Brisbane and back again. Our school holidays were divided between those long drives north and visits to my mother's family in one of Adelaide's poshest suburbs. There our grandmother took us as childhood emissaries to sing and chat at old folks' villages and for those living in the cruelly named 'Home for Incurables'.

Trips to Queensland took longer, through shimmering mirages that would eventually evaporate. We bounced on hard bench seats, endlessly I-spying through the Wimmera, over the Hay Plains, sleeping overnight in the car beside the road in granite boulder country alive with wild pigs and the ghosts of bushrangers, and on, over the border, to Kingaroy. There, in my paternal grandmother's dark old Queenslander, we settled into the very different routines of potato and pumpkin farms, in a town that smelled of roasting peanuts. Our visits drew an inevitable query from the police, *why we weren't at school*, easily answered as holidays varied between states. Then we'd spend a few days fishing and paddling on the beaches of Moreton Bay, followed by a slow drive through the hilly city, over its snaking brown river and past distinctive-smelling factories that turned rough pineapple into sugary slices, hops into beer and wheat into sweet biscuits. It was impossible to ignore that Queensland was not only hotter and steamier but was rougher, poorer, with little gloss, closely tied to the agricultural production that happened beyond the ranges and further north. Secrets hung heavily in the air, occasionally aired late at night when eavesdropping children were not meant to hear—hand-me-down memories of trips down the pass from the Darling Downs to Ipswich on drays laden with produce, and skirmishes with Aboriginal warriors.

IT TAKES A lot to challenge the reluctance to say shameful things out loud, to find a way of evoking the memories, examining them, learning the lessons to find a more robust truth. Keith Hancock published *Australia* just 30 years after Federation, producing a bestseller that put the short history of the nation in its imperial context. The first chapter was called 'Invasion of Australia' but focused on the blank slate that was remade, not the 'predestined passing' of the First Australians.[13]

In 1992, the Queensland Education Department withdrew a primary schoolbook that had been used for years but was by then considered racist and discriminatory. Two years later, the department issued a new Social Studies sourcebook for Year Five students, and advised teachers to use terms like 'discovery, pioneers or exploration' thoughtfully and in their historical context. The *Courier-Mail* 'investigated' and found plenty of fodder for politicians and readers who saw an attempt to 'rewrite history' by discussing why some might consider European settlement as an invasion. Wayne Goss, the state premier who had first made his name working for Queensland's Aboriginal Legal Service, attempted to defuse the politically orchestrated pressure. But he cautiously concurred that 'invasion' went too far, the sourcebook should be rewritten and students should make up their own minds.

Badtjala artist and academic Fiona Foley grew up learning about her mother's K'gari country, then known as Fraser Island. She has made it her life's mission to find ways to tell truths and share the confronting knowledge she has learned. Hers are brutal stories of death and destruction, and survival against the odds. She presents them with poetic power in important public artworks that challenge the silence and force passers-by to notice. Some of her big public works include listing the names of 94 massacre sites where some of the estimated 66,680 killed in the Queensland frontier wars died, engraving them in tombstone-like paving in the footpath outside the Brisbane Magistrates Court; the evocation in the State Library of Queensland reading rooms of the way opium was used to poison, pay and placate First Nations people; an installation of aluminium sugar cubes on the banks of the Pioneer River in Mackay, naming and remembering some of the kidnapped Melanesians who were brought to work on sugar plantations; and, with Janet Laurence, the representation of the 29 clans of Sydney Harbour outside the Museum of Sydney, on the site of the city's first Government House that is now dwarfed by luxury hotels and office towers. These works, like much of her art, aim to bridge the 'abyss' of ignorance. It is designed to challenge and provoke. Only after *Witnessing to Silence* outside the Brisbane Magistrate's Court was completed did she reveal that names in the paving stones were massacre sites. She feared that if she had been truthful it wouldn't 'get up'.[14] She did not expect a silent response, which she found was another way of rendering invisible her 'work, intellect and voice'.[15] This haunting work outside the court where countless thousands of First Nations' people have been found guilty, evokes absence in the way the Holocaust Memorial in the shadow of the Brandenburg Gate in Berlin commemorates the Holocaust. Unlike that hauntingly famous memorial, *Witnessing to Silence* does not register on lists of the top ten things to visit in Brisbane.

This habitual silence is not limited to understanding the rightful place of the First Australians. It infects every aspect of life. It is there in the immigrant family who chooses to leave the trauma and stories of their past behind and not learn their parents' language, in the secrets and shame that prevent long-term residents from confronting the past, in the returning soldiers who cannot speak of the horrors they have witnessed, in the victims of institutional and sexual abuse, racism and homophobia who have until recently felt too ashamed to speak.

At the time W.E.H. Stanner gave his celebrated lectures, the number of professional historians in the country had grown to several hundred, but their field of vision was still limited and resoundingly uncritical.[16] Only six years earlier, the revered historian Manning Clark, who later became the much-vilified bête noire of the Murdoch press and conservative politicians, published the first volume of what was to become his six-volume magnum opus. It began: 'Civilization did not begin in Australia until the last quarter of the eighteenth century.' As the footnote at the bottom of the page carefully explains, the author considered the pre-existing cultures did not pass the threshold of coming 'out of a state of barbarism'. The same year, Rachel Perkins' father, Charles Perkins, a student at the University of Sydney, heard about the 1961 Freedom Ride in the United States that aimed to desegregate the south. Perkins gathered a group of students who, like him, were destined to become some of the most influential people in the nation. They decided to use the same tactic in country New South Wales, where segregation kept First Nations peoples in what was considered 'their place'.

Some of the most original thinkers and writers did not feel comfortable in this somewhere where much could not be spoken. Instead they took their brilliance to the world to shape global debates about the rights of women, homosexuals, animals and the environment. That has changed; the world has come closer. We know more and are discovering even more but uncomfortable truths are still avoided, critics are told to shut up. And now we apologise for things that those who were paying attention always knew were wrong. We have apologised to the stolen children and their parents and descendants, to those subjected to institutional abuse, to the unwed mothers whose children were taken, to the children who were forcibly removed from British orphanages, to those Australian-Germans who were interned and deported, to the welfare recipients who were penalised and hounded by ill-considered algorithms for debt they had not incurred, to the

From Somewhere

Afghan people who suffered at the hands of rogue soldiers. No doubt, in time, we will apologise to the refugees incarcerated on yet another set of remote islands. First, we need to be comfortable saying difficult things out loud and accepting the consequences, looking at both of Janus's faces rather than cringing from the dark.

WRITER DAVID MALOUF is a close observer of this country, particularly the patch of south-east Queensland where he grew up. When he described ramshackle country-town Brisbane, its weatherboard houses perched precariously on hillsides, high enough to survive floods and catch the cooling breezes, the place became a literary character. In it the walls were thin; gossip spread easily and enforced social control. He viscerally recalls a time when much could not be spoken, when even great works of literature that had escaped the hyperactive censor's wrath—like James Joyce's *Ulysses*—were hidden under the chief librarian's desk. Malouf argues that television, which launched in Australia in 1956, taught Australians to talk.[17] Women had found a public voice a decade earlier when radio created a public audience for things that might once only have been said privately or in small groups.[18] As people watched and listened, things that had once been left unspoken worked their way into conversation. There were fewer subjects that drew the response *You can't say that*. Not long before his 95-year-old mother died, the demographer Bernard Salt asked her when things had changed the most in her lifetime. She said it was the 1960s. Not for the reasons he expected. She remembered that as the decade when school changed. 'In the 1960s, kids were asked their opinion. They were taught how to think. I was taught what to think.'[19]

That was my experience. Our tiny two-teacher school, Number 84 at Tabor, was an unlikely beneficiary of the shortage of local teachers: a young graduate and his wife were brought out from Chicago.

The Idea of Australia

I am forever grateful that Jim and Joyce Born arrived in our isolated hamlet, a day's walk from the nearest township and a 30-minute drive to Hamilton. I am even more grateful that they were open minded and interested in the world. We could have got a fundamentalist. Instead, after singing 'God Save the Queen' and raising and folding the flag, we started each day creating a scrapbook of current events. It was probably our teacher's way of staying in touch with a world that must have seemed extraordinarily remote. But it was still, as it had been in 1880, a 'land of newspapers'. We clipped the *Penshurst Free Press*, *Hamilton Spectator*, *The Age*, *The Herald* and the *Sun News-Pictorial*, tracking stories about the huge number of road deaths, crime, censorship, disasters, assassinations of American leaders, politics, the Vietnam War, the execution of Ronald Ryan, referendums and local events. It was a lesson in civics and life. Whatever the limits of the newspapers, he encouraged us to think and wonder about life beyond the pine-fringed compound.

In his sermons in that bluestone church, my father spoke a lot about the soul. He crafted his sermons with meticulous care and spent Saturday evening, after the football, memorising the twenty-minute address he would deliver in the morning. The details suffused me, and the idea of a soul remained. These sensory experiences put a stamp on me; just like the aroma of the Straddie wallum and the smell of composting pine needles, it is etched in my brain. Like many other experiences they helped shape the way I perceive the world. In my search for the soul of the nation and her people, these experiences have become useful tools to make sense of the big picture and find meaning from small details and little stories. These sensitivities have helped inform the way I see things and the meaning I draw from places, events and people. They are my guide in this journey through the undercurrents of life in this *somewhere*.

4

Stories We Tell Ourselves

FRONTS OF ICY air swept across Australia in the late autumn of 2021, sending a signal that the second plague winter could be chilly. Thermometers plunged to new lows and records were broken. This year there would be no easy escape from cities that are not well designed for even mild winters. With international borders closed, the perpetual equatorial warmth or Northern Hemisphere summer that lured the tens of thousands most winters were off limits. There was no chance of a quick, cheap trip to the beaches and hills of Bali or Thailand, or a leisurely European summer in the south of France; no Greek islands, Italian lakes or English countryside. And worse, no chance of visiting family in one of the nearly 200 countries where half the Australian population has relatives. Those who ventured inland were reminded that the plains and deserts beyond the Great Dividing Range experience bone-numbing cold as well as world-beating summer heat. At home, borders closed erratically, making even the tropical north and well-powdered ski fields unreliable destinations. Like dominos, cities, states and local government areas progressively locked down. Grey nomads and school leavers taking their gap year at home rushed to cross desert borders and avoid quarantine.

Over the previous year, Australians had adapted surprisingly well to life in their 'Hermit Democracy', as the nation had been called when the barriers of the White Australia policy first provoked international ire.[1] Now, more than a century on, the borders were more firmly closed than ever. In the first six months of 2021, half the 100,000 citizens who wished to go *over seas* were told they could not. Permission to leave had to be sought through a complicated online form that demanded supporting documents and statutory declarations, and a promise not to seek consular support should anything bad befall you. Meanwhile, public money sloshed like water across floodplains, propping up businesses and giving some more income security than they had ever known. At the end of plague year one, Australia was doing well, although the sources of advice were narrowly medical and economic. Here, at least hospitals, cemeteries and crematoria were not overflowing as they were elsewhere, the worst-case scenarios of up to a million cases a month avoided.

As had happened before in other less-threatening circumstances, the cultural strut had soon masked the cringe, and with it the unavoidable boastfulness that puffed up the 'Blatant Blatherskite, the God's-Own-Country, and I'm-a-better-man-than-you-are Australian Bore'.[2] But this time, all but the most diehard braggarts were tinged with muted anxiety as the plague took its toll and industries were reshaped, jobs disappeared, house prices skyrocketed, domestic abuse soared. Cheery platitudes were insufficient. All was not as it first seemed. What threatened to be an exceptionally cold winter gave way to one of the warmest on record, just as the climate-change models predicted.

The less-assured cultural strutters worried that the hubris that had accompanied the apparent early success in flattening the curve of severe illness was making people hard-hearted. Many wondered out loud what being Australian now meant. In no time at all, more than 11,000 people liked a tweet by Geoff Kitney, a former foreign correspondent, who declared: '[I] feel like crying for my country. Right wing conservatism has sapped the life out of Australia, stunting its humanity, ambition and potential. Hard to be optimistic.'[3]

It seemed a once-abundant generosity of spirit was again at risk of being mugged by fearful self-interest.[4] Anxiety leached empathy. Everyone who bothered to look was reminded that there was no definition of the rights of citizens in the Australian Constitution, that international covenants promising the right to return to your homeland were a weak back-up.[5] As the first plague year had demonstrated, regulations could be changed by ministerial decree and announced (or not) by media releases in the middle of the night.

EXCLUSION LURKS DEEP in the national psyche. Many Australians like to think of themselves as active cosmopolitans. They are at home in grand cities and remote villages but hiding under the doona or disappearing to a deserted beach also have a strong emotional pull. Isolation—personal, community, national—is what happens when barriers are raised. Sometimes for very good reasons, sometimes not. In Australia, isolationism recurs as a by-product of a lingering utopian dream that an ideal society of like-minded people could be created on the blank slate of the continent. But the pervasive fear of abandonment[6] has more often held sway in a population shaped by exclusion ever since the nation was signed into being by a dying queen in another hemisphere.

The romanticised, sometimes well-justified view of Australia as a land of mates where Jack is as good as his boss, a global leader in social and political reform, has always depended on the almost invisible scaffold of exclusion: of First Nations people, who were not counted until the 1971 census; of anyone who failed the arbitrary dictation test set by immigration officials, until the language test was abolished in 1958 and the White Australia policy ditched fifteen years later; and of women, until 1984 when they were at last deemed legally equal under the Sex Discrimination Act, which passed with the help of Liberal Party MPs who incurred the wrath of their party to support it. As modern Australia opened her borders and adjusted bureaucratic processes and social systems to create space for more immigrants and to welcome their diversity—of culture, history, language, ethnicity, gender, experience—the society was transformed. Australia at the beginning of the 21st century looked and sounded very different. It had become browner, busier, richer, more confident in the world. Women outnumbered men.

Even as cities and towns, schools and universities, offices, building sites and shops look less like a provincial British outpost, the Federation's founding dream of a white utopia under threat from Asian interlopers has proved hard to dislodge. *Go back to where you come from* remains a potent form of abuse. In 2015 the first head of Australian Border Force described its role to *protect our utopia* and announced plans to randomly check that people in central Melbourne could prove their right to be there.[7] Deciding who could come and who could not has become a contemporary version of the old imperial tactic of divide and rule. Those who are approved through the carefully curated, slow and costly immigration program sign up with a sigh of relief. Those on good visas with a promise of permanent residence count their lucky stars with barely a glimpse back at those destined to remain on the other side of the customs barrier. The nation had prospered despite the tyranny of distance, with relatively robust institutions, a selected immigrant population and a blind eye turned to repeated attempts to obliterate the world's oldest continuous civilisation. As Blatant-Blatherskite-in-Chief, Prime Minister Scott Morrison, repeatedly asked—rhetorically, without inviting a response—*How good is Australia*? Clearly his answer was 'God's Own Country'.

Even in an age of instantaneous digital communication, when planes can cover a thousand kilometres in an hour and a third of the population was born *elsewhere*, a palpable sense of remoteness lingers, thanks to the scale of the continent and the vast oceans that pound her ancient coast. Many found this willingness to close the borders, limit flights and cancel visas during the plague years a burdensome artefact of another age when isolation was as much a product of distance as fear. But the polls in the winter of 2021 were conclusive: those who objected were in the minority. Most people were happy to snap the gate shut, even if it meant other Australians could not return home. Those inside liked the feeling of safety, confident they had outsmarted the spiky microscopic virus. In the age-old manner of hermits, they became grumpy and didn't want anyone disturbing their peace, even fellow citizens who happened to be abroad when the music stopped at the end of March 2020. Like the lucky few at a child's birthday party, they grabbed the nearest chairs and sat tight.

Isolationism was nurtured by fluoro-garbed political leaders alert to the power of fear, as they amped it up on social media and reiterated their warnings in quick interviews with like-minded interlocutors. In May 2021, the federal health minister Greg Hunt declared in a midnight media release that Australians of Indian descent would be jailed or levied huge fines if they sought to return as the Delta mutation of the virus claimed millions of lives on the Indian subcontinent. The government was then visibly surprised to find that this decision did not pass the much-vaunted *pub test*. Even the most strident defenders of the old ways thought it was a step too far, too reminiscent of the rules that had once protected the old fortress. Forcing those who happened to have Indian heritage to take their chances in a country that was failing to keep its people safe morphed into heartbreaking stories involving real people who just happened to be in the wrong place. As the stories were told publicly the outrage grew to the point where restrictions were slowly relaxed.

For decades, the public had been lectured about why the harsh treatment of refugees was necessary. Migration had become ever more complicated as new categories of visas proliferated. But the horrific personal nature of this threat proved too much. The people trapped in India were citizens or permanent residents from what had become, over the previous decade, one of Australia's most important sources of new immigrants. The frog was not prepared for the water to become quite so hot, at least not so fast, and slowly, slowly, some of the stranded Australians of Indian heritage and others who had made their lives there were allowed to return—but not before others died gasping for breath in hospitals that had run out of oxygen. A month later, as the virus made its winter surge and a new round of lockdowns began, earwigging conversations in the street made it clear that the search for someone to blame had started. The problem was caused by 'Indians'; the blunt political sledge had taken a month to find its mark but landed with force.

Isolation's janus face is practical self-reliance—preferably with a rich, powerful friend on speed dial. A practical people can work around their leaders, as Australians have done by installing solar panels on their roofs in world-beating numbers, in defiance of politicians who refused to rise to the challenge. But there are some things that can only be done by governments. And this gap was on display as the virus caught a ride on the icy winter air. Australians like to think of themselves as a pragmatic people, an antipodean breed wary of 'golden promises'[8] who default to getting on; residents of a place that generally works, where trust has not been irrevocably destroyed by corruption, self-interest or incompetence. But as temperatures in the biggest city briefly fell to the lowest since records had been kept, and its people were confined to ever-shrinking bubbles, confidence in this can-do spirit waned. Selecting, authorising and ordering enough vaccine for a nation under threat of a pandemic did not have a viable personal workaround. The failure to secure adequate supplies of vaccines became a matter of national outrage. It meant twelve million people were confined to their homes and neighbourhoods for months, forcing businesses and schools to close, increasing anxiety, stress, domestic violence and loneliness.

On the first weekend of 2021, the *Sydney Morning Herald* had splashed, 'Vaccine can wait, says PM'. The front-page story paraphrased Scott Morrison's warning that 'it would be dangerous to rush a coronavirus vaccination rollout even if it could lead to restrictions and border closures easing sooner'. There had been 28,408 cases and 909 deaths in 2020, a remarkable achievement, but just a way station on the pandemic's inexorable journey. Even as border closures disrupted summer holiday plans across the nation, there was no reason, he was reported as saying, to bring forward the national cabinet meeting scheduled for 5 February. By March he had memorised a mantra about the slow pace of vaccination that would haunt him all year: *It's not a race. It's not a competition.* It was an eerie echo of his detached response a year earlier when he had lingered on holiday in Hawaii as the summer fires raged, declaring he *did not hold a hose.*

Over the next summer, images of overcrowded hospitals in the Northern Hemisphere were replaced by photos of vast, crowded vaccination centres, full of people with sleeves rolled up ready for the 'jab'. Outrage about the failure to secure enough appropriate vaccine and distribute it efficiently was growing, even as the prime minister urged caution. The carefully managed media moment when he became the second person in the country to be inoculated with the hard-to-come-by Pfizer vaccine was undermined when Jane Malysiak, the 84-year-old Second World War survivor who received the first shot, unwittingly held her hand up the wrong way and turned the prime minister's victory sign into the more colloquial 'up yours'.

As winter began, only about half a million people in Australia were fully vaccinated against the virus that was turning the world inside out, and a robust quarantine system was not yet on the drawing board. The leader of the opposition, Anthony Albanese, rehearsed the line that would become his incantation for the next six months as the inoculation tally slowly rose: 'Scott Morrison had two jobs this year: the rollout and quarantine. He has failed at both.'

The quarantine station in Manly, above the beach where Arthur Phillip first decided Sydney Harbour was the 'finest in the world', served its purpose for 152 years. In 2004 it became a luxury hotel and conference centre—itself a metaphor for the new globalism in which international travel was ubiquitous, cheap and virtually risk free. Planeloads of incoming passengers were no longer sprayed by quarantine officials in overalls before they disembarked; the only real threats became agricultural and environmental—food, wood, and mud on boots from exotic locations. Even as epidemiologists warned of a 21st-century global pandemic, Australia stopped active planning. The system of quarantine developed not long after the spores of smallpox arrived on the ships from Britain, decimating those who had lived around the harbour for millennia, was abandoned.

Surely a practical people with effective systems of administration should have taken the expert advice, heeded the history and planned a response once it was clear that a pandemic was raging. The images of catastrophe elsewhere were a chilling daily reminder. How could Australians brag that they had handled COVID-19 better than other nations when such a tiny proportion of the population was vaccinated before the virus's inevitable winter surge? Returning travellers were sent to air-conditioned hotels where the virus recirculated. The much-vaunted practical self-reliance seemed hollow, triggering dismay at the apparent ineptitude of those charged with safeguarding the nation. And another wave of anxiety.

———

THE RESOURCEFUL ELEMENTS of the national psyche were not at first the most visible as the ferocious winter storms of 2021 destroyed whole regions and dry, icy winds sent electricity usage soaring. Instead, a darker marker—harsh judgementalism—bubbled to the surface. Every day of lockdown, thousands of people reported their neighbours to the police. Ever since the First Fleet arrived, the mob had been quick to judge, blame and shame. Somehow the absence of politesse had become a perverse measure of authenticity, as though speaking your mind stripped you of the need for courtesy. During the Frontier Wars, when tens of thousands of First Nations people were killed, those who objected to the brutal violence were dismissed as indulging in 'ridiculous' spectacles of 'periodical fits of morality'.[9]

The first example occurred just days after Arthur Phillip claimed the country from the northern extremity of Cape York to Tasmania's South East Cape 3685 kilometres south, and 2400 kilometres west to lands unseen. The Union Jack was again hoisted up the stripped trunk of a eucalypt on the other side of the harbour from Quarantine Beach, on 7 February 1788, a fortnight after the abandoned attempt to make a settlement at Botany Bay. The enormity of the project must have seemed overwhelming, just as it has done ever since for each wave of new arrivals. Phillip soon discovered that assurances of a scarcely populated land, made by those who had mapped the east coast eighteen years earlier on Lieutenant Cook's *Endeavour*, were wrong. The Gweagal and Bediagal people had seen them quickly depart but their curiosity about the new arrivals quickly gave way to hostility.

It was inevitable that a settlement of 548 male and 188 female convicts, predominantly young thieves,[10] and their overseeing officers, established after nine months at sea on crowded boats, would be predisposed to rough justice. Many convicts had escaped to a fate worse than death on the other side of the globe when they found themselves under the cursory rule of a military judge advocate. Some had the imaginative capacity to thrive, but survival more often dictated brutal directness, even cruelty. At its best it was dressed in process; at its worst it was arbitrary, subject to the mood and whim of the reigning official.

Modern Australia is unrecognisable from these merciless origins, but a brutal brashness sometimes still reverberates. Public shaming remains one of its most powerful manifestations. The Murdoch press has refined it to an art form, especially when there is a Labor premier, or misbehaving *other*, available to be blamed. As the pandemic dragged on, inadvertent carriers of the virus were pilloried and mocked—the barbecue man, limo driver and removalists and partygoers from Sydney, the pizza guy in Adelaide, the refugee border jumpers in Brisbane, the mourners at a Wilcannia funeral, even the Toorak doctor. The most vulnerable got the full News Corp treatment and complained, unsuccessfully, to the Australian Press Council.[11] The rush to blame, humiliate and harangue was swift and ruthless, even when the targets had done nothing wrong.

In the second plague winter, the judgementalism in its contemporary manifestation had people asking: *What has happened to this country? What have we become? What does it mean to be Australian?* The stories that became public during the long winter of 2021 when millions were locked down illuminated this institutionalised harshness. Sydney divided along its oldest lines: those in the west confined to quarters and under curfew, those closer to the ocean living with lockdown lite. Lives were turned upside down as visas and travel permits were refused: *Computer says no.* The messy reality of people's lives was not easily reduced to algorithms. Many who needed to visit dying relatives abroad were denied permission to leave. The algorithm did not consider parents close family members. Some stories were heartbreaking, such as that of a fully vaccinated woman briefly taken out of quarantine for an emergency caesarean but not allowed to touch or even see her premature baby until her fourteen days in isolation expired. Expensive visas were voided and families were prohibited from seeing one another, adding trauma to costly heartbreak. Isolationism dressed in the safety garb of national security prevailed.

Stories We Tell Ourselves

It was the image of a gravely ill little girl who had spent the previous three years in detention on remote Christmas Island as her parents fought for the right to remain in Australia that powerfully, if briefly, crystallised the bubbling sentiment *What has happened to this country? What have we become? What does it mean to be Australian?* The Murugappan family was among hundreds who had been caught in purgatory by changing government policies. A new low was set when Prime Minister Kevin Rudd in 2013 embraced the brutal exclusionary sentiment and declared that any refugees who arrived by boat in the 21st century would never reside in Australia.

This sideshow had been running with successive layers of cruel determination since 2001. It didn't take much historical imagination to see the replay with a twist of a foundation story of criminals and their overseers who had arrived by boat. The theft of land in the name of King George III went unremarked, but those who stole food from the settlement's precious stores were punished with death or deportation to a smaller island. During the COVID-19 years, the numbers of would-be refugees released, sent abroad or moved arbitrarily around the country reached new highs—the average time in detention exceeded 600 days. Protesters picketed the two-star hotels that had become detention centres and the powers that be responded by moving detainees, under cover of night, to unspecified locations.

Not since offending convicts were sent to ever-more remote islands had Australia treated new arrivals with such calculated brutality. Sending people to islands as a 'Dreadful and Awful Example to Others' had been imprinted as a punishment since the earliest days of white settlement. Joseph Hall and Henry Lovell were the first examples in February 1788. Thanks to a petition from their fellow thieves they escaped the gallows for stealing butter, peas and pork just weeks after the boats arrived, but were sent to penitentiary islands: Lovell to Norfolk and Hall to a week in irons on bread and water on the sandstone islet Mat-te-wan-ye (Pinchgut), within sight but just offshore. Life in irons not far from the makeshift convict settlement was better than death, but the lesson was impossible for other hungry men and women to ignore. Old habits die hard.

Turning living, suffering human refugees into numbers is hard administrative work but a task that had been well practised. Lesson number one since time immemorial in establishing a caste system is to strip people of their humanity, their name, their language.[12] Frequently this was done in the name of protection, but it was always designed to shame and undermine. The silence about deliberate official brutality has been broken since colonial times by periodic public inquiries and trials, even parliamentary debates, where some people of conscience complained about the harsh treatment of First Nations people, indentured Melanesians, and poor women. In contemporary times the unlikely Royal Commission into Human Relationships in the mid-1970s encouraged thousands of people to tell stories of their lives, of shame and guilt, punishment and brutality. Experiences once excised from the official language became public. Since then, one royal commission after another has heard the evidence of institutionalised, officially condoned abuse, of orphans, stolen children, people with disabilities, unmarried mothers and people in custody. The pattern was consistent. Strip people of their humanity, shame and humiliate them, ignore and silence them, deny them agency or respect. If they are just numbers they can never be truly human.

The Murugappans broke this rule. They had names, backstories and friends who were prepared to pursue every avenue they could to keep them close. The campaign to enable Priya and Nades Murugappan and their Australian-born daughters to return to Biloela, where they had been living and working since 2015, had been running ever since they were forcibly removed from their home in the early hours of 5 March 2018. After seriously ill three-year-old Tharnicaa's photo won headlines at home and around the world in June 2021, their case gained new momentum. Hundreds of thousands of people signed petitions, wrote letters to their MPs, called talkback radio, swamped social media, and created the evidence of community support that underpins ministerial discretion—discretion that allows hundreds of chosen people to remain each year.

———

STORIES MAKE US fully and uniquely human. They are the way we make sense of the world, our lives and relationships. They may not always be true, completely, or even substantially. They may be tinged with hyperbole and hope, fiercely contested or modified by hand-me-down retelling. Key characters and memories are conveniently or painfully lost in the miasma of pride, shame and trauma. But the best stories retain a flicker of emotional truth, a resonance that outlives the events, people and places they describe. The questions they raise are, as the philosopher Richard Rorty observed, 'part of the process of deciding what we will do next, what we will try to become'. Some provide the key to atonement, others a safe or challenging place to consider the lessons of the past. Others, over time, make the journey to myth, where they console and distract from more confronting truths.

This applies to nations as well as individuals, families and communities. Stories 'underlie the necessary fiction that is "us"', the Irish commentator Fintan O'Toole wrote as he pondered *what is the Irish story.*[14] The challenge is to allow multiple stories. Identity is not an either/or. It is possible to be attached to different places, beliefs and ways of being at the same time. To share an inner life with others of a complex place where belonging, not exclusion, prevails. In Australia, O'Toole's question is more often phrased as a negative accusation: that's unAustralian. In the early months of the pandemic former prime minister Tony Abbott declared it was time to again ask: *who are we?*[15] It was ironic that he should ask. His side of politics had scoffed at this question for decades as they wrapped themselves in the flag, with its dominant Union Jack, and repeated selective tales of the past. Discussions about national identity were dismissed as 'obsessive' and 'frantic', an endless seminar.[16] The necessary fictions of the official foundation story, the one that starts with European sailors and offers a cursory nod to those who were already here, have become an increasingly threadbare, lazy shorthand for a much more complex identity. A nation that does not know its history well enough to interrogate it, extract meaning from it and challenge its received wisdoms cannot imagine a robust future.

So much has been forgotten, or never known. False statements enter public discourse from the mouths of people who should know better with only belated clarification. Could any other prime minister so misunderstand the celebrated journey of his nation's foundation as Scott Morrison did when he suggested a re-enactment of James Cook's 'circumnavigation' of Australia? Cook, for whom Morrison's electorate is named, did not circumnavigate Australia. Matthew Flinders and the Kuring-gai man Bungaree first made that voyage. Yet the prime minister was prepared to allocate $6.7 million to build a replica of the *Endeavour* to 're-enact' the mythical voyage as a learning experience for the nation.[17] Can we just dismiss the ignorance of a nation's leader who could suggest that slavery never existed, when the legislation to deport indentured labourers from the Pacific (slaves by any other name) was one of the first bills to pass the national parliament a little over a century earlier?[18]

While the stories on the main stage all too often resemble the carcass of a dead animal on a drought plain, those percolating elsewhere are rich with nuance, inclusion and possibility. The ancient stories of the peoples our official narratives tried so hard for so long to extinguish are being coaxed back from memory and official records; languages once banned are now taught in schools and appear routinely on signs, television titles, and even envelopes. Australia Post announced in 2021 that mail would be delivered to addresses that included First Nations place names 25 years after the revealing patchwork map was published. The lands and languages of First Nations peoples were now named. Speakers once shamed and jailed are now honoured for rescuing words and stories to buttress the uniqueness of a continent that is now a nation.

Fintan O'Toole has described the profound challenge to national, personal and community identity that followed the collapse of respect for the Catholic Church as Ireland's pre-eminent institution. 'People do need a sense of collective purpose, a sense that there is something that they belong to and that belongs to them,' he wrote. 'All the evidence is that if one set of stories no longer makes sense, people do not simply become realists. They become prey to any old story at all, especially one that has potent contrast between Us and Them.'[19] This is not the only response.

Inquiries in Australia have also revealed the limitations of once-trusted organisations. Institutions created to make a democratic system robust, accountable and ethical could no longer be relied on. Brutal stories of abuse and betrayal that were once held as tightly as state secrets were revealed in heartbreaking royal commissions and aired on endless news bulletins, helpfully tagged with the numbers of charities to call to manage the grief. Joyful stories of opportunity and transformation also jostle, but don't fit the catastrophic definitions of news and are harder to hear. Still, most Australians supported their sons and daughters being able to marry irrespective of sexual preference. Stories that stretch narrow stereotypes are welcomed. Stories that extend belonging do not destroy society, as some feared, but make it stronger and more interesting.[20]

In 2007, I, like most Australians, voted for a change of government. I enjoyed trying to figure out who among my neighbours were the 338 people who had pushed the Labor vote up 17 per cent in one of the most traditionally Liberal polling booths in Sydney. Earwigging at the corner shop, on dog walks around the harbourside parks or on the ferry meant they weren't hard to identify. Even in this rich old suburb named for a tyrannical governor, home to more than its fair share of life's winners, I was not alone in feeling that the momentum, which had made the country I knew as an adult more interesting than the one I had known as a child, had stalled.

Well before the new nation first raised its flag with a nod to empire and geography, the idea of Australia was a contest between the inward- and outward-looking, between ambition and complacency, between human rights and disempowerment, between labour and capital. There is a clear pattern: inquiry comes in energetic waves and then dissipates. Conversations begin and are all too often shouted down or dismissed. Surveying the topography of an evolving national identity reveals peaks of great change and long valleys of fearful, censorious complacency.

The journey to redefine the nation began after Prime Minister John Curtin announced in late 1941 that Australia would look to the United States for her defence. This was an important marker in the beginning of a reconstruction that would gather momentum for decades.[21] As decolonising movements swept the world, a positive, inclusive, home-grown nationalism eventually delivered new stories and long overdue reforms. The often painful assimilation of new Australians in time gave way to a celebration of multiculturalism; the economy diversified, more people were better educated, Australia became confidently in and of the region rather than looking across continents for a European home.

As the new nationalism of the 1970s gave way to the Labor government's modified neoliberalism of the following decade, Australians grew richer, less defensive and even more engaged with the world. When the Coalition government returned to power in 1996, the principles of the market economy were given even freer rein. It was surprising to see the myths of the Australian legend reinvented by John Howard.

Stories We Tell Ourselves

The symbolism was clear when the quintessentially suburban prime minister donned an Akubra, opting for the 'Squatter' design. What the new nationalists had evoked in books and on screen as a myth of egalitarianism morphed into a story of self-interest and individual success. Symbolism became another commodity. R.M. Williams boots embodied this evolution. The now expensive designer boots were first made from a single piece of leather during the Great Depression by a man in the remote Flinders Ranges who felt the force of that catastrophe. By the time they became a national icon, the company was owned by Rupert Murdoch's right-hand man in Australia. Then another luxury brand owned by Louis Vuitton, and the footwear of choice for prime ministers and presidents. More recently, the boots became a bauble for another rich man who made his extraordinary fortune shipping iron ore to China. The irony was unmistakable.

The egalitarian myth was stripped of its collectivist spirit to become a glossy fantasy. In the same sweep, unionists became self-employed tradies, private and religious schools created one of the world's most segregated education systems, union membership plummeted, fragile institutions of First Nation self-determination were dismantled, cities bristled with McMansions in ever-growing suburbs and the bush was transformed by industrial mining. The malleability of myth was best demonstrated in 2010 when some of the world's biggest companies, whose wealth came from the minerals they extracted from the land, invoked the spirit of the Eureka Stockade to campaign against a super profits tax, taking a Labor prime minister down with them.[22]

A new age in Australia should have dawned with the centenary of Federation in 2001. Committees were formed, conventions held to consider not just the creation of a republic but a fundamental rethink of the constitution, recognition of First Nations people and more. Then the agenda shrank and became increasingly preoccupied with process. The first step—to create a republic and replace the monarch with a local head of state, an idea that once enjoyed overwhelming support—failed, even with the support of the Murdoch press. As time went on, Australia become more divided and cynical, less imaginative and generous. Politics become more transactional, more 'professional', less visionary, too often captive to bullies, designed to resist the change that is essential in any living system.[23]

Similar patterns played out in other nations where the market was given its head and myths commoditised in the neoliberal realignment in the last decades of the twentieth century. In Britain, and America as well, institutions of self-government were undermined. Public good became harder to define and even harder to defend. Apathy was fostered and trust eroded. George Packer the American author of *Last Best Hope*, is deeply troubled by the deliberate destruction, in the name of the market, of institutions of self-government in his country. He fears visionless political leaders 'hold on to power and fatten corporate allies. Corruption—financial, political, intellectual, moral—set in like dry rot in a hollow log.'[24] It sounds familiar.

The big patterns were not so clear in the 2007 election when Prime Minister Howard lost his seat and even the most traditionally conservative electorates signalled they were ready for a change. It was time to resume the discussion about how to thrive in the 21st century. A decade earlier Pauline Hanson was condemned in the national parliament for her inflammatory racist views, but her views had been normalised. They were embodied in 2005 in the most serious racially charged riot in Australia's post-war history. The sunburnt blond boys of Cronulla battled to force the swarthy lads from further west off *their* patch of sand. Many feared irreparable damage had been done.

Still, I hung on to the knowledge that things had once been worse, more closed down, less welcoming for those who did not quietly fit themselves into the mainstream. In 2007 when people lined up to vote and buy a sausage sandwich there was still a sense of hope. In my mind, despite the disappointments of the previous decade, the arc was still bending upwards towards a more inclusive and respectful society.

Stories We Tell Ourselves

Listening to a group of brilliant young people, men and women a generation younger than me, at the 2020 Summit in Parliament House in 2008, brought me up with a start. They said they were almost embarrassed to be Australian. They felt no affinity with the *Crocodile Dundee/Throw a shrimp on the barbie/Where the bloody hell are you?* version of the country. The idea of Australia they saw being projected did not reflect the diversity they knew, or the stories they wanted to hear and tell. The 'history wars' had raged during their schooling with officially sanctioned attacks on the historians who revealed darker tales. These brilliant young people felt Australia's reluctance to face the past meant the nation was going nowhere. They preferred to think of themselves as citizens of the world, ready to detach, and make their lives elsewhere. This was before banking fraud triggered the global financial crisis, before Trump, before Brexit, and before professionalised politics spun the revolving door so fast it spat out five Australian prime ministers in a decade.

I could see how this had happened. The momentum that had driven national transformation had slowed in 1996 with a change of government. It stalled in 2001 when Australian leaders refused assistance to hapless boats of refugees and hundreds drowned in the ferocious waters of the Indian Ocean. The language of exclusion and fear that characterised the Federation parliament was again invoked. Those poor Hazari asylum seekers were wrongly accused of throwing their children overboard, echoing the claims a century earlier that 'blackbirded' Melanesian labourers in Mackay ate their babies.[25]

Old tropes shaped by fear once again became the new normal. When John Howard announced in 2001, with righteous fury, that 'we will decide who comes to this country and the circumstances in which they come', the angry political rhetoric that enabled the White Australia policy again bubbled to the surface. Not since Governor Phillip had sought offshore islands to punish the most intractable convicts had there been such a search for islands—this time as a dumping ground for the unwanted. It was not just rhetoric. Legislation was passed that adjusted Australia's territorial boundaries. Boats were turned back and discussion about 'on-water matters' banned. Tears welled in politicians' eyes as they talked about the drownings at sea, and their tone switched to anger when describing evil people smugglers. Meanwhile, refugees whose lives had become intolerable in their homelands suffered under Australian administration. It was a textbook example of George Orwell's definition of political speech as the euphemistic defence of the indefensible.[26]

We don't like to dig too deeply into these stories. Unlike some nations that suffer under the burden of too much history, it sometimes seems Australia doesn't have much. Instead the habit of a lack of curiosity has prevailed, preferring to look away, perhaps fearful of what might be found. But harsh, officially sanctioned suffering is as much a part of the formation of a national ethos as self-reliant pragmatism. It recurs in public and private life. The times should favour openness, but secrecy—the first cousin of incuriousness—is deeply embedded. This is fertile territory for the oldest tropes to bubble up like groundwater, bitter with excess salt and polluted by the detritus of mining and industrial agriculture. I wonder how these institutional cruelties endure when they are nurtured by neglect, and how they might be displaced by ideas that enable us to create an Australia that knows its past well enough to foster an enduring open, innovative, generous society.

5

Architecture of Silence

FORTY YEARS AGO, when the Australian population was only about half its current number, Bernard Smith delivered the ABC's Boyer Lectures. The great art historian wanted to talk about the legacy of *being a bastard*, but the powers that be made it clear that this emotionally challenging subject was strictly off limits. The stigma of being born illegitimately in 1916 was still real 64 years later. He was told he must not stray beyond the invitation's 'intended parameters ... the visual arts', although none had been included in the formal invitation.[1]

As they listened to his 1980 lectures, the ABC's commissioners must have wished they had heeded the sage advice to 'be careful what you wish for'. *The Spectre of Truganini* is arguably the most politically and morally challenging lecture series the national broadcaster has ever transmitted. It was informed by Bernard Smith's deep knowledge of the nation's cultural history in literature, film and visual arts, and his personal insights accumulated over a lifetime as a successful *bastard*. Smith declared that a culture's 'vitality and capacity for survival will depend largely on the quality of the moral values it brings to the solution of human problems ... values born of its own historical experience, values which are continuously tested'.[2]

Over five weeks he described the way the 'white blanket of forgetfulness' had been repeatedly thrown over the carcass of genocide that haunted the nation, and wondered whether the deep fear of change would render the country unviable in the next century. Yet he dreamed that a Makarrata would be in place before the bicentenary eight years hence. Thirty-seven years later, the plea for a Makarrata formed the centrepiece of the *Uluru Statement from the Heart*, a plea that was rejected rather than just ignored.

Bernard Smith based his optimism on the transformations he had observed in the Australian population as a 'lucky young bastard' who was raised with generosity and openness by those who looked beyond the stigma of 'illegitimacy' to find real people eager to learn and empathise. The knowledge and understanding that came from listening, learning, researching and writing had evolved over his lifetime. Its cultural expression in books, films and art was more widely shared and valued. He hoped that those with informed consciences would prevail, that the benefits of inclusion would outweigh the fear that powered exclusion. Now it's likely that Bernard's Smith's personal story of being 'born a bastard' but much loved and without shame, which the ABC commissioners once considered off limits, would gobble the airtime, rather than a deeper discussion about how this lived experience shaped his serious and challenging ideas.

Knowledge about the history of this place and its people has increased exponentially over the past four decades, but there are still many gaps. People from diverse backgrounds, people who would once have struggled to find a place in the tight private school–dominated world of ideas—*bastards* of all sorts—are asserting the right to tell their stories. The number of professional historians has grown from five before the Second World War to thousands today.[3] More history is revealed; more diverse and complex stories are told. It should now

Architecture of Silence

be impossible to say that the idea of the place started when the British ships hove into view. Yet in September 2021, then federal Liberal minister for education Alan Tudge declared that some history was off limits. The undisputed loss of 62,000 Australian lives in the First World War commemorated on Anzac Day was, he declared, too sacred to be described as 'contested',[4] although its complex meaning demands constant re-examination. Under his administration, he told parliament he wanted 'a positive, an optimistic and patriotic view of history embedded in the curriculum'. When history teachers responded to ask how they might teach more optimistically, their questions were deemed offensive by the administrator of the minister's Twitter account. Their accounts were blocked.[5] Ignoring, and refusing to hear or discuss, are powerful silencing tools.

A decade after his death, one can only imagine the despair Bernard Smith, like the other great scholars, advocates, politicians and public servants of his generation, would feel about this. The gap between a culturally informed and concerned national conscience and a brutal, nitpicking politics intolerant of dissent has grown to become a chasm. It is taking much longer than Bernard Smith had optimistically predicted for the truths that were swept out the door to blow back in through open windows.[6]

SILENCE IS NOT just an absence. Sophisticated scaffolding is needed to keep the dark hole open and empty. It takes determination for a nation created out of reports and official inquiries to hide. Bureaucracies thrive on records. The early administrators sent to establish an open-air penal settlement documented everything in fine copperplate. Reports, documents and accounts were written on parchment, tied with blue ribbon and sent back to Whitehall. There they were considered, reviewed, filed and tucked away in archives. Later records from the colonies and states were typed in triplicate. But many decisions and documents crumbled like the paper they were written on. Institutions sometimes prefer to hide their secrets in plain sight. Families with shameful stories, like nations, develop a habit of secrecy and will go to extraordinary lengths to maintain the silence. This is not confined to the distant past. Those in power and with something to hide, and a flexible attachment to liberal conventions, will stretch the tools at their disposal to protect themselves, closing courts, redacting documents, pillorying individuals, invoking defamation laws.

For a nation with a bureaucratic creation story, its recordkeeping has left a lot to be desired. There are stories of lost and inadequate records in every state and territory. Queensland is home to several of the most instructive. It took decades before the destruction of many Native Police archives in 1939 became public.[7] It meant there were apparently no diary records to test the rumours of the 'collisions'—killings—by the Native Police. Tales of its terrorising impact were left to hand-me-down stories, the distortions of memory and mask of defensiveness. And grief.

The part colonial police force, part military organisation operated in Queensland from 1860 to 1910, its ill-disciplined leaders drawing on the oldest lesson of colonial administrations: divide and rule native populations. Its remit was to 'suppress Indigenous resistance to colonisation',[8] so elders with cultural knowledge and young people who could nurse their anger for a lifetime were particular targets. Carl Feilberg, who was inducted into the Australian Media Hall of Fame in 2018, more than 130 years after his death, paid a high price for his campaign against the brutality of the termagant force. He lost his job as editor of *The Queenslander* after documenting the 'promiscuous massacres'. 'Every resident of Brisbane,' he wrote in 1880, 'who, becoming aware of what is going on, neglects to do what he can in his capacity as a citizen and voter to wipe out the stain which rests on the whole colony, shares the disgrace of it.'[9] In recent years, the

Architecture of Silence

disgrace has again been revealed. There was every reason for officials to wish these records lost to fire. When historians and archivists decided to look harder, they found that much remained, hidden in dusty files. Even though the police diaries had evaporated, there were hundreds of letters to and from the colonial secretary, records of coronial inquests and newspaper reports. Jonathan Richards, the author of *The Secret War*, noted that many were replete with 'clerical errors' designed to compound a 'frontier culture based on secrecy, discretion and suspicion'. The extent of the violent attacks, reprisals and massacres was vast and undeniable, resulting in many tens of thousands of deaths that were 'profligate, furtive and unprosecuted'.[10]

The greatest secrecy always attaches to records that threaten to reveal what was known about politically inspired or sanctioned abuses of power. Forty years after the Native Police was disbanded in Queensland, the Cold War elevated another threat that needed a dedicated force. In 1948, the Special Branch of the Queensland Police was established, a year before ASIO was founded, to monitor a new breed of those with 'dangerous' views—communists. Special Branch's remit grew and became more political under the quasi-authoritarian administration of Joh Bjelke-Petersen. Following his inquiry into police and political corruption in the state, Tony Fitzgerald QC recommended that the Special Branch be abolished, and Freedom of Information be made law. Even before these recommendations could be implemented by the first state Labor government in 32 years, the recently arrived police commissioner, Noel Newnham, directed that the Special Branch records be destroyed. One hundred and thirty-three political activists who hoped to gain access to their files, historians with a more general interest and others asked the Supreme Court to prevent the destruction. They hoped that access to the information would reveal the extent of the politicisation of the police under the Bjelke-Petersen government. By the time the court considered the matter, it was too late: 24,216 branch files and 107,398 index cards had been trashed.[11]

The Queensland state archivist authorised the destruction on the same day the police commissioner made his request, before the new government took office. She feared 'public mischief would be caused by access to sensitive and confidential documents'.[12]

WHEN PAUL HASLUCK travelled east from Perth in 1941 to take up a position in the federal Department of External Affairs, the journalist and academic who later became a Liberal government minister and governor-general was astonished to discover the inadequacy of the recordkeeping. Hasluck was one of a new breed of public servants drawn to Canberra by the existential threat of war, even before Darwin was bombed and Japanese subs entered Sydney Harbour. His skills as a researcher, oral historian and journalist were invaluable in the reconstruction effort that began before the war was over. Shortly after he arrived in the department, he asked for highly confidential cables on Syria to prepare a brief on a possible Allied intervention. He was instead brought a file on Tasmania. The clerk who brought them, he later recounted, said she 'could not find Syria in the index of files but one of the boys told her it was a town in Tasmania'.[13] The department files were a mess, recordkeeping chaotic, access to information and past decisions dependent on memory and networks. Hasluck was appalled. He knew the importance of official files from his research into the failure of protectionist and segregationist Aboriginal policies in his home state. It took another twenty years before the archives were given some autonomy, though still in the prime minister's department, and it was 1983 before legislation was passed to form an independent authority. Four score years and two since the nation had come into being.

Buildings often reveal priorities more robustly than words. Walter Burley Griffin and Marion Mahony Griffin's[14] design for Canberra included a National Archive in the parliamentary triangle of the national capital. The American designers drew on the institutions of their own capital, where a grand neoclassical archive takes pride of place between Congress and the White House. As the Australian institutions grew on the banks of the lake named for Walter Burley Griffin, plans for the archives literally fell off the drawing board. First it was to be a wing of the National Library, then on a site overlooking the precinct that has since become the ASIO headquarters, then a separate building near the library.[15] Two competitions were held to find the best design and two winners selected, but nothing was built. Instead, much of the lakeside site was used to build Questacon, a science museum, funded in large measure by a bicentennial gift from the Japanese government. Today, the National Archives of Australia leases one of the modest Art Deco buildings on the outer edge of the precinct, its records stored off site in a stylish building in an industrial estate on the outskirts of Canberra.[16] Its place in the hierarchy is plain to see.

It should not have been surprising that the archives showed up in one of the COVID X-rays. Like all the cultural institutions, it had been struggling for years, weakened by a lack of respect, recognition and resources. The waiting time for requests had grown so embarrassingly long that the archives stopped including the clearance rate in its annual report. It emerged that despite the legislative requirement of a maximum 90-day wait, 10,000 requests had been unanswered for a year, 10,000 for five to ten years and 256 for more than ten years.[17] In early 2021, the minister responsible for the national memory bank, Senator Amanda Stoker, dismissed a report that found the neglect was such that the archives was unable to do its job. 'Time marches on and all sources degrade over time,' she declared. With one throwaway line, the former lawyer galvanised a campaign by historians and prominent public figures. They knew in their bones that ensuring access to sources was essential to good government, and to a cohesive and informed society. *The Australian*, in a homage to its founding nationalist ethos, joined the campaign. Rupert Murdoch's newspapers like to boast about shaping policy and political decisions, so when the minister saw the error of her ways, the paper bragged, in its time-honoured way, that its intervention had persuaded the government to act. Nearly $70 million became available within days to digitise some records and make the archives cyber secure. Even *The Australian*'s reflexively grumpy readers, who could spot any sign of incipient socialism from the nineteenth hole, agreed that records were needed and shouldn't be allowed to degrade.

Allocating scarce public funding requires judgements about priorities. Some of those involved in the campaign wondered whether a cash-strapped, avowedly pro-disclosure organisation should have spent millions of dollars and the time of its most senior officials over a decade trying to prevent access to its documents. As authoritarians everywhere know, even old official records are not neutral artifacts. Jenny Hocking has made a brilliant career researching and writing about the characters who drove transformational change in Australia. Her two-volume biography of Gough Whitlam won many awards and helped to flesh out the personal and political motivations of the politician who did more than any individual to shape modern Australia.[18] He had touched every aspect of life in a whirlwind three years in office before being dismissed by the governor-general, Sir John Kerr, in what many consider a constitutional coup. Whitlam drew the ire of the old establishment but inspired others who were surprised to discover that after twenty-three years of conservative rule, change was possible. Thirty-five years after Whitlam's dismissal, Hocking was denied access to hundreds of letters between Kerr and Queen Elizabeth II from that time. The National Archives claimed the letters were 'personal' and embargoed by the queen.

In July 2011, the ever-optimistic historian requested access to an unexpectedly located copy of this correspondence that had been deposited, without restrictions, by the Kerr family. She was surprised to discover a month later that not only would she be denied the records, but that the open-access classification had been retrospectively revoked.[19] Hocking's hopes of discovering the behind-the-scenes discussions that had preceded that epoch-defining event on 11 November 1975 were dashed. Her niggling fear that the archives was not an organisation that defaulted to disclosure was set to be realised.

A Kafkaesque battle began, reaching into the heart of government and public administration in Australia and the United Kingdom; Queen Elizabeth II, who preferred to operate with an invisible hand, did not want the letters released. It did not matter that at different times over the decade-long battle, an Australian attorney-general and a prime minister had wanted the documents released. The archives fought to keep the records private, a battle that had cost the cash-strapped organisation more than $2 million by the time its recommendation was eventually overturned by the High Court. These were not private and personal letters but matters of national significance between the two people at the top of the pyramid of Australian government—one in Yarralumla, the other in Buckingham Palace.

There is no better example of the way a commitment to secrecy, and the enduring determination to protect imperial interests, still pervades Australian society. More than a century after the British parliament approved the Australian Constitution, the palace still had more than a symbolic role in Australian governance. Not long after Jenny Hocking's quest to open and read the 1200 pages of correspondence had begun, the Archives was reclassified as an agency of national security rather than culture. This reflected the way national security was displacing economics as the dominant lingua franca of policy in Canberra. It was there in ministerial statements, retail politics and bureaucratic hierarchy.

Again, buildings spoke volumes. A Museum of Aboriginal Australia was considered an important priority in 1975, but nearly 50 years later, after it was stalled by one inquiry after another and on the eve of another election, Prime Minister Morrison, wearing a Dreamtime tie, promised it again. In the meantime, the National Museum had been tormented by political opposition but Questacon, the National Portrait Gallery and Magna Carta Place sprouted in the parliamentary precinct. New headquarters for the spy agencies were built in a prime position overlooking the national capital. Half a billion dollars was allocated to expand the Australian War Memorial into a war museum but still excluding the most Australian wars—the frontier wars. The Griffins had imagined its elevated site on the Parliament House axis as the place for a pleasure palace, a 'casino' in the parlance of the day. The devastation of the First World War, where the live-or-die game of two-up had distracted men facing death, shifted priorities. Pleasure palaces slipped off the agenda and instead the site would house a memorial, which was built and opened as another war took its toll in lives. The sweeping views from the Eternal Flame, over the Pool of Reflection and over the lake to parliament, put the human cost of war at the sober heart of national life. There were howls of opposition to the plans to undermine the ethos embedded in the expansion, and allocate so much money to the top tourist attraction in Canberra while other cultural institutions resorted to crowdfunding to maintain their operations. Former generals, curators, historians, politicians and architects argued the vast development was inappropriate, and would desecrate a sacred site.[20] But national security was ascendant, tourism numbers spoke and approvals were given.

THE ATTACHMENT TO official secrecy has deep roots. It took the High Court four score and eleven years to discover an implied freedom of political communication in the Australian Constitution. Even then the right was not a personal guarantee of freedom of political speech. It was limited to the effective operation of responsible and reasonable government as befits a nation with a bureaucratic, not revolutionary, foundation story. There were many ways of limiting the freedom of speech that is central to political communication: administratively, legally and by custom and practice dressed in the clothes of protection and security.

Censorship regimes operated by all governments prevented tens of thousands of books, journals, movies and reports being made available to the public until the early 1970s, when they collapsed under the weight of public opinion and legal challenges.[21] Secrets are the currency of the intelligence services, including the state Special Branches that were used for years without impunity against political opponents. Despite increasingly fervent declarations of fealty to the Magna Carta's right to open trials, closed courts, legal proceedings hidden from public view and mandatory confidential cross-examinations became unremarkable features of laws enacted in the 21st century.[22] Constitutional scholars argued, with little impact, that the government's willingness to undermine democratic rights by closing courts and redacting evidence threatened the core principles of liberal democracy. Openness had been a short-lived and patchily implemented preference. Freedom of information laws became a minefield where delay rather than disclosure prevails; government contracts limited by confidentiality clauses, official corruption scarcely scrutinised. Australians like to think they are open and direct, but still much happens behind closed doors without an accessible paper trail.[23]

Freedom of information had been slow to arrive in Australia; the first legislation passed in 1982, fifteen years after the US Congress enacted similar laws. The principle of openness has struggled to be firmly established, and governments have found ways to wind it back ever since. The instinct is to find ways to hide—take revealing documents to cabinet, declare them commercial in confidence, redact them beyond meaning. Life was made so uncomfortable for whistle-blowers who spotted corruption and maladministration that some became a modern 'Dreadful and Awful Example to Others'. Ministers talked themselves hoarse declaring important issues of public policy could not be discussed because they were 'operational matters'. During the dark period, when scores of boats a year were being turned back to prevent would-be refugees landing on Australian soil and claiming their rights under the international convention Australia had signed, 'on-water matters' were cloaked in secrecy.

It was scarcely surprising that this became another fault line revealed in the COVID X-ray. After the prime minister created a national cabinet of premiers to manage the pandemic response, an overseeing Senate committee struggled to get access to the documents it needed. Feisty former submariner and independent senator Rex Patrick took the matter to the Administrative Appeals Tribunal, which ruled that the ad hoc body was not subject to cabinet confidentiality. The government's response was to introduce new legislation to further entrench a culture of secrecy, despite furious opposition by constitutional experts.

Fear is another plank in the scaffold of silence. Public servants like many employees are contractually bound to keep the secrets of those who employ them. Those compelled by conscience to disclose soon discover a new meaning of loneliness. It doesn't take long to realise that caution is secrecy's big sister. Listen to public servants, politicians and political advisers earnestly discussing how any complicated issue could look reduced to five words and a picture on the front page of the local tabloid and the lesson is clear. Best not to be too ambitious. Don't rock the boat; keep the status quo.

Peak bodies of lawyers, and critics with long memories and deep experience, argued that silence was at odds with the best traditions of accountable government, that openness was a virtue that could ensure the best decisions were made, that citizens were familiar with the options. They were batted aside in the brutal *realpolitik* where the winners wrote and supervised the rules. Fears about national security, about the threat posed by foreign agents of influence, of political embarrassment, of hints of corruption and political favours were deemed to be more important. Freedom of information requests were refused,

Architecture of Silence

documents redacted beyond meaning and whistle-blowers targeted. This suggested the system was more fragile and existentially threatened than was apparent in the sunny uplands of daily life in the world's most liveable country.

CULTURE WAS THE chief target of the censorship regimes that prevailed for decades. Novels, films, paintings and magazines were caught in the web. In 1971 Don Chipp, then the Liberal customs minister, invited journalist Jane Perlez into what he called 'censorship's inner sanctum'.[24] In a fibro office in a neon-lit reading room at the National Library, he showed her the thousands of books that had been censored by customs and the literature censorship boards. First editions of James Joyce's *Ulysses* and T.E. Lawrence; number 26 of the *Kama Sutra* on parchment; books banned for their blasphemy, erotica and politics. Don Chipp's growing frustration with the reactionary conservatism of the Liberal Party led him six years later to found the Australian Democrats 'to keep the bastards honest'. The censorship regime eventually imploded and the books were forgotten. Thirty years later, literary historian Nicole Moore started to hunt for the censor's library. It seemed to have disappeared. Eventually, in 2005, staff at the vast National Archives storage facility at Chester Hill in western Sydney noticed an exceptionally large, uncatalogued customs file titled 'Miscellaneous'. When they looked for it, they found the 'file' seven storeys underground. It defied the usual understanding of a file. There were 793 boxes of books, nearly 12,000 titles, all neatly covered in brown paper and catalogued. It was, as Nicole Moore noted in her book *The Censor's Library*, a 'metonym for the secret exercise of power over knowledge'.

Censorship aims to keep knowledge and critical thinking at bay, but it can be limited by less obviously heavy-handed means. In 1980, Bernard Smith's critical Boyer Lectures were infused with hope. At the time, a spontaneous cultural flowering had emerged; censorship collapsed under its own weight. It was nurtured with public funds for artists, writers and filmmakers, and new and restored galleries and performance spaces. Australians were ready to face the world directly and had begun to absorb and enjoy more interesting stories about themselves; many were inflected with history, while others shattered the silence born of shame and fear.

Ever since the Commonwealth Literary Fund was created in 1908, support for the arts has been a dance with patronage and politics, generally with bipartisan support. When Bernard Smith was preparing his Boyer Lectures, he could not have anticipated that public support for culture would one day become so fraught. Or that the free-market ideas of Milton Friedman's barnstorming lecture series a few years earlier would find such fertile soil, and give birth to a robust libertarian network of think tanks and politicians. In the increasingly market-driven context of the early 21st century, culture became less about meaning and sense making and more like another commercial enterprise. Those that measured their achievements in dollars were rebranded 'creative industries', and some areas of popular music, publishing, film and television flourished. But public support for culture as a public good languished and was bitterly contested. As concern about national security increasingly takes centre stage, cultural expression is particularly troublesome. It depends on openness, encourages critical reflection. Its social value cannot be simply measured in sales.

Culture is, to hark back to its original meaning, a form of cultivation that nurtures the mind and spirit—the soul. It is not something that responds well to a utilitarian public domain. It needs space and time, creativity and openness, skill and thoughtfulness. Cultivation transforms seeds into plants, which nourish and sustain; similarly, culture transforms lives, turns the shadows of insight into meaning. Its restlessness is dangerous, and it is not comfortable with the status quo. Sense making mugs us by surprise—the painting that distils a dimly perceived truth, the music that captures emotion, the play or film that forces you into the experience of another, the novel that allows the unspeakable to be written and its impact explored. All produce stories that break the silence.

Culture is more complicated than the prevailing commercial framework allows, its value less easily quantified but its absence easy to spot. Political attempts to control and limit cultural expression and inquiry have a history that dates to Governor Philip Gidley King's decision to raze Sydney's first theatre in September 1800.[25] The governor, like many of his successors, sensed the danger was real. It is through culture that authority is challenged and meaning is made. Its foundations are in people, place, language, imagination and morals. By the time the COVID X-ray was taken, its fragility was undeniable—hundreds of thousands lost their jobs, audiences evaporated, companies collapsed. The stories, music and images that had clothed the scaffold of silence became increasingly threadbare.

CULTURE GROWS FROM language. Without language, stories are lost and knowledge disappears. Culture depends on language. Criminalising the use of the languages of the First Australians, requiring immigrants to pass a language test and treating new arrivals who had not yet mastered English with disdain were all part of the scaffolding of silence.

For more than two centuries, those who had lived with the land for millennia were subjected to one policy after another to render them silent. But the stories, so deeply entwined in the place, survived, and the languages people had been jailed for using were recaptured thanks to elders who remembered, scholars who recorded and young people hungry to learn. New words and concepts broke the silence.

The human spirit was stronger and prevailed. The journalist Stan Grant wrote how his father felt compelled to accept a mission to save the Wiradjuri language. 'As a boy, he had spent time with his grandfather Budyaan out in the scrub . . . Budyaan yelled out to Dad one day in the main street of town and a cop heard him. The old man was arrested and jailed. When he came out, he said he would never speak our language again. He saved it only for when Dad was with him, out where no white man could hear him.'[26] Brave-spirited people preserved and restored languages, and encouraged their children to treasure and share them. The Wiradjuri dictionary that Stan Grant senior created became the backbone of Tara June Winch's Miles Franklin–winning novel *The Yield*. The artist Fiona Foley followed the footsteps of her mother, who recorded the Badtjala language of the people who lived on K'gari and traversed the waters of the Fraser Coast. As novelist Kim Scott slowly discovered his heritage, he embarked on a Noongar language reclamation project. Dictionaries are being recreated, school children are being taught the original languages of their neighbourhoods, even *Gardening Australia* calls the areas it features in its prime-time television slot by their original names. When the governor of New South Wales welcomes visitors to the original seat of settler power in the state, with its sweeping views up Sydney Harbour, past the sentinel islands to the heads, she does so, at length, in Dharug—the language of the people who were displaced—breaking the silence of centuries, allowing new stories to be told.

As people began sending the painful, shameful, secret and joyous stories of their lives to the Royal Commission into Human Relationships, the public wall of silence around lives as they were actually lived began to break. Twenty years later, in 1995, when the Labor attorney-general Michael Lavarch prepared the terms of reference for a national inquiry into the separation of Aboriginal and Torres Strait Islander children from their families, the dyke burst, and painful, shameful, humiliating, distressing stories have gushed out in official inquiries ever since. Over the following two years, the inquiry just scratched the surface as it heard the stories of 535 people who had been removed from their families as children. The painful vignettes of their lives were recorded in the 690 pages of the *Bringing Them Home* report: people who had been separated from mothers, fathers, brothers and sisters; people who had been tricked and shamed; people who had spent a lifetime trying to put the pieces back together. Heartbreak, shame, fear and trauma spring from every page. So does survival.

Sometimes not telling was a necessary part of survival, sometimes that cost was impossible. As the novelist Melissa Lucashenko observed, 'All over Australia there are elders who won't tell young people what happened because they don't want anger and hard feelings stirred up. I think we need both. How do you tell the truth and yet have a narrative that ends in hope, that ends in a possibility of redemption for the country? It's a difficult thing when political resolutions haven't happened yet.'

Miriam-Rose Ungunmerr-Baumann had known for a long time that she, and the Ngangikurungkurr people of the Daly River in the north-west of the Northern Territory, had a gift for the nation.[27] For a nation where the habit of secrecy was deeply ingrained, the 2021 Senior Australian of the Year knew the gift her people had to offer may not be easy to accept. She knew it would take time, but she was accustomed to waiting and challenging accepted norms. The first Aboriginal person to qualify as a teacher in the Northern Territory was convinced that despite centuries of policy that had sought to make the First Australians 'traumatised outcasts in their own land',[28] her people were not the problem captured in the seemingly intractable statistics of disadvantage, but the key to the future. They were, in the jargon of the day, part of the solution. Much more than window dressing in tourism campaigns that evoke an ancient land where, as Stan Grant once wrote, 'an Aborigine is a marketing tool'.[29]

Dadirri is a word from the first of her six languages, one that survived the bans and punishments that pushed many languages to extinction. It encompasses deep listening and hearing, and a respectful contemplation that seeks to understand, becoming a way of life and informing action. There are similar concepts in other First Nations languages. In the Dharug and Dharawal languages, it is *ngara*.[30] It is a concept that makes it clear that listening is not passive; to really hear, one needs to hover over and *listen*. Its anagram is silent, and listening the key to the secret code.

Miriam-Rose Ungunmerr-Baumann first described the ancient cultural practice publicly at a teachers' conference in Tasmania in 1988. Five years later, when her paper was published in an academic journal, it entered the literature and changed the paradigm for teaching students with entrenched disadvantage. Even before the scientists started exploring epigenetic transfer she knew that trauma lingered and extracted a toll from one generation to the next.

Judy Atkinson had worked with Aboriginal communities in Queensland for years before she came across Ungunmerr-Baumann's work. As a community advocate in North Queensland who traced to Jiman, Bundjalung and Celtic-German in her heritage, she had become increasingly desperate to find a better way to understand and address the violence that ravaged so many First Nations communities, violence that corroded and destroyed so many lives. She participated in endless discussions about policies and procedures, and endless meetings that seemed to miss the point. People in positions of power thought that the old methods of segregation, protection and assimilation would eventually work. One senior bureaucrat in 1988 told her that 'the solution is clear . . . just stop them from breeding'.[31] As a respite, in the evenings she took to sitting under the mango trees in the impoverished settlements of north Queensland, listening to the elders. Years later she told the story in a TED talk at the Sydney Opera House that has since reached the world. She spoke of how this active listening set her on a path to understanding the language of violence, and the many layers of anger and grief that powered it. Listening, she realised, was the beginning of healing. 'With listening to long-repressed stories comes a responsibility. It forces us to listen to ourselves and challenge our own inherited assumptions, judgements, prejudices, the resistance we all have individually and as a nation.'

In workshops and retreats around the country, Atkinson worked with Ungunmerr-Baumann to apply *dadirri*—using respectful listening, talking and contemplation to inform action and transform lives and communities. Breaking the silence was the crucial first step. She soon realised that its benefits did not only apply to First Nations peoples living with multigenerational grief, but more widely in a nation marinated in trauma. 'There is an anger across this nation that we choose not to acknowledge,' she told the full house at the Sydney Opera House in 2017:

> It is an anger fuelled by racism, prejudice, discrimination and poverty. A distressed discontent that is growing, not just here but around the world. But under anger is always grief . . .
>
> There is a truth in this country we must confront as we move into maturity. The grief of separation and loss, of shame, of pain, deep and unresolved. A woundedness that is much more than the commemoration of the Anzacs and much, much more than the celebration partying and boozing that we have on Australia Day. This country is more than that. It has to be. It holds the trauma of many people across many generations. The Indigenous. The invaders. The immigrants. All seeking refuge from pain and disorder that we humans are so good at creating in this world.
>
> It is time we started the work of deep listening. We, all together, the 'I's coming to 'we'. Working with each other for transformation. Listening. Listening deeply to one another in contemplative reciprocal relationships, a mindfulness to the multiple stories embedded in the lands we call home . . . Miriam-Rose said, 'Dadirri is the Aboriginal gift to this nation, a gift that we all have been waiting for. It is this gift of listening.' If you accept this gift, as a nation we can all grow together.[32]

Secrecy is a difficult habit to break; it hides shame and masks grief, it makes a virtue of silence and leaves individuals isolated. Even in the blather of internet chatter it is deeply ingrained, a protective mechanism. Secrecy, silence and the desire to wipe clean the slate of the past have taken many forms since those prison ships first made their way between the cliffs of Sydney Heads. 'The past,' as Judy Atkinson, emeritus professor of Indigenous Studies at Southern Cross University, wrote in *Trauma Trails*, 'is very much with us today.'[33]

Listening requires talking, and fills the gaps with story, knowledge and insight. Whether by accident or design, the three women who became Australians of the Year in 2021 alongside Miriam-Rose Ungunmerr-Baumann also spoke about the once unspeakable: sexual abuse of children, domestic violence in immigrant communities, and access to menstrual products. The COVID X-ray revealed the flaw of silence, but as the year rolled on, secrets tumbled into the public domain and more of Bernard Smith's white blankets of forgetfulness slipped off. Stories that had once shamed were now broadcast and repeated over and over, shouted and whispered to shatter the void and destroy a powerful tool of control. It is likely to take more than the advocacy of this exceptional quartet to break, because the talking is just the first step of many in reimagining a different, more just future.

Despite the revelations of many royal commissions and other inquiries, the public response was most often an attempt to deal brusquely, but not conclusively, with these essential, often defining truths. Victims were blamed. Apologies were made but invariably compensation lagged, and lives were needlessly and painfully lost by those who were reminded they were victims. *We shouldn't feel guilty. We didn't do these things*, some in power shouted when the finger of responsibility pointed to them. *Ignore them. It will go away.*[34] Their angry retorts ignored the bigger truth that shame, not guilt, was the more corrosive emotion, and that it attached itself like sweat to perpetrators as well as victims, providing a reason to hide and deny.

Architecture of Silence

Those who spoke out, signed petitions, joined protests and wrote to their MPs about the dark consequences of using race and gender to deny a shared humanity were frequently mocked by commentators and public figures. Their dismissal as doctors' wives, black armband–wearers, chardonnay socialists and bleeding hearts obliged them—rather than those who exercised the power—to question their judgement. As if a conscience were a luxury for the few. As if black armbands were not a time-honoured symbol of respect and grief.

Decades ago, Bernard Smith described the morality gap between 'our sympathies and our achievements'. He suggested, taking his cue from Lewis Carroll, that Australians were living then in the Years of the Walrus, a time of 'manifest hypocrisy'. His optimism that new generations of more informed and curious people open to understanding and making reparations for the past was tempered by the diffidence of counting the 'arithmetic of our shame'. That was, he thought, a 'small price to pay for the moral right to live in the Lucky Country'.[35]

Four years later Bernard Smith explained in his elegant and prize-winning autobiography, *The Boy Adeodatus*, how this was personal for him. In the middle of the First World War, his recently emigrated Irish mother had had no choice but to relinquish her infant son as a ward of the state. He was lucky: his foster family loved him and recognised his potential, teaching him to read—two chapters a night and word quizzes each morning—from the Bible before he started school. He was luckier than thousands of other children who were raised in care, as his mother remained in his life. The generosity of strangers is rarely so freely given or richly rewarded.

The idea of Australia, like the idea of a life, is as much shaped by the silence as the stories we tell ourselves and the institutions we create. There have been dramatic leaps in understanding, but the architecture of silence remains unaddressed and corrodes the soul of the nation. Until it is, everyone loses, and the nation remains trapped in aspic. Secrets need to be heard with compassion and without judgement, not to retraumatise but to release and so that reparations can be made and the old power structures changed There are lessons of how this might be done. In 1985, Richard von Weizsäcker, the German president, gave a speech that set the framework for modern Germany. The horrors of the genocidal war still hung heavily, but he said it was not a matter of coming to terms with a past that could not be undone. 'However, anyone who closes his eyes to the past is blind to the present,' he said. 'Whoever refuses to remember the inhumanity is prone to new risks of infection.'[36]

6

Hidden in Plain Sight

SYDNEY HARBOUR IS one of nature's greatest gifts to the world. So sumptuous are its sparkling waters, protected beaches, hidden coves, island sentinels, soaring cliffs, and its verges clad in angophora, fig, cabbage tree and silky oak, that human beings are put in their place. Its meandering coastal trails dare you not to fall in love with its seductive majesty, rock by rock, tussock by tussock, as the briny air fills your lungs. All admire. Some seek to acquire, bulldoze and conquer. But the storied waterway, which formed as sea levels rose in the delta of ancient rivers and has been home to the people of the clans of the Eora Nation for thousands of generations, resists domination. Long after the grand mansions and apartment buildings on its foreshores have slipped into a rising ocean and the contaminants dumped into its depths dispersed, the sandstone-encased harbour will prevail.

For the best part of a decade in the new millennium I awoke every morning to a view of its glistening waters. Sometimes accompanied by the sound of horns as ferries gingerly edged through the fog, more often by the clatter of cleats. After work I watched yachts in competitive formations powered by the brisk afternoon breeze, before the sun set and turned the sky red behind the Harbour Bridge. As darkness fell, the lights of North Sydney and the densely packed suburbs behind the tree-studded sandstone foreshore transformed the bay into a brooding rainbow. When conditions were right, the red, orange, yellow, green, blue, indigo and violet of the synthetic rainbow would stretch out from the bushy fingertip of Booragy (Bradleys Head), sweep over Billong-olola (Clark Island) and reach the shores of the beach a hundred metres from my window. The first time I saw the display I thought I must be hallucinating. How was it possible for light and water to play such a joyous trick?

I had never thought of myself as a 'harbour view' sort of person. I was not born into privilege; I punched the ticket that led to this glorious view when I enrolled at the University of Queensland in 1974. Tertiary education was newly free, but still less than one in ten people found their way to uni. Networks were tight, but not closed; tribes looked out for their own, but the right pedigree mattered less then than it would come to in the contemporary resentment-generating machine of meritocracy. Australia was much smaller, more homogeneous, it was possible to believe egalitarianism was within reach and women might get a seat at the table. People who in a more class-bound society would not have had the opportunity to rise to some prominence liked to quip that 'if you've been to university and worked as a journalist, you probably know everyone (who matters)'. My career was marked by the usual stops and starts, but like many others of my generation I learned how to take risks and play the game. Then, thanks to an unusual slump in Sydney house prices, and a vendor with an urgent need for cash that could be resolved by selling his surplus apartment, I had a new perspective on the harbour city.

Every day there was a gift from the gods. The natural beauty in the most densely populated part of the biggest city on the continent was breathtaking. When I had first moved to Kings Cross a couple of decades earlier, it had been exciting enough to stand on tiptoe, peer around buildings and find a sliver of a view. Thirty years later it became the never-predictable backdrop of my life.

When guests arrived, they inevitably took a deep breath and walked across the room to the balcony that opened to the ever-changing watery vista. The view from the other side was almost as beguiling: a giant silky oak, a kauri pine, cabbage tree palms and a jacaranda had found the means to flourish for more than a century in the sandstone shelves that gave the garden its structure.

Property was the seemingly simple reward for success in Sydney, but it was very complicated. Jibes that the quest for a view in the Emerald City sucked meaning out of life only told some of the story; its beauty distracted, but also captivated and beguiled. Many stories lurked just below the surface, hidden in plain sight. Buckhurst was one of the red-brick mansion apartment blocks, replicas of buildings in the posher parts of London, that had sprung up during one of the city's perennial property booms. The eight apartments, with a caretaker flat in the basement and box rooms in the attic, were built in the grounds of a former estate. Just as many of their London counterparts came with access to a locked park square, a key to the beach at the end of the cul-de-sac came with these titles.

I imagined what it must have been like for the first owners to sit in the sunroom and watch the Harbour Bridge take shape and then miraculously join, connecting and transforming the city forever. I wondered whether the people who had lived there during the Second World War were awake late on the night of 29 May 1942 when a tiny enemy seaplane flew just metres above the harbour to check out the defences at Garden Island, or two nights later when the Japanese subs fired torpedoes at the USS *Chicago*, sank a naval ferry and killed 21 sailors.[1] I knew the owners had worried about the war; the stark red-and-black Red Cross sticker on the back stairwell window—THIS HOUSE HELPS TO SUPPORT AN AUSTRALIAN PRISONER OF WAR—survived countless renovations and was still there when we left. But maybe, like so many people of means, they had retreated to the Blue Mountains or the Southern Highlands. I could see the tell-tale signs that, during the years when the working harbour became the city's smelly, dirty sewer and the rich folk moved up the hill, the building had been neglected. I never heard the very early stories—the elderly lady who was the block's longest resident had only been there since the 1950s—but she had plenty to say about shady deals and self-interested owners.

Walking up the stairs one day, trailing sandy towels, beach bags and kids, our neighbour stopped us and said how pleased she was to see us using the beach, 'That was the point of the battle,' Mrs Morris said, 'to let the children enjoy the beach.' In a city where property had increasingly become both the defining symbol of status and the source of wealth, the land around the building had been subdivided, and subdivided again, to make the most from the booming post-war population. Those with the new waterfront houses on Seven Shillings Beach complained about noise and asserted what they considered their rights. The beach was theirs. Our now elderly neighbour had a young family when she and her husband found that the key that came with their apartment no longer worked—their property rights had been breached. More importantly for the new waterfront residents, everyone else was locked out of the beach. In a city that prided itself on its raffish bonhomie, this had become one of only a handful of beaches off limits to all except those with sand pushing up against their front fence or with boats who could drop anchor in the shallow waters.

It took a decade of intense legal and political manoeuvring before Valda and Stanley Morris's key worked again, and another ten before a council officer began arriving in a small car at dawn and dusk every day, bounding out of his illegally parked vehicle, door left open, to unlock and lock the gate. The hoi polloi, and readers of the *Lonely Planet Guide to Sydney* and *Time Out*, have been making their way to the unremarkable sliver of beach in increasing numbers ever since.

Hidden in Plain Sight

'Isn't it lovely to see the beach being used?' Mrs Morris remarked whenever we passed on the stairs. She knew the crowds of heavily tattooed, virtually naked young people made the beachfront owners, who scattered grass seed over sand to push out the high-water mark, fume. I sensed that, from her point of view, that was almost enough revenge. Small victories count. The harbour had again asserted itself. The egalitarian, fun-loving Sydney values, forever under attack from rapacious self-interest, had prevailed. There was always a contest. A story of winners and losers waiting to be told and deserving to be noted and remembered. The silences are more interesting than the manufactured tropes of popular culture. Teasing out the threads in the white blankets of forgetfulness more revealing than the myths, which are designed not to be unpicked.

THIS WAS NOT the first battle over access to the cove on the eastern edge of Double Bay that forms the armpit of Point Piper's peninsula. The battles have recurred for generations. The first had commenced when Arthur Phillip called it Blackburn in honour of David, the master of the HMS *Sirius*, one of the eleven ships in the unlikely flotilla of prison hulks that edged their way on the prevailing breeze from the open expanse of Botany Bay in January 1788. The charts Phillip had been given in London had suggested this huge protected harbour was just a dimple on the coast, so he was astonished to discover its secret fingers and deep waters beyond the windswept cliffs. Although every site already had a name, hundreds of new ones were scattered like confetti on landmarks, beautiful places and new settlements by the masters of the exile colony. Some were prosaic—Manly, Double Bay, Bellevue Hill—while others drew on the words that acknowledged prior settlement—Woollahra, Woolloomooloo, Bondi; some were reminders of home, but most were gifts to powerful people, mementoes of faraway places and distant loved ones. The rising and falling fortunes of occupants of the offices of Buckingham Palace, Westminster, Whitehall and the Admiralty were noted. Their names bestowed on random sites across the length and breadth of Australia, giving local maps another dimension, an honour board of eighteenth- and nineteenth-century political power in another hemisphere.

Naming became the enduring reward for patronage. James Cook had branded the natural harbour Jackson, for Sir George, the Admiralty's judge-advocate, who in the tightly knit class-bound world of eighteenth-century England was also the brother of the woman he had served as a child. It was an honour that became somewhat confusing after Sir George changed his name to Duckett a few years later when he became a baronet. Warrane became Sydney Cove, named for the British home secretary who drew up the orders for the First Fleet; Bradleys Head for William, the fleet's cartographer; and the island Billong-olola became Clark Island after Ralph, who established a potato and onion garden on the island to help feed those who had arrived on that journey. Although the vegetables grew, Clark gave up on his garden; the Gadigal people who had husbanded the produce of the bay and its islands for millennia beat him to the crops. They were not going to give up on Blackburn Cove's shallow waters, rocky mollusc-encrusted shelves, plant-laden inlets and abundant seafood without a fight.[2]

It took a few decades before the settlers moved east along the southern shore of the harbour. Double Bay remained distant, a place for fishing until it was gazetted a village in 1834, and a century later synonymous with property developers.[3] Governor Phillip's vision of turning the land he had taken without compensation into a large-scale open prison worked by young convicts did not last long. Gifts of land and leases soon became the currency of reward. Land was a gift of an administration that had 'acquired' it without a hint of the punishment that was meted out to the thieves who had been sent across the seas for 'acquiring' much less valuable spoils. Ironically, once they had done their time, these miscreants also became the beneficiaries of the gifts at the disposal of the penal administration.

Land was then, as it continues to be, the key to personal fortune and political power. The eminent historian of the early colony, Grace Karskens, noted that just five years after the ships had sailed through the harbour's sandstone gateposts, 'it was already clear that land *was* a commodity in New South Wales'.[4] An enduring tone was set. The abstract promise of common land in an open-air penal settlement crumbled, and over time an armed garrison with convicts who were treated like slaves took its place. The much more tangible promise of fortunes from acquisition, speculation and profiteering prevailed. 'Nothing could be more "Sydney",' the former NSW chief justice Jim Spigelman noted in 2008, in a speech explaining that the 1808 coup by military officers commonly known as the Rum Rebellion was more about property ownership than booze.[5]

Those who paid the not inconsiderable price to lease the land on Blackburn Cove, decades after the coup collapsed and the rule of imperial law restored, had to commit to building expensive mansions on the expansive north-facing cove. This is well documented in official records, many now digitised. There you can trace the leases bought and lost, money made and squandered, the story of once grand houses left to decay, neighbourhood disputes (rats and possums dumped in wells), ambitious dreams, the ignominy of jail, and the perpetual movement between provincial colony and homeland. The pre-history, what came before the ships, is noted more cursorily in the same records and concedes that Aboriginal people were still living on the beach in the 1860s. The construction of Redleaf, the grand building and its gardens that perch on the rise above Blackburn Cove, is recorded in meticulous detail. The old building has been carefully reworked to include remarkably light-filled underground offices, and is now the home of the Woollahra Council. Redleaf is now best known for the deep green waters and pontoons of its meshed harbour pool and as one of the most popular destinations in Sydney.

Therein lies a more instructive tale, which still resonates. The first owner of Redleaf, William Walker, returned with his family to England, after which the lease was sold to William Busby for a substantial £7000—an amount that would make the dollar-obsessed property gossip pages today—and his family lived there until the end of the century. They became keepers of some of the secrets of the colony, secrets like many others that were pushed to the dark reaches of memory as each new wave of people washed in.

Nearly a hundred years after the first flotilla had arrived, ownership of the land around the harbour was still a matter of active and acrimonious dispute. Gurrah,[6] a Gadigal man, his wife 'Nancy', her sister 'Sophie' and their clan lived on the seashore at Double Bay. They were descendants of those who had survived the decimation of the smallpox plague that swept through the harbourside settlement in 1789, when bodies of the dead Eora people lay everywhere.[7] Seventy years later, despite 'trauma on trauma on trauma',[8] they continued to make their lives on the beach as the land around them was diced and sliced and passed from one wealthy, well-connected white man to another.

In 1950, Dora Busby, one of William Busby's descendants, was quoted in a letter to the editor of the *Sydney Morning Herald* drawing on her grandmother's diary and asserting that the colloquial name of the beach, 'Seven Shillings', on whose shores the newspaper's owners lived, was of the Busbys' making. Her letter was designed to settle a squabble that had bristled in the stuffy pages of the paper since a book about the houses built in the early settlement of the area had been published. The book bristled with gossip. It was one of several written by Glynda Nesta Griffiths, to preserve 'the recollections of an earlier generation'. At stake was whether the Busbys or the Walkers could claim credit for the name that begat a legend before it became a popular beachside destination.

Hidden in Plain Sight

According to Dora, her grandmother wrote in her diary that after her husband William bought Redleaf, they had 'continual trouble with members of [Gurrah's] tribe', who 'lived just outside their fence':

> Mrs. Busby tried to buy their fishing rights, and offered them blankets, clothes, and flour. Gurrah said he would sell for seven shillings. Mrs. Busby was afraid this would only be spent on rum, and tried to persuade Gurrah to take more useful goods. But at last so many fowls and eggs were stolen that she gave Gurrah the money and the tribe moved up to . . . the Rona Garden on Victoria Road.[9]

While other reports suggest that it was Mrs Walker who reached the settlement, none dispute that the amount paid for the beach was seven shillings—a lot less than the £7000 William Busby paid for the estate abutting the beach.[10]

Years later, Gurrah buried 'Nancy' with the seven shillings in the heart of Double Bay, a gesture now rich with symbolism. The suburb today is distinguished by the number of real estate agents who pound its carefully laid pavements, ever alert to whispers of properties for sale and the desires of buyers. For Gurrah, it was clear: the money meant less than the principle, the connection to the land infinitely more important than the 'shilluns' he was given to acquire it—and go away.

For Tim Fairfax, who grew up in Elaine, the first of the houses the Fairfax family acquired on the Seven Shillings waterfront—houses now owned by young men who made their fortunes from software—this story was personal.[11] For some people who have lived here for four or five generations, the history is so close you can almost touch it. Tim Fairfax was a boy when the exchange of letters in the family's paper about the origins of the name of the beach was published. His family's newspaper, the *Sydney Morning Herald*, was the firm-handed gatekeeper of the city's stories and gossip. It was a paper that ensured that the castes—Protestant, Catholic, Aboriginal, Irish, New Australian—were clearly delineated and kept in their place. I happened to meet Tim at a dinner one night. As we talked, it became clear we shared an interest in this little-known history. 'My father used to tell me about Gurrah and the old ways when I was growing up,' he said. 'That little beach was so important.' As the second son in a family where the rules of primogeniture still applied, he had left Sydney to make his own way, building a life on the land in Queensland, as his mother's forebears had done. Later his active social conscience, developed in part by his observation of the growing inequality of the Sydney in which he grew up, guided the distribution of millions of dollars by his family foundation.

Earwigging on the beach, it was not unusual to hear visitors wondering about the name. *Why is it called Seven Shillings?* some would ask. There are no visible clues. Some recalled learning that seven shillings was the first daily minimum wage for a family, set in 1907; others recalled the film that described it as the amount provided as 'susso' during the Depression.[12] But few beachgoers knew these arcane facts. Those most attuned to the property-obsessed neighbourhood and its $100 million waterfront estates wondered if maybe the name was ironic. Could it be a dig at the greedy neighbourhood? An elaborate play on knowing the price of everything and the value of nothing? Or a signal that Sydney is so egalitarian that some pay millions, and others shillings? There is no plaque to tell the story of the eons of Gadigal life on the beach, the derisory price paid for an unequal trade, or even the battle the Morrises waged for public access. A little further east, a tiny terraced garden named for Bungaree, who died nearby after he accompanied Matthew Flinders on the circumnavigation of the continent, is perched on the edge of the traffic-clogged New South Head Road. Best we forget, scrub the past away.

Hidden in Plain Sight

SYDNEY DOES NOT pretend to be an imperial city. It is more a playground, a watery gateway to the Pacific, a coastal outpost sheltered from vast inland plains by escarpments and mountains. This may explain why, for a city of its size and significance, there are relatively few statues. Matthew Flinders is memorialised outside the State Library, but it is the bronze of his cat Trim clinging to the window that generates most interest. When the statue of James Cook was unveiled in the then open plain of Hyde Park, a century after his journey, it triggered the biggest public rally in the city's history. Tens of thousands of people flocked to the then hot, dusty 'park' for the commemoration.

It took two centuries after Governor Lachlan Macquarie put his transformative stamp on the city for his likeness to rise in Hyde Park. By 2013, statues of colonial figures were less likely to draw a crowd of wellwishers. All over the world they were being torn down. Where they remained, plaques were amended with the more complicated story of what they represented. Governor Macquarie's statue noted his role but failed to mention his warlike pronouncements. At the height of the Black Lives Matter movement in the first stage of the pandemic, Stephen Langford stuck an A4 piece of paper with an 1816 declaration by Macquarie—marked *For public education. Please do not remove*—to the plinth of Macquarie's statue: 'All Aborigines from Sydney onwards are to be made prisoners of war and if they resist they are to be shot and their bodies to be hung from trees in the most conspicuous places near where they fall so as to strike fear into the hearts of surviving natives.' Not long after this declaration, more than fourteen Dharawal and Gandangara people were shot and run off the cliff at Appin, south of Sydney. A memorial now marks the site.[13] Langford was, however, arrested and charged with malicious damage for his attempt to provide some context to the life of the inanimate object in a park.[14]

After living in the densely populated inner suburbs of Sydney for much of my adult life, I had developed a sixth sense for the nuances of the city's status markers and hierarchy. Ever since Captain John Piper used his responsibility for customs and 'all harbour matters' to enrich and big-note himself, the eastern suburbs have been home to countless brilliant innovators and thoughtful professionals, but also to crooks, rent seekers, and people ready to charm, bully or blackmail their way out of a tight spot.

Sometimes ironic references to history sneak through, but more often they are lost. Governor Macquarie gave his name to an investment bank with a holey-dollar insignia. It became known as 'the millionaires' factory' as a new generation of swashbuckling bankers found a way to multiply their wealth. Macquarie had addressed the shortage of coins by importing Spanish *reales* and punching out the middle to create two: a five-shilling coin with a hole in the middle, and a smaller one worth a few pence.

Those suburbs are the sort of places where fortunes can be spectacularly won and lost. Captain Piper built the biggest mansion on the harbour in 1822 and entertained lavishly—so lavishly he had to embezzle the customs he collected to pay his bills and settle his books. The fall from grace for the man who was paid twice the salary of the governor was spectacular. After he was declared bankrupt, he arranged to be rowed out into the harbour, a band playing on the shore. He intended to take his own life. He survived, but set a pattern in the neighbourhood on the point that was named for him. It has been repeated with variation ever since by self-aggrandising crooks who hog the limelight, Gatsby-like, drawing others into their aura by entertaining more extravagantly than they can afford until they crash. John Piper's mansion was demolished, making way, eventually, for another grander building. It is a pattern that has been repeated ever since: the ambitions embodied in one building are destroyed by others with bigger dreams, who, with the terra nullius of the mind that has typified the settlement since its first days, saw only land waiting to be developed, on the shores of a spectacular waterway.

Hidden in Plain Sight

By the time we left our harbourside eyrie, it was not unusual to see men who had once dominated the business pages with their spectacular acquisitions and developments walking the picturesque streets with locked police security bracelets around their ankles—enjoying the views, observing what was being built and sold, talking loudly on their phones, and savouring as much as they could before they were eventually jailed.

Nearly 250 years after the First Fleet arrived, echoes of the old hierarchies still reverberated. Apartment buildings replaced mansions, leaving only remnant gateposts, some lumps of convict-hewn sandstone and the oldest trees.

THE SOCIAL ARCHITECTURE was more resilient, absorbing wave after wave of new arrivals. The luxurious, segregated schools that take up prime positions trace their origins back a century or more and provide the scaffold on which the social ecosystem grows. Still at the top, increasingly wobbly but buffed by philanthropic largesse, is the old money of the descendants of squatters, early business owners like the Fairfaxes, whose compounds presided over the harbour from Seven Shillings Beach for a century.

During my time in this postcode, those at the top of the hierarchy were nudged by the latest breed of excessively remunerated bankers who had proliferated since the mid-1980s, when finance began its inexorable rise to the pinnacle of an increasingly freewheeling economy. These masters of the universe helped ensure that the already rich got richer as the economy was deregulated, public-sector businesses were privatised and financialisation touched every aspect of life. Next in the hierarchy came the comfortably off, multigenerational professionals and owners of family businesses who were confident about their longstanding place in the social hierarchy and asserted it quietly but without equivocation. Then came those who had arrived from everywhere and grown rich from finding a niche supplying low-cost, high-margin goods that everyone wanted—shopping centres, magazines, car parks, fast food, clothes, handbags, appliances, mortgages, poker machines, minerals, apartments, food and grog—'new money', theirs was once called. The princelings from China, business visa buyers from South Africa and Russia, and transient senior executives of global firms all had deep pockets; they lubricated the economy but rarely made it inside the club for long. Then came the raffish, charming, energetic, conscientious, eccentric people who had made a beeline for the densely populated, uniquely beautiful suburbs on the southern shore of Sydney Harbour. Until very recently, the descendants of Gurrah and his clan were conspicuously absent from 'the Woollahra mob'—as Leah Purcell called them in her play *Box the Pony*—who sat on pavements drinking coffee.

All of them were *into* property. It was Sydney's most important commodity, as it had been since 1788. During the pandemic, the property market defied the predictions of falling prices, caused by unemployment and stalled immigration, to reach ever-new heights. In the Sydney COVID X-ray, property is the spine.

Real estate advertising had secured the fortunes of newspaper owners for generations. Even the gossip pages were given over to chatter about who was buying, who was selling and for how much. The front pages reported every movement; weekends were as much shaped around viewings and auctions as school sports; dinner parties deteriorated into dreary recitations of *what, how much and who*, tempered by the well-founded anxiety about how the next generation would ever get a foothold in a city that had become one of the most expensive in the world.

A special class of traders—property developers—were the spiritual descendants of the officers who staged their military coup in 1808. Those officers incarcerated Governor Bligh for two years and succeeded in turning the colony into a dictatorship of entrepreneurs for a few years, setting a pace for unchallenged authority that some would like to see return. The first coup in Australia's history created a moment that is still dimly acknowledged—a moment when those who sought to get rich by making up the rules for themselves undermined the remotely imposed rule of law. The rules that prohibit property developers donating to political parties in many jurisdictions are the most visible modern manifestation.[15] The new breed of property developers generally, but not always, operated within the law. But like their forebears they were always poised to exert the influence their wealth bestowed to get a better deal on zoning, density, construction standards, public infrastructure.

They, and their handmaidens the deregulated banks, fuelled the wave that saw the median prices of a house rise from $39,390 when I first moved to Sydney in 1981, to $1,211,000. The deregulation of finance made housing an asset first and a home second. Those who could focused their investment on property and saw it soar over forty years, as house prices escalated but wages rose just threefold. Money for doing almost nothing, except greasing the perpetual mill of renovation. It was striking, and a mark of an unsophisticated economy, that in the 21st century a third of those atop the rich lists derived their wealth from property, and all the others had extensive holdings. It was fitting, and predictable, that the young men who made a fortune building a software company should pay record prices to become the new owners of the two Fairfax houses on Seven Shillings Beach.

Everyone else who could, like surfers off the point at Bondi Beach, hung on for the ride, counting their windfalls as they traded up, struggling with mortgages in bad times, while calibrating their anticipated windfall capital gains, using the stored capital in their homes, which effortlessly accrued, to fund holidays and school fees, at the same time worrying about how their children would ever afford a house, how homelessness was increasing, and how stupid to have an economy that puts so many eggs in one basket. Even as the banks froze interest repayments and governments mandated rent relief during the first wave of the pandemic, still the prices soared, rising more than a fifth in one year.

Every city has similar enclaves. Sydney's unique topography—harbour, peninsulas, beaches, rivers, mountains—defines the boundaries more clearly. The people in the east are no better or worse than anywhere else, but they are richer, better educated, more cosmopolitan, yet less diverse, than the rest of the city. As a group they enjoy the opportunities chipped out of the sandstone for centuries. At their most smug they are the beneficiaries of a meritocracy that for others is a resentment-generating machine. But the dynamic of human relations is eternal.

During Sydney's long winter lockdown of 2021, the privilege this enclave had long enjoyed was on clear display. The early cases of COVID-19 reported in Bondi, Vaucluse and Double Bay—the limo driver and barbecue man—did not immediately provoke a lockdown. At the time, New South Wales exceptionalism was flourishing. In May the *Australian Financial Review*, which had a jaundiced view of lockdowns and their economic cost, lauded Premier Gladys Berejiklian on the cover of its glossy magazine. She was 'The woman who saved Australia'.[16] Unlike other premiers who were locking down at the slightest sign of infection, she hoped to use the still scarce vaccine, rather than lockdowns, to prevent the pandemic spreading. Until it spread.

The first lockdown targeted the eastern suburbs, but within days it extended to the whole city. Restrictions tightened as the virus infiltrated to the more populous west and south, home to most of the city's essential workers, whose jobs could not easily be done from home. While police patrolled deserted streets in the west and helicopters hovered, socially distanced crowds still gathered on the famous beaches for daily exercise. Rarely had the city's class divide been so visibly on display.

Hidden in Plain Sight

THE EMOTIONAL TEXTURE of a place and its people is shaped by gossip and the things not spoken, hidden in plain sight—the stories untold, the convenient amnesia that stretches back to first settlement but embraces much that has happened since. It is not confined to public events, people or places. Secrets are held tight: that is a truth not limited by class.

Everyone has a little backpack filled with shame, trauma, grief, embarrassment and fear. Things that are difficult to speak about. It is hard to own your own life burdened by this unexamined baggage. It is impossible for a nation to resolve its idea of itself if the events and behaviours that produce these emotions are ignored or wished away. Public life is hardened and coarsened, wrapped to form an almost impenetrable carapace, emotion consigned to the personal domain. Until it is pierced.

Hidden stories edged onto the national agenda when sexual assault survivor Grace Tame was named 2021 Australian of the Year for her own bravery and courageous advocacy of child survivors of sexual abuse. The stories of other women escalated when former ministerial adviser Brittany Higgins made public what she remembered of an assault in Parliament House. The experiences of these two women struck a chord and entered the mainstream when the attorney-general tearfully denied that as a schoolboy he had raped a woman who had since taken her own life. Tens of thousands of other women joined impromptu rallies in cities and towns around the nation to protest the pattern of persistent misogyny.

No doubt Grace Tame and Brittany Higgins had heard the horror stories of abuse that had filled the airwaves during their adolescence. Inquiry after inquiry recorded the tales of children taken from their families, of mothers forced to relinquish their babies, of others abused in institutions by the people they were supposed to trust; of domestic violence, elder abuse, deaths in custody, shocking numbers of children taking their own lives; of people living with disability without support. They were hard to miss. For years the media reported them with horror and outrage and a touch of salacious glee, tagged with the number of an outsourced community service to ring in case of distress. Little was done to address the real and intergenerational damage of trauma, or to make structural and legal amendments that ensured the actions that caused it were not repeated.

Redefining consent, making workplaces safer and taking victims seriously were ideas whose time had come. It was somehow appropriate that the momentum for this should grow out of the experience of young people in one of the most privileged enclaves of Sydney. If it happened there, it happened everywhere.

Chanel Contos was a university student in London when she posed a question on Instagram, created a shared document and set up a petition about sexual assault in eastern suburbs schools. She knew that her experience of assault was familiar to her friends and assumed they were not alone. She asked her followers to tell of their experiences, and watched her online document grow at an astounding pace. Within weeks, 30,000 people had responded. Page after page was filled with horrifying stories of sexual abuse, betrayal, shame, humiliation, rage and fear.[17]

Affluence, and the attention provided by schools that resemble five-star resorts, was no protection. In story after story, consent had not been sought or given. As an old girl of one of the schools with the most sweeping harbour views, Chanel Contos's focus was on the most privileged dozen or so schools in the eastern suburbs and a handful on the other side of the harbour. All were sorted by price and segregated by gender, class and religion, places where the offspring of 'old girls' and 'old boys' were given preference. Schools that cost half the median annual wage per child per year for up to thirteen years; schools that promised to bequeath an excellent education, but more importantly networks and opportunities that would set them up for life. Schools that provide the status that is the foundation of success in a society that people liked to think was classless. Schools that are subsidised by the public purse and boast such luxurious facilities that anyone who enters the gates with even a residual attachment to education as a universal good must recoil to see such entitlement embedded into the lives of a few.

The stories in Contos's shared document revealed a cruel and uncaring environment. Many young women had found that mixing with boys from their partner schools—some the sons of family friends—came with abusive extracurricular activities that taught them caution and fear, a training for a life of acquiescence, laden with unwarranted shame for the things done to them. Too many young men learned how to wield the power of fear and humiliation for the fleeting satisfaction of bragging about their victims—'rehearsing and projecting', as a heartbroken Tim Winton observed. Winton, one of Australia's most celebrated authors, has been chronicling class and masculinity in his novels for decades. 'Boys and young men are so routinely expected to betray their better natures,' Winton wrote, 'to smother their consciences, to renounce the best of themselves and submit to something low and mean.'[18] Seventy pages of stories in a couple of weeks. The pattern was the same: betrayal by friends, humiliation and fear. The legacy was a burden of shame that seemed almost impossible to dislodge, and a brazen shamelessness by those who knew they had gotten away with it. Until the stories were told, and new conversations began.

Complaints to police skyrocketed, and public officials were forced to address the issue without averting their eyes. These were the children of the most privileged, linked by personal experience to everyone else. The great unspoken truth that while the statistics show that young men are the most likely victims of violence, it grows in the bedrock of the often-unspoken violence against women, as it has for centuries.

The Idea of Australia

MY GENERATION OF women grew up in the intense cauldron of grievance and outrage that fuelled second-wave feminism. We swapped stories of slights and abuse, and fought to change laws and increase opportunities, not just for ourselves. We knew that the personal was political, and as we devoured the best books and engaged in passionate debate we learned how to make this more than a slogan. Much was passed on to our daughters and sons, but like every generation they had to discover the enduring, brutal, nasty essential truths for themselves. But as the stories Chanel Contos gathered showed, this intergenerational knowledge transfer had gone seriously awry. It seemed to be swamped by the distractions of striving and success. Pointing to the powerful perversions of social media was not sufficient. The reports of brutal encounters in bedrooms and sitting rooms told of neglect and inattention wrapped in privilege. We had stopped stoking the cauldron, protecting the vulnerable.

The editor who hired me at the *Australian Financial Review* had paid enough attention to 1970s feminism to realise that there was a talented generation of women keen to become journalists. Other editors still thought careers in teaching or nursing were more appropriate. Women were, Max Walsh liked to joke, 'the new Irish'—people who, like him and his mates with their Irish Catholic pedigrees a generation earlier, would work harder for less pay. Attractive young women, he said, might also be able to draw out the secrets of businessmen unaccustomed to attention from professional women. 'You'll be able to find out their stories better than the blokes,' he joked. At the time it felt a bit like being pimped, but he had a point. The art of active listening, of paying attention and asking more questions, was a lesson from those feminist consciousness-raising sessions, and a path to the stories that were rarely told.

I was well prepared for this role. As a daughter of the manse, I was brought up to be an observer, *in* the community but not really *of* it; to politely ask questions and listen to the answers; to find patterns of relationships, but not get involved. I learned, watching my parents engage with their parishioners, how to actively listen, to empathise and draw out the background that was otherwise rarely explained.

The stories I found most interesting as a business journalist were rarely the ones that generated front-page stories. I was drawn to the context, to the social relations, to the personal background that made sense of the decisions that made the news.

In the mid-1980s, I wrote *Steel City Blues* about the recession that had decimated the steel industry in Wollongong. It took the rest of the city with it, turned coalmining from underground extraction into vast, open-cut mechanised enterprises and left thousands of people unemployed and with little prospect of jobs in traditional manufacturing industries. At its simplest, it was a story of labour and capital, of a failure to adequately invest or accept social responsibility, and of governments' reluctance to drive the structural economic change that was so obviously needed. I interviewed scores of people who were touched by this catastrophe and a much more complex story emerged. Executives who had lain awake at night worrying about the consequences of their decisions. Management consultants who were troubled that their business models left no space for human consequences. Miners who thought they had no option but to stay underground for days and days to force the company to negotiate. Men worn down by decades in the steelworks, once known as 'wogs' and 'dagos' who had practised enough Aussie slang to survive in the most multicultural region in the country but now worried what would happen to their children as industrial jobs disappeared. Women who had fought for years for the properly paid positions once available only to men but found that because they were the last on the payroll they were the first to lose their jobs. Apprentices who saw their futures evaporate and blamed 'slopes' and 'towelheads' (more recent migrants) even if they were themselves the sons of 'wogs' and 'dagos'. Boys sure they would never get a break, who drank too much, took too many drugs and talked about the abuse they had suffered at their Catholic schools. Kids from the poorest, harshest neighbourhoods with big dreams and tiny prospects. People whose parents were starting to gather the confidence to tell stories of being stolen and sent to abusive institutions on their way to menial jobs. For months I listened to stories laden with trauma, anger and grief. To those who were so angry at not being heard they broke through the glass doors and stormed into King's Hall at Parliament House. Stories of the real people who were invisible in the rooms where decisions that shaped their future were being made.

It was good training, and the book hit a nerve. Many felt the pain as industry was restructured and the economy became more outward looking. I learned that it was impossible to understand public events without grappling with the emotional impact that lurked in the subtext. It was clear that class, gender, ethnicity and religion could be used to keep people feeling ashamed, thinking that there was something wrong with them, not that they were pawns in a system.

The playing field is not level. As Chanel Contos's survey showed, under the surface of even these most privileged, indeed truly lucky Australians there lurked unresolved trauma and shame. Some felt guilty, others angry; others preferred the shamelessness of not hearing, not knowing and therefore not believing in any awfulness, satisfied with terra nullius of the mind.

I realised almost everyone had a story they held close, which under the right circumstances they might tell. After writing *Steel City Blues*, I practised active listening, alert to the moments when people might tell me their secrets, often in the most ordinary circumstances. The son of Lebanese immigrants who arrived at primary school and proudly said his name was Wassim, and his teacher replied, 'No, you are Sam.' The foreign policy expert whose Australian mother had to wait until the end of the White Australia policy before she could return home with her 'brown' husband and children. The Aboriginal leader who dropped out of university when her professor declared he had made a mistake giving her the top mark in the class because 'that's impossible'. The diplomat who knew she had been adopted but discovered as she travelled the world that, thanks to her Catholic mother's fear of sinning by using contraception, she had unacknowledged siblings in several countries. The pillar of the establishment whose grandparents had married in the US because his divorce was not recognised in Australia and then sailed across the Pacific for the birth of each of their children. The well-connected Chinese engineer, a political refugee, who channelled his ferocious intelligence into his children and taught the Australian passengers in his taxi the lessons he had learned from his study of their history and culture. The man who received a letter asking why their grandmother was described as his aunt in her death notice and tumbled across the truth that both his parents had been born illegitimately in the same year, offspring of men and women refused permission to marry because of class and religion, who carried the secret with them to their graves. The woman who, at 87, realised that the abuse she had endured as a child could no longer be wished away, and after fearfully Googling her abuser's name found he had died in disgrace as his repeated assaults of young women had come to light.

None of these stories, or the countless others I heard, came easily. None were the fault of the person who felt ashamed. They all spoke to a deeper, darker truth about the human consequences of public policy—impacts that were ignored and exploited—and about political language that glossed over the human consequences. They were all hiding, just below the surface, where they unwittingly shaped contemporary behaviour, an uncanny reflection of the secrets that lurk below the surface of even the most beautiful places.

7

A Fair Go

As the potential horror of the COVID-19 pandemic was revealing itself in March 2020, Prime Minister Scott Morrison eventually announced that an allowance to supplement lost income would be available for all. Regardless of how much they normally earned or how many hours they usually worked, everyone whose employer was impacted by the mandatory shutdown would get $1500 a fortnight. He declared that to do otherwise would 'not be the Australian way. If one person falls on a hard time, if anyone falls on a hard time, it's the same hard time. We're all in this together. That's what's fair. That's what's Australian.'[1]

He spoke with passion and conviction and just a touch of panic. The private briefings were dumbfounding: officials warned of the possibility of millions of infections, tens of thousands of deaths, a deep recession and a paralysed workforce. A week before, when businesses were ordered to shut and hasty lists of emergency workers were drawn up, images of people queuing for blocks to register for Centrelink payments were a shocking reminder of institutional fragility. Centrelink phone lines jammed; the MyGov website crashed. Frustration and fear were palpable.

A Fair Go

No one who had been an adult during the Great Depression 90 years before was alive to tell those tales, but black-and-white images of hungry children, desperate workers and anxious women were etched into the collective memory. Political decisions in the 1930s had made that crisis worse than it needed to be. Wages fell, unemployment rose, bankruptcies skyrocketed, and when the government refused to spend the depression became deeper and went on longer than in every other country except Germany.[2] In Australia there were no leaders remembered as heroes, 'just men overcome by events, dogmatists and ratbags'. It punished people unevenly and continued to take a toll for a decade, until the demands of war started to reconfigure the economy. Fifty years later the *Steel City Blues* recession that devastated Wollongong, and other industrial heartlands, also revealed a Liberal–National Coalition government incapable of responding even to circumstances within its control, and drought that was not. Judgement was harsh, the people stripped the long-dominant Coalition of its power, for the first time a prime minister who lost his job cried on television. The 'recession we had to have' in the early 1990s was shorter and deeper and set a time bomb that eventually exploded under the Labor government.

A repeat of the suffering (not to mention the possible electoral consequences) was unconscionable, even for a newly elected government that boasted it was debt free—*back in the black*—before the numbers came in. This was a cabinet made up of a generation of leaders with no lived experience of a deep recession or of Keynesian pump-priming except to criticise its application during the global financial crisis on their way into power. Their careers had been forged with little reason to question their faith in the market-driven economics of neoliberalism. COVID-19 was potentially a health and economic catastrophe beyond the imagining of even the scenario-planning games once favoured in Canberra that had fallen out of favour when the Coalition resumed the green benches in Parliament House in 2013.

The Idea of Australia

Day after day, as the potential enormity of the pandemic grew, the prime minister stood in front of a carefully draped Australian flag and delivered long, rambling sermons. He was prickly and defensive, smothering the crisis with, at times, incomprehensible detail, describing what could and could not be done, what must close and what could remain open, in one breath banning large gatherings, in another saying he would go to the footy, outlining activities that were in and out before hastily amending them.

The panic was palpable. Images of people being bolted into their apartment buildings in Wuhan had outraged those who sensed overreach by an authoritarian Chinese state. But when screens filled with the catastrophic scenes of overcrowded hospitals and makeshift morgues in northern Italy—the wealthiest and most sophisticated part of a country that hundreds of thousands of Australians knew well—perspectives shifted. *This could happen here too*, they whispered. In the twelve days from 13 March, the number of Australian cases jumped from 200 to more than 2000. The potential devastation in the worst-case scenarios of an exponential increase gave rise to a new mantra: *to flatten the curve*. The most urgent task was to preserve and manage hospital resources and prevent them being overrun; privately, the government was being warned about tens of thousands of potential deaths.

All around the world governments were scrambling to contain the virus, marshal hospital resources and keep people safe. Businesses closed, borders shut, cities emptied. New Zealand astonished the world on 19 March when it set the pace, closing her borders and providing a wage subsidy for those sent home; Britain followed a few days later with a furlough scheme to subsidise lost incomes. For an anxious week there was no news about how Australians who found themselves without work, by government decree, would survive. It was clear that Centrelink would find it hard to cope.

Then, on the second-last day of the month, there was a collective sigh of relief when the prime minister announced that the coffers

A Fair Go

would open and those without work would be supported, and their employers would be subsidised to keep them employed. It was the first good news in the cascade of disaster. Scott Morrison, the country's first Pentecostal leader, spoke like a preacher. In his rambling sermon, the word of the day from the text of the Bible of National Identity was 'fair'. He applied the advice of his charismatic pastor Brian Houston: 'Leave people feeling better about themselves.'[3]

What's not to like about fairness? the prime minister might have asked in his distinctive patois. It is just and proportionate, not distorted by personal preference, favouritism or discrimination. It favours equilibrium and suggests that the giver is open minded and generous. Survey after survey shows that Australians put the highest value on fairness—it is much more important to them than freedom or independence.

Fairness is, however, a word made for a marketing handbook. It is slippery enough to mean almost anything, but its absence clear enough to trigger emotional responses laid down in unresolved childhood squabbles: *That's not fair!* You know it when you see it, and you sharply feel its absence. Scott Morrison's announcement cut through in a way that the convoluted descriptions of what was in and what was out could never do. It's the Australian way. We're all in it together. That's *fair*.

THE PRIME MINISTER could have been channelling his famous ancestor Dame Mary Gilmore. For Australians like him, whose convict forebears arrived in the late eighteenth century, history is short and personal; with good genes, timing and longevity, five generations can span three centuries. In 1998, in one of the periodic flurries of Canberra-led public history-making, Dame Mary—Scott Morrison's great-great-aunt, a socialist poet and unlikely celebrity—became the aged face on the ten-dollar note. She was present but invisible in countless transactions for decades before cards virtually displaced cash. This grand old dame, born in country New South Wales in 1865 to a Scottish father and a mother conceived shortly after her parents arrived from Ireland, gave the country's unlikely leader a unique personal link to one of the founding ideas of Australia.

Many Irish settlers who had left the hardships of life in colonial Ireland were acutely sensitive to the prospect of the patterns of abusive entitlement repeating in the new colony. 'Among the sports of the military officers and landed gentry, was hunting the blacks,' Gilmore wrote. 'Grandmother told me they went out after them with packs of dogs just as they hunted foxes in Ireland . . . when it was over they made a feast and had a ball.'[4] Her grandparents were forced out of their Hunter River farm—their paddocks burned and cattle shot—for sheltering Wonnaura people who were hunted by these officers and landed gentry. For Dame Mary's family and thousands of others the notion of fairness grew in this shallow soil of hardship and dispossession, as the spoils of hard work were shared with those deemed to be mates. Fairness became a touchstone, the bedrock of a nationalism that became more sentimental with time.

The Australian ideal of fairness had its roots deep in the history of a settlement that was, by definition, unfair. A 'fair go' was apparently grounded in instinct, but always lurked in the eye of the beholder. The legend of an egalitarian and irreverent people had been revived in the books, films and television shows that were produced as the new nationalism emerged and flowered during the 1960s and '70s, then reduced to fodder for advertising campaigns.

So when the prime minister declared 'That's what's fair. That's what's Australian' on 30 March 2020, his words cut through, and their deep emotional resonance reverberated. The promise of support for all lifted spirits.

It was a long time since fairness had been central to political talk. For most of the previous quarter century the prime minister's party had been in power, and 'fairness' had been reworked as 'reward for effort'. Scott Morrison had revived it in the election campaign the year before with his can-do slogan *Have a go to get a go.* Like every successful politician, his antennae were attuned to public sentiment, and he distilled this version of fairness from the noise. Henry Parkes, the father of Federation, had done this by what he proudly called 'ear-wigging'[5] on the footpath outside his toy shop; now polls and focus groups generate the data to detect mood and sentiment. Listen hard enough and respond; carefully chosen words always cut through.

For decades self-interest had prevailed, and its entitled reward, personal gain, was by definition unlikely to be fair. Politicians spoke with a knowing smirk about 'lifters and leaners' and demanded ever more complex regulations to determine who was entitled to public support and how much they might receive. Economists had gone grey lecturing us that self-interest was the only rational choice, as if life decisions were as simple as choosing from a crowded supermarket shelf and everyone had a full wallet.

But at the end of March 2020, for a fleeting moment it seemed that the moral core of Dame Mary's vision for Australia might bear fruit, channelled through the stories that John Morrison, the prime minister's father, must have picked up when he visited her at her Kings Cross flat as a young policeman on the beat.[6] The idea of Australia Dame Mary advocated in her writing and activism was highly political and placed a premium on fairness. For most of her life she was at odds with the prevailing conservative political order. Her complex politics evolved over many years, and as she aged she continued to use her fame to make a case for women, soldier settlers, Aboriginal people and the poor. For nearly a century until her death at 97 she had been a complicated embodiment of a dream of Australia that had been seeded before she was born. It was, on the surface, very different to the country her great-great-nephew would lead.

The Idea of Australia

EVEN AS A young girl in rural New South Wales, Mary Cameron showed a precocious intelligence. She was a teacher's assistant by twelve and a teacher in the Silverton mining township, near Broken Hill, a decade later. Broken Hill had long been a hotbed of industrial activism as the miners battled against the mines' owners, who became known as the Collins House Group, their well-manicured fingers in the books of almost every industrial pie. It had been a place of opportunity, and struggle. For those who made the arduous journey on foot or dray north from Adelaide or Melbourne, across the dry land beyond the great inland rivers, to find work in the mines or the shops, pubs and businesses that supported them. It was also the source of wealth for a handful of mining companies that would become the most powerful in the land, whose owners and managers grew accustomed to asserting their power and influence. Mary Cameron was touched by the radical social and political movements of the time, and became a feisty writer and activist so committed to socialism and equality that she helped arrange the finance for the New Australia movement—the 238 antipodean idealists who decided to set up Colonia Nueva Australia in Paraguay in 1893.

Despite its political energy and innovations, Australia in the turbulent 1890s had disappointed these utopian nationalists and their humanitarian colleagues. The country was not shaping up to be as fair as they had hoped—workers were underpaid, strikes were bloody, union leaders were jailed on prison islands, landowners and droughts held sway, businesses were collapsing, battles in the north were still killing large numbers of First Nations people, and opium, alcohol, and segregation were destroying families and communities. Colonial governments could be as capricious as the weather. Banks collapsed, unemployment rocketed, the economy shrank. By the turn of the century fear was on the rise, and Australia was the source of more dystopian than utopian fiction.[7] One group of idealists, led by the charismatic journalist and union organiser William Lane, who at that time was inspired by Adam Smith and Karl Marx and the grand social movements of the day, saw their dreams evaporating. Socialism was out of reach in the Australian colonies. Lane promised a place where men and women could 'live together in perfect peace and contentment' with 'absolute equality and absolute mateship . . . the basis of the movement'.[8] So they left. In the spirit of the times, they found new land across the sea to colonise and conjure a utopian community.

Two years later, the 31-year-old teacher responded to the plea to join them and set up a school. Mary Cameron set sail, her trunk filled with schoolbooks for the children and enough white hailstone muslin to make a wedding dress should she find someone to marry. As she did. Her betrothed, the happy-go-lucky shearer William Gilmore, fashioned her a ring by hollowing out a shilling. Lane's commune did not hold them long after their son was born—Colonia Nueva Australia had not lived up to its utopian promise. With their dreams dashed on the rocks of ego, personal ambition, hardship and grinding poverty, John Morrison's favourite great-aunt returned to the much-loved country of her birth.

The Australia that had literally been born in her absence demanded her attention. Unlike Lane, who became an angry, racist imperialist after his dream collapsed, Mary Gilmore became more radical. In the new nation founded on racist exclusion, she fought for inclusion. She used her gifts for writing, activism and self-promotion to try to change the country. After a few trying years in the Western District of Victoria, she returned to Sydney and before long was a towering figure in the city's small literary community. She edited the Women's Page of *The Worker* for 23 years and devoted her life to improving the lot of those who had not drawn a winning ticket in the Australian Lucky Dip. Her mantra, captured in poetry, embodied the stoical silence that has characterised the nation since before it was founded. 'Never admit the pain,/Bury it deep;/Only the weak complain,/Complaint is cheap.' By the time she died in 1962, Dame Mary had lived through nearly a century of low-key national experimentation. She knew fairness was not a gift. It required a fight.

Not long after he won the 2019 election, the prime minister detoured off the planned route in a drought tour of north-western Queensland to visit the Cloncurry Cemetery. Bounding across the bleached grass, he searched for the grave Dame Mary shared with her husband and son, who had continued to work on the land; both died in 1945, almost two decades before her. When the prime minister found the gravesite, he joked to his entourage, with evident embarrassment, 'She was a communist—I'm not kidding.'[9]

This awkwardness about his radical family history had been on display a few months earlier when US president Donald Trump hosted an unlikely state dinner at the White House. The bombastic president with an ear for a good story that would connect with his supporters canvassed a romantic, sanitised shared history of settlement: 'Our two countries were born out of a vast wilderness, settled by the adventurers and pioneers whose fierce self-reliance shaped our destiny. The first settlers carved out a home on the frontier and forged our defining national traits . . . From the wide-open landscapes of the West and the Outback, rose up cowboys and sheriffs, rebels and renegades, miners and mountaineers.'[10]

President Trump then introduced the carefully selected audience of business and political leaders—but not the prime minister's spiritual adviser Brian Houston, who was excluded by White House protocol— to the unlikely connection between the Pentecostal prime minister and an icon of early Australian radicalism. Trump's speechwriter was no doubt relieved to find in Dame Mary's extensive politically charged output a nationalistic battle hymn. She had written 'No Foe Shall Gather Our Harvest' in 1940, well before Japan joined the war, before Singapore fell, before Darwin was bombed or the Japanese subs bombarded the USS *Chicago* moored in Sydney Harbour: 'Our women shall walk in honor,/Our children shall know no chain,/This land that is ours forever/The invader shall strike at in vain.' A visibly surprised Scott Morrison responded, 'Well he got me . . . Dame Mary, my great-great-aunt, would be very, very proud.'[11]

EVER SINCE THE first legislation was passed in the newly formed Federation parliament, Australian ideas of fairness have been colour coded. The laws had long since lapsed but their shadow remained as news of the mysterious virus in Wuhan began to make it into the relentless news cycle in January 2020. First a case in Victoria, then three in New South Wales and one in Queensland. The close ties between Australia and China meant that this was news that touched many.

Over the previous decade, Chinese-born people had become the second-largest group of immigrants in Australia. Fifty years of active diplomacy had set the scene. Mandarin and Cantonese became two of the most spoken languages, China became Australia's largest trading partner, and Chinese capital an increasingly important source of investment. People of Asian appearance, many with Australian accents, filled the major cities, universities and workplaces, and announced that the nation had changed. It was a long way from the bans on Chinese immigrants for much of the previous century, and even further removed from the bureaucratic obstacles, higher fees and racial attacks that had targeted Chinese settlers in the nineteenth century.

It had seemed that the new face of Australia would inevitably become Eurasian to embody its geography and demography. The outrage that had followed Pauline Hanson's 1996 declaration that Australia was being 'swamped by Asians' had dissipated, but fear still lurked in the subtext of public discussion. For those with an Asian heritage, and many of their friends and relatives who have never set foot in Australia, this was disappointing but not surprising. The shadow of the founding racist White Australia policy still lingers, a humiliating collective memory easily triggered by words and action.

Wuhan, we soon came to know, is one of the vast Chinese metropolises on the Yangtze River, a city with a population just under half Australia's total. With a sophisticated economy and cultural life, it had become a centre for medical and scientific research, the sort of place visited by many who had been pursuing the logic of government-endorsed trade and scientific diplomacy in the Asian Century.

Over the fire-singed, smoke-laden summer, news from Wuhan got progressively worse. There were reports of lockdowns and a belated but heavy-handed response by the Chinese state. Plans to bring home some of the 600 Australian citizens and permanent residents in Wuhan swung into action. Planes were chartered, tickets were sold.

The offer announced by Scott Morrison on 28 January 2020 was admirable, swift and generous. It removed people from a looming crisis. During the 1900 bubonic plague in Sydney, people of 'Chinese appearance' from Haymarket, The Rocks and Botany were rounded up and sent to the North Head Quarantine Station.[12] They were put in tents on the foreshore to ensure they were sufficiently distant from others who were in isolation in the buildings up the hill. When it was announced that the Wuhan evacuees, who were potentially infected, would be sent to Christmas Island, a four-hour flight from Perth, it seemed that the deep, racially shaped fissure in the national fabric had still not mended.

For nearly two decades, Christmas Island, 1500 kilometres from the Western Australian coast, had been used as the out-of-sight, out-of-mind place to deposit refugees who were seeking to come to Australia by sea, people who were told they would never be welcomed on the mainland. More than 200 years earlier, not long after Joseph Hall was sentenced to a week in irons on bread and water on Mat-te-wan-ye, Governor Arthur Phillip despatched convicts to Norfolk Island, establishing a pattern that has been followed ever since: the utility of islands to remove, exile, quarantine and punish has been an Australian article of faith. First Norfolk, then Van Diemen's Land, and Maria, Sarah, St Helena and Cockatoo islands for convicts; Flinders, Rottnest, Palm and other islands for First Nations peoples; a network of island and peninsula quarantine stations; and, in recent years, Pacific islands for refugees.

The decision was not intentionally racist, but using Christmas Island—better known for its costly, well-barricaded detention centre—to quarantine Australians of Chinese descent was freighted with embedded meaning. It suggested that this was not a normal quarantine process with ready access to medical facilities and other support services. Sending Australian citizens and permanent residents who happened to have Chinese heritage to the remote island felt punitive. It revived memories of racial exclusion. The president of the Christmas Island Shire, Gordon Thomson, told an ABC reporter via text message, 'Create convict settlement for innocent people, now we'll be a leper colony. These ideas were abandoned in the mid-20th century.'[13] Another woman told *ABC News*, 'The government wouldn't send its citizens to Christmas Island detention centre if those who are trapped in Wuhan were white Australians.'[14] Peter Dutton, then the bellicose minister for home affairs (and a former police officer), declared he couldn't close a hospital to accommodate the evacuees, although NSW Health suggested they could be screened at the Richmond RAAF Base and moved to hospitals.[15] Therese Rein, wife of former prime minister Kevin Rudd and the grandmother of two children with Chinese-Australian heritage, chipped in on Twitter to urge the government to put the returnees into a hotel close to a major hospital. Tony Bartone, then head of the Australian Medical Association, declared it was 'not the appropriate or humane solution'.

It was hard to avoid the conclusion that this solution played to the fear that had always driven racial exclusion in Australia. Those pleased to be safely out of the epicentre of the plague were grateful, as far as we could tell from the television vox pops. For some, the enchantment of the Australian lifestyle prevailed. No doubt some brought a lesson learned in their homelands: the well-practised art of keeping critical thoughts to themselves. Evacuees who had embraced a more distinctive Australian commitment to directness were less circumspect. One said, 'If we were Caucasian, coming from America or Italy, we wouldn't have been sent to Christmas Island.' The well of memory is deep, and humiliation, like shame, is not easily displaced.

The plague that had disrupted the Federation celebrations more than a century before had also been blamed on Chinese people—it was thought to have originated in Hong Kong. As people fell ill, it reinforced the determination of the newly elected members of parliament to enact the White Australia policy in the first year of nationhood. The 'fear of Chinese immigration' was, as the first prime minister Edmund Barton declared, capturing the carefully cultivated national mood in the writer Charles Pearson's influential words, 'an instinct of self-preservation, quickened by experience'.

Quarantine was one of the responsibilities that the sparring colonies had ceded to the federal government in the earliest drafts of the Constitution. Until the 1980s, Australia had a network of stations on islands and peninsulas far enough away from population centres to limit the risk of infection, but close enough for medical attention. Ever since smallpox first decimated the Eora people a year after the first ships arrived, preventing the devastation of infectious diseases had been high on the agenda of administrators. In an eerie precursor to 2021, Governor Philip Gidley King in 1801 pleaded for more smallpox vaccines to be urgently sent from England. They took two years to arrive, and many people died. The age-old way of dealing with epidemics—quarantine—remained a fail-safe. Yet after more than a century, the transformation of these stations into holiday destinations and luxury hotels spoke to modern hubris, even as the world became more connected and risks increased. These ghostly places were redundant; medical science was thought to be sufficient.

It did not take long for the practical limits of using Christmas Island for quarantine to become obvious. After the second group of Wuhan evacuees completed their two weeks in isolation, those evacuated from the infected cruise ship in Japan were sent to Howard Springs in the Northern Territory. By April, quarantine became a lifeline for hotels in capital cities whose normal business had evaporated.

Although Australian leaders did not echo the language of the US president who shouted to his supporters, and the rest of the world, that the COVID-19 pandemic was a 'China virus', the subtext was unavoidable. The prime minister's first ministerial statement cast the virus as an enemy alien and his job one of 'defending and protecting Australia's national sovereignty'.[16] It also marked the beginning of a rapid deterioration in the trading relationship with China that had been so carefully nurtured for decades. Gone was talk about the endless possibilities of trading with the vast Chinese economy, of scientific diplomacy and student exchange. Instead China again became an unpredictable threat, requiring expanded national security laws and highly charged political rhetoric, even talk of war. There were good reasons to take a more sceptical view of the behaviour of the authoritarian state, but the belligerence of the official language took many by surprise, and gave competitors an opportunity to claim many of the lucrative markets Australian exporters had cultivated for decades. On the ground, the response was swift and personal. Reports of racist attacks skyrocketed. In mid-October 2020, three academics with Chinese heritage were asked by Tasmanian Liberal senator Eric Abetz to 'unconditionally condemn the Chinese Communist Party dictatorship'.[17] By channelling the notorious demands of US senator Joseph McCarthy at the height of the Cold War, Abetz revealed how the deep-seated discriminatory politics that had shaped Australia remained, even in those who were themselves, like Senator Abetz, born abroad.

The Idea of Australia

The previous 25 years had fundamentally changed the face of Australia in an unheralded and undigested way. The population had increased by more than seven million people in that time, jumping at one of the fastest rates since Federation. For the first time since the 1890s, those born overseas made up one-third of the population. The right to live here became explicitly linked to work, regulated by a complicated web of expensive visas and categories, citizenship safeguarded by civic knowledge and values tests. Along with mining, migration had itself become an economic lynchpin. Every new arrival needed a place to live, food, clothing, schools for their children, entertainment and money to travel. They made the overall population younger and better educated. The arrival of new residents generated hundreds of billions of dollars a year. Suddenly it stopped. In 2020, the total number of new arrivals fell to its lowest in a century. Soon the message became clear: in fortress Australia we look after those we decide are our own.

As QUICKLY BECAME evident after the prime minister's 30 March 2020 announcement of income support, fairness was not universal nor, when the rules are applied, simple. This was policy on the run, made by politicians and public servants unaccustomed to handing out money but acutely attuned to polls and the demands of their supporters. Within days of his announcement, Scott Morrison was explaining why 'fairness' didn't apply to some businesses, some types of employees, casual workers, visa holders, international students or universities. Everyone was not entitled to income support—fair did not mean equal. The 'conditional fair go' that had been the hallmark of his invocation of fairness in the election campaign returned.[18]

Those who were excluded heard the drumbeat of another tougher, less inclusive idea of Australia, one that had become the new normal.

A Fair Go

It was a place where moral questions that underpinned such a discussion were belligerently dismissed, and where old enmities were not far below the surface. *We have to draw the line* became a new mantra.

A year later, when the scale of the income support was revealed, the line-drawing revealed another X-ray of power and influence. Modern monetary theory had provided a technical economic tool that allowed governments to print money. Ninety billion dollars dropped electronically into bank accounts and then washed across the nation. It was unprecedented. People whose jobs evaporated or were unable to leave their homes because of the closures and lockdowns survived, the living standards of those on unemployment benefits improved, but those who missed out were forced to rely on charities and the kindness of strangers. By September 2020, three million people were receiving the JobKeeper allowance, and nearly four million who liked to think they were self-reliant withdrew money from their superannuation accounts. Tens of thousands of businesses claimed their entitlements.

If you were included it seemed fair, but without knowing who received what it was hard to know. A parliamentary inquiry questioned officials and asked for details, but in a land where the architecture of silence has such strong foundations, there was no official register. Instead, news snuck out as annual reports were released. Some had done very well, their financial success reflected in bonuses and dividends. When a year later the Parliamentary Budget Office reported on its review of the $90 billion payments, the fact that some of the welling public money had funded executive bonuses, dividends and increasing profits touched the fairness nerve. Twenty billion, more than the economic output of 70 countries, $2000 from every Australian household, had gone to corporations that flourished during the lockdown. It was 'avoidable wastage', the generally even-tempered *Herald* columnist Peter Hartcher raged, 'the single greatest act of national profligacy in modern Australian history'.[19] Some paid the money back; others, like Gerry Harvey, whose homewares stores had thrived during the lockdown, considered it a legal entitlement and only reluctantly responded to public outrage with fragmentary reimbursement

The dirty little truth about the Australian attachment to fairness is that it has always been partial. It was not long after Federation that a social contract was struck with white Australian men to ensure a minimum standard of living for most. It was a bit like mateship. You choose your mates. You look out for them, rather than committing to an all-encompassing principle of the French *liberté, égalité* and *fraternité*.

Right from the beginning, some were left out—First Nations people, indentured Pacific Islanders, Chinese and others deemed non-white, and women. The landmark judgment of the Arbitration Court in 1907 required employers to pay men a minimum wage of seven shillings a day. The first age pension, introduced in the next year, extended this principle, but excluded 'Asiatics, Aboriginal natives of Australia, Africa, Pacific Islands and New Zealand'.[20] Race was a convenient proxy for class and Aboriginal people were at the bottom of the ladder, working in the most menial and demanding jobs for pennies they rarely saw. For decades these safety nets were crafted to keep white men afloat and reinforced a mythic egalitarianism, but even this was greeted with sustained opposition from employers and economists.

DAME MARY GILMORE lived for most of her life in a little flat not far from the Darlinghurst police station, a box seat from which to observe the winners and losers of the Australian settlement up close. In the early 1960s, when she died, Gavin Souter noted that the adjoining suburb of Kings Cross was a place charged with emotional electricity, where conversations were louder and more interesting than elsewhere in Sydney. At the time the Cross boasted 27 restaurants, 42 coffee lounges, sixteen frock shops, eleven fruit shops, nine nightclubs and strip shows, and eight florists. But it was, Souter wrote, more than the sum of its commercial parts, more than a magnet for suburban visitors: 'It sings to these innocents, strips for them, feeds them, shocks them, solicits them, laces their coffee with vodka, takes their money and sends them home feeling that they have done something exciting, perhaps even faintly illicit.'[21] Decades later, Dame Mary's former neighbours took pride in this evidence of the raffishness of their neighbourhood, and its practical, welcome-all-comers manifestation of egalitarianism: 'She's probably the only Dame of the British Empire who's ever lived up here.'[22]

When I moved to Kings Cross in 1981, the raw underbelly of winners and losers was on display in a way it rarely was elsewhere in Sydney. This was the most densely populated and diverse pocket of the biggest city. Walking to the train it was wise to look down, not only to be sure to sidestep the needles and syringes that littered the streets, but to avoid the entreaties of pimps and shysters and the desperate eyes of junkies. Its notorious corruption was palpable.

In that tight little urban village, judgement was largely withheld. As Malcolm Fraser, prime minister of the day and the beneficiary of intergenerational wealth, liked to say, 'Life is not meant to be easy.' Most of those who lived in the Cross in those days, when unfairness was so easy to spot, would have taken more comfort from the rest of George Bernard Shaw's aphorism 'but take courage: it can be delightful'. At night Kings Cross burst with energy, fuelled by drugs and booze in stylish clubs and smoky, crowded bars, and the raffish possibilities of a city that enjoyed flaunting its sensual beauty.

Its charm always had an edge. One of the most delightful, when I lived there, was the chance encounters with the old ladies who had made the area their home for decades. Some had moved out of the grand houses that once distinguished the area into gracious apartments in sought-after buildings, but most lived in small Art Deco flats with creaking lifts, antique gas cookers and wall after wall of highly polished timber. Widowed, or never married, women who had broken the rigid rules of class, religion and gender; refugees; workers; escapees from domestic violence, the bush and small towns; and storytellers. They slowly walked the streets, chose their books at Miss Norma Chapman's Clays Bookshop, picked up a pastry from Croissant D'Or, visited the community centre behind the El Alamein fountain, took the 311 bus along the leafy avenue of Macleay Street, past the Garden Island naval base and rotting wharves of Woolloomooloo into the city and their favourite department stores. They kept a weather eye on the comings and goings of the newer residents, just as they had been alert to the violent protests that had accompanied and stalled the redevelopment of Victoria Street.

Many had found their tribe in this most urban part of the largest city. 'Here joy, if not unconfined, was less restricted than it would be in suburbia or Boolamakanka. Live and let live was the attitude and still is,'[23] one wrote in a 1981 compendium of memories of life in the Cross that grew out of a local oral history project. The old ladies remembered the wartime blackouts, the grief of loss, the fun of the dances. They enjoyed the new foods and clothes that followed the influx of people who arrived on the migrant ships that docked at Woolloomooloo. The drollest even wondered, as the beautifully coiffured drag artists perched next to them in coffee shops, if the area should return to its original name: Queens Cross.

As THE OLD ladies died, their apartments were redesigned and became fodder for glossy magazines and real estate agents. Old egalitarian ideas were eroded by money. Within a couple of decades the triangle of Kings Cross, Potts Point and Elizabeth Bay was again home to some of the richest people in the nation, living in some of the most expensive real estate in the most expensive city. Those who had drawn the short straw in life's lottery were still present but less visible, pushed out to distant suburbs and cheaper regions.

By the time COVID-19 arrived, well over three million adults and 700,000 children in Australia were classified as living in poverty. They lived in the thirteenth-richest country in the world, but did not have enough money to feed, clothe and house themselves. Dame Mary would no doubt have welcomed the dollars that flowed like floodwaters across a parched plain in the first year of the pandemic. Never had so much money moved so swiftly from government bonds to bank accounts. The aim was to keep the economy moving, to prevent catastrophic hardship and intolerable images of people queueing for support. Accommodation was miraculously found for the homeless people who routinely slept on the streets; unemployment and disability benefits nearly doubled. People who had struggled to feed and clothe themselves and their families could at last afford the necessities that had become luxuries. Many casual and low-income workers found that life was easier with a little more money. Like a grand experiment of a universal basic income, lives were transformed by the security that even a modest guaranteed income provided. Until it stopped.

The COVID years have demonstrated that it is possible to find more money for those in need if the political urgency is real. For decades the public domain had been filled with stories of welfare fraud, of cheats and dole bludgers. Centrelink's devastating robodebt experiment had demonstrated how misguided dreams of administrative efficiency could be. The proposition for those who suspected that welfare recipients were leaners, not lifters, had seemed simple—compare the income data from the tax office with welfare support provided and demand the difference be repaid. Experts advised that the flaws were obvious, that income could not simply be averaged over a year, that the rules of entitlement were complicated and time dependent. It took several years, but eventually the courts found that the scheme was not only unjust but illegal. The settlement required that $1.8 billion be repaid to those who had been wrongly punished by a flawed algorithm.[24] No politician accepted personal responsibility. There was no special compensation for the loved ones of those who took their own lives under the pressure of government debt collectors. There was no recalibration of the messages about fairness.

Levels of income support had not increased in real terms for 25 years as Australia became more unequal, the rich much richer, the majority in the middle stagnant and the poor poorer. The pandemic threw the reality of this disparity into sharp relief, and the campaign to raise the level of income support won new advocates in unexpected quarters. Journalists quizzed public figures—*could you live on $40 a day?*[25]—and economists, business leaders and union leaders all agreed that this was not enough. They argued that an increase of $95 a week would help those in need get back on their feet and benefit the economy as they spent the money they received. It would also lift Australia from the bottom of the OECD table of income support. Instead it was increased by just $50 a fortnight.

Trust in government depends on countless micro-judgements about what is fair and honest, and those who had drawn the short straw in the Australian lottery were losing faith. The Edelman Trust Barometer revealed in 2021 that even as trust in Australian institutions was at an all-time high, for the second year running Australia had 'the largest trust inequality gap on record globally'. The less well off knew they were being ignored.[26]

Arguments based on fairness, on a right to support, still got less traction in a society that had looked askance at those in need ever since Prime Minister Malcolm Fraser declared life wasn't meant to be easy. The COVID X-ray had shown that the old Canberra argument—there is not enough money—could be ignored when priorities shifted, but the paltry increase was a reminder that public support was always given begrudgingly. Fairness struggled to get a foothold in a polity arbitrarily divided between lifters and leaners.

8

Lucky, Not So Smart

IF FAIRNESS IS one guiding Australian ethos, luck is another. It is as though no one can quite believe the good fortune that has come their way, rarely acknowledging the appropriation of land or the trade in finite minerals that form its bedrock. Luck neither requires nor rewards effort. It has been dug deep into the compost of national identity. Since the earliest days of British settlement, fortune has come from the land—wool, wheat, gold, silver—and enjoyed by those who claimed the treasure it yielded. Over time the nature of the most lucrative products, and their beneficiaries, have changed but the principle has remained. The phrase 'the Lucky Country' had been conjured by Donald Horne in 1964 as an ironic quip, but has since been taken literally.

At the end of COVID Year One, when it appeared that Australia had been spared the worst of the plague, an almost bewildering sense of luck came back with full rhetorical flourish. Over Christmas, people reflected on the country's good fortune in comparison to the catastrophic toll elsewhere. *This is really the Lucky Country*, they said to each other with a note of disbelief, as images of overcrowded hospitals and cemeteries in faraway places filled the screens. Australia had in 2020 managed to escape the worst of the deadly virus, with less than a thousand deaths that year. This was just another example of what happened in the Lucky Country even when, as Donald Horne had written more than half a century earlier, it was 'run mainly by second rate people'. But, as became clear in the second and third years of the pandemic, luck is random and cannot be channelled, even if some believe you make your own.

As always, the objective circumstances made it clear that Australia's relative success was not a matter of luck. As an island continent, Australia could close her borders, prohibit her citizens from leaving, and enforce the oldest method of disease control in human history—isolation. The country should have been a model for the region, with its large landmass; a relatively small, well-informed population temperamentally inclined to behave as directed; still-strong institutions; deep resources of money and expertise; even with a relatively unsophisticated economy that had come to rely too much on the Ponzi scheme of migration to fuel growth. Hubris balanced palpably on a tightrope. The fall—bad luck—arrived as a nudge from China, Australia's largest trading partner. China's need for iron ore kept the economy ticking over, while it prohibited the import of one commodity after another and refused to take calls from ministers.

Donald Horne famously popularised the ironic phrase when he and his publishers decided to use *The Lucky Country* instead of *The Anatomy of Australia* as the title for what became his nation-defining book analysing Australian complacency and possibility.[1] It was a good call. *The Lucky Country* sold 120,000 copies within four years; the phrase almost immediately entered the vernacular and helped galvanise a transformation. At the time, Australia faced an existential threat: her largest trading partner, Britain, which many still considered the motherland, had given up on the last vestiges of empire and switched her focus to Europe. To survive, new markets were needed. As the memory of the terrors of the Japanese aggression in the Pacific receded, the region began to look less like a threat. Japan had been an important trading partner before the war and now more than ever needed resources to fuel its recovering economy; in return she offered cars, electronics and consumer goods. Korea was emerging from the devastation of her civil war and Singapore was beginning the journey to city-state powerhouse. Australia had much of what they needed, and a more diversified and sophisticated economy began, slowly and under the burden of tariffs, to emerge.

Horne's focus was not just on trade; he was seeking in 1964 to answer a recurring big question: *what kind of people are we?* It was an urgent quest, and the book and the debate it fostered sounded a wake-up call that was cultural as well as economic, and eventually political. Critics initially hated Horne's book but readers loved it, not least because Horne stroked them and described them as smarter and more decent than those who held the levers of power.

Donald Horne grew into his role as a wily and passionate advocate for his country. Over the following years he himself added to the crowded bookshelf of books that riffed on his title, with *Death of the Lucky Country* and *The Lucky Country Revisited*. He became more radical and more sceptical about his country's capacity for change. As his ironic title became a synonym for Australia, his optimism faltered. Luck is not a rational basis for the life of a nation, but a good predictor for complacency. *Why bother if it is just a matter of luck?* In a 1990 election speech, Prime Minister Bob Hawke flicked the switch: 'No longer content to be just the lucky country, Australia must become the clever country.' Donald Horne responded, 'I think we should realise that the lucky country provides a descriptive phrase, condemning Australia for what it was, whereas the clever country is a prescriptive phrase, suggesting to Australia what it might become.'[2]

This should have been uncontroversial. But unlike fairness and luck, cleverness has not taken root strongly in the national psyche. It is tempting to find an elaborate metaphor in the fact that few have heard of the Adelaide University professor of physics and his Australian-born son, William Henry and William Lawrence Bragg, who, uniquely, jointly won the Nobel Prize in 1915 for X-ray crystallography. Their work, much of it undertaken at the University of Adelaide, made it possible to determine the structure of molecules at the previously invisible atomic level. It was fundamental research that revealed the structure of matter and provided the essential tool to more than twenty subsequent Nobel Prize winners in medicine, physics and chemistry. It remains work of enduring significance, but rarely invoked by those who point to the Hills hoist or stump-jump plough as evidence of Australian smarts. Unlike the Braggs, Australians have persistently shown a reluctance to go back to first principles, to try to understand the underlying structures and adjust accordingly. The much-vaunted sentiment—*she'll be right*—encourages people to operate at the surface level of feeling without too much thought and with trust that good fortune will deliver a good enough answer.

Inventiveness and pragmatic adaptation are celebrated, but being smart, like being imaginative, has rarely ranked highly. In 1987, Hawke had promised that no child would be living in poverty by the 1990 election. It was an ambitious claim that galvanised the campaign and forced the government to deliver on policies that would reduce poverty, but was pilloried for setting the bar too high.[3] Hawke was criticised for making impossible promises, as though poverty were an immutable force of nature, not a product of human decisions and responses to unforeseen events. His 1990 ambition for Australia to be known for being clever generated a similarly hostile response, even though the country was already on track to achieve it.

IN THE SIX years to 1990, the number of students completing high school had doubled to two in three. Getting students to stay at school long enough for an education that would prepare them for an increasingly complex world had been a long, slow process. When Hawke talked about Australia becoming a clever country he knew many families would need support to make it possible. He included increased scholarships for students, support for parents who would otherwise need their kids to start working, and generous rewards for the top 500 high school graduates. There were extra funds for First Nations students, adult literacy and disadvantaged schools, retraining options for the unemployed. And funding for university research centres to create a thousand jobs for promising scientists, and keep them in Australia. The aim was to reignite one of the young nation's most distinctive signatures as a well-educated society. It had languished for decades.

To put this in its historical context: by 1880 all the Australian colonies had passed laws making schooling free, compulsory and secular, and most had implemented them. The hunger for education was real, and books were devoured in huge numbers to make the Australian colonies the most profitable market in the British Empire. At the time, there were three universities serving a population of just two million.[4] The colonies had come a long way in a century from being the dumping ground for those Governor Lachlan Macquarie had described as Britain's 'most ignorant, most wicked and most abandoned wretches'. By Federation, Australian men and women were among the most numerate and literate people in the world.[5]

This spirit was revived during the Second World War. Labor prime minister John Curtin and his advisers, including H.C. 'Nugget' Coombs, were determined that this crisis would not be squandered. The austerity programs adopted by conservative prime minister Joseph Lyons during the Great Depression had continued to extract a toll for years as his government reduced spending, balanced the budget and repaid loans to international lenders. At the same time, the United Kingdom and the United States experimented with the then-new model of Keynesian spending to build infrastructure, putting a floor under the economy. As the war continued, an increasingly urgent commitment to learn the lessons from the past grew.

The Idea of Australia

Charles (C.E.W.) Bean, the journalist charged with documenting the detail of the First World War that had so devastated the new nation, completed the final volume of his history of that war in 1942. He was acutely aware that its promise to deliver a stable new world order had not been realised, and that the claim to racial superiority that had shaped Australia had 'passed beyond recall'. As another conflagration raged, it was a time to redress the failures of the first. In his book *The War Aims of a Plain Australian*, he wrote, 'When we ask, what is the main step towards bringing about this kind of New Order that we want,' the answer is 'Educate, Educate and Educate! . . . It doesn't matter much what else you do—educate and you solve the problem; fail to educate, and nothing else can save you.' Education would nurture talent, expand opportunity, break down selfishness and prejudice and strengthen democracy and national life.[6]

At the time, four out of ten children left school at Year 8, another five left at Year 10, and only one in ten completed secondary school. A tiny proportion of those students went on to one of the five universities, the preserve of the wealthy and recipients of a handful of scholarships. Charles Bean's message was heard by politicians and policy makers. As they returned from active service, thousands of soldiers found new opportunities to study and enter the professions. A Universities Commission was established in 1943 to exempt students from war service so they could continue their studies, and returning soldiers did not have to pay fees. The number of university students more than doubled from 1939 over a decade to more than 32,000, a third of them ex-servicemen. It became an article of faith, as the young MP Gough Whitlam said in 1953, that Australia 'should not limit university education by leaving it primarily to the states'.[7]

Even with direct grants from Canberra, the states failed to give the universities sufficient means to meet the growing demand. By 1957 the universities had become so overcrowded and under-resourced that a report into Australian universities by Sir Keith Murray, chair of the

British University Grants Committee, declared that 'immediate action' was needed to ensure the 'position [of the universities] is not to be catastrophic'. It was a policy that won bipartisan support. Education was an unalloyed public good, its benefits proliferated. Scholarships increased and new universities opened.

Robert Menzies, the Liberal prime minister who dominated the post-war years, had been one of only 25 students in Victoria to win a scholarship to the University of Melbourne in 1913. His personal understanding that education was a privilege bestowed on too few had influenced his decision to increase scholarships and expand the number of universities. Over his parliamentary career, the Labor leader Gough Whitlam gave dozens of speeches about the need to expand opportunities for education. In a 1972 campaign speech, he made this tangible when he promised to remove university fees. 'Education should be the great instrument for the promotion of equality,' he said. Years later he declared that the most 'enduring single achievement' of his government was the transformation of education which enhanced the 'future of all Australians . . . by a tremendous uplifting in our educational expectations and achievements'.[8]

It took a long time to change an education system that was selective, and limited by state government spending, family circumstance and gender. My father was the youngest of thirteen children, and the only one from his father's two families who completed high school. My mother's father refused to allow her to go to university, deeming it inappropriate for a girl, but less than a decade after the Whitlam government abolished tuition fees she completed her doctorate.

THE ROAD WAS much longer for First Nations families, not because they were less able but because the structural obstacles were greater, making it harder to finish school, let alone continue to further education. Jackie Huggins arrived at the University of Queensland as a mature student in the early 1980s. A bright student, she had been told in high school she couldn't go to university, 'You couldn't possibly do Senior because Aboriginals have no brains!'[9] It took eleven years to begin to recover from that psychological blow, before she found a seat in Raymond Evans's history class at the sandstone-clad cloisters of the subtropical university. When she did her life changed. As she sat in the 'Problems in Australian History' class, she realised that Raymond Evans was talking about her experience. It hurt that he 'knew so much about my own people and I knew so little'. Years later she reflected that studying with him 'saved' her, enabled her to 'recover the dignity and self-respect' her high school teacher had almost destroyed. It set her on the path to becoming the national leader she is today, former co-chair of Reconciliation Australia and of the National Congress of Australia's First Peoples. She was not alone.

Colin Tatz grew up in South Africa when race defined everything: where you could live, where you could go, who you could mix with, who you could marry, what work you could do, how much you were paid. Mental barriers held the clamps even tighter. For members of the Jewish community whose families had been shattered by the Holocaust, the parallels were painfully easy to draw. Tatz, like many others, was drawn to the protest movement that captured world attention in 1960 when 69 people were killed in a massacre following a protest in Sharpeville, outside Johannesburg. Those opposed to the regime felt its brute force. When he was offered a scholarship for a doctoral degree at the Australian National University, with full access to the records of Canberra's administration of Aboriginal affairs in the Northern Territory, it was an offer he could not refuse.

He had not anticipated the tight ties between the university and the government. The minister, Paul Hasluck, who in 1951 had made his name advocating for 'assimilation to ensure all Aborigines and part-Aborigines would attain the same manner of living as other

Australians', took a personal interest in his research. He directed Tatz to 'look at full blood affairs, not at the *emancipated* community', thereby excluding the catastrophe of forced child removals. Hasluck later intervened to make and withhold documents, vet and in the end censor Tatz's findings.[10] There was no escaping the tight rein of power, and the power of the prevailing established viewpoint.

After the heated, passionate and informed debates Colin Tatz and Sandra, his wife and collaborator, had been party to in South Africa, he was astonished to discover how effectively the Australian form of apartheid segregated, excluded and marginalised. The most sophisticated debates in Australia were likely to occur in Aboriginal rights organisations supported by unions, the Communist Party and some churches, but not in the universities, which were still mostly limiting their interest in First Nations peoples to archaeology and anthropology. Until 1959, black students had been allowed to enrol in South African universities; Nelson Mandela had graduated in 1944; scores of Black colleges were opened in the United States after the Civil War.

There was no such history in Australia. The pathway to a formal education was informal and capricious, most likely to be shaped by churches or trade unions. For the First Nations people confined to missions and reserves luck played too big a part—which church ran the mission, the pastor's character, the willingness to accept traditional ways and knowledge, the resources of the community. David Unaipon's father, James, was the Congregationalist mission at Point McLeay's first convert, and became a powerful Christian evangelist. When David was just thirteen, the exceptionally brilliant Ngarrindjeri boy from the haunted watery reaches of the Coorong was sent to Adelaide as a servant. He was lucky: his master was interested in philosophy, science and maths and encouraged his young servant to pursue these subjects. When he returned to the Coorong five years later in 1890 his path as an inventor, preacher, writer and advocate was set.

The Idea of Australia

At the same time as the Braggs were discovering how to X-ray molecules in an Adelaide lab, upstream on the Murray River David Unaipon had begun his lifelong quest to invent a perpetual motion machine, had won his first patent and revolutionised shearing, was writing the first of his three books, and advocating for a self-governing Aboriginal territory. The man whose image now authorises the 50-dollar note was even then considered Australia's Leonardo Da Vinci, but was arrested for vagrancy, his work stolen, his patents lapsed.

David Unaipon was 87 when the first Aboriginal student to graduate from an Australian university, Margaret Williams, was awarded a diploma in physical education from the University of Melbourne. Three years earlier in 1956 the Casino student had become one of two First Nations high school graduates to qualify for university admission.[11] It took the university decades to publicly claim this 'first', years after Williams-Weir had returned to Australia from Canada and completed a doctoral degree.

In 1966, when Charles Perkins graduated from the University of Sydney and Margaret Valadian from the University of Queensland, Perkins' public profile ensured that this was a first that could not be ignored, although Valadian's quieter advocacy also made an impact. This was to be a transformative moment. Fifty years later 30,000 First Nations students have completed tertiary degrees, hundreds with doctorates. Thousands more join their ranks every year, a key to economic security in their testamurs, proudly taking their places in professions and public life, the arts and business, honouring community and demanding more. They are the generation who powered the *Uluru Statement from the Heart* which will, sooner or later, fundamentally reshape the idea of Australia.

EDUCATION HAS A value in itself for individuals, who by knowing more and learning how to think critically are better able to make life decisions and sense of the world. It also has a public benefit that can most readily be measured in economic terms. The other prong of Bob Hawke's clever country rhetoric was to again acknowledge the explicit role of government in industry policy. Nudging companies to be more innovative, more outward looking. Providing a network of incentives and penalties, opportunities for retraining, easier access to capital for those with a bright idea. Companies that had grown fat and lazy behind protective tariff barriers recognised the need to recalibrate, to become more productive, more innovative. Some succeeded before the full force of market-driven globalisation stripped the economy back to its sun-bleached bones of raw materials, property, finance and people. Some did not, and manufacturing crumbled, services predominated, the biggest companies relocated offshore. For others, clever met luck, and abundant minerals, privatisation and the financialisaton of everything made them very wealthy. The economy still displayed the scar tissue of its lopsided foundation—banking, agriculture and minerals—and a policy framework that hid government support behind an opaque network of grants and rebates.

The business sector slowly became more ambitious, but people were hungry for more. Reducing the cost of education in the early 1970s pushed the proportion of the population who studied at university from 2 to 6 per cent, and the expansion during the 1980s continued to nudge the numbers higher, transforming lives and creating once unimaginable opportunities for hundreds of thousands of people. By 1990, that proportion had grown to 15 per cent. Half a million students were enrolled, and the federal government provided just under 90 per cent of university funding. By 2021 one and a half million students were enrolled at university, 68 per cent of the population had a post-school qualification. But government funding accounted for less than 40 per cent, local student fees for a fifth and international students another 20 per cent.[12]

When Bob Hawke promised that Australia would become a clever country by investing more in education and research, I had a direct personal and professional interest in seeing this occur. I was teaching journalism at the recently minted University of Technology, Sydney. The reforms expanded the number of universities and introduced deferred income-dependent fees, which allowed the sector to grow but pushed some of the cost back onto students. It introduced new complexity to the funding system, which became increasingly fraught. Overnight there was money for research, an expectation of higher degrees for staff, and opportunities to broaden the curriculum, welcome new students and create new programs. University was not free, but the fees were modest and could be deferred. Education was still considered a public good with private benefits, not just another business.

The Bachelor of Arts degree in Communication at UTS was a sought-after qualification. Half the students were chosen on the basis of their life experience and expectations. This meant that to secure a place in the small program, school leavers needed grades comparable to those that would have earned them a place in a medical school. This produced a vibrant environment and a group of people who would go on to become leaders in their fields—as journalists, novelists, filmmakers, historians, scholars and politicians of all hues.

Ever since I had graduated from the University of Queensland in the mid-1970s, I had found it a struggle to explain to editors why well-educated journalists might do a better job. Suddenly it was accepted. Work-experience placements led to jobs for a brilliant generation. Australia began to look more like other developed countries, with a well-educated population. The promise of a clever country within reach.

———

A DECADE LATER another Labor leader, Kim Beazley, a Rhodes scholar whose father had shepherded the metamorphosis of education in the Whitlam government, attempted to again raise the bar. He promised to increase educational opportunities and pathways, branding the idea

Knowledge Nation. The public initially welcomed the idea, which suggested how, in an increasingly complex, information-driven world, government might act as a catalyst to increase capacity. His promise was poorly packaged and quickly ridiculed, with shrieks of outrage over a clumsily drawn diagram that sketched the 21st century's new economic and social complexity. Journalists tagged it 'Spaghetti Nation'. *Sydney Morning Herald* columnist Alan Ramsay set the tone: 'In one mad moment, with his incomprehensible bird's nest sketch of 23 circles and 40 train lines, Barry Jones made Kim Beazley's Knowledge Nation an instant national joke ... One look at that absurd drawing ... must just about have killed Knowledge Nation as a politically saleable product, at least for now.'[13]

Alan Ramsay was right. Instead of an achievable aspiration, it became a joke. Prime minister John Howard and his education minister David Kemp—a highly educated former professor—led the charge. Under their leadership, for the first time in decades, government support for higher education failed to keep pace with the growth in student numbers. The proportion of Commonwealth money going to universities fell from just under half of the education budget when they took office in 1996 to under one-third by the time they left, although more money was directed to schools that derived most of their income from fees.

Public money available for university education increased again during the Labor years, but with the re-election of the Liberal–National Coalition in 2013 the proportion of Australians going to universities fell. Higher education was no longer an unalloyed good with bipartisan support. Instead, as the economic commentator George Megalogenis wrote, 'The Coalition came to see education politically, through the eyes of parents.'[14] Schools trumped universities. As the government contribution to Australia's thirty-nine public universities fell, resourceful administrators found a receptive international market and tertiary education became the fourth-largest export earner. The first Chinese student to study at an Australian university came from Wuhan in 1923, and after a market for full fee–paying international students was made possible in 1990, the numbers grew spectacularly. In 2013, there were nearly 250,000 international students enrolled in Australian universities, many on a pathway that would lead to permanent residence, and by 2019 this number had nearly doubled. Just as Chinese goldminers once paid more for their licences than other miners, these Chinese students, and their classmates from India, Nepal, Vietnam and elsewhere, paid much more for their degrees than local students. As the universities' government funding fell, international students kept the universities afloat—until the pandemic. Border closures made it impossible for students to come to Australia.

THE UNIVERSITIES WERE a canary in the mine of the policy response to the pandemic. Rather than taking pride in the success of the higher education system, both as a business and for its achievements in educating tens of thousands of students from home and abroad, Coalition members sneered. Victorian Liberal senator James Paterson declared in May 2020, as the enormity of the pandemic threat was becoming painfully real, 'Over the last few decades our universities have bet big on the international-student dollar. Their institutions have boomed from what has been a very lucrative business, but they have become badly overexposed.'[15]

The same could be said about almost every other sector of the Australian economy: their fortunes had risen as China became richer and integrated further with global markets and communities. Industry policy had been forgotten; the faith in the market was overwhelming. Despite the contrary evidence from South Korea, Singapore and China, it was an article of faith in Australian policy-making that government should not pick winners: the market should be left with only the lightest touch of regulation, but with plenty of embedded subsidies and grants for the chosen. It was an environment that inevitably increased the gap between the richest and the rest. The extraordinary wealth of the two wealthiest people in the country was inextricably bound to China's need for quality iron ore, and the willingness to pay ever more for the commodity that was once considered little more than dirt. Fortunately for them, there was no ready alternative and iron ore was not subject to quarantine. Nonetheless, in the earliest days of the pandemic private ministerial briefings in Canberra were preoccupied with the problem of finding enough workers to keep the mines running should the pandemic prove as devastating as the early modelling suggested.

When, on the last day of January 2020, the prime minister announced that Australia would close its borders to people travelling from China, vice-chancellors all over Australia huddled in disaster-management planning meetings. Would it be possible to teach the students remotely? Could ways be found around Chinese internet firewalls to make online materials available? Could they be flown to countries whose Australian routes were still open? Chinese students accounted for 10 per cent of students in a few universities, but up to 50 per cent in some courses in some of the biggest, oldest and richest institutions.[16] The fees they paid bankrolled research and other operations. They had become an important part of the social and employment ecosystem in the suburbs that wrapped around the universities. There the students found accommodation, food, part-time jobs and friendships.

Less than two weeks after the first COVID-infected person arrived in Australia from China, the aerobridge was pulled in. The increasing dependence on international students had been making university administrators nervous for several years. Critics asked if this was undermining the core offerings and experience for local students. Were they providing enough support to help the students settle? Would other countries steal the market? Would new Chinese universities lead to more students studying at home? The possibility of a pandemic closing borders and preventing students from travelling was the black swan none had anticipated.

Over the following months, the government made it clear that the universities would be punished for their success in creating an international market to offset local cuts. The rules attaching to the JobKeeper scheme were adjusted three times to ensure that the local public universities did not qualify. Tens of thousands of academics and support staff lost their jobs. The then University of Sydney vice-chancellor Michael Spence described a call from a departmental official in Canberra who asked, 'What do we have to do to make sure that the universities don't qualify for support?' The message was clear: universities would not receive any of the support that was flowing to other enterprises that had been savaged by the pandemic.

Classes moved online and researchers swung into action; university-based professors of epidemiology became ubiquitous, sought-after talent on television current affairs shows. In each of the universities, in every field, important research was undertaken—from the most high-profile quest for a vaccine and genomic sequencing, to measuring and mitigating the pandemic's impact, participating in global studies, and highlighting the hidden costs in social cohesion, safety, mental health and equity. A dossier prepared by a group of leading academics that highlighted world's best practice in mitigation and control was delivered to Canberra and ignored.

This was just the opening salvo. In June 2020, without prior consultation, the federal education minister announced one of the biggest, most short-sighted, changes in university funding for decades. It was dressed up as providing more job-ready graduates, and in a flurry of numbers suggested that it was actually providing more support to the sector. Rather, it doubled the cost of arts degrees, reduced funding for key teaching areas, led to massive internal reorganisations and a new round of job losses. By the end of the year more than 20,000 full-time academics had lost their jobs, as had tens of thousands of casual academics and administrative staff—with no prospect for them to return. Education was treated neither like a business nor a public good, marooned in a wasteland of almost incomprehensible ideological contempt.

Jacqui Lambie, the independent senator from Tasmania, seemed to understand the value of education better than a cabinet room full of ministers with degrees. She was acutely aware of how education was the key to both fairness and luck. She declared in the Senate on 7 October 2020:

> I'll be damned if I'll vote to tell those kids in those rural and regional areas of Tasmania that they deserve to have their opportunities suffocated in a way they'll never even know . . . I refuse to be the vote that tells poor kids out there, or those sitting on that fine line—no matter how gifted and no matter how determined you are—'You might as well dream a little cheaper, because you're never going to make it. Because you can't afford it.' I won't take that from them—I won't be a part of that.[17]

The Morrison government's legislation passed with only minor amendments. International students did not return for another year. Local student numbers increased, as they always do when jobs are scarce. Research ground to a halt in some areas but continued in others. At least 40,000 highly qualified people lost their jobs; researchers scanned advertisements for positions abroad. The universities managed, but were on the brink of catastrophe, the very independence that had guaranteed their success under threat. The bipartisan commitment to education since the post-war reconstruction had evaporated. It was not fair and it made little sense—the pathway out of this crisis would depend on education, and carefully considered and implemented industry policy, just as it had in the past. Luck would not be enough.

9

Utopian Dreaming

THE JOURNEY BETWEEN the heads that guard the entrance to Sydney Harbour promised me, as it did millions of others before and since, safety. Calm water at last. For days the MS *Wanganella* had struggled with mountainous seas, making her way to the top of a wave only to fall into its accompanying trough. It was a long time since the *Wanganella* had offered luxury travel between Auckland and Sydney, and her battles against the wild winds and waves had taken a toll.

By the time my family boarded, sailing across the Tasman Sea had become the cheapest way to make the journey from New Zealand, where my 24-year-old father had been sent to start his career ministering to Lutherans across Aotearoa's north island. There was no money to waste on young pastors and their families moving to a new parish. Water gushed over the decks, and those passengers not tormented by seasickness watched their gelatinous scrambled eggs slide off plates while chairs and cutlery flew across the dining room. This was one of the ship's last voyages before being offered for scrap. I was nearly four years old, and the terror of those enormous waves, followed by the relief of the calm Port Jackson waters and the wonder about whether the *Wanganella* would hit the Harbour Bridge as we sailed underneath, fed my imagination. The memories found their way into my childhood paintings for years. In 1959, the working harbour was fouled by the industrial waste that flooded into its upper reaches, the inner harbour polluted by effluent, Bennelong Point a building site, and just a handful of baby skyscrapers closed in the city's horizon. But it was still magnificent: between the ugly red brick buildings the shoreline suggested an older, more bounteous natural beauty, the quay jostling with people. It was brash, dirty and busy.

This encounter was the first step in my lifelong quest to make sense of a place and its people. My twentysomething parents were relieved to be returning to the land of their birth, even if it meant another six-hour drive over the mountains to the hot flat plains of the Central West of New South Wales and a town they had barely heard of. The relief was palpable when we were met on the quay by a kindly couple. We learned they had made their lives growing and harvesting grain in vast paddocks that stretched to the horizon.

Fanciful ideas of what lay on the other side of the imposing Blue Mountains had long drawn those who arrived by sea to go further west. They watched the stars and made their way on ancient walking paths along the ridges, eyeing towering sandstone escarpments and deep valleys. After Gregory Blaxland, William Lawson and William Charles Wentworth achieved a certain sort of immortality by crossing the mountains they called Blue, convicts felled trees, chopped and hauled sandstone to turn the well-worn paths into roads suitable for horses and drays. On the plains Wiradjuri warriors fought the NSW Mounted Police for decades, until settlers claimed the spoils of land and gold just below the surface. Some were felled by hardship and driven mad by disappointment. Land prone to flood and drought tested the spirit.

By the 1960s, when agriculture needed fewer workers and no longer dominated the economy, the connection with a life on the land for many people was still real and personal. My father had spent his childhood on a hardscrabble farm in South Burnett in Queensland, where his father and brothers battled the prickly pear and scrub to clear fields. He, no doubt, had some idea of what to expect—floods, droughts, plagues of locusts, stoical people who didn't talk much. For my city-bred mother, it was a throwback to an era she had known only from a distance, through books and paintings and stories around the dinner table. Our destination in the Central West was a long way from the urbanity of Melbourne, where she had briefly worked, or the stuffy gentility of Adelaide where she grew up.

With four adults and two children squeezed into an old Chevrolet, our trip that October took us through the towns named for explorers. There were no markers to the battles by the Wiradjuri to protect their land. We continued beyond the mountains, along winding roads, through the hills and gullies on the other side of the Great Dividing Range, over the open plains and on to the town of Gilgandra. We were no longer seasick but it was a long, boring drive—positively suburban in comparison to the journey that had made Gilgandra famous.

On a hot day in October 1915, 26 men, responding to the urgings of the captain of the local rifle club, left their marginal farms adjoining the town on the banks of the Castlereagh River and embarked on the patriotic adventure of a lifetime. News of the catastrophic landing at Gallipoli that had claimed the lives of 3158 Australian soldiers that April and May was reverberating around the country.[1] More young men were needed to defend the motherland and her empire. Gilgandra's spontaneous wartime recruiting drive quickly gathered attention and official support.

Two hundred and thirty-seven country recruits joined the Coo-ee March as it trundled towards the coast along dusty roads, through other river towns—Wellington, Dubbo, Molong—and over the mountains. Before long the ragtag adventure had fulfilled its propaganda promise. In Dubbo they were given dungarees, in Orange army greatcoats. No doubt they stopped at the new Freemasons Hotel in Molong, and on and on they marched through Bathurst, then Katoomba, before arriving in Sydney in November. After a few months' training they were shipped to the Northern Hemisphere to fight in what was supposed to be the war to end all wars.

It was the first of nine 'snowball' walks. Each had a name that distinguished the new nation—Waratahs, Kangaroos, Wallabies, Cane Beetles, Boomerangs. The walks gathered young men from farms and towns across New South Wales and Queensland and swept them along to almost certain death or injury in a war they could not yet imagine.

What began as an adventure for hardy young men from the backblocks of the newly federated nation soon became something much darker. Many never returned. The war divided the new nation in ways that had been unimaginable when the founding fathers sailed to London in 1900 with a draft Constitution they hoped the British House of Commons would approve. The carefully crafted provision guaranteeing religious freedom, which eliminated the need for an official faith, was about to be tested by sectarian battles between Catholics and Protestants that would poison politics, and tarnish lives, for generations.

An imposing red-brick 'Lest We Forget' memorial now stands on a grassy bank just near the bridge over the Castlereagh River that marks the entry to the town. It bears the names of the 75 locals who died etched in bronze. Those who did return came back to a country sapped of its youthful energy by the deaths of close to 62,000 men and the injury of many more. In the process, Nationalist Party prime minister Billy Hughes, who many still regarded as a turncoat for leaving the Labor Party in 1916, declared that in a country riven by the bitter debates that had twice rejected conscription, 'the spirit of Australia, the spirit of our race, the spirit that has made free men, that has carved out the Empire and that alone can hold this country a White Australia and a free government . . . If Britain wins and we stand with her, the White Australia policy is forever safe.'

The Idea of Australia

By the time the surviving Coo-ee walkers returned, their country was, as historian Peter Cochrane wrote in *Best We Forget*, 'a distracted and divided land, a people riven by vast human loss, by economic hardship, state repression and fierce antagonisms of class and caste'. Myths were being burnished. Keith Murdoch had set the tone with his letters and reports criticising the British command, but urging that more men be sent. As the conscription referendums had shown, not all Australians were convinced their men should be prepared to die for the motherland, and those who had left Ireland with enmity in their hearts against the colonial power across the Irish Sea were resolute in their opposition. After the war, Billy Hughes, fresh from his role at the Paris Peace Conference where he had led the charge against a racial equality clause in the treaty, returned as a conquering hero. In his triumphant September 1919 parliamentary speech, Hughes became the first of many prime ministers to declare that the war had 'made the nation'.[2] Death in battle as a precursor to the formation of nations has a long history. The protracted guerrilla battles and massacres of the frontier wars were not factored into Australia's bureaucratic formation story. Despite the occasional court case and newspaper report those struggles were even more firmly locked up in the memory-jar labelled *Forget*.

As the country licked its wounds and tended to the thousands of injured, Gilgandra experienced a small taste of national attention. It was rewarded for the spirit of its romantic, brave, foolhardy young men who were prepared to kill for King, Empire and White Australia, with a new Church of England church. It beat Moosejaw, Canada, in a competition for the place in the Dominions that most deserved recognition for its contribution to the British war effort, according to the church authorities of St Ambrose in Bournemouth. Eleven days after the second Remembrance Day, the state governor, Sir Walter Davidson, took the long journey west to lay the church's foundation stone. Another St Ambrose grew on the site, a hybrid Arts and Crafts/Gothic–style red-brick church, its coloured windows filled with native

Utopian Dreaming

flora and fauna rather than biblical iconography. It was perched on unstable foundations, thanks to the high water table that had already claimed one brick church, and became the first memorial to loss in a town that had only existed for 30 years.

This imposing red-brick church was not our destination in 1959. We were heading to a reinforced concrete church and its next-door fibro manse with an outside toilet, a canna-covered septic pit and its own windmill, on a dusty corner opposite the primary school. The community that was about to make us welcome was made up of Lutherans. Their families had travelled north as land once claimed by squatters and held by businessmen with vast holdings was sold to wheat and sheep farmers, and some allocated to soldier settlers. There were 3000 people, five churches, half a dozen pubs, elegantly spare Art Deco buildings, a swimming pool and a hospital. This was a town that embodied the idea of rural Australia that had captured the popular imagination and remained unchanged for decades: a tough but good-natured place shaped by the unforgiving whims of nature, isolation, dogged will, fickle land-use policies, sectarianism, class and racial exclusion.[3]

Tin Town was a shanty settlement perched on the banks of the river parallel to the main street. This was home to some survivors of the Wiradjuri, Kamilaroi and Wailwan nations, who had used this reach of the sandy-bottomed quick-flowing Wallambungle (Castlereagh) River as a spiritual and social meeting place for millennia. Even if it wasn't much discussed, the settlement was hard to ignore. It must have evoked feelings of shame, embarrassment and anger for many who drove over the rickety wooden bridge above the river.

In early 1965, after we left the town, a group of 29 Freedom Riders set off from the University of Sydney to confront and challenge the racism and segregation that was the norm throughout the state. They wondered whether, like the ride to the American South that they were emulating, there would be violence. Gilgandra was on the original itinerary for the 2000-kilometre journey. But a few days before they left in their shabby white bus, the Gilgandra Church of Christ minister sent a message that although Aboriginal people needed a guarantor to buy at the timber yard and main store, the situation was worse in Gulargambone, 50 kilometres further north. There the cinema was segregated, and Aboriginal people could not sit at a table in the town's cafe.[4] In Gilgandra, restrictive regulations controlled the lives of First Nations people who lived in town and those who lived in state-run reserves, but it was considered less racist than other towns in the region. As the Freedom Riders—led by Charles Perkins, soon to be the first Aboriginal man to graduate from an Australian university, and Jim Spigelman, future NSW chief justice—discovered, segregation damaged everyone. Difference was accentuated. Their journey was extensively covered by journalists who shared the anger and urgency of the protesters. Photos of Aboriginal children frolicking in formerly segregated swimming pools became enduring images. Over time, the Freedom Ride would come to mark the beginning of a new era, the end of segration, land rights, and a new way of understanding and being, that is still evolving.

EVEN BEFORE A faltering Queen Victoria signed the new nation into existence on 9 July 1900, Australia had been a notional place rich with possibility. In 1676, the Frenchman Gabriel de Foigny described the Southern Land as a 'place of hybridity, monstrosity [and] extreme otherness'.[5] The low-key administrative act of national creation in the British Parliament and Windsor Castle paid little heed to any utopian imaginings, embodied myths or deep knowledge of the continent. The words in the document that were signed that summer's day conjure an almost blank slate.

Two years before Queen Victoria put her pen to the paper of Australia's founding document, Ethel Pedley died of cancer in

Utopian Dreaming

Darlinghurst after completing the manuscript of a book that would have a much longer life than its author. While visiting her brother on his property at Walgett, north of Gilgandra, Ethel Pedley wrote *Dot and the Kangaroo*. It is a book that has not been out of print since, later adapted into a much-loved film. In it, she reimagined the magical wonderland Lewis Carroll had created for Alice, in the north-west of New South Wales. Dot, a young child, is lost in the bush, but is looked after by a kangaroo whose joey has disappeared after one of the many hunts that decimated the unique animals. 'White Humans are cruel, and love to murder,' the Kangaroo says. 'We all must die.' Dot asks the Kangaroo 'to forgive human cruelty and hope that future Australians will reassess their relationship to the natural world'.[6] A decade later, the nation put an emu and a kangaroo on her coat of arms. Ethel Pedley's book was a powerful metaphor for a new nation keen to celebrate her unique fauna while averting eyes from the human 'hunts'. Easier to talk about the First Australians as a dying race. Ethel Pedley was one of many artists who grappled with the darker, more complex and richer subtext of the place that many sensed but found hard to say out loud.

A few thousand years earlier, when the prevailing wisdom in Western centres of knowledge held that the earth was flat, seers and philosophers conjured a land so remote and different that it was replete with possibility. Stars, holding secrets of life for those who had always lived in the southern land, hinted at possibilities for others. In ancient Greece, Pythagoras imagined the earth as a sphere and, later, Aristotle concluded that the map of the known world needed to be balanced by another continent.

How such ideas entered the minds of men in ancient Greece on the northern shore of the Mediterranean, hundreds of years before Christ, 200 million years after Gondwana broke up, is hard to know. Some documentary fragments hint at Greek voyages to a mysterious southern continent.[7] Ideas hide and memories get lost but, mysteriously, their tendrils endure.

The Idea of Australia

Four hundred years after Aristotle defined global equilibrium, his disciple Ptolemy sketched how this remote southern land might look. The great mathematician and cartographer was born in Alexandria around AD 100, a century after the city's library was largely destroyed by fire but still a great centre of learning and culture. The elaborate maps Ptolemy drew in *Geographia* conjured a vast southern land; although Islamic scholars were intrigued, the maps languished for another millennia. Even after Byzantine monks reworked them at the end of the thirteenth century, it took another 300 years before they informed scores of competitive European voyages of discovery and plunder—first the Spanish, then the Dutch, British and French. And that was just one route south. The Chinese also sent explorers and nearer neighbours shared a vibrant trade in the unique produce of the north of the continent.

A hundred thousand years before these exceptional men from another age conjured spherical global balance, extraordinary journeys had brought other human beings to the place they would later imagine. The creation stories of First Nations cultures say they were always here. Science suggests a backstory and that intrepid people made their way out of Africa to the southern shores of the Mediterranean, east across the seas to India and Indonesia. They arrived in a land of megafauna, extraordinary forests and vast inland seas. It would be home to them and, over time, tens of millions of their descendants.

In many ways the First Australians' sense of time is better understood in geological terms than by using the Gregorian calendar that pivots backwards and forwards on the life of Christ just 2000 years ago. They didn't so much settle as seamlessly inhabit the land. Over time, a spiritual and practical idea of the place evolved. Its essence of connections, power and mores was recorded in drawing, story and song and passed from one generation to the next forever. This despite changes wrought by rising and retreating seas, droughts, ice ages and an occupation that forced them from ancestral lands to settlements

Utopian Dreaming

like Gilgandra's Tin Town. Against this ancient timeline, the 250 years it has taken modern Australians to begin to understand how people survived and thrived for tens of thousands of years is a celestial blink.

Australian society prides itself on pragmatism, yet scientists, philosophers, writers and artists have always had a place. The story, art and culture of the First Nations peoples imbued this antipodean somewhere with timeless meaning for millennia. It describes a spiritual world view as complicated as any ancient religion, and more interconnected. Making sense of it required more patience and humility than most of those who landed from another hemisphere possessed. Artists and writers sought to make sense of what they encountered, scientists and researchers categorised and defined, but without *dadirri* they could never really know.

HALF A CENTURY before King George III gave James Cook his instructions to follow the stars and track the transit of Venus, competing imperial voyages of exploration had captivated the popular imagination.[8] Some were recorded in diaries and journals, others in ochre etchings in caves and rock galleries. In 1719, Daniel Defoe transformed the journey of the Scottish explorer Alexander Selkirk into the bestselling *Robinson Crusoe*, creating a novel that 300 years later ranks as one of the most important in the English language. A few years later, Jonathan Swift brought a more cynical and disaffected eye to imperial ambition with another bestselling novel, *Gulliver's Travels*. Generations of children have listened to the abridged tale, not knowing that its settings were drawn from descriptions of what was once known as the Great South Land.

Gulliver's Travels became an instant bestseller in 1726, with its elaborate parody of contemporary English politics and skewering of fashionable tales of exploration and exploitation. Swift was born not

The Idea of Australia

long after vast swathes of Ireland had been transferred to English companies and landowners. By the time he wrote the book, a century before the potato famine sent Irish settlers across the seas and two centuries before the Irish won independence, his homeland was 'a nation of petty tyrants and trampled slaves'.[9] English occupation chafed, and Swift set himself the task of denouncing it, along with the literary genre of exploration and appropriation that it inspired. Seven years after Robinson Crusoe's tale of survival and endurance was published, *Gulliver's Travels* fancifully imagined a land of dwarfs and giant invaders.

Swift drew on the writings of the pirate-explorer William Dampier, who on his journey to New Holland described those he encountered as 'the Miserablist people in the world'. The storyteller imagined them differently. The little people of Lilliput, who occupied a place somewhere north of Tasmania, and the Houyhnhnms, who lived on a fictional island that bears a passing resemblance to Noongar land in the south-west of the continent, existed in harmony with each other and the land. Swift's characters were a product of his imagination, but true to a well-established type they were noble savages who lived without government, war, law or punishment. Unlike the grasping, self-serving English.

For generations people have ventured to Australia inspired by, and in search of, its exotic uniqueness. Missionaries and anthropologists were drawn by a desire to convert and document the people who had lived here for time immemorial; scientists gathered flora and fauna and swapped human remains and developed preposterous theories. The diaries of countless voyagers and, later, immigrants and refugees record how hearing alluring tales of alien creatures and places fostered their founding idea of Australia. For many, this was enough. Still the physical attributes of ancient deserts, reefs, forests and rivers, even as they are diminished by climate change and an extraordinary pace of extinction, remain the country's most visible calling card. As the economist Heinz Arndt wrote as he railed against the national identity discussion that fostered unprecedented conversations in the 1980s, 'A country that can boast of kangaroos, koalas and platypods needs few other symbols of national identity.'[10]

MATTHEW FLINDERS WAS one of countless boys whose imagination soared after secretly reading *Robinson Crusoe* as a child. Seventy years after it was published, Flinders set his heart on a life at sea—his imagination filled with exotic tales of survival and derring-do. By the time he was 25 he had twice sailed around the globe and set himself the task of filling in the blank spaces on the navigational maps used by the Royal Navy. In *A Voyage to Terra Australis*, the journals that record his journeys around the Great South Land at the beginning of the nineteenth century, he observed 'marks of the country being inhabited everywhere'.[11] Flinders set out on the 33-metre refashioned collier, HMS *Investigator*, with a small crew and the ever-resourceful Bungaree, a Kuringgai man 'of good disposition and manly conduct'.[12] His was the most challenging role: to make contact and peace with the people who lived on the seemingly endless shoreline, communicating with them despite different languages and norms. Flinders noted that those whose land he observed and defined by physical description, latitude and longitude 'had no idea of any superiority we possessed over them'.[13] The vast continent they mapped was not the 'Terra Australis' the ancient seers had imagined. Flinders concluded there could be no other land further south, and after his book was published the name stuck. (The French, with whom he was competing, preferred to call it Terre Napoleon.)

It is one of the truths of human behaviour that we recognise only what we expect to find. First we define and then we see. *Robinson Crusoe* and *Gulliver's Travels* helped define ideas of the Great South

Land and its people for generations of seafarers and settlers who found themselves trying to make sense of the land in the eighteenth century. James Cook adopted a typecasting that owed a lot to imagination fostered by the popular culture of his day. European empires had by then accumulated a great deal of experience in conquering and subduing those they encountered on their voyages. Laws guiding appropriate responses had also begun to establish a framework that went beyond plunder. As Henry Reynolds has noted, even before James Cook reached Possession Island at the peak of the peninsula we now call Cape York—after more than three months sailing up the east coast, naming landmarks as he went—the law was clear. The Dutch legal scholar Hugo Grotius had defined it 50 years earlier: 'It is equally shameless,' he wrote, 'to claim for oneself by right of discovery what is held by another, even though the occupant may be wicked, may hold wrong views about God, or may be dull to wit. For discovery applies to those things which belong to no-one.'[14]

Cook was a man following orders. His claim of possession was largely symbolic. It was designed more to satisfy the king's vanity and send a message to other empires than a physical assertion of ownership. The descriptions in his journals suggest his frame of reference had been shaped by views of noble savages: 'The Natives of New-Holland ... are far more happier than we Europeans,' he wrote. 'They live in a Tranquillity which is not disturb'd by the Inequality of Condition: The Earth and sea of their own accord furnishes them with all things necessary for life.'[15]

It took another 222 years before the Australian High Court rediscovered this essential truth, one we now consider blindingly obvious. The luminous Mabo judgment established that the concept of *terra nullius*, which was asserted when Arthur Phillip hoisted the Union Jack at Warrane on 7 February 1788 and claimed all the territory westward to 135 degrees longitude, was without foundation. The people who had lived on the continent for tens of thousands of years had a complex and sophisticated system of belief, trade and social networks. Able to survive in an environment that baffled more recent arrivals. It had not taken Phillip long to realise the flaw in the official instructions he had received, which had described a 'thinly inhabited' coastal region and an unpeopled hinterland.

On 3 June 1992, just a few years after the prospect of appealing decisions by Australian courts to the Privy Council in London was finally and unequivocally revoked, six of the seven High Court justices found that native title survived the British claim of sovereignty. Four years later, just before Christmas 1996, the court extended its findings in the Wik decision, which established that pastoral leases also did not extinguish pre-existing native title. The court overturned a 1971 judgment in a case brought by the Yolngu people of Arnhem Land, who had challenged the establishment of a bauxite mine at Yirrkala on the western coast of the Gulf of Carpentaria. At the time Justice Blackburn had found that although a 'subtle and elaborate system of laws' adapted to the country existed, it had been voided by settlement.[16] The linked Mabo and Wik judgments challenged the founding principle of the nation. Native title had not been voided.

By challenging the foundational principle of land ownership, these judgments upended many of the accepted wisdoms that had shaped the nation. As their meaning was unpacked, it was clear that they demanded the re-creation of a half-formed nation and what historian Tim Rowse has called 'moral community based on a common complex understanding of entitlement to land'.[17] The Labor prime minister Paul Keating embraced this transformative possibility in his famous Redfern Address six months later in December 1992. This was a time for national reckoning, truth-telling and reparations. Not everyone agreed.

The big questions the judgments pointed to—ownership, recognition, restitution, compensation—and their deep undercurrents were 'overlooked in chasing things that matter much less', as the historian

Alan Atkinson wrote in the third volume of his ground-breaking *Europeans in Australia*.[18] The Coalition parties were happy to harvest the votes of those who feared that this fundamental truth of prior occupation, and continuing attachment, would destroy their businesses, homes and livelihoods. John Howard was the Liberal prime minister by the time the Wik legislation extended the Mabo principle to pastoral leases, but again clipped the rights of traditional owners. Although many pastoralists and some miners were prepared to negotiate new ways of sharing the land, legislation based on Howard's ten-point plan appeased the more vociferous critics. The foundational issue at the nation's heart was sidestepped, buried in process.

In response, a new tribunal, new administrative processes and new rules for proving native title were established. Traditional owners became claimants who sought to prove their connections, arguing their cases with supporting documents and anthropological reports. It was onerous. Within three decades a third of the continent had once again become, in various forms, the estate of First Nations peoples. Some land came with compensation, some with access to economic rights, some as cultural property. This gave new meaning to the slogan Barkandji elders coined in their long-running but eventually successful campaign to have a national park in the far west of New South Wales returned to their custodianship. It was 2015 before their native title over 128,000 square kilometres was recognised, but by then their catchcry had entered the vernacular: 'Always was, always will be, Aboriginal land.'[19]

FOR A GENERATION after James Cook sailed up the east coast of the Australian continent, British interest in the Great South Land abated. King George's mission was complete. The flag had been planted. The punctured Gweagal Shield taken from Botany Bay warrior Cooman deposited in the British Museum. Specimens of plants and animals distributed to other collections. Diaries collated. And the map of the Southern Hemisphere filled out some more. A generation is long enough for a one-off encounter to enter the realm of memory. Long enough for explanations to evolve about what, if anything, it meant. Scholars note that some Eora people remembered the time when the *Endeavour* rested in what became known as Botany Bay as a 'miasma'. The white-skinned men who had come ashore for a week became an almost mythic memory. It was eighteen years before the ghostly men returned. Children at the time of the first encounter with Cook and his entourage had become adults; elders had died, and a new generation had been born. The idea that the pale voyagers might this time remain demanded a huge imaginative leap.

As is so often the way, revolution triggered a transformative response in another hemisphere. The American War of Independence dragged on for eight years from 1775. It provided the impetus for the first big idea of what was to become modern Australia: a vast island prison. The British had been sending convicted felons to its thirteen American colonies since 1618. Seven years earlier, the governor of Virginia had asked authorities in London to send convicts across the ocean to help build the colony. At the time it seemed like a brilliant idea, one that today, if it weren't so depraved, could be described in management speak as a virtuous circle. It provided free labour for colonists, removed undesirables from Britain and established a potentially lucrative new business in human transportation.

Over the following decades, more than 50,000 convict servants were 'bought, sold, gambled and willed or mortgaged by their owners' in the American colonies. As the settlers' grievances with the mother country's taxes and control grew, so did their dislike of the felons. They 'corrupted and spoilt other servants and Negroes'.[20] People from West Africa had been sold to landowners in the American colonies since the year after the first British convicts arrived. They quickly became 'the preferred drudges'—they may have initially cost more, but the enslaved people were property for life, not just a few years. After the British conceded in 1782 that they had lost control of the colonies, the newly independent United States made it clear it would no longer be a dumping ground for the 'worst of mankind'. The virtuous circle was broken. Convicts whose crimes did not merit execution quickly overfilled hulks on the River Thames and penitentiaries across the British Isles. Officials in Westminster urgently surveyed other colonies and considered, with full imperial fancy, islands they might acquire to dump the felons. An American-born midshipman who had sailed on the *Endeavour*, James Matra, wrote a letter to the Admiralty in 1782 suggesting that the land mapped by James Cook might serve the purpose.[21]

Fifteen years after James Cook made that journey, his travelling companion Joseph Banks, by then the president of the Royal Society, urged a parliamentary inquiry to consider the proposal by Matra, his friend and fellow voyager on the *Endeavour*: send the convicts to New South Wales. Only a few years before it had been regarded as an outlandish notion, but depositing them in West Africa had failed. There they died from tropical diseases and, worse, became a disruptive influence on the slave trade, which was scarcely surprising as some convicts had themselves once been enslaved.

The mysterious, almost forgotten land mapped by Cook appeared, at last, to have a purpose. Banks's grand vision generated a debate that raged in the popular press. Some argued that it was too dangerous even for these reprobates—worse, even, than Africa, a place of cannibals and strange creatures. Others declared that it was a paradise, unsuited to penal settlement because it was too good. Many anticipated, as Manning Clark later wrote, a barren land where everything was topsy-turvy, swans were black, kangaroos incomplete—a place 'where God, or nature, had fallen a-doting, or had had an attack of the sillies' on the afternoon of the sixth day of Creation.[22]

After years of agitation, Banks and Matra eventually prevailed and on 12 May 1787 more than 700 mainly young, mainly male, law-breakers from the four corners of the empire were loaded onto eleven ships bound for exile on the other side of the Earth. They were the first of 164,000 people sent on 806 ships over the next 80 years. It was a maritime trade. Some ships had previously been used to transport slaves to the Americas, others collected tea, fabrics and porcelain from China on the return journey.

Like original sin, the stain of criminal forebears seeped into the perplexing soil to shame future generations. For those seeking a place in a national foundation story, convicts in the family tree became a badge of honour only recently. Scott Morrison did not announce his plans to visit a Cornish cemetery while representing Australia at a G7 meeting of world leaders in 2021, the second year of the pandemic that had closed the borders to most. For a man who managed his profile with meticulous attention to detail, this invited varying interpretations. Was he ashamed? Guilty about visiting a relative abroad that his locked-down electors could not? Or just enjoying the entitlements of office? A local Cornish newspaper was alerted to his search for the graves of his forebears, the parents of his thieving fifth great-grandfather William, who had arrived on the First Fleet. Their headstones could not be found, but like a minor celebrity on *Who Do You Think You Are?* Scott Morrison portentously wrote in the visitor book, 'It has been wonderful to return "home", in memory of William Roberts.'[23]

It had taken a long time to dislodge the idea that Britain was home, even for those who had never left Australian shores, or whose forebears had arrived centuries before. As it turned out, Australia was neither topsy-turvy nor the product of a distracted creator. After a few precarious years, and the decimation of those already living here, the 'gift' of land enabled the new arrivals to begin to thrive and tuck away old memories of trauma and dislocation.

10

Gliding Forward

WHEN BILLIONS OF television viewers sat transfixed by the opening ceremony of the 2000 Sydney Olympics the old ideas of Australia as a cultural desert, a boorish redoubt, an unworthy recipient of luck were shaken to their core. Many of us who had won the ticket lottery and secured seats in the vast, overfilled stadium that brisk September evening wondered, as scores of horses cantered into the arena, whether we were in for yet another clichéd recreation of bush myths. The Man from Snowy River may have been a household name when Banjo Paterson wrote his poem in 1890, but a century later when life on the land was remote for most, he was little more than a flickering celluloid image. Then, as if by magic, the horses disappeared and the arena was filled with hundreds of First Nations people from across the continent, dancing, singing and showing the world that they and their traditions had defied the cruelly assured prediction that they would die out.

The buzz around the stadium grew. We put on the flashing wristbands from the yellow vintage school cases we found under our seats and waved our arms to the music. This was a ceremony celebrating a nation that had a clear image of itself; it was able to treat her myths with irreverence and honour her uniqueness. For two hours, depictions of the land and sea, suburban pastimes (mowing the lawn) and stories of bushrangers, builders, dreamers and immigrants were re-enacted with spectacular choreography and soaring music. We saw ourselves and liked what we saw.[1] This was no predictable or cringe-making re-enactment. It was brilliant storytelling, ambitiously drawing on a deep well of art, dance, song and history to describe a diverse and inclusive society. Australia was no longer a simple, unworldly, racist outpost, but cosmopolitan, sophisticated and grounded.

Clive James personified a generation who felt the need to escape provincial Australia in the early 1960s, as ships loaded with European immigrants were arriving. He and his brilliant but frustrated colleagues left to find sophistication and fame in the Northern Hemisphere, repeating the age-old colonial pattern—lured 'home' to the beguiling centre of power from the insular provinces. By the time of the Olympic Games, he had realised the country was not the same as the place he left: it had grown up. 'Pundits who bewailed Australia's philistinism missed the point,' the prodigal son wrote in the opening ceremony program:

> Culture was not to be had by elevating our pretensions, but by broadening our range of spontaneous enjoyment. And that was exactly how it happened. Music had always been a natural form of Australian expression. Long before the First Fleet arrived, there had been music in the air . . . Before World War One Australian impressionists had already proved that their country was a natural open-air studio . . . in recent years our writers have begun to carry themselves with the confidence of our painters and musicians—which is to say, with the same confidence as our athletes who have always wanted to take on the world, and always known that there was nothing incongruous in such a wish.[2]

The Idea of Australia

The spectacle that evening, and the equally exuberant and revealing closing ceremony a fortnight later, were the culmination of a process of redefining the idea of Australia that had taken a long time to mature. Over the decades since Clive James left, writers, artists, historians, journalists, politicians and citizens had interrogated the legacy of the old inward-looking Fortress Australia. The reconciled, outward-looking, inclusive nationalism they dreamed of was bearing fruit, as revealed in the Olympics ceremonies. The world had changed and so had the nation. The Australia on display at the beginning of the new millennium was ambitious, open minded and joyful. It was a country that most of us recognised and lived in. Former prime minister Paul Keating was not alone in thinking, as he left the stadium after the final event, that it was good to get the 'jolt of surprise' of recognising ourselves as we really were: bold, imaginative, generous, inclusive.[3]

The rock band Midnight Oil embodied this new spirit. Over two decades, the five musicians had gone from playing Sydney pubs to becoming national icons, topping the charts at home and abroad, always with a distinctive, newly sophisticated Australian accent. They were a troupe of hard-rocking musos imbued with the politics of those who had grown up during the comfortable 1960s and '70s—curious, spirited and brave.

Just how brave became clear on the windy Sydney night at the end of the Games. The westerly arrives in Sydney each spring, its icy gusts carry a sobering message from the inland—the 'Aboriginal wind', the Scottish-born *Sydney Morning Herald* editor J.D. Pringle called it, a wind that Gavin Souter suggested 'tastes of blood'.[4] It proved a fitting environmental cue. Midnight Oil was best known for songs that passionately made the case for recognition of the rights of the First Australians. 'Beds Are Burning', the song they decided to play for the two billion people watching the closing ceremony, embodies this passion. Its chorus has been etched into millions of minds convinced that the time had come to be fair and pay back what was owing. Towards the

Gliding Forward

end of the ceremony, towering bald-headed lead singer Peter Garrett made a nervous dash through the subterranean passageways backstage towards the stage. He was preparing to prove yet again that sport and politics and music are a potent mix. In one of the biggest surprises of the Olympics, the five members of the band mounted the stage and dropped their overalls to reveal clothes emblazoned with 'SORRY'. The word was unmistakable from every angle. The gasp from the audience, followed by applause and cheers, said they had hit their mark with the precision of a gold medal–winning archer.

In many ways, this was a performance for an audience of one: Prime Minister John Howard, sitting in the VIP area, his discomfort obvious for the world to see. Humiliation is rarely a good political strategy, but many felt this was justified. For years the 25th prime minister of Australia had belligerently refused to apologise to First Nations peoples for the state-sanctioned removal of thousands of children from their families over generations. He said repeatedly that he, and the current generation, could not be held personally responsible for decisions of the past. When Midnight Oil sent a message of contrition to the world, they demonstrated that the culture had embraced the need to accept responsibility and recalibrate. But the old, unapologetic Australia still held the power.

What was on display at those theatrical ceremonies, just as it had been in the extraordinary dedication and achievements of the athletes who competed with distinction, was a new sense of a country that was willing to stretch the myths, interrogate the past, and dream of a different future in and of the world. Paul Keating was not alone in wondering, as he left on that final windy evening, whether he 'had just seen the beginning of something new or the concluding fireworks of the period of reform and ambition in Australia in the 1980s and 90s from which the Games had sprung'.[5]

HE WAS RIGHT to wonder. Just twelve years earlier, the celebration of the 200th anniversary of the arrival of the First Fleet had demonstrated just how hard it was to re-examine the past. In 1979, three years after an expansive national conversation had been triggered in the US by the anniversary of the American War of Independence, Liberal prime minister Malcom Fraser decided to emulate the model. He appointed a government-funded, independent Bicentennial Authority.[6]

The prime minister declared, with more than a touch of wishful thinking: 'Deep in any human community is a consciousness of its origins and its hopes and resolutions for the future.'[7] At the time, less than a quarter of the population could accurately name the year of the anniversary. If there was such ignorance of the basic facts, it was scarcely surprising that Malcolm Fraser's rather innocently optimistic embrace of the past would in time be seen as provocative. Discovering, examining and integrating the past is an important part of anyone's development, and so it is for nations. Nations, like people, are only as sick as their secrets force them to be. Owning and interrogating the past is particularly challenging for countries that depend on immigrants for population growth. The story is constantly being added to. Perspectives change, and demand new ways of telling the old tales. To reveal hidden dimensions that were once overlooked and prevent boring repetition. Or a retreat into mythic sentimentality. The move from intimate stories explored by family and friends as people find forgotten truths that enable them to belong and make sense of the place to the stages of public life takes time and depends on opportunity, but is the crucial first step.

Public understanding almost always demands and finds cultural expression first. Homosexuality was still criminal in 1975 when Reg Livermore filled the Bijou Theatre in Balmain for eight months with rapturous audiences celebrating *Betty Blockbuster's Follies* and helped make the law change inevitable. Watching a concert hall full of primary school children singing along with Yothu Yindi as they belted out 'Treaty', not long after Bob Hawke had tearfully conceded one would not be signed on his watch, left little doubt that this was an idea whose time would come when these children were adults. Being one of many moved to flooding tears as we watched a young Deborah Mailman embody Dreaming, Invasion, Genocide, Protection, Assimilation, Self-Determination, and Reconciliation in *7 Stages of Grieving*, and knowing that she and her co-creator Wesley Enoch were stars who would in time irrevocably change the way things were seen by countless others. Listening to Maroochy Barambah in *Black River* fill the Opera House with keening wails for those who had died in custody. Sitting on uncomfortable benches in a huge Adelaide festival venue as the personal and political complexity of Sri Lankan emigration unfurled in *Counting and Cracking*, which elegantly, joyously and searingly destroyed years of harsh political rhetoric about refugees.

These shifts happen organically through the cultural expression. Its mission is to break the silence, upend the official story. Conscientious and ambitious leaders accept the responsibility of finding ways to synthesise the past and learn from it. As French president Georges Pompidou observed when he opened the avant-garde art centre in the heart of Paris that bears his name, often it is through art that the most uncomfortable truths can be given voice and people can begin to reckon with the past and imagine the future.

Others with less imagination and a greater desire for managed control prefer to wage war with the uncomfortable revelations that may be brought to the surface. This is a universal phenomenon: those who have most benefited from the status quo are least likely to examine its origins. As British historian Eric Hobsbawm noted:

> The destruction of the past, or rather of the social mechanisms that links one's contemporary experience to that of earlier generations, is one of the most characteristic and eerie phenomena

of the late twentieth century. Most [now] grow up in a sort of permanent present lacking any organic relation to the public past of the times they live in. This makes historians, whose business it is to remember what others forget, more essential . . . than ever before . . . to explain why things turned out the way they did, and how they hang together.[8]

David Armstrong, the founding director of the Australian Bicentennial Authority, made it clear he was up for this challenge. He did not want a 'safe' bicentenary. He had a big vision for what could be achieved with a 'warts and all, serious, broadly educational and cultural' year. He had a long agenda. He wanted it to be a time to remember the past, reaffirm the best values. To rededicate the country 'to the immense task of solving problems that still confront us as a people—racism, philistinism, materialism, lack of national pride, widespread inequalities of opportunities, desecrated historical sites, polluted streams, ignorance of our collective past'.[9]

This vision quickly generated a heated political debate. The unexceptional notion of treating First Nations people, women and people of colour equally had festered since well before Federation. Even though their rights had since been acknowledged, and Australia had changed, it was clear that this was an itch that still needed to be scratched. Armstrong's vision inflamed conservative critics. British history, Christianity and core values were being ignored, they shouted. Their noise in the media drowned out nuance or reflection. It intimidated politicians who found administrative shortcomings to justify a change of focus. In 1984, the new Labor government requested the ambitious plans be modified.

In the same year, Australians finally stopped singing 'God Save the Queen' as the national anthem. Detaching from Britain was still a work in progress. Australians struggled to learn the arcane words of the new anthem, 'Advance Australia Fair'. It had narrowly beaten

Gliding Forward

'Waltzing Matilda' in a plebiscite to choose a new song. Two years later, in 1986, legislation quietly passed in both British and Australian parliaments to remove the British Privy Council as Australia's final court of appeal, after 1988. Symbolic and legal independence had finally arrived though it had taken four score years and seven.

Like many transformative reforms throughout Australia's history, this hugely significant step was made administratively, after two political glides backwards, without fanfare. Similarly, in the middle of 2021, John Howard's political heir Scott Morrison announced that the once-unimaginable reparations to survivors of the stolen generations would be given. The heat and noise of John Howard's refusal to apologise or consider compensation had 23 years later evaporated like a summer mist. The news was barely reported.

On 26 January 1988, more than a million people flocked to the banks of Sydney Harbour to watch a flotilla of oddly assorted skiffs, naval and merchant ships, motor boats and yachts join eight tall ships that had recreated the journey. It was noisy but oddly lacklustre. There they heard long speeches from the Royal Family and fireworks as darkness fell. But the most enduring image of the day was that of the tens of thousands of Australians who opted instead to join the large and peaceful March for Freedom, Justice and Hope led by Aboriginal activists through the streets of Sydney. The protests signalled that the 'immense task of solving problems' remained undone. This was the first sustained battle in what came to be called the culture wars. It focused, as tussles over values always do, on the weakest point, the festering legacy of what Jeremy Bentham had predicted would be an incurable flaw. The opponents of change may have publicly prevailed, but the ground on which they stood was shifting, as was the idea of Australia itself.

This was a noteworthy moment. The strident debates in the bicentennial year signalled that the discussion about national identity had reached beyond university common rooms, cultural salons and little magazines. Now everyone noticed history-laden films and pub bands belting out songs about coming from a land Down Under where men plunder and women glow. National pride had soared in the previous couple of decades. As the novelist Robert Drewe wrote in *The Australian* in 1973, 'Unless you're a 67-year-old mining magnate who's a member of the League of Empire Loyalists, you're aware of a certain rare feeling of national self-respect these days . . . Go into any pub and criticise Australia. If you're not a good fighter you'll have to run like buggery.'[10] National identity with a critical edge had begun a sentimental journey towards a marketing tool. *Aussie, Aussie, Aussie! oi! oi! oi!* Pride comes before a fall.

———

THE TWO CENTURIES before the bicentenary had been punctuated by fluctuating periods of national pride, bravado, embarrassment and cringe. The core defining idea that Australia was a land free for the taking by the first European Empire that raised its ensign provided a troublingly provisional foundation. The acquisition was not accompanied by any signed deed of transfer; for those who like to go back to first principles it felt more like squatting than owning. After the ancient traditional society was assaulted, the prison settlement over time gave way to a place of opportunity where land, gold and other resources were virtually free for the taking with a levy for the state. Then a spirited quest for independence and self-determination, with idealised notions of equality, gave way to a self-satisfied democracy for a racially selected few. Before an outward-looking and engaged society transformed by the need to 'populate or perish' developed in its wake. By the time the globalised ethos of neoliberalism swept all before it, the prospect of a positive notion of national identity had been irreparably tarnished. The shames of the past and embarrassment about an easily discredited, exclusionary, triumphalist nationalism made an

Gliding Forward

expansive conversation awkward. National identity could be inclusive and multi-layered, but that required attention, not slogans. So at each point, the frame changed and a different idea worked its way to the top of the pile defining national identity. Like waves breaking on the shore, they were similar but different, building and crashing as events and circumstances changed, leaving most of the population, happily enough, in a permanent present where the past never needed to be synthesised.

The reassessment of how an outward-looking society might integrate its past, present and future could be traced back to debates that had developed momentum half a century earlier. A month after the Japanese bombed Darwin in February 1942, when war was an urgent and existential threat for the seven million people who called Australia home, the literary critic Vance Palmer wrote:

> The next few months may decide not only whether we are to survive as a nation, but whether we deserve to survive. As yet none of our achievements prove it, at any rate in the sight of the outer world.
>
> We have no monuments to speak of, no dreams in stone, no Guernicas, no sacred places. We could vanish and leave singularly few signs that, for some generations, there had lived a people who had made a homeland of this Australian Earth.[11]

Two months later Japanese submarines found their way into Sydney Harbour, where the USS *Chicago* rebuffed the attack.

The profound pessimism of Vance Palmer's assessment was widely shared. The opportunity the war provided to reimagine the operating idea of Australia was grasped, just as it had been in countries around the world. That conflagration ushered in an era defined by a widely shared agreement about the primacy of human rights, self-determination for nations, individual rights to freedom of speech and worship, and freedom from fear and want. Within a few decades the Opera House at Bennelong Point, a building site when my boat from New Zealand arrived in Sydney Harbour, grew into a monument beyond Vance Palmer's imagining. Recognised on the UNESCO World Heritage Register as 'one of the indisputable masterpieces of human creativity, not only in the twentieth century but in the history of humankind'.[12] It is one of four Australian cultural sites on the register, including the Budj Bim cultural landscape in the western district of Victoria near where I grew up, twelve grand natural sites and four others where long-term human habitation has enhanced the physical environment. Again the cultural recognition of the ancient heritage of First Nations people was ahead of the political. Australia remains a global outlier, the only remnant of the British Empire without formal recognition of its first peoples. The Second World War profoundly disturbed the equilibrium of the 40-year-old Commonwealth of Australia. The external shocks of British abandonment, Japanese incursions and the relocation of the US Pacific command to Brisbane marked the beginning of a process of reassessment that continues to play out. Deep in the DNA of the nation is a fear of abandonment that recurs in unlikely ways and is generally addressed by almost sycophantic adulation of the great power de jure. Before the war Australia had been more British than Britain. Even two years after it ended, less than 2 per cent of Sydney's population had been born outside Australia or Britain.[13]

The provincial fortress mentality that had prevailed since Federation eventually gave way as millions of people arrived to provide the labour needed for a rapidly industrialising economy. This eventually upended the founding idea of racial selection and homogeneity. The campaign to revoke the White Australia policy took a long time to gain momentum. It grew during the 1960s in response to both domestic and international pressure. Many in Canberra considered it a shameful policy, but few were ready to stir the hornet's nest of carefully nurtured foundational values. There were intense debates in the political parties; the old ethos would not just die. Malcolm Fraser, who was then minister for the army, described the beginning of its legislative dismantling in 1966 when variable waiting times for naturalisation were abolished: 'I can remember the speech in parliament. It was very carefully worded and [you] almost had to get the speech again and say *What is this meaning?* Nobody in those days wanted to stir up a backlash and say *No this is wrong*. We didn't want people going around saying the White Australia policy should remain.'[14]

Gough Whitlam revoked the policy as one of his first acts as prime minister. He later recalled:

> Right up to our election in 1972 there had to be, from any country outside Europe, an application for entry referred to Canberra and a confidential report on their appearance . . . But in practice they still made it very difficult for people who were not white skinned to come to Australia . . . The photograph wasn't enough, because by a strong light or powdering you could reduce the colour of your exposed parts. It was said that the test was in extreme cases, 'Drop your daks' because you can't change the colour of your bum. We changed all that.[15]

The journey to transform a racially determined nation into a colour-blind, open and inclusive place had begun.

THE SURGE OF migration immediately after the war, now celebrated for changing the nation, was at the time colour coded and subject to bitter political debates. Many 'New Australians' struggled, focusing as best they could on better lives for their children. Preference had been given to fair-haired refugees from the Baltic states and northern Europe, and assisted immigrants from Britain and Ireland. Exclusion was still at play, as the treatment of Jewish survivors of the war tellingly reveals.

There had been at least eight Jews on the First Fleet. The Grand Synagogue in Sydney opened in 1878. General John Monash and judge Isaac Isaacs had demonstrated outstanding national leadership. But the big lesson from the genocidal Second World War had still not been learned. Refugees and displaced people were asked if they were Jewish, and if they answered in the affirmative limits applied. An angry campaign waged by the Returned Sailors', Soldiers' and Airmen's Imperial League of Australia, along with much of the press and many politicians, ensured that most Australians were opposed to providing a refuge for displaced Jews. They feared they would not integrate. As a result, only 500 of the 190,000 displaced persons brought to Australia immediately after the war were Jewish. But over the following decade 17,600 Jewish survivors found their way here, often using informal networks.[16]

Good neighbourhood councils were formed, and campaigns were devised to encourage locals to exercise tolerance and advise new arrivals how to forget their past and integrate.[17] The historian Raymond Evans was one of thousands of children who arrived as assisted immigrants. A Welsh uncle gave him a tiny red-covered book of wafer-thin rice paper pages, *The Australia Book for English Boys and Girls (and Their Parents)*. His father read it to him to reassure him that Australia was:

> exactly the same as England ... with a stirring [history] of explorations by stout hearted Britishers ... resolute and determined men from the British Isles ... although Australia had only been discovered by white people a comparatively short time ago ... it was inhabited by a race of black aborigines, but these have generally died out. There are a few thousand left in the uninhabited areas. Now they are almost civilised and there is no need to be frightened if you should see one, which is most unlikely.[18]

Australia persisted with a policy of assimilation long after it had been internationally discredited as inhumane. Expecting people to forget where they came from, to jettison their history and culture and forge a new identity, was cruel. It was another form of terra nullius of the mind—a continent-wide experiment, tested first with disastrous consequences on generations of First Nations peoples and applied, albeit in a less draconian form, to new arrivals. Language came first. First Nations peoples had been jailed for speaking their languages. Some endured, but scores of languages became extinct. The language test for new arrivals to Australia had been deliberately set 'to serve as an absolute bar'.[19] For many years, new arrivals were mocked and sneered at if they spoke the languages of their homelands, but were given few opportunities to learn English.

Assimilation operated alongside segregation. Eliminating difference. Pretending everyone shared the same heritage. That belonging was a zero-sum game and only one identity could be chosen. This was a perverse yet brutally pragmatic act of 'national imagining'. Labor minister Arthur Calwell oversaw the early post-war migration program, despite his commitment to the White Australia policy and instinctive racism. He did not want Australia to become a 'mongrel nation'. So the idea of the Australian Way of Life—relaxed, egalitarian, tolerant—was conjured. It was one that new arrivals were expected to fit into rather than add to.[20]

Anna Haebich grew up in Wollongong, the industrial city an hour or so south of Sydney, in a community of post-war European immigrants who had been 'spun out to the other side of the world to end up as labourers in the Port Kembla steelworks'. Years later she wrote that as a child she had 'no inkling of how our little household was being shaped by an official policy that gave minimal government assistance to European migrants and urged community organisations and churches to take up the slack'.[21] Her parents, whose forebears had arrived in Australia generations earlier, helped people adjust from hostels to houses, to find and keep work, to source familiar food, to learn English and withstand racist taunts. On the other side of the country, her future husband's family was learning how to adjust to the assimilationist policy that meant Noongar people were expected to 'blend in' despite entrenched racism and punitive government actions. Among her many important books, two stand out: *Spinning the Dream*, the story of migration and assimilation, and *Broken Circles*, which documents the long history of removing children from their families and its consequences.

In a small country, Anna Haebich and I were probably destined to meet. It still came as a surprise to find someone who had such a similar background in an adjacent office at Griffith University in 2004. We were both daughters of Queensland Lutheran ministers, unusual men who were prepared to challenge—at considerable personal and professional cost—the reactionary conservatism of their church as they learned more. We both found a non-traditional path into academic careers; Anna grew up in Wollongong, the subject of my first book. When we met, Anna had moved back to Brisbane from her home in Fremantle to care for her father, Bert, as he struggled with dementia. Over the years, as she sat with him in the family home in Ipswich, she worked her way through the boxes of books and papers he had accumulated over a lifetime of ministry, teaching and community activism.

One day she called and said I had to come to her office; she had found something amazing. There in Bert's papers was a series of essays my father, Noel, had written as a high school student in 1949. One was about the Housewives' Associations that had once flourished in Australia, an embodiment of maternal feminism devoted to self-sufficiency, growing fruit and vegetables, keeping chooks in backyards as post-war rationing continued. Another was a contemporaneous report about the Chinese Revolution. The essays revealed a critical and thoughtful mind, not a captive of cant or propaganda; the comments in the margins revealed Bert as a teacher who cared passionately about his students and was curious about the world.

Gliding Forward

Of his father's thirteen children, Noel was the youngest son. When the teacher at his isolated Darling Downs primary school suggested he sit for the state exam, which would make it possible to continue to high school, his parents were thrilled. Only a handful of children in country Queensland primary schools were invited to sit for the test, and even fewer passed. No one in the family had made that journey—all the boys went on the land, although one elder brother, child number twelve, escaped to join the police force.

Noel passed the entrance test with what seemed astonishing results, and was enrolled in a brand-new Lutheran school taking shape in an old mansion in Toowoomba. He and his parents arrived a week earlier than school was able to start, but wartime petrol rationing made it impossible to make the 150-kilometre journey twice—so the teary teenager was left to bunk in with the staff until school began. Before long he was swotting Latin, Ancient Greek, Classics, History, Science, Maths and German, a language he hated for reasons that seem obvious in retrospect as his brothers and cousins were at war with Germany. It was a long way from the farm, from the 11-kilometre horse ride to and from primary school each day, from the schoolyard harassment of children with German surnames, and from his former classmates who were learning woodwork and sheet-metal work. Bert Haebich was his inspirational teacher.

They met again many years later, when Noel was sent by the Lutheran Church to review the ministry Bert was running for the recently arrived immigrants whose labour powered the steelworks and other heavy industry in Wollongong. Education was their secret handshake to a very different life, one that would have been unimaginable a century earlier when Noel's grandfather first set foot in Queensland.

In 1862, my illiterate forebears arrived at the pilot station on Moreton Island, Mulgumpin. Vast sandhills shape the island that lies adjacent to

Minjerribah and forms a cap on Moreton Bay. Journeys across oceans almost always took lives, but their trip on the *Caesar Godeffroy* was better than most; just six infants and one adult had died at sea. The ten-member Schulz (as it was spelled on the arrival documents) clan and the other 285 German passengers had been at sea, with no stops, for 94 days. They were not alone: more than 17,000 German-speaking people settled in the colony over the next couple of decades, taking advantage of cheap fares and land. After they passed health checks, they made the slow journey up the Brisbane River and eventually over land. They crossed the Great Dividing Range to the 30-acre 'selection' that had been allocated to them by the agent who had arranged their passage. My great-grandfather signed the ownership papers with an X.

At the time there were 30,000 white settlers living in what had become the separate Colony of Queensland just three years earlier. In the preceding years 40 squatters had filled the region with millions of sheep and 140,000 cattle. The murderous frontier wars had already killed half of the Queensland Aboriginal people who would die before Federation. Before long the owner of the *Caesar Godeffroy* grew rich on the trade of people across hemispheres. He sent scientific emissary Amalie Dietrich to collect 'plants, corals, shells, insects, spiders, fish, reptiles, birds, mammals', photos of human remains, Aboriginal skeletons and skulls for his museum in Hamburg.[22] In the volatile, brutal, land-hungry colony, a caste-like hierarchy was taking shape. My lot were in the peasant farmer category.

Like the generations of migrants who followed, but unlike the generations of Aboriginal people who have remarkably managed to keep their stories, no one talked about the great relocation much— where they came from, why they left, what they found. Each settlement in the colony had at least one newspaper, but my forebears were not big correspondents. Their stories were buried in the earth they cleared. When Noel started to trace his family history using internet-enabled genealogy tools, he found shipping records, land title records and the

Gliding Forward

other documentation of the modern state. But the stories that fleshed out their lived experience were elusive. There were more questions than answers buried in the official records.

Assimilation is a tool of forgetting. Even today it is not unusual to hear people whose families arrived in Australia in the long tail of post-war immigration bemoan how little they know about their origins. How the shame of speaking their parents' language means they never learned it, making it hard to connect with their ageing parents as they revert to their mother tongue. Assimilation made people apologetic about their backgrounds. Encouraged them to change their names so job applications could slip through and they could quietly just get on with a new life. Scratch the surface and stories of escape from war-torn Europe tumble from the mouths of people whose names suggest they arrived from the Home Counties. Those who didn't change their names too often felt the blunt hand of abuse, name calling and exclusion. I recall being taken aback when Andrew Jakubowicz, a fierce champion of multiculturalism who had hidden behind an abbreviation of his name for many years, asked whether my family had arrived before or after the war. Longstanding settlers had generally been anglicised into an assimilated norm.

During the 1950s, as a tool for dealing with the changing human fabric of the nation, annual constitutional citizenship conferences were held. The aim was to broaden the definition of what it meant to be Australian. When a Greek-Australian group asked if they could attend, they were told in no uncertain terms that their input was not needed. But if they would like to put on a dancing display for the evening's entertainment that would be welcome. The insularity of 1950s Australia is almost unimaginable now. The 1956 Melbourne Olympics started to break the mould. The Games could demonstrate that Australia was not a racially selective nation—but when it came to the practical realities, the truth was clear. Feeding, housing and entertaining the visitors was outsourced to citizens in suburban houses. Melburnians were taught how to cook meals that might appeal to different palates—but with less than a year to go, it was clear to the organisers that this would not be sufficient. Special political dispensation, and funding, was sought to fly to Europe and recruit chefs who would be able to prepare French, German, Italian and other continental cuisines to the standard that would be appropriate for the international visitors. Just a month before the Games, the organisers realised they had forgotten the dietary requirements of the rest of the world, and Indian, Chinese and Japanese chefs were seconded from P&O ocean liners to fix 'more exotic' meals.[23] Many of the chefs decided to stay. Melbourne's prized reputation as a centre of foodie culture and culinary expertise was born as its population swelled with immigrants, and locals found they enjoyed something more than meat and three veg boiled to tastelessness.

The celebration of cultural diversity that followed the acknowledgement of multiculturalism in the 1970s changed this. Just as the legacy of the convict forebears ceased to be personally shameful at some point, so the richness of history and place informed by different experiences, cultures and expectations was embraced. The prevailing viewpoint shifted without apology, although racialism still lurks in the groundwater and bubbles up whenever a crack emerges.

VANCE PALMER AND his wife Nettie were members of an active group of writers and intellectuals who advocated a distinctive and internationally relevant Australian story. They were both just fifteen years old when Federation turned the colonies into a commonwealth, so they were members of the generation whose lives were intimately entwined with that of the new nation. They celebrated a progressive past but were well aware of its darker underbelly. They wrote, published and promoted novels and treatises, exhuming the past to try to make sense of the present and shape a future.

Gliding Forward

They were not oblivious to the depth of the cultural history of those who were on what Vance called 'this Australian Earth' when the British arrived to set up a prison. But the act of appropriation and murder was not embedded at the core of their national view. Instead, they looked back to the class struggles, camaraderie, and environmental and economic catastrophes of the 1890s to find an idealised egalitarian nation with contemporary relevance. In his landmark 1954 book *The Legend of the Nineties*, Vance Palmer traced the way these events morphed into myths to provide a crucial platform for the cultural development of the nation.

Reading and writing were key in a highly literate society. Poems and short stories distilled meaning into pithy evocations that lasted longer than the worlds they described. Novels explored the often-traumatic experiences of convicts, bushrangers, drovers, First Nations peoples, women, city dwellers and Native Police. Politics and art were indivisible. The stories that made an impact taunted the censorious taste makers. They became bolder, braver and more at odds with the benign official narrative as the twentieth century progressed.[24]

Thanks in large measure to the Red Page of *The Bulletin*, the 'real nature' of the country in the years before Federation was thick with rural adventurism, in what was even then an urban society. As the nation became more sophisticated and integrated with the world, this provided a bedrock of national identity. By the 1970s many could still name the town where their family had first put down roots. This was not confined to those who had arrived in the nineteenth century. The great twentieth-century migrations spread across the land, leaving a patchwork of Greek milk bars, Chinese cafes and Italian greengrocers as physical reminders of a changing society.

On the afternoon of 11 November 1975, I was in the luggage department of Myer Indooroopilly, in Brisbane's jacaranda-dotted inner-west. I was there to choose a suitcase for a journey starting the next day, to interview a new generation of bush poets scattered all over the country. I selected a shell-like brown Samsonite and went to the counter to pay. Even in those days it was hard to find someone to pay in a department store. This time it was for good reason. Staff and the handful of other customers in the department store that hot afternoon had gathered around a small transistor radio on a counter near a window. They were listening to a crackly broadcast of momentous events in the national capital. I joined them and realised why everything had stopped. We listened in stunned silence. A few hours after his government had been dismissed, Gough Whitlam was speaking with passion and astonishment from the steps of Parliament House, declaring in sonorous tones, 'Well may we say "God save the Queen", because nothing will save the governor-general.'

The next day I travelled to Eagle Farm, to the old metal shed that stood as a reminder of Brisbane's wartime history and passed for the city's airport terminal, to fly to Cairns. It was the first leg of a trip that would unexpectedly shadow politicians on the divisive election campaign that began after the parliament was dissolved: Cairns, Innisfail, Townsville, Charters Towers, Rockhampton, Griffith, Cooma, Gosford, Colac, Shepparton and Frankston, and finally Melbourne on the day of a huge election rally in its City Square.

I was travelling with the support of a small grant from the newly well-endowed Australia Council. The English department at the University of Queensland, where I was studying, was at the time led by a group of postcolonial scholars who were eagerly exhuming Australia's literary past. Filling the enormous gaps in Australian studies preoccupied a group of academics who were increasingly confident that all knowledge was not from over the seas. It was an ethos that touched every discipline. I was one of the unworldly group of young people who had unexpectedly been given the key to our future lives when university fees were abolished. The nationalism of our lecturers shaped a new curriculum. We studied Henry Handel Richardson, Christina Stead, Marcus Clarke, Xavier Herbert and Patrick White alongside Charles Dickens, Henry James and James Joyce. It was an emerging, highly contestable canon. We were encouraged with a striking absence of theory to compare and contrast local novels with other great English-language works.

In tutorials we wondered whether the tradition of bush poetry that had played such an important role in shaping national imaginings was still alive—or relevant—in the overwhelmingly suburban Australia of the 1970s. Three of us had the somewhat daft idea to write to country newspapers around the nation, inviting local poets to send us their work. We were inundated. Much was doggerel, but some captured the experience of the writers' lives with passion and insight. Just as it had been for the farmers and townsfolk in Gilgandra and the Western District of Victoria when I was a child, life in the bush was still hard. The pain for those who had been forced off farms and into suburbs and towns left a void some sought to fill with verse. The tradition had continued to flourish. Australia had profoundly changed since *The Bulletin* ceased to publish new creative work on its Red Page. It had even changed since Donald Horne directed a typesetter to chip out the lead font spelling out 'Australia for the White Man', a logo that had graced the magazine's masthead since the American Navy first visited Sydney Harbour in 1908.

The 1975 election campaign, and my journey through what is now called regional Australia, highlighted the tensions in a nation that had been transformed. Agriculture employed a smaller percentage of the population than ever, since Britain had switched its focus to Europe. Manufacturing jobs had disappeared as tariffs were reduced. The policy that prohibited non-white migration eroded under the weight of international opprobrium and local shame. The decision to join and then leave the American war in Vietnam had been bitterly contested. Women, who at last had control over their fertility, were asserting their rights. Universities no longer charged students fees. First Nations people were able to leave missions and reserves without asking, to vote, and beginning to have their land rights recognised. Three score years and fourteen after she became a nation, Australia had a national library, an independent national archive and a national gallery under construction. The arts were flourishing. The honours bestowed on the most distinguished citizens were no longer dispensed from Buckingham Palace. The cultural change that had been a long time coming happened in a flash. For some the shock was profound.

But hundreds of people were still sitting at their kitchen tables writing poems on lined notepads, trying to capture a fast-disappearing rural life, to put into words the pain of watching old towns shrink as one family after another left. In their verse they tried to recapture a utopian ideal of self-sufficiency in the bush. As I sat with them in their poor houses on farms, in towns and suburbs, I realised just how vast the gap was between my idea of Australia and theirs. Even though I had spent most of my nineteen years living in the bush, I knew that the myth was overblown. The remoteness, hardship and bluster were real, as was the love of the land despite its punishing routines. The people I met on that journey were, like the folk who made my family welcome in Gilgandra, courteous and curious, eager to share the stories that had shaped them and their communities. They loved its beauty and knew the places where the ghosts of bad things still roamed.

It was easy to understand why their kids wanted to escape to the city. That was where the jobs were, where the past could be put aside and lives reinvented. The old German saying *Stadtluft macht frei nach Jahr und Tag* resonated as much in post-war Australia as it had a century earlier in rural Germany. *City air makes you free after a year and a day.* Those who remained in the bush as the exodus peaked in the mid-1970s spoke with a defensive sense of missing out, of living out of step and out of time with the world they saw on television. It was clear that many of them were ill-prepared for the change that

Gliding Forward

those attending Gough Whitlam's big rallies so passionately wanted to see continue. It was also clear that, if they felt their unease was not recognised, their sense of abandonment could turn to anger.

———

JUST OVER THIRTY years later, in April 2008, I found myself talking to a very different group of people at a Canberra summit that was meant to imagine the country's future, and to provide a space for new ideas to percolate and develop. It was the ill-fated Australia 2020 Summit at Parliament House, and a group of brilliant young people who worked in the arts were discussing their idea of Australia. How it shaped and influenced their work. Over their lifetimes nationalism had become a dirty word, co-opted as little more than a marketing tool, a redoubt for those who clung to myths that seemed more than usually arcane in globalisation's market-driven conformity.

It was one of those perfect Canberra days, with an endless blue sky, the sun bouncing off the autumn leaves and a crisp breeze from the mountains promising a snowy season keeping the temperature down. This new generation of creative minds was every bit as ambitious as Vance and Nettie Palmer had been. Each of them had begun to make an impact, build recognition and plot a career. They were bursting with ambition, conjuring ideas that they would bring to life through their art. Just like the Palmers, they wanted to make a mark, and they wanted it to be distinctively Australian, but of the world. It was an exciting and exhilarating conversation.

All of a sudden, the discussion touched a nerve. 'Sometimes I find it hard to think of myself as Australian,' one said. 'It makes me sad, but I sometimes don't even know what it means.' This was just three years after the 2005 riots on Cronulla Beach revealed that the deep wellspring of racism had not evaporated; indeed, it was still nurtured by some with megaphones who should have known better.

The Idea of Australia

The others quickly chipped in. They saw their futures elsewhere, in bigger, more exciting places, places where they could make their names on a world stage unencumbered by the curiosities of a land of platypuses and kangaroos. I was struck that their comments echoed what Patrick White had said when he won the Nobel Prize for Literature in 1973, not long after the Opera House had opened. 'I had to experience the outside world, and would have felt deprived if I didn't have that behind me,' he said. 'But it's from the Australian earth, Australian air, that I derive my literary, my spiritual sustenance. Even at its most hateful, Australia is necessary to me.'[25]

In the intervening years, Fortress Australia had been breached and her children had become detached global citizens. 'I might come back, but apart from my family there's nothing to hold me,' said another summit delegate. 'Australia is stuck in an unexamined past, constantly retelling the same threadbare stories . . . I don't want to have to constantly re-enact Ned Kelly, Donald Bradman or Gallipoli or watch re-creations of baby boomer pop culture from the seventies and eighties. How many times do we need to see *Puberty Blues* or *Picnic at Hanging Rock*? This isn't the Australia I know and live in.'

I was surprised. They were surprised that I was surprised. Generations matter. I tried to imagine what being Australian meant from their point of view. I was only fifteen years older than them, yet their experiences and perspectives were quite different to mine. They had been children in the 1980s, when my generation thought that Australia grew up. The backdrop of their lives was filled with cultural shifts that had taken decades to materialise—severing almost all ties with Britain except the monarchy, jettisoning the notion of terra nullius, floating the dollar, embracing Asia, exploring unexamined history and conjuring a creative nation. The witty, expansive, self-reflective opening of the Sydney Olympics—with its synthesis of ancient and new, celebration of suburban life, diversity and mythic tales—marked their coming of age.

Gliding Forward

And then it stopped. Maybe Paul Keating was right that the 'best Games ever' marked the beginning of an end rather than the mid point. Since 2000, nitpicking fights over historical fact had made inquiry dangerous. Old myths of mateship had been appropriated and stripped of their collectivism. First Nations recognition was still a dream, even as Cathy Freeman showed that big dreams could come true, and the gold medal–winning runner from Mackay in Queensland became the new face of the nation.

When I tried to describe how things had changed, how Australia really was a much more open, self-aware and reflective society than it had been before they were born, I was met with polite silence. I realised there were consequences for failing to keep the perpetual quest of interrogating the defining ideas of Australia going. This was especially acute at a time of globalisation when unprecedented numbers of people were arriving every year. We had grown complacent, happy enough to assume that our children and the millions of new arrivals from every continent would absorb this knowledge and these stories by osmosis, and share their stories, dreams and expectations to deepen ours. We thought that vague talk of values would be enough.

Over those twenty years before the 2008 summit, the country had been transformed at least as much as it had been in the 1960s and early '70s. Some was the result of deliberate economic and social strategies introduced by governments in response to momentous movements that shook the world. Some was the result of persistent scholarship and advocacy that forced redefinitions of the past and apologies to those who had been treated inhumanely. The narrow economic priorities of global neoliberalism had sapped marrow from the national bones and made a progressive transfusion of new ideas almost impossible. But big change had happened quietly, in the way people live their lives. The gap between cultural expectations and public life had never been greater.

11

The Incurable Flaw

GALARRWUY YUNUPINGU IS one of the most consequential men of his generation. He was just 30 when he was appointed Australian of the Year in 1978, jointly with Alan Bond, a young entrepreneur. It was a pairing that embodied the unresolved polarity at the heart of the Australian story, between ancient custodians and ne'er-do-well arrivistes with big dreams. Within a few years of immigrating from England as a child, Alan Bond, aged fourteen, was charged with theft; four years later he was arrested again for planning a burglary. Within a few decades he was an extraordinarily rich man. Like many immigrants, he was a dreamer who put his faith in the power of reinvention. Alan Bond's dreams were bigger than most, and his flamboyant bravado captivated those he did not betray—until his career imploded under a mountain of debt. His name was not removed from its plinth on the walk of Australians of the Year beside Lake Burley Griffin even when the bankrupt billionaire was jailed for fraud. Three and a half years later he was released on a constitutional technicality.

Constitutional technicalities did not work so well for the man with whom he shared the Australia Day honour. Galarrwuy Yunupingu is a

The Incurable Flaw

traditional man born to leadership, a former chairman of the Northern Land Council and leader of the Gumatj clan of the Yolngu Nation in the north-eastern corner of the Northern Territory, on the edge of the Gulf of Carpentaria. His father, Mungurrawuy, taught him to be both grounded in tradition and to navigate the modern world, and as he was dying gave his chosen son his clapsticks and his authority.

Fifteen years earlier, in August 1963, after the Menzies Coalition government approved plans for a bauxite mine in north-east Arnhem Land, twelve Yolngu leaders crafted and signed the Yirrkala bark petitions. The carefully typed petitions, each mounted on a traditionally painted bark, 'humbly pray[ed]' for respect, the recognition of sacred sites, and the recognition that the Yirrkala peoples had been living on the land since time immemorial. Bauxite had, by the late 1950s, become the new gold, the essential element to a new, fast-paced, globalised age of multinational business. When refined with vast amounts of electricity, bauxite produced the aluminium that was needed for the high-rise buildings, cars, planes and consumer electronics that were proliferating all over the world in the new industrial age.

Geologists had known for decades there were vast supplies of rich ore on the fringes of the far north, but in the years after the Second World War its value increased. Australian governments overseeing both coasts of the Gulf of Carpentaria wasted no time signing agreements with ambitious international mining companies. Legislation was changed so there was no consultation or compensation for the traditional owners, or for the missions on which they lived. The Yirrkala petitions sought them and a parliamentary inquiry.

The same story played out more brutally 600 kilometres across the gulf, where the Dutch had made landfall in 1606 to the north of Duyfken Point. Rights to a vast bauxite deposit near Mapoon had been granted to Comalco by the Queensland government, also without consultation or compensation. This was just three months after four copies of the Yirrkala bark petitions were lodged in Canberra. In November

The Idea of Australia

1963, Queensland police arrived at the impoverished Presbyterian mission at Mapoon with orders to remove the remaining families. They were loaded onto boats, their houses destroyed. Some were sent 80 kilometres south to Weipa; others who had spent their lives in the searing heat and humidity of the tropical north were despatched to Stanthorpe, the coldest place in the state, nearly 3000 kilometres away.[1] Fifteen years later, in what the First Nations advocate Noel Pearson has described as 'an act of gross political violence', the Queensland government undertook another 'colonial takeover' with the support of the Privy Council. Brisbane and Canberra combined to strip the Uniting Church of its effective and valued administration of the Aurukun Mission. By giving rights to the bauxite to a French company, Australian governments threw the Wik people into 'their descent into hell'.[2]

Mining reshaped everything, but it also triggered protests that would eventually change the law and mark the beginning of a new start for the nation. The Yirrkala bark petitions signalled the public beginning of the modern land rights movement. The typewritten plea by the First Nations elders now hangs in Parliament House. In 2013, Labor prime minister Kevin Rudd described it as the Aboriginal Magna Carta.[3]

ALAN BOND TURNED his fame and ambition into personal wealth and power. Galarrwuy Yunupingu's dreams, marked for decades by petitions, small victories and major setbacks in winning rights, were about recognition for First Nations peoples. Often his negotiations were with men and women who, in his assessment, recognised the moral flaw at the heart of the nation but felt paralysed, unable to do anything about it.

When Alan Bond's yacht *Australia II* won the America's Cup in 1983, the recently elected Labor prime minister, Bob Hawke, in a flush of excitement, declared a national holiday. Still wearing his heart on

The Incurable Flaw

his sleeve on his last day in office eight years later, he wept as he hung the Barunga Statement in Parliament House alongside the Yirrkala bark petition. Like the Yirrkala petition, the Barunga Statement is a typed plea for recognition, rights and a treaty, wrapped in a beautifully detailed bark painting rich with symbolism. Bob Hawke signed it at the end of the bicentennial year and promised a treaty by 1990. It was a promise he did not keep, like his 1983 promise of national land rights legislation. Mining companies in Western Australia, which feared they had much to lose, vigorously campaigned against it. The state premier, Brian Burke, who was also president of the Labor Party, heeded their call. A treaty became politically impossible. Brian Burke was later jailed for corruption, but not for his moral cowardice.

When Hawke, as outgoing prime minister, unveiled the beautiful Barunga bark and its embedded statement in Parliament House, it became yet another symbol of the failure to resolve the original sin at the core of the nation. Still, Galarrwuy Yunupingu, the heartbroken Yolngu leader, remained generous to Hawke. 'I am sure that his tears are for his own failure,' he said. 'We have no treaty; his promise was hollow, and he has not delivered—but they are genuine tears from a genuine man who tried leadership and was caught out by politics.'[4]

The pattern had repeated for centuries. Galarrwuy Yunupingu kept trying, just as Aboriginal leaders had always done, ever since Bennelong first negotiated with Governor Phillip. The Palawa, exiled to Flinders Island, petitioned Queen Victoria to remove the abusive supervisor; Kulin leaders put the case for their land to Queen Victoria through the governor of the colony that carried her name;[5] eleven years after the Federation parliament denied Aboriginal people the vote, David Unaipon, the polymath genius who fronts the 50-dollar note, called for Ngarrindjeri autonomy over the Point McLeay mission; and 25 years on, William Cooper petitioned King George V pleading for legal status and land rights—a petition the Australian parliament refused to forward, on another constitutional technicality. Then, another decade later, Pastor Doug Nicholls beseeched Labor prime minister Ben Chifley for Aboriginal representation in federal parliament.[6] Over and over the case for a respectful relationship had been made, only to fall on deaf ears or be beaten by the politics of fear or denial.

The toll on those First Nations leaders who accepted the responsibility of leadership was immense; many found it overwhelming. The responsibility and repeated failure grew heavier with the years. 'I am seeing now that too much of the past is for nothing,' Galarrwuy Yunupingu wrote in 2008:

> I have walked the corridors of power; I have negotiated and cajoled and praised and begged prime ministers and ministers, travelled the world and been feted; I have opened the doors to men of power and prestige; I have had a place at the table of the best and the brightest in the Australian nation—and at times success has seemed so close, yet it always slips away. And behind me, in the world of my father, the Yolngu world is always under threat, being swallowed up by whitefellas.[7]

At the time he wrote this heartbroken plea, the most senior *delak* (representative forum) of East Arnhem land had once again 'humbly petition[ed]' the prime minister 'as the chief adviser to Her Majesty Queen Elizabeth the Second' for constitutional recognition. He followed the line of authority to London, the seat of the original flaw, again to no avail. Those with political power at home were still captive to the politics of fear that their predecessors had assiduously cultivated and rarely challenged for more than a century. As historian Tim Rowse observed, 'a surviving and articulate Indigenous population provokes a morally troubled imagining of the nation'.[8] It remained unresolved.

The Incurable Flaw

YEARS OF INTERMINABLE, unproductive, bureaucratic process, of expert groups, advisory councils and crocodile tears, provoked a change of tactics. In 2017, another moving and respectful request was developed, this time after an extensive consultation with First Nations leaders and communities across the country. Rather than appealing to the queen or prime minister, this time the request for recognition, the *Uluru Statement from the Heart* and its three-pronged proposal of an enduring structural means to end the 'torment of our powerlessness', was addressed directly to the Australian people.[9]

A new generation of First Nations leaders had emerged. Some already had high profiles; many had felt the sting of betrayal and the frustration of preparing reports that had been filed away and forgotten. This was a chance to change the public conversation, and it was led by people who had learned to play the Canberra game: the charismatic Noel Pearson, whose brilliantly analytical and unflinchingly powerful speeches could inspire and infuriate, owed some to a childhood listening to Lutheran ministers at the Hope Vale Mission on Cape York; Megan Davis, a Cobble Cobble woman whose determined mother moved the family to Brisbane's 'black belt' and inspired her to become not only a professor of constitutional law but the first Aboriginal person appointed to a United Nations body and chair of its Permanent Indigenous Forum; Pat Anderson, the co-author of the *Ampe Akelyernemane Meke Mekarle: Little Children Are Sacred* report into child abuse, who after a lifetime of public service felt betrayed when the Howard government used it as a cover for the Northern Territory intervention; and Rachel Perkins, the brilliant filmmaker who, as Charles Perkins' daughter, had been raised for a life of advocacy. These men and women, and many others, had learned the lessons of the past. Their education, and their professional, cultural and personal experiences, meant they could walk in both worlds with confidence and authority. As the Canberra process spun its wheels, they spent the latter part of 2016 arranging dialogues in First Nations communities all over the continent. They wanted to inform, listen, and learn how to address the failure that had festered for so long. It was clear to them, and anyone who paid attention, that the wound Jeremy Bentham described in 1803 as 'incurable' needed to be healed for the nation to mature.[10]

This was an exercise in true consultation. It was deliberative democracy, rather than a ratification of solutions drafted by anonymous officials in air-conditioned offices. The thirteen meetings were held in community centres in cities, towns and remote communities over five long hot months from December 2016.[11] Each dialogue followed the same intense, three-day agenda, with 100 delegates chosen to represent traditional owners and community members, leaders, young and old, men and women. As the meetings progressed it became clear the solution needed to be both symbolic and practical—to address the past and provide a robust framework for the future. To have one without the other would be meaningless.

After months of meetings, on the day before the final statement was prepared, Noel Pearson realised that the words alone would not be sufficient. Rachel Perkins then began the search for a painting that would encapsulate the spirit and intent of the statement. The Anangu communities in the Uluru-Kata Tjuta area are home to some of the nation's most renowned desert artists, but a painting that conveyed this complex, sophisticated and haunting message was not something that could be conjured overnight. Instead, the *Uluru Statement from the Heart* was signed on a blank canvas in the red desert sand by more than 250 delegates at the First Nations National Constitutional Convention on 26 May 2017, the fiftieth anniversary of the referendum that started to repair the Constitutional flaw. It is an eloquent, considered and heartfelt plea *to the people of Australia*.[12] The poetic words were crafted in a final all-night session, distilling years of debate and discussion, frustration and hope. Later the canvas was filled with paintings by renowned Anangu artists to become a beautiful object, continuing the tradition of synthesising art, history and law. It called for a constitutionally enshrined Indigenous Voice to Parliament,

The Incurable Flaw

a Makarrata Commission to supervise a truth-telling process, and treaties that would truly be 'a coming together after struggle'.

The Uluru Statement turned years of rejection, disappointment and bureaucratic obstruction into a triumph. The process was almost as interesting as the outcome; it was as Megan Davis, the scholar who actively guided the process, wrote, 'an example of the transformative potential of liberal democratic governance through civic engagement beyond the ballot box'.[13] As one obstacle after another blocked meaningful recognition, it took a leap of faith to take the question of the best way forward to the people who were most affected.

As a result, and an infuriating frustration to the leaders in suits who thought they knew it all, the outcomes changed. The process of deliberative democracy engaged with the local, respected opposition and when, at last, a tearful, emotional agreement was reached, an enduring political treatise and cultural object was created. To unite the disparate voices and perspectives was an extraordinary achievement. When the delegates emerged from the meeting room at Yulara, near Uluru, to read the invitation to the nation to walk with them, it was an astonishing moment. Survival is not an end, but an essential first step. As Megan Davis wrote in an essay describing the process that marked an important milestone, 'Uluru is the beginning of the process, the coming together after a struggle.'[14]

> The process of creating the Uluru Statement was a breakthrough of epic proportions for people who had been subjected to calculated policies of divide-and-rule since 1788, and a legacy of internalised shame and lateral violence. A few delegates walked out of the Convention and refused to sign, but most remained, overwhelmed by emotion and the achievement centuries in the making.
>
> We, gathered at the 2017 National Constitutional Convention, coming from all points of the southern sky, make this statement from the heart:

The Idea of Australia

Our Aboriginal and Torres Strait Islander tribes were the first sovereign Nations of the Australian continent and its adjacent islands, and possessed it under our own laws and customs. This our ancestors did, according to the reckoning of our culture, from the Creation, according to the common law from 'time immemorial', and according to science more than 60,000 years ago.

This sovereignty is *a spiritual notion: the ancestral tie between the land or 'mother nature', and the Aboriginal and Torres Strait Islander peoples who were born therefrom, remain attached thereto, and must one day return thither to be united with our ancestors. This link is the basis of the ownership of the soil, or better, of sovereignty.* It has never been ceded or extinguished, and co-exists with the sovereignty of the Crown.

How could it be otherwise? That peoples possessed a land for sixty millennia and this sacred link disappears from world history in merely the last two hundred years?

With substantive constitutional change and structural reform, we believe this ancient sovereignty can shine through as a fuller expression of Australia's nationhood.

Proportionally, we are the most incarcerated people on the planet. We are not an innately criminal people. Our children are aliened from their families at unprecedented rates. This cannot be because we have no love for them. And our youth languish in detention in obscene numbers. They should be our hope for the future.

These dimensions of our crisis tell plainly the structural nature of our problem. This is *the torment of our powerlessness*.

We seek constitutional reforms to empower our people and take *a rightful place* in our own country. When we have power over our destiny our children will flourish. They will walk in two worlds and their culture will be a gift to their country.

We call for the establishment of a First Nations Voice enshrined in the Constitution.

The Incurable Flaw

Makarrata is the culmination of our agenda: the coming together after a struggle. It captures our aspirations for a fair and truthful relationship with the people of Australia and a better future for our children based on justice and self-determination.

We seek a Makarrata Commission to supervise a process of agreement-making between governments and First Nations and truth-telling about our history.

In 1967 we were counted, in 2017 we seek to be heard. We leave base camp and start our trek across this vast country. We invite you to walk with us in a movement of the Australian people for a better future.[15]

Quandamooka man Dean Parkin, who became the director of the From the Heart campaign, later recalled 'people who had previously been arguing furiously with each other embraced with tears in their eyes'.[16] In time, the beautiful statement will hang alongside the Yirrkala and Barunga barks in Parliament House. Hopefully that time will not be too far hence, and will celebrate success, not mark another failure.

Opinion polls showed that their fellow Australians welcomed the statement almost immediately, and their support continued to grow and consolidate as time passed and it was bounced like a piece of kryptonite from one committee to another, from one inquiry to the next.[17] Politicians prevaricated and then brusquely rebuffed its recommendations. Unlike his predecessor, Prime Minister Malcolm Turnbull did not shed a tear when he announced that his government could not accept the Uluru recommendations. As if to rub salt into the wound, his timing was rich with powerful negative symbolism. His rejection of the recommendations was reported on 26 October 2017—the 32nd anniversary of Uluru's return to its traditional owners, a date that was more often celebrated as a marker on the road to recognition. In the manner of modern political information management, half-truths were leaked to the press, playing to racially charged fears. The misstatements included claims designed to frighten, assertions that accepting the recommendations would produce a 'third chamber' that would weaken the authority of parliament. This phrase had been refined by the Institute of Public Affairs, the free-market think tank that counts Gina Rinehart and Rupert Murdoch among its most prominent supporters. It has more often sought to highlight Aboriginal dysfunction than facilitate structural solutions that necessarily challenged the status quo that had served them so well.[18]

Prime Minister Turnbull knew—and he knew personally and painfully better than most who have occupied that office—that the Commonwealth of Australia was the product of constitutional conventions. Yet his opposition to the intent of the statement was unwavering. The reasons were unclear. Was it because his historical imagination could not embrace this more inclusive and representative 21st-century convention? Because it suggested a restructure of power that went back to the incurable flaw at the heart of the nation? Or had his ego been bruised by the process that sidestepped his own envisioned solution of a technical constitutional amendment? Or had he lost ambition as he struggled with his opponents? The man who had said the country's heart was broken when John Howard played the politics better than him and killed the republic referendum that would have severed the link with the Royal Family did not resile. At the time he was preoccupied with the fraught practical politics of holding power within the ideologically divided Coalition. The *Uluru Statement from the Heart* was, he wrote later in his memoir, 'a beautiful piece of poetry, a cry for a say, for agency, for respect . . . but contained no detail about how such a Voice would be designed'. Having found the limits of his prime ministerial power, he washed his hands of the 'incurable flaw' rather than seek to mend it, declaring: 'Social problems centuries in the making cannot be resolved in any one government.'[19]

The Incurable Flaw

THE PARALYSIS OF politics suggested to the shrewd Yolngu leader Galarrwuy Yunupingu that it was time to revive an old strategy. Respectful pleas to local politicians had repeatedly fallen on deaf ears; maybe it was time again to go to the source. The nation may have been a product of colonial ambition and nineteenth-century conventions, but it was ultimately formed as a gift from the elected representatives of enfranchised men in the British House of Commons, and from a monarch in Buckingham Palace.

The Yolngu, like traditional owners in other territories colonised by the British, understand the dynamics of hereditary power probably better than those raised in a world of representative democracies. In the homes of many old First Nations aunties, the portrait of a young Queen Elizabeth has pride of place, just as it had in the homes of the latter-day bush poets I visited in the 1970s.

For centuries the Indigenous peoples of colonised lands had known it made more sense to negotiate an agreement with a monarch than to try to pin down the moveable feast of those who held fleeting political or bureaucratic power. Signing treaties—reluctantly, enthusiastically or under duress—has always been the business of kings and queens. British politicians were well aware of this as the empire grew, negotiating treaties, paying compensation or leasing land via agreements signed by the Crown. International law was clear. The first of the 70 treaties in Canada were signed in 1701.[20] Over the border, in 1778 the newly independent United States signed a treaty with the Delaware Indians, the first of some 370 treaties with Native Americans signed by 1871. The lessons learned by the failure to reach an agreement in the Australian colonies in part inspired the 1840 Treaty of Waitangi between the Crown and Māori leaders, which became the foundational document of New Zealand.

The failure to do the same when Arthur Phillip landed in Sydney Cove, or subsequently as the penal settlement and colonies expanded, and battles were fought and lost, was not just a result of forgetfulness.

His brief to 'conciliate' with 'amity and kindness' was framed by the expectation, fostered by Joseph Banks's recollections, that the Great South Land had very few inhabitants, and that those who were there would 'speedily abandon the Country to Newcomers'. One of Phillip's first despatches to London highlighted Banks's error: 'the natives are far more numerous than they were supposed to be'. It was shaping up to be an 'audacious territorial appropriation'.[21]

As the settlers moved beyond Sydney Cove, this truth became ever clearer. It is now accepted that the population of the continent numbered at least 800,000 people, and probably more than a million.[22] Still the policy that determined there was no need for a formal, compensated settlement because the land was unoccupied did not change, despite recommendations from the British Colonial Office. An increasingly humanitarian ethos was developing in London, with campaigns to end slavery and transportation. But the flaw was not addressed in Australia. John Batman's problematic and deeply flawed treaty with the Kulin Nation in Victoria was rejected for fear it 'would subvert the foundation on which all Proprietary rights in New South Wales at present rest'. By the time the colonies became self-governing and, later, when the Commonwealth of Australia was formed, the 'misunderstanding had crystallised into expedient deceit', and the First Nations population reduced by 90 per cent.[23]

Despite their lack of active consent in the process of nation formation, First Nations people are citizens of the nation that emerged from this imperial project. Since 1984 they, like all other Australians over the age of eighteen, have been compulsorily required to vote. But Galarrwuy Yunupingu and the clans of East Arnhem Land 'acknowledge no king, no queen, no church, no state'.[24]

While Australia remains one of the few Commonwealth countries that still recognises the British monarch as head of state, time-honoured traditions suggest hereditary leaders should meet. For centuries kings and queens have played a role in allocating the spoils of war, dividing

The Incurable Flaw

and aggregating territory by birthright and marriage. Australia has been the destination of countless royal tours since Prince Alfred, Duke of Edinburgh, first visited the colonies in 1867, but no king or queen has suggested a treaty, even after meeting First Nations leaders. Queen Elizabeth II was welcomed to Alice Springs in 2000 by Arrernte elder Max Stuart, then chairman of the Central Land Council. He presented her with a submission, but it went the way of so many others. Stuart was in the final stage of a life he could not have imagined in 1959, when he had been jailed and sentenced to death. Stuart's case gave Rupert Murdoch his first taste of media power when his newspaper, the Adelaide-based *News*, campaigned successfully to have his death sentence overturned. By the time Stuart met the queen, he was regarded as an elder. 'I thought she'd talk in big language but really [she was] like one of us, really like a bush woman,' he recalled. There was no discussion of a treaty.[25]

In the 21st century, notwithstanding the Brexit fantasy that the British Empire might be restored, its most visible remnant is the Commonwealth Games, when athletes from the former colonies run, jump, swim and play against each other, presided over by a ranking royal. In 2018 it was the turn of Queensland (another state named for Victoria) to again host the Commonwealth Games, this time under the watchful eye of the Prince of Wales.

As the political response to the Uluru Statement foundered on harsh ideological shoals, Yolngu leaders from north-east Arnhem Land invited the prince to visit while he was in Australia. Prince Charles had been familiar with the country since his days at Geelong Grammar in the 1960s, and he had once hoped to become Australian governor-general.[26] He and Galarrwuy Yunupingu were both men born to leadership. They were contemporaries, arriving in the world just five months apart, who might have been classmates at Timbertop, the bush campus of Australia's most elite college, had Galarrwuy's father not decided against sending his brilliant young son to the school on the south edge of the continent.

The ageing prince's sixth visit to the Northern Territory was quite different to the flag-waving, flower-giving, baby-kissing tours of the past. Local elders met him and his entourage at the Mount Nhulun sacred site, with its panoramic views, and a story of the spirit man Wuyul who journeyed through the land searching for *guku* (honey), and greeted the prince with respect and formality. He was given a dilly bag and a traditional headdress—gifts from one head of state to another—and television cameras captured the unlikely images of the pale, elderly prince, in a beige linen suit, wearing a white-feathered headdress and walking with a group of children whose faces and bodies had been painted with ochre. After a spectacular traditional ceremony, a 'diplomatic meeting' took place. At that private exchange, the Yolngu Nations Assembly presented the heir to the British throne with a message stick. It reiterated the Yirrkala bark petition: the Yolngu were a sovereign people who had never been conquered. 'It's probably about time,' an organiser told *ABC News*, 'the great, great, great, great grandson of the person who ordered someone to stick a flag in and claim the whole continent fronted up and actually met the landowners.'[27]

12

Making the Nation

To DESCRIBE THE YIRRKALA bark petition as the Aboriginal Magna Carta, as Kevin Rudd did in 2013, highlights the fact that Australia does not have her own grand founding document. Her practical, cynical people are reputed to be allergic to glorious rhetoric, and there is none in the Australian Constitution. There are no words that stir the heart, no pithy lines that trip off the tongue. It is hard to get excited about a document that begins: 'Whereas the people of New South Wales, Victoria, South Australia, Queensland and Tasmania, humbly relying on the blessing of Almighty God, have agreed to unite in one indissoluble Federal Commonwealth under the Crown of the United Kingdom of Great Britain and Ireland . . .'

It is also hard to find inspiring language with a contemporary ring in the Magna Carta. The royal charter of rights was first crafted in 1215, when King John briefly conceded some power to his restless bishops and barons. As the long-serving clerk of the Australian Senate, Harry Evans, declared in a speech 800 years later, the Magna Carta is mostly a 'very tedious recital of feudal relationships which not only have no relevance to modern government but which would be of interest only to the most pedantic antiquarian'.[1] Over the centuries it has been revoked, reworked and reinterpreted many times. Some copies were sold to raise funds for war, to cover debts or for personal profit; others were lost. It has, however, won almost mythic status as the 'bedrock of English liberty', thanks to the interpretation of several famous clauses: promising freedom from arbitrary arrest, no taxation without representation, and justice for 'free men'.[2]

In recent years conservative politicians have reclaimed the Magna Carta, asserting with increasing frequency that it should be considered as Australia's defining document. The free-market Institute of Public Affairs has been at the forefront of this movement—sponsoring research, seminars and speeches, even publishing a scholarly book to make the case. Politicians have become attuned to the institute's agenda and its public reach, particularly through News Corp commentators in print, television and online. With increasing frequency, politicians have proposed in private forums and at public events that the existence of the Magna Carta obviates the need for a formal bill of rights (which Australia does not have) and distils the essence of the nation. This argument was first made in 1925 by the High Court Justice Sir Isaac Isaacs, who later became the first Australian-born and first Jewish governor-general. He adjudged that the Magna Carta better asserted the 'right to life, liberty, property and citizenship' than Australia's own Constitution. He was right: the Constitution is silent on many 'rights'. The founders left them to be discovered by judges, not conjured by legislation or international covenants.

A decade before James Cook was despatched on his imperial voyage, the Magna Carta was displayed, in a specially made glass case, in the newly opened British Museum. The exhibition was labelled *The Bulwark of our Liberties*. Thanks to a book by then-unknown Oxford jurist William Blackstone, the most recent iteration of the Magna Carta was enjoying 'a reviving cult' of popularity. Iconic texts of identity and rights had a certain cachet, as forward-thinking Russian and Swedish monarchs made concerted efforts to develop them.[3] British and Irish radicals and reformers also found hope in the Great Charter, but not everyone was convinced. 'Common people,' wrote one conservative commentator in 1766, were being 'encouraged to discover in the Magna Carta liberties these ancient patriots never dreamed of.'[4]

As he prepared for the journey of the First Fleet, Arthur Phillip, who had spent the previous few years as an English spy in France, was well aware of the rights that were stirring spirits in Europe and in the newly independent United States. But when he found himself presiding over a penal colony, the ancient Magna Carta was not uppermost in his mind. He appointed no juries, nor promised freedom of speech, and punishments were harsh—'corpses rotting from swinging gibbets on the harbour'.[5] The campaign in Britain to end transportation—and the loss of its stained, virtually free convict labour—had prevailed by 1868. By then, limited self-government had been granted to six Australian colonies; each had a constitution, elected representatives, jury trials and a more or less free press. These principles were assumed by the authors of the Australian Constitution. They failed to fully define the rights of citizens.

The only copy of the Magna Carta in the Southern Hemisphere has been on display in Parliament House—when not being repaired, which is much of the time—since 1961. The badly damaged 1297 edition of the document was found in an impoverished English school after the end of the Second World War. Its principal sensed a solution to his school's pressing financial problems by finding a buyer with deep pockets. The British Museum didn't want to have to compete for the ancient document, and a game that could have come from an episode of *Yes Minister* played out, before it was sold by Sotheby's and allowed to leave the UK. The £12,500 asking price was considered so extortionate in 1952 that a hire-purchase scheme was proposed to pay it off. Now the boffins would probably recommend crowdfunding, as they did for the National Archives and Library.

The Idea of Australia

Eventually the prime minister, Robert Menzies, found a solution. A devoted Anglophile who famously waxed lyrical about the young Queen Elizabeth—'I did but see her passing by and yet I love her 'til I die'—Menzies convinced Treasury to make a special dispensation to release funds so he could acquire the culturally significant document. It turned out to be a good investment. The going price these days for one of the remaining 23 copies of the Magna Carta is more than $25 million. In the absence of an iconic local document, 21st-century Australian school children on their end-of-primary-school trip to the nation's capital traipse past the cabinet where it is housed and are invited to write a Magna Carta for Australia—only the opening phrase is set as 'I grant that Australia should . . .'

In 2001, as a gesture to celebrate the centenary of Federation, the British government gave more than $500,000 'to the people of Australia' to build a Magna Carta memorial. It was a gift rich with irony for the anniversary of national independence. It emphasised the absence of an authentic local declaration of rights, an enduring tie to an ancient struggle over the power of a king and unbroken links with the motherland.

The copper-domed monument stands on ironbark columns, its crown-like ring etched with lines from the ancient text, with bronze plaques below, for rubbing—like in an old English cathedral, but under southern skies. It is not high on the list of must sees in the national capital, tucked away in an otherwise desolate corner of the parliamentary precinct.

In a sign of how bound Australia was to the motherland during the Menzies years, in 1952 Langton Crescent, which circles what is now called Magna Carta Place, was named after Stephen Langton—the Archbishop of Canterbury who had been instrumental in having King John seal the Magna Carta in 1215. More prosaically, Magna Carta Place is across the road from the Hyatt Hotel, which started life as the residence for members of parliament, and near the rose garden of

Making the Nation

Old Parliament House, now repurposed as the Museum of Australian Democracy. Across the road from the modest building, the Aboriginal Tent Embassy remains—a reminder of principles foregone in the half-century since it was first pitched.

In 2001, as part of the centenary of Federation celebrations, Prime Minister Howard's wife Janette buried a time capsule under the foundation stone at the centre of the monument. Forty years earlier, Prime Minister Menzies' wife Pattie was the first person in Australia to view the copy of the restored Magna Carta that her husband had twisted arms in London and Canberra to acquire. Whether this has all just been a historical fantasy or something of enduring relevance and merit remains to be seen. The continuing relevance of the memorial will be evaluated next in 2101, when Janette Howard's time capsule is opened. One can only ponder what mementos of the first year of the 21st century await the scrutiny of the prime minister's 'wife' in the first year of the 22nd, and what the reaction might be.

Already the memorial seems insufficient for the rights and aspirations of an independent nation with its own distinctive history. The memorial itself makes no mention of the way the Magna Carta was honoured in the breach when the settlement was first established, nor that its principles did not extend to the custodians of the land already in residence. But the National Capital Authority's guide to the often windswept memorial notes that the Magna Carta applied 'in a particular way in Australia':

> When Europeans arrived, their new colonial society was often in conflict with Aboriginal and Torres Strait Islander peoples. The early colonial settlements, founded mostly on convict labour, also imposed a system of justice at odds with the rights and liberties expressed in Magna Carta. However, as penal settlements evolved over time into free colonies, Magna Carta's principles could no longer be ignored. Ultimately, with the federation of Australia's

colonies in 1901 . . . the rights expressed in the Magna Carta were confirmed to suit the unique conditions of our Australian society.[6]

The document's enduring resonance highlights that there is no sweeping promise that encapsulates a particular Australian dream, no inspiring words against which we can be measured or held accountable. The Australian Constitution was one of many constitutions written in countries around the world in the nineteenth century, but Australia's is one of the least changed, revered by people who are largely ignorant of its contents. Long queues of people inch forward every day to see the original 1337-word US Declaration of Independence; it is displayed with reverence and illumination in the National Archives in Washington, DC. There is no comparable Australian experience. The Museum of Australian Democracy is still a work in progress. The National Archives only in 2021 put the vellum on which Queen Victoria gave her assent in Windsor Castle, and the small silver case containing the wax seal with a royal insignia, on display. The new exhibition—'Voices/Dhuniai: Federation, Democracy and the Constitution'—was provoked by the Uluru Statement's plea for a First Nations' Voice to parliament. The frequently leaf-littered Magna Carta Memorial behind the rose garden is an inadequate monument to a more complex polity.

SINCE IT OPENED off-Broadway in New York in 2015, people around the world have queued for hours, willing to hand over extraordinary sums of money for tickets to *Hamilton*. The hip-hop musical celebrates the life of one of the lesser-known American founding fathers. As a result of Lin-Manuel Miranda's creative genius, a civics lesson became a hit. The show begins with a big and unlikely question: how did a bastard who grew up in impoverished squalor, and longed to be part of something bigger, become a hero?

Making the Nation

Similar questions could be asked of the characters who played leading roles in the Australian process, although they are unlikely to be recognised as heroes or become stars of screen or stage. The 45 men at the heart of the process of creating the Commonwealth of Australia had tasted the excitement and possibilities of political power as premiers and cabinet ministers. They had experienced the frustrations of compromise, the violence of settlement and the complicated heritage of being colonials. Most were well travelled and well read, and all were creatures of the intellectual fashions of the time. Some had seen the frontier wars at terrifyingly close hand; others had been at the forefront of crafting representative democracies and compulsory secular education. They had engaged in debates over self-rule, territorial autonomy and land ownership. They had seen labour disputes grow violent, and business owners and banks grow more demanding. They recognised the power of fear and fostered anti-Chinese sentiments. They became preoccupied with how to 'protect' a people whose 'dying' they had witnessed and, in some cases, expedited. Some had absorbed progressive ideas from abroad; others had embraced what Charles Darwin called the 'unique civilisation' taking form on the Australian continent. Some opposed what was a slave trade by another name, of Melanesians from the Pacific, and introduced minor reforms that allowed First Nations people to give evidence against settlers; others responded to popular movements and legislated to allow women to vote and stand for parliament. As a group they walked the tightrope of asserting independence while keeping republicanism at bay.

If an antipodean Lin-Manuel Miranda were given the task of creating an Australian *Hamilton*, Alfred Deakin would command a leading role. He was a gifted orator, handsome and passionate. He was also a colourful character—a transcendentalist who believed in the spirit world, and whose seance and prayer diaries would provide a dramatic colour. He was born within years of Ned Kelly, but took a very different path to the violent, angry man who became an unlikely national icon. In Judith Brett's award-winning biography *The Enigmatic Mr Deakin*, she describes him as too unusual to be a mate: 'too intellectual, too respectable for the larrikin masculinity . . . that runs from convicts and bushrangers . . . through the drovers and shearers and men from Snowy River, the early labour unions and the Anzacs, to Crocodile Dundee and footballers'.[7]

Tasmanian-born Andrew Inglis Clark, who wanted Australia to be her own nation, not a provincial outpost to an empire, would deserve a role. When the Hobart *Mercury* dismissed Inglis Clark as a 'communist', he responded by declaring his faith in Abraham Lincoln's description of a 'government of the people, by the people, for the people'. He hung portraits of Giuseppe Mazzini, the Italian republican, in every room of his large house.[8] Inglis Clark explicitly wanted something like a US Bill of Rights to be included in the Constitution. He was strongly influenced by American republicanism as well as Italian, and he travelled to Italy to talk to leading jurists. He was an advocate of proportional representation and women's rights, aligning with South Australian reformer Catherine Helen Spence and delivering Tasmania's unique proportional, multi-member Hare–Clark electoral system. A small man towered over by the big-whiskered crew of founders, he was described by Deakin as 'small, spare, nervous, active, jealous, suspicious, awkward in manner and ungracious in speech'. Had he prevailed, a different Constitution and nation might have emerged.[9]

No dramaturge could deny the duelling, philandering South Australian Charles Kingston a leading role. Physically he was Andrew Inglis Clark's opposite: a towering former athlete and volunteer sergeant, a man always ready for a fight. Despite their physical differences, they shared some progressive dreams. Kingston's complicated world view might be a challenge to distil. He was present at the first Australasian conference in Sydney in 1888 when the idea of making a nation—possibly one that included New Zealand and other Pacific

Making the Nation

islands—was explored. After a turbulent decade, he was also at the final hard-fought negotiations in London when he and Alfred Deakin lost the argument with the Colonial Secretary to remove the British Privy Council as the new nation's last court of appeal. Kingston was an advocate of female franchise, a state bank, tariffs, factory regulation, income tax and land regulation. He was also vehemently anti-Chinese. He picked up the gauntlet from Henry Parkes, who had declared at the end of the 1888 meeting that 'our purpose is to terminate the landing of the Chinese on these shores forever', and who became known as the father of the White Australia policy—'success' has many fathers, so it was for a time an 'honour' others also claimed.[10]

A point of dramatic tension in the antipodean stage show would be created by Rose Scott, a suffragette and fierce opponent of Federation who wielded influence from her salon. Scott was one of a rapidly growing group of educated women who believed 'woman has been a slave too long'. These feisty feminists, including Louisa Lawson and Vida Goldstein, had different perspectives, and would form the ideal chorus to critique the prevailing male wisdom. Scott imagined a new form of government to remedy this fundamental inequity. Her vision was one that would resonate with contemporary audiences watching the Federation stage show. To her mind, local representation was crucial. This still echoes. The Independent Voices campaign, which gathered momentum during the pandemic 120 years later, was its successor. Every Friday night the Australian-born heiress hosted guests in her Woollahra home, where they explored a different model of the nation—one without political parties, where women were heard and daily life mattered. Rose Scott's idea was of a nation that was decentralised, where people had direct contact with their representatives. 'For heaven's sake,' she argued, 'let us divest ourselves of the old-fashioned idea that a great nation is made-out of huge national debts, standing armies, expensive buildings, much territory, artificial sentiment, fat billets for some people, whilst others starve.'[11]

The Idea of Australia

Despite the possibility of caricature, Sir Samuel Griffith, the Ipswich-raised son of a Congregationalist minister, would deserve a role as an earnest character, conscientiously doing his job, ready to spin on a dime, as slippery as his nickname. Edmund Barton would embody the protectionist business elite, with his libertarian sidekick, the portly George Reid. And the two heroes who face the five-dollar note would hover above the stage: Catherine Helen Spence, advocate for the rights of women, children and the destitute, could be the omnipresent conscience, while the ghost of Henry Parkes would observe proceedings, wishing he had lived long enough to see his dream come true.

In contrast to the global fascination with the contradictory characters who drove the creation of the United States, Australia's founders remain virtually unknown. The process by which 422,788 white men, a few women from South and Western Australia and a smattering of First Nations people in the antipodean colonies voted to ask the House of Commons to create a national constitutional democracy forms an invisible foundation. They have no memorial, let alone a global stage show. There has not even been a screen dramatisation, and the few books that attempt to personalise the stories of the founders fail to capture the imagination. Australians are diffident about a history that involves whiskery men in greatcoats.

The Queensland flagship *Lucinda*, where the draft of the Constitution was largely settled in 1891, ended her days hauling coal down the river from Ipswich. An attempt by the Brisbane legal community to save the *Lucinda* and turn her into a national monument came to nothing, and the boat was scuppered in the Brisbane River. The best that could be done was a replica of the ship's smoking room where Sir Samuel Griffith held court. This was a personal project for Brisbane's conservative silks, who traced their lineage back to Sir Sam. The smoking room they recreated in the Queensland Supreme Court included the original beautiful woodwork, stained glass, furniture and paintings they retrieved. Even the silverware, whiskey decanter and glasses were in place, as if to invite visitors into a conversation with the nation's first chief justice.[12] That too was demolished when the state's new Supreme Court opened in 2012, one that embodied a very different ethos. Gone was the stuffy clubbiness, replaced with a building that, in its glassy essence, celebrates transparency and openness.

Most of the grand monuments that were planned at the turn of the century did not materialise. Canberra was Federation's best embodiment, but even the national capital, which some wanted to call Utopia, was a defensive compromise by the Australian colonies, midway between the two largest cities. The diminutive Billy Hughes, still a Labor politician at the time of Canberra's inauguration in 1913, said the nation was unfolding 'without the slightest trace of that race we have banished from the face of the earth. We must not be too proud lest we should, too, in time disappear. We must take steps to safeguard the foothold we now have.'[13] He was a man of his word, and secured his own foothold: by the time he died in 1952, he had been a member of the parliament for more than 50 years, the nation's seventh prime minister, and a member of six political parties, of which he led five, outlasted four, and was expelled from three. 'Turncoat' was his nickname. He too would have a role in the Australian Federation stage show.[14]

THE SLOGAN 'One People, One Destiny'[15] was the best that could be conjured during the campaign for Federation. This was a society that oscillated between racial bravado, confidence that they were 'a coming Sun-God's race' and racial angst. Threatened by 'Asian engulfment, rampant miscegenation, birth-rate decline and tropical enervation'.[16] It was, historian Raymond Evans has noted, 'the largest and most tremendous experiment ever tried in race building'. He quotes the nativist journalist Randolph Bedford, who in 1911 reflected that 'Australia had been handed a sacred duty of breeding a pure race in a clean continent'.[17] The official claim was more measured and optimistic: 'Ours is not the federation of fear, but the wise, solemn, rational federation of free people.' The ideal of a wise federation without fear was forgotten almost as soon as it was conjured. It did not last long enough to take root, as John Hirst records in his masterwork *The Sentimental Nation*.[18] Instead, fear shaped the nation: fear of abandonment by Britain, fear of being swamped by Chinese people, and the shame-tinged fear of failing the moral challenge of the First Australians.

Few promises were made to future generations on 1 January 1901 when the nation was finally signed into existence, with working arrangements that would enable a group of bickering colonies to find a common purpose. The founding document was preoccupied with how to make a federation work. It did not guarantee universal suffrage, define rights, or stretch with the ambition that distinguished other great constitutions (even scores of mediocre ones) that had been written over the previous century. The Commonwealth of Australia was tied to Britain, an unapologetically bureaucratic work in progress. In many ways it was the product of a committee. The nation's second prime minister, Alfred Deakin, who persuaded Victorians to become its most ardent supporters, described Federation as a 'series of miracles'.[19]

It occurred more than a decade after the long-term premier of New South Wales, Henry Parkes, first proposed a national union in a speech in 1889, in Tenterfield. By then, the legislation he had drafted to claim the name 'Australia' for his colony had lapsed. Personal ambition drove him, along with the challenge of defending the 'unprotected coasts' of a continent that had still not been fully 'explored'. It was hard to generate enthusiasm for what the press liked to call Henry Parkes' 'whim'.[20] He had boasted to the governor of New South Wales, Lord Carrington, that he could federate the colonies in a year, to which the governor archly replied, 'Why don't you do it?'[21]

The man who considered himself the father of the nation faced a bigger challenge than he expected. The first conference, in Melbourne

Making the Nation

in 1890, with delegates from all the colonies and New Zealand, was held in an 'atmosphere of strain'.[22] The delegates were well read, but deeply divided between three options: the United States model that Andrew Inglis Clark advocated most strongly, the more distributed power of Canada, and essentially a British province. The early visions of utopia that had gained momentum as each of the colonies established self-government, saw their white native-born populations grow, established free compulsory education and passed laws to restrict Chinese immigration were a long way from these outlines. By the time the discussion began in earnest, tensions were running high; strikes, lockouts, recession and drought divided and preoccupied people. 'Nothing seemed further from the minds of the elderly politicians,' Vance Palmer noted in his 1954 evocation of the legend of the 1890s, 'than the subterranean conflict that was going on in the community.'[23]

As the decade progressed, interest grew. The predominantly Australian-born population welcomed direct elections by citizens 'owning no class distinctions or party influence', and the promise that a federation would 'advance the cause of Australian patriotism'.[24] Trade was uppermost in the minds of those shaping the founding document. Each colony had its own rules and tariffs. Those living along the Murray River, where bridges had 'customs houses at both ends',[25] were daily reminded that borders were barriers—just as their descendants were, more than a century later, as they stuck special pandemic permits to their windscreens and drove slowly past checkpoints.

The Constitution was substantially drafted over the wet Easter of 1891, on the Hawkesbury River aboard the *Lucinda*, under the leadership of Queensland's premier Samuel Griffith, who had held many high offices in his colony's short history. While the men on the *Lucinda* refined the Constitution, the Queensland government authorised troops to break up the shearers' strike in the west of the colony and sent its leaders to an island prison in Moreton Bay.

It was Andrew Inglis Clark's draft that the men on the *Lucinda* worked on that Easter weekend, a document he derived from the US Constitution.[26] The young Inglis Clark had an expansive republican vision. He was inspired by the end of slavery in America; his family had actively opposed the brutal treatment of convicts and transportation. He was swept along with the same anti-Chinese sentiment that gripped them all, and was silent on the frontier wars and the decimation of the Palawa nations in his island colony. He had fallen ill and was not aboard the *Lucinda*. He thought Griffith had taken them on a Hawkesbury River picnic and made a mess of it. Had he been present, and been a more forceful and persuasive individual, a different document may have eventuated. Instead, Andrew Inglis Clark became virtually invisible, the only founding father who does not have a suburb in the national capital named for him, although a statue of him was eventually erected in Civic in 2020.[27]

The document continued to be revised for the rest of the decade as conventions and parliaments debated the provisions, especially the principles of 'one vote, one value' (for men) and free trade, and whether the smaller territories would be overwhelmed. 'They were times that try men's souls,' Alfred Deakin declared in an impassioned speech in Bendigo in March 1898 that turned the tide to support. It was, he implored the audience, an unstable era, a time of unprecedented crisis for the Empire, one in which the toll of separation left the self-governing colonies 'hampered in commerce, weakened in prestige . . . jarring atoms instead of a united organism'. It was not the time to surrender, he declared, even as 'the classes resist us, the masses may be inert; politicians may falter; our leaders may sound the retreat'; instead, it was time to 'embrace the enlightened liberalism of the Constitution'.[28]

A series of formal meetings and more organic people's conventions followed before a proposal to become one nation was put to several votes in each of the colonies. Sixteen polls were held in the five years to 1900. Sydneysiders were reluctant, and if a few thousand people

Making the Nation

in Queensland had voted the other way Federation would have been further delayed.[29] Western Australia did not agree to join until after the British House of Commons had passed the bill.

Even this product of compromise and negotiation was changed by the Colonial Office, but the core that Samuel Griffith refined over that Easter weekend remained: a federal structure ensuring autonomy of each colony, a House of Representatives selected by a one-vote-one-value system (men only and a promise to women), and a Senate that equally represented each state. The Senate was drawn from the Americans, the parliamentary model that ensured oversight of the executive, from Britain. A complex web of state and national responsibilities evolved. It was as minimal as possible, and future change was designed to be as difficult as possible.

Six months after Westminster approved the document and Queen Victoria gave her assent, the nearly four million people who had made their home in the colonies—but only a few of those First Nations people who had been here forever—took the first steps towards nationhood. They were still British subjects but ready to assert a distinctive cultural identity. There was a paradox, as Vance Palmer noted: in the bush, where there was little talk of Federation, people shared a strong sense of being Australian, but in earnest urban conversations Federation was 'regarded almost as an alliance between countries foreign to one another and having rival economies'.[30]

A century later, when Australians' focus had been on Canberra for decades, the pandemic was a reminder that the states did have real power. Dim memories of once being called a Sandgroper (from Western Australia), Banana Bender (from Queensland), Croweaters (from South Australia), Cabbage Patchers (from Victoria) and Taswegians were revived. Thanks to the divisions of responsibility from another age, premiers could close borders and impose curfews. State insignias on driver's licences determined rights and access. By then, the states had updated their constitutions, begun to negotiate treaties, introduced human rights charters, created institutions to formally investigate corruption, and adopted targets to mitigate the risks of climate change. For the first time in many decades, the states were more likely to be innovative than Canberra. Many found the variable rules frustrating, but it was an unexpected gift of Federation: power was not completely concentrated in a bush capital remote from ordinary lives.

———

ON A HOT, windy summer day in Sydney, the first of 1901, about 200,000 people made their way from the Domain to the thirteen-year-old Centennial Park to celebrate the polygamous marriage of the colonies. Although most Sydneysiders had opposed the union, about half the city's residents came out to enjoy the festivities. On the way, they walked along Oxford Street under grand arches decorated to celebrate elements of the new nation: flowers, fauna, wheat, wool and coal were represented, as was the military, foreign allies and citizens. Melbourne had her own arch. Finally, on the first day of the second year of the new century, a 21-gun salute signalled 'a thing called Australia had been created . . . looked upon with affection, pride and curiosity' but meagre applause.[31]

The practical business of creating a nation resembled a wedding. There were documents to be signed, obligations to dispense with and celebrations to be had. On the table used by Queen Victoria to sign the Royal Assent, that Edmund Barton had asked her for, each of the new ministers appointed by Governor-General Lord Hopetoun signed his name. To the amusement of some and horror of others, the hot wind blew the papers off the table. The Federation Stone, which embodied the moment, was placed in a six-sided, 14-metre-high plaster of Paris pavilion, ornately decorated with native flora and fauna and the royal coat of arms of Great Britain.[32]

Aboriginal people were not included in the Federation conventions and were mentioned just twice in the Constitution, both in the negative—they remained under state control and could not be counted in the census. The 'incurable flaw' at the heart of the nation had worsened under competing colonial administrations. In a little over a century, the population of First Nations peoples had fallen from about a million to around 100,000, the result of brutal policing, battles, disease, drugs and abuse. The preferred Darwinian-inflected theory of a vanishing race worked as a cover-up. Still, 25 men from Queensland, under the control of the colony's Protector of Aborigines, had been pressed into service for a re-enactment of the *Endeavour*'s landing. They were brought down to entertain the partygoers, singing, dancing and menacing those playing James Cook and his party. The next day the press reported that they looked 'exceedingly weird and barbaric'. The New Zealand Minister for Native Affairs had a different view, and told guests at a celebratory lunch that he hoped that someday the First Australians would be treated as well as the Māori, a view reported as a 'discordant note'. This unease was reflected in the photographs of the nervy, worried faces of those who had 'seen too much violence in the frontier days'.[33]

Women were not quite so invisible, but no woman, apart from Queen Victoria, had her hand on the founding document. Catherine Helen Spence had led the way in making South Australia a world leader in allowing women to vote and stand for parliament. She had been campaigning for half a century, but as she approached her 76th birthday, women were far from equal. Women took freedoms that were once unimaginable, pursuing education and careers, independence, and the right to vote, write and be heard, but theirs was not full equality.[34] Women's groups were not invited to join the Federation leagues, but many were passionately engaged with the debates and the possibilities a new nation might offer. Instead they were offered the promise of a political deal.

After the marches, speeches, and gun salutes in Centennial Park, the good and great gathered for a major celebration in the ornate

Sydney Town Hall. The men ate and drank (a lot) and basked in the glow of boozy self-congratulation. The 'civilising' women, who had been active behind the scenes in the decade-long campaign, were confined to the upstairs galleries, where they watched the men carousing below. Attempts to include universal suffrage in the Constitution had been mocked and trivialised. Women's suffrage would not have been a unique breakthrough. There were local precedents: New Zealand had enfranchised women in 1893, and Pitcairn Island, where the mutineers from the *Bounty* had found refuge, adopted a constitution in 1838 that mandated education, protected the environment and allowed women to vote.[35]

What should have been a right was replaced by a sotto voce compromise, and an undertaking to legislate after Federation. It was the new nation's first political deal. It took almost eighteen months before white women aged over 21 were allowed to vote, seven years before they could vote in every state, 22 years before they could stand as candidates in all elections, 42 years before a woman was elected to federal parliament, and 109 years before Julia Gillard became the first female prime minister.

A little over a week after the ten days of dinners, sports and other celebrations concluded, Queen Victoria died. The first Australian elections were held in March, and two months later the new king, Edward VII, reluctantly allowed his son George, then the Duke of Cornwall and York, to travel and preside over the opening of the first parliament in Melbourne. *The Bulletin*, in full nationalist fervour, noted that 'the men who made the Commonwealth' were eclipsed by 'a thin, undersized man who has never done anything save be born, and grow up, and get married, and exist by breathing regularly, and be the son of his father, who did the same things'.[36]

The royals then went to Brisbane to continue the celebrations. An outbreak of bubonic plague had closed the city's port, so they travelled by train. As they crossed the new state borders, the gauge of the track

Making the Nation

changed and they disembarked, as travellers would be forced to do for decades. When they got to Brisbane, the local celebration included another two arches, one dotted with primary produce and topped with a crown, and another acknowledging the 'vanishing race' of First Nations people. The royal private secretary noted, 'Of the fauna also we notice one genus which was conspicuous by its absence in Melbourne—the aboriginal population . . . In Queensland they are more numerous, and on this occasion they are used for decorative purposes.'[37]

THE ORNATE PAVILION first constructed from plaster of Paris to house the Federation Stone of the nation was flimsy. Within a couple of years, it had eroded so badly it was destroyed, the wooden scaffolding sent to Cabarita Park beside the Parramatta River, where it languished as 'a shabby and forgotten memento of Proclamation Day'.[38] It was a metaphor that spoke volumes; an idea had been realised but it needed to be reinforced. The hard work of nation building lay ahead in a society that was torn between dreams of utopia and fear of dystopia with an anxious grip on a continent.

The Federation Stone then rested on a pedestal surrounded by an iron fence until 1988, when it was placed in an elegant new Federation Pavilion, in a low-lying grassy field tucked below an elbow of remnant bush in Centennial Park. Even this is diffident. It is not a full-throated celebration of the event it commemorates. The architect who designed the pavilion, Alec Tzannes, captured the conflicted spirit of the times: 'I wanted to make an intriguing or slightly mysterious object. What I wanted the viewer to do was to engage in the concept of history and time, and I tried to make it relevant to that moment in history.'[39]

It is certainly an enigma. The Federation Stone lies at its heart, but there is no re-creation of the journey to independence, no statues of the founders, no copy of the Constitution in a special glass box. The mosaic artwork on the ceiling by Imants Tillers came later and fills only a small part of the dome, which is dominated by a void, symbolising the 'vast emptiness of the Australian inland'. The montage of 440 panels includes an iconic European who might be a convict or settler, and an Aboriginal man who also features in the forecourt of Parliament House in Canberra. It is a beautiful evocation but one that demands explanation and says little about Federation.

Just below the Federation Pavilion's dome, an inscription in giant capitals on the sandstone frieze—'Mammon or Millennial Eden'—is even more mystifying for passers-by. It was designed to capture the contested spirit of Federation. These four words were chosen by the historian Manning Clark, who was at the peak of his fame in 1988. They paraphrase the 1901 poem 'Australia' by Bernard O'Dowd, who had opposed Federation; unlike Alfred Deakin, he did not consider it a miracle. The four words are designed to evoke the question asked then and still resonant: will Australia be a country of corrupt, 'ill-gotten' wealth or a paradise that will last for 1000 years?[40] As debates about corruption and integrity raged in federal parliament during the pandemic years, this question still resonated in the negative.

When the governor-general, Sir Ninian Stephen, and Prime Minister Bob Hawke opened the new pavilion in 1988, Aboriginal protesters stormed the dais, providing an answer to another question that had not been asked in 1901 and still made politicians uncomfortable four score and seven years later. As they walked onto the stage, they shouted: 'We are a sovereign people.'[41]

13

Small Brown Bird

PATRICK KEANE IS a justice of the High Court who likes to refer to the Australian Constitution as 'a small brown bird'. These mythical creatures have flitted through High Court judgements for decades, but it is his way of contrasting it with the American bald eagle. That grew from a Declaration of Independence replete with lofty rhetoric—*We the People . . . all men are created equal*—soaring high. For a judge of the highest court in the land, whose job it is to interpret the founding document and resolve the most complex legal matters, this may seem somewhat pejorative. But he uses the image to underscore the understated modesty of the founding document. What others see as a lack of ambition, Justice Keane regards as evidence of caution that has served the nation well and encouraged political engagement. Imagine, he asks, if the values of the day had been incorporated into the Constitution?[1] Rather than a declaration of equality, the racial prohibitions that became law in the first year of Federation may have been cast even more firmly in stone.

Rather than a grand document that embodied a unifying and uplifting idea of the first new nation of the new century, it was a prosaic, working rulebook. A guide that would regulate relations between the states and leave final legal authority in London. It lacked a definition of citizenship, universal suffrage, freedom of expression or movement, acknowledgement of the rights of those whose system of governance it categorically displaced or clarity about limits on the role of the executive. It was a small brown bird prepared for a fight.

The metaphor of a small brown bird is more powerful if you imagine it with actual feathers and wings—a real bird, rather than an abstract aid in a complex argument. I don't know if Justice Keane had a particular bird in mind when he conjured the image. There are plenty to choose from: brown treecreepers, speckled warblers, brown quails, jacky winters, thornbills and more. Some are beautiful, others nondescript.

From where I sit in northern New South Wales there are several contenders, but only one delivers the full metaphorical promise. The guidebooks say that the noisy miner is grey. From my desk, as I watch the native honeyeaters soaring and squawking, feasting on nectar and bathing in the ponds I kindly provided for them, they look brown to me, with a fashionable but unlikely flash of yellow eyeshadow. Visiting ornithologists first gave the noisy *buthaibuthai* an ancient Greek name in 1801. Since then, while more than 100 other native species disappeared, they thrived. They are aggressive and territorial, thrive in the margins, mob predators and form temporary alliances. They are braggards given to 'flight displays, postural displays, and facial displays . . . chasing, pecking, fighting, scolding, and mobbing occur throughout the day, targeted at both intruders and colony members'.[2] It could be argued that they embody so many Australian characteristics that they, not the emu, should be the national bird. The changes made to the environment in the last 200 years have suited the noisy miners. Now *they* are considered a threat to the environment, and scientists and environmentalists debate how they might be culled.[3]

This stretches the judge's metaphor beyond his intent. But it is a compelling image of the way powerful groups behave, always ready for a fight, even when all that is at stake is holding their ground, stalling.

Small Brown Bird

Like the noisy miner's greige plumage, it is hard to get excited about a document that begins: it may, where 'expedient', allow other colonies and queenly possessions to join, pending 'the advice and consent of the Lords Spiritual and Temporal, and Commons'. The Commonwealth of Australia Constitution Act then reaches across time to give generations of royals the right to exercise authority in perpetuity. And in perpetuity it was cast, just like the thriving noisy miners.

Just how hard it was to change quickly became clear. Even in the decades immediately after Federation, when the debates were still fresh in the minds of voters, only two of sixteen amendments were approved. Over the twentieth century, 44 amendments to the Constitution were put to the people, but only eight passed. Change requires a majority of voters in a majority of states, making the support of all the major parties essential. Those amendments that found the approval of voters were generally technical—allowing concurrent elections and Territorians to vote in referendums, and adjusting the retirement age of judges—or designed to increase the power of the Commonwealth, especially over money. What should have been uncontroversial amendments proposed by the Hawke Labor government in the 1980s—to mandate four-year terms of parliament, recognise local government in the Constitution, enable the states and Commonwealth to voluntarily interchange authority, ensure fair elections, and extend the right to trial by jury, freedom of religion and fair terms for property acquisition by government—were overwhelmingly defeated. None had the enthusiastic support of the Coalition. All would have been timely and enduring improvements that would have enhanced the quality of civic life in the nation.

The last referendum, the one that 'broke the heart' of half the nation, was held in 1999. It followed the 1998 Constitutional Convention, the first held since 1977. A mix of appointed and elected delegates considered competing models for an Australian republic and a new constitutional preamble crafted by poet Les Murray and a less revered wordsmith, Prime Minister John Howard. Their preamble declared Australians valued 'excellence, as well as fairness, independence and mateship'. It was widely ridiculed.[4] The next iteration was not much better, and Les Murray distanced himself from it.

The minimalist republican model was supported by all the News Corp papers, with a nod to Rupert Murdoch's youthful republicanism. Still, a narrow majority voted against recreating Australia as a republic, removing the queen as head of state and replacing her with a president appointed by a two-thirds majority of both houses of parliament. An even larger majority disapproved of John Howard's cynical attempt at a preamble to symbolically, but not substantively, acknowledge First Nations people. Les Murray joked 'the Australian people had mercifully taken it out the back and shot it'.[5]

The noisy miners prevailed again. It was a victory for tactical politics that maintained the status quo and fostered apathy by encouraging people to think they had little real capacity for input. It cynically revived the disinterest that had accompanied the debates in the 1890s. People were prepared to be persuaded that the system was not broken and didn't need to be fixed—a bit like the adult child who doesn't see the point of leaving home. In 1999 a newspaper headline got it in a few words: the battlers had given the republic the kiss of death. At the time, the novelist David Malouf sensed the trailing coat of history had been embraced by those discomfited by the changes over the previous decades. '"No" was not a vote for the queen, or for direct election,' he observed, 'but a cry from the heart from those who do not feel like full participants in the new Australia.'[6]

PUBLIC DEBATE ABOUT change is now invariably cast in terms of impossibility, rather than about why evolution is essential for any living system to adapt and thrive. Had the 1980s amendments passed,

Small Brown Bird

Australia would now be a healthier organism. If a majority of people in a majority of states had voted for a republic, and ignored the cynical politics and lure of royal photos in glossy magazines that played them as fools, Australia would not look so obsequious on the world stage, still so mystifyingly beholden to the protection of Britain and the United States.

In the same period that Australians have resisted amending a document that few have read, hundreds of constitutions have been written around the world as nations formed, sloughing off the bonds of empire and reinventing themselves after war and catastrophe, and in response to changing norms. Most lasted on average only twelve years. This was not a mark of failure but a sign that they were adapting as their societies evolved.[7] South Africa is the best example. The former British Dominion, an epicentre of racialism for decades, became an independent nation in 1996, with a new constitution fit for purpose in a very different world. It took years of struggle, argument, debate and commitment, enabled by an electorate that took its future seriously and found leaders who were prepared to imagine and act to make it possible.

Thomas Jefferson, one of the fathers of the US Constitution, famously argued at the time that it should not bind another generation. This sentiment was echoed by the most 'dangerous' voice at the 1891 Constitutional Convention in Sydney that preceded the drafting on the *Lucinda*. Sir George Grey was the most experienced administrator and democratic leader at the meeting, having been governor of South Australia, the Cape Colony in South Africa, and New Zealand (twice), and as premier head of its government. At 78 he was also the oldest delegate, a man who had become more radical with age. His participation had a liberalising effect on the convention and brought what Vance Palmer called 'the breath of a more spacious world than the political one'. He argued for the principle of 'one vote one value' so that the landowners would not be advantaged; stressed that the

The Idea of Australia

Constitution should not be so rigid, lest it hamper future generations; and proposed that the governor-general should be elected, so the head of state would be chosen by Australians, not imposed from London. Rather than heed his experience, other delegates patronised him and dismissed him as naive. The earnest provincial nationalists were infuriated by his insistence on going back to first principles about what the founding framework might represent.[8]

This debate had been raging in the colonies for decades, often with the pugnacious John Dunmore Lang on stages and podiums winding up the audience. He was a larger-than-life character who played a crucial role in the settlement of Queensland, arranging for ships of English and German immigrants when the colony was still part of New South Wales. His name now fittingly adorns the football stadium in a noisy, sports-mad state. Lang had migrated from Scotland in the early 1820s, and became Sydney's first Presbyterian minister, actively involved in building churches and schools. The settlement was the ideal channel for his hyperactive nature, as the politician, editor and advocate for an independent Australasia pursued one vision after another. He was infuriated by English hypocrisy. Lang was alert to the similarities between the shortcomings of colonial administration and the divorce note of complaint and grievance included in the American Declaration of Independence. He was inspired by California's adoption of her own constitution in 1849. He raged that, 'like common beggars, British colonists must take what is offered them by their betters and be thankful'.[9]

Australians have been encouraged to think of their Constitution as one of the first in the world, but constitutions had become very fashionable over the preceding century, artefacts of increasingly literate societies. Two hundred and eight had been adopted by 1820, most with provisions for trial by jury, and for freedom of speech, assembly, religion, trade, movement and the press.[10] By the time the bill that was to become Australia's founding document made its way to the House of Commons, constitutions had been adopted in countries and states across North and South America, North Africa, Europe and Japan.

The men who later gathered on the *Lucinda* over Easter 1891, struggling with influenza and seasickness, crafted a document that was provincial, not republican. It was less a document of enlightened liberalism than one that, as Vance Palmer wrote decades later, 'reflected the timidity and conservatism of an elderly generation of politicians who were primarily concerned with the interests of their own provinces'.[11]

IT COULD HAVE been worse. Patrick Keane is not alone in seeing virtue in the small brown bird of a document that was finally authorised by Queen Victoria. He fears that if, like the US Constitution, it had been more ambitious it could have been intolerably racist. The ethos that had shaped the grand statements in the American document a century earlier had faltered. By the time the Australian drafters were at work, racism was a prevailing ethos, protecting the distribution of power on spurious biological arguments. At least racist legislation could eventually be revoked; changing the Constitution would have been even harder. Enshrining the White Australia policy in Australia's founding document, Justice Keane noted, would have been 'a fetter upon the existential choices of future generations'.[12]

Ever since the Americans had stopped receiving British convicts and triggered the establishment of the Sydney penal colony, 'the land of the free' has exercised considerable, if sometimes invisible, influence. It continues today as Australia is the superpower's most active deputy in the region. The eighteenth-century principles embodied in the statement that all men were created equal may have been honoured in the breach when the First Fleet arrived, as they were in the slave-owning republic, but the principles were still influential. Ever since people and ideas have travelled back and forth across the Pacific Ocean—with a lag. The Yankee influence sits deep in the national psyche. We say, with a shrug and sometimes a note of fear, *Where America goes we follow*, or *It'll happen here too*.

Now we watch American television at the same time as our cousins in the land of the free, and follow the daily cut and thrust of American politics as if it were our own. In the early days the lag was physical; it literally took months to cross the ocean by sail and weeks by steam. Although John Dunmore Lang was advocating the Californian Constitution in public meetings in Sydney less than a year after it had been adopted on the other side of the Pacific, distance was a tyrant. News of Abraham Lincoln's assassination on 14 April 1865 did not reach the colonies for two months, but when they heard of this death, Sydneysiders dressed in black and lined the streets to demonstrate their grieving outrage, and a memorial service was held in Melbourne in July.

These spontaneous events honoured the president who had done the most to enact the principle of equality and the abolition of slavery in the United States. This came three decades after Britain abolished her slave trade, though its corrupting legacy lingered. The convicts sent to Australia were not enslaved, but they were not employees either. The brutality with which many were treated, like the brutality of the treatment of First Nations people and kidnapped Melanesians, could trace a direct line to the treatment of enslaved people throughout the empire. The main opposition to ending convict transportation to the Australian colonies came from those who depended on the cheap labour the convicts provided. It was abolished in 1850, but convicts kept landing in sparsely settled Western Australia until 1868. Entrepreneurs lucratively filled the end-of-transportation labour shortage in the colonies with kidnapped Chinese workers; other landowners and traders 'blackbirded' Melanesians and brought them to Queensland as 'indentured labourers'. Then, as now, business always wanted cheaper labour, happy to source it from places where people had fewer options.

Some of the enormous compensation, a government debt it took two centuries to settle, paid to those who owned the plantations, and the people who worked them, and shares in the companies that operated the British slave trade became capital for building the colonies: funding universities, pastoral ventures, buildings, public works and private business.[13] Ships once used to transport slaves continued to be repurposed for the journey south, and some recalcitrant traders in human lives who refused to believe the era had ended were charged, convicted and despatched to the colonial jails.

Over time, the mentality that made it possible for people to treat other human beings as possessions was displaced; disavowal and denial were normalised on the way to future amnesia. Commonwealth legislation ended the blackbirding of Melanesians in 1901, but First Nations workers were treated as indentured state labour for decades. Many are still fighting for compensation for unpaid wages. Again places and names are a good guide to change that has arrived, to the slow victory of opposition voices. Still it was only in 2021 that the outrage that had been building for decades was formally acknowledged. The National Park that wraps around Eden on the far south coast of New South Wales and named Ben Boyd in 1971 for the man who decided to reinvent slavery in the South Pacific after it was abolished in Britain, was stripped of this name 50 years later. The street named for him in Sydney's affluent Neutral Bay remained. In the same year, councillors from Moreland, in Melbourne's northern suburbs, were 'shocked and saddened' to discover the name of the local government area was a memento of a Jamaican slave estate. The Mayor of Bundaberg, the home of rum made from the sugarcane harvested by blackbirded slaves for decades, formally apologised and signed a sister city agreement with Luganville, Vanuatu, where many of the 62,000 kidnapped people brought to Queensland had begun their reluctant journey.[14]

By the time the promise of 'One People, One Destiny' was being rendered into a practical document, there were new lessons to learn.

The slave trade had ended in Britain in 1834, and the compensation provided capital for colonial outposts. It took another three decades to cease in the United States in 1865 following the civil war that killed 600,000, but by the end of that century racial inequality and violence were still entrenched. By the time the Australian colonies were voting to decide whether to federate, the political mood in the United States was fractious. The constitutional amendments ensuring equality that were approved after the civil war sat uncomfortably alongside the brutal political reality. Reconstruction soon gave way to a new nativism; the first laws limiting immigration were passed and white supremacy was again on the rise.[15] Chinese people were being redesignated as a threat. 'Negroes' were considered the enduring problem, so mass deportation to Africa was actively debated in legislatures and the press. Yet Black colleges were established and people like the polymath W.E.B. Du Bois found a voice and power that still endures. In many states the formerly enslaved people and their descendants were considered unfit for political rights, and record numbers were lynched by marauding mobs in the American south.

This was the American expression of the racialist intellectual movement of the time. People were categorised, race was a proxy for caste. In Australia, First Nations people were categorised by proportionate assessments: full blood, half-caste, quadroon, octoroon. The ideal that all men were created equal was highly qualified. As British foreign secretary Lord Balfour said at the Paris Peace Conference after the First World War, 'all men of a particular nation were created equal, but a man from Central Africa is not equal to a European'.[16]

The experience of living in the colonies shaped Charles Pearson's thinking. He was the first Australian intellectual to decisively influence thinking around the world—the forefather of the brilliant Australians who have since shone on a world stage. With a perspective provided by distance, he challenged the unquestioned supremacy of European civilisations and predicted a postcolonial world. 'The day will come,' he wrote in his hugely influential 1893 treatise *National Life and Character: A Forecast*, 'when the black and yellow races will no longer be under European tutelage, but in control of their own destinies, welcomed as allies by the civilised world.'[17]

This scandalised his critics, who believed that civilisation was something that could be created and enjoyed only by Europeans who lived in temperate climes. Yet the fear of humiliation that he predicted struck a chord and was interpreted defensively in Australia and the United States. Racial purity became the key to national 'self-preservation', a protection against 'contamination' and 'difficulties within our borders', the first and defining goal of the new nation whose 'egalitarianism' derived from a democracy built on the 'unity of race'.

DECIDING WHO COULD come and the circumstances under which they could enter the country has been central to the management of the Australian utopia since 1901. It still is, as Australians, permanent residents and visa holders were again reminded during the COVID pandemic. As the British social and political theorist, philosopher and historian of ideas Isaiah Berlin noted, 'The idea of the perfect society is a very old dream, whether because of the ills of the present, which lead men to conceive what their world would be like without them [or because utopias] are social fantasies—simple exercises of the poetical imagination.'[18] Australia at the time of Federation was awash with bad poetry by mediocre poets. So, if conceiving the nation was an exercise of the poetical imagination, it was inevitably flawed.

The first step towards the creation of Australia's white utopia was brutal and relentless. It depended on the humiliation and elimination, by design and neglect, of the First Nations peoples, their population decimated by 1901. The men who debated the legislation for the new

Federation parliament preferred to avert their eyes from this unpalatable fact. They were as Raymond Evans has noted, 'surrounded by a genocidal cultural *Zeitgeist* . . . providing permission and excuse for unrestrained assault'.[19] Instead, they looked to the future and drafted laws to create their utopia. But they were not ignorant of what had gone before. Even in a world increasingly shaped by race, there was debate, opposition and some shame.

Months after Australia became legally, unequivocally, white with the passage of the Immigration Restriction Act in late 1901, the men in parliament debated whether to recognise the survivors who preceded them. The Senate leader and future High Court justice Richard O'Connor argued that just as the right to vote was being extended to women—in some states, they already had the franchise—the same principle should apply to First Nations people who, if they were registered, had the right to vote in four of the former colonies. 'It would be a monstrous thing, an unheard of piece of savagery,' he declared, 'to treat the Aboriginals, whose land we were occupying, in such a manner as to deprive them absolutely of any right to vote in their own country.'[20]

Not everyone agreed. The former Tasmanian premier Edward Braddon summed up the majority sentiment: 'We are told we have taken their country from them. But it seems a poor sort of justice to recompense those people for the loss of the country by giving them votes.'[21] This argument prevailed. White women and Māori were the only exceptions: 'no aboriginal native of Australia, Asia, Africa or the Islands of the Pacific' could enrol to vote. Suffrage was not to be universal in this utopia.

At the heart of the Australia embraced by those who met in Melbourne in the first federal parliament was the idea of a model society populated by men like them. Utopian dreams had played out in many ways in shaping the new nation. The lesson learned here from the American Civil War was not primarily one of equality but of the long tail of disruption slavery could bequeath. It was this fear, not humanitarianism, that animated the campaign to end the use of kidnapped Melanesians in Queensland agriculture and deport them.

Prime Minister Edmund Barton, in the middle of the second year of the new century, drew on his interpretation of Charles Pearson's writings to firmly ground the new nation in the 'instinct of self-preservation, quickened by experience'. It was optimism tempered by fear. What became known as the White Australia policy was necessary, he said, because 'we know that coloured and white labour cannot exist side by side; we are well aware that China can swamp us with a single year's surplus population'.

In 1923 Myra Willard, a recent graduate of the University of Sydney, paid Melbourne University Press to publish its first monograph—her book *The White Australia Policy to 1920*. She wrote with a contemporaneous eye. The debates in the colonies before Federation were still recent enough for the lines between them and the 1901 legislation to be thickly etched with detail. She grimly recounted the way each colony penalised and excluded 'coolies' and 'Celestials'. 'The desire to guard themselves effectively against the dangers of Asiatic immigration was one of the most powerful influences which drew the Colonies together,' she wrote, describing the desire for uniform measures as overwhelming but much misunderstood in the rest of the world. She quoted with approval the now infamous speech by Attorney-General Alfred Deakin—regarded as one of the more moderate supporters of the policy—in which he described the principle of white Australia as the universal 'motive power' that had dissolved colonial opposition to Federation. At heart, he declared, was 'the desire that we should be one people, and remain one people, without the admixture of other races'. The Australian utopia depended on a 'united race', one that could safely 'intermarry and associate without degradation on either side'.[22]

The Immigration Restriction Act was finally, and somewhat reluctantly, signed by Governor-General Lord Hopetoun just before

Christmas 1901. London was discomfited by the determination of the new nation to exclude, and proposed amendments to save face with Britain's imperial allies in Europe and Japan. A discretionary dictation test in a foreign language was the tricky solution. As Willard noted in 1923, 'Australia's policy does not as yet seem to be generally understood and sanctioned by world opinion.' It was, she maintained, despite the negative connotations, a positive policy that ensured Australia would be a productive global contributor of resources and supplies. The nascent nation was determined to shape her own utopia despite the 'mother country' chiding 'her daughter colonies'.[23]

By the time the national legislation passed, there were fewer people with Chinese heritage in Australia than there had been in the nineteenth century. It did not take long before Indian residents who had lived in Fremantle for years, as British subjects, were denied the right to return to Australia after visiting their birthland.[24] The Australian iteration of a caste system in the making was determined primarily, but not exclusively, by skin colour.[25] Only two members of parliament, free trade advocates, objected to the legislation that was to define the country for decades. They had plenty of arguments: freedom of movement, race prejudice, the achievements of Chinese civilisation and old-fashioned Christian principles. By 1903, two books opposing the policy had been published. Challenges 'came from conservatives and socialists, men and women, white and non-white', and increased over the following years.[26] Meanwhile, US President Teddy Roosevelt praised the Australian experiment, and the South Africans copied it. London was not convinced, and Fleet Street newspapers in 1908 described Australia for the first time, but not the last, as a 'hermit democracy'.[27]

A few years later the deportation of Pacific Islanders generated such damaging publicity that the policy was modified. British unease about the new nation's determination forced the law makers in Melbourne to modify the dictation test, from a European to a 'prescribed' language, to assuage Japanese complaints to London—*japonoise* was the fashion and Japan another recognised empire. A school friend of Alfred Deakin wrote to him in 1908 when he was prime minister, imploring him to revoke the law: 'I beg of you to kill the "White Australia policy" as it is now being administered. Depend upon it the curse of God will rest upon us as a country unless we withdraw from an enactment, that is inhuman, cruel and God dishonouring.'[28]

He was right. The nation would be unapologetically white for the next seven decades. When the White Australia policy was (partially) revoked in 1966, there was no public apology to those whose lives had been damaged, no public recalibration. Instead, time and the intergenerational impact of new arrivals changed the country for the better. The idea of Australia as a racist, inward-looking country has been hard to shake and has left a shadow, even as politicians happily boast about being the most successful multicultural nation in the world. Only the most nativist politicians now invoke race out loud, whispering and insinuating on social media those views that had once formed a screeching, unapologetic chorus.

———

A CENTURY AFTER Federation, the first formal event to celebrate its centenary was a service in Westminster Abbey, a grand dinner and boisterous party of famous, successful, provincial Australians—*look at me, look at me*—in London in 2000. The irony was striking. Commemorating a separation by returning to its source is unusual. It suggested that the mother country was still uppermost in the minds of those in power, that turning 100 did not mean you were really an independent adult. Former prime minister Paul Keating 'declined to join the great trek of present and former leaders to London', choosing to mark the moment at home.[29]

The contrast from just five years earlier could not have been greater. In June 1995, Paul Keating had received a highly unusual standing ovation in the House of Representatives when he presented the report of a bipartisan advisory committee that concluded it was time for the country to become an independent republic. Public support for the change had been growing, and by then polls indicated that nearly three-quarters of the population favoured the move. When it was put to the people, three years later, tactical politics prevailed, and Australia remained a constitutional monarchy. Gavin Souter was as perplexed by this reluctance as anyone. In a postscript to a new edition of his book *Lion & Kangaroo*, he likened it to a geometrist's trick question: 'If you travel half the distance from A to B, then half the remaining distance, and keep on halving it, when do you reach B? Answer: never.'[30]

The new nation had remained tied to the mother country symbolically and literally for decades—for defence, law, capital and a continuing supply of people. The legacy of the First World War had not emboldened demands for more independence; indeed, Australia was reluctant to take what was offered. The 1931 Statute of Westminster removed the right of the House of Commons to overrule legislation passed in the Dominions. Rather than welcoming this, the conservative opposition leader John Latham campaigned against it, and galvanised the states to join him. Britain regarded Australia as independent, but Australia did not agree.

After the fall of Singapore in 1942, and the realisation that Australia could no longer depend on Britain, the Labor government of John Curtin at last incorporated the statute into legislation. Australians became Australian citizens but remained British subjects and sang 'God Save the Queen' until 1984. The umbilical cord frayed after the Empire imploded, when Britain embraced Europe and 'abandoned' Australia in 1963. Yet it took until 1988 before the argument that Charles Kingston and Alfred Deakin had put to the Colonial Office—that the Privy Council should not be the final court of appeal—was realised in legislation passed in both countries. Still the umbilical cord did not rupture.

The coincidence of a nation being formed at the beginning of a new millennium was tantalising, and the prospect of repeating the symbolism by revising the Constitution at the beginning of the 21st century irresistible. While still prime minister, Paul Keating spoke at the 1996 Constitutional Convention in the NSW regional centre of Bathurst and set a challenge: revise the founding document. A group of local Bathurst organisations agreed. With the support of AMP, when it was still a non-profit mutual society, they invited 130 people to Bathurst in late November 1996 to revisit the convention that had occurred there 100 years earlier. It was an ambitious local initiative, chaired by the state's governor, Gordon Samuels, and attended by a wide range of people. This highly focused re-enactment was to become the first of four conventions that emulated the conventions in Adelaide, Sydney and Melbourne held in the lead-up to the vote for Federation in 1898.

The ambition of the first contemporary convention was striking. It was held eight months after John Howard's election as prime minister, but its agenda was clearly a product of the politics that had preceded the change of government. This was a convention steeped in understanding of the past and openness to the future, and the recommendations it developed should have set the agenda for transformative discussions. It was not a party-political exercise, but active deliberation by a group of engaged citizens imagining what their country might be like in the next century. They recommended that a revised Constitution include a preamble, defining a nation that was a republic, recognised Indigenous rights and prior occupation, defined citizenship, clarified rules around the houses of parliament and the role of the executive, and worked towards the incorporation of a bill of rights. The communiqué captured a moment of potential transformation, historically grounded and forward looking.

Over the next three years, under new conservative political leadership, the agenda of each of the three conventions that followed became narrower, more bureaucratic and process bound. The big picture shrank. Those who attended were the modern reincarnation of the founding fathers who had sneered at Sir George Grey for being too naive, too idealistic, too preoccupied with first principles. Whereas the November 1996 communiqué from Bathurst suggested a path to the next century, the final Commemorative Convention in Melbourne focused on process: treaties, foreign capital and micro-economic reform. Much like the founding document, this was not designed to inspire the collective imagination or challenge the status quo. It failed to set the course for the next century. Instead, apathy and the impossibility of change was conjured. Only 8000 people turned up for the re-enactment of Proclamation Day at Centennial Park in 2001; the most enduring reminders of the year were probably the 4000 Centenary of Federation numberplates.

EIGHTY-FIVE YEARS after the celebration in Sydney marked the birth of a nation, the tripwires built into the Constitution had served their purpose. Australia was legally independent, and the worst aspects of the legislation that did even more to form the character of the nation—ignoring the First Australians, diminishing women and excluding people of colour—had been jettisoned. Yet the rather prosaic document crafted to address the competing interests of a very different time, people and place had been put in aspic.

The inauspicious ten days of celebrations in 1901 may have been a good party—and Australians love a party, especially one paid for by the government—but it did not deliver a defining idea. The prevailing mood was sentimental and defensive. Debate about national identity still rumbles here in a way it does not in much longer settled nations, or those forged more recently from conflict. The challenge in 1901 was to create a nation in the absence of threat, without a deep cultural history, where the wars of settlement were not acknowledged. It needed to be both pragmatic and romantic. That this was done is remarkable, but more than a century later the challenge is still alive. Ambition remains the fault line. On one side are those who say we can do better; on the other are the noisy, smug, territorial boosters of 'the best country in the world'.

Although the Constitution lacks a rhetorical equivalent of similarly grand dimensions, no other nation has such a commanding physical presence. Australia is the only nation that is also a continent. Yet, as was clear during the pandemic, our public ambitions are generally defensive, protectionist and prosaic. Why this is the case is puzzling. Maybe because Australia is so vast, too physically diverse to be easily defined. Maybe because the land is so sparsely settled; cut into a jigsaw puzzle, each person would be at the centre of a piece a third of a hectare in area. Maybe because we have been so relatively rich for so long, complacency and entitlement rather than innovation and aspiration have become the norm. Maybe because the habit of not looking back has become so ingrained we are incapable of imagining what we might become, having little idea of how we got here. Maybe because we have for so long accommodated bullies, we have retreated to smaller dreams in manageable spaces. Maybe because so few of our political leaders have had courageous imaginations, they have to be led by others. Maybe because we are so ashamed of our racialist past, we forgot how to hold on to the good bits. Maybe being home to the oldest continuous culture is just too difficult to comprehend.

By channelling a small, noisy brown bird that thrives in the margins and is always ready for a fight, rather than the large, unique, flightless brown bird that insouciantly props up the coat of arms opposite another unique marsupial, the federation's founders sent a clear message. Australia was an independent nation with precisely defined rules about elections, trade, quarantine, border control and state's rights, but in practical terms it was a remote province that would remain defined by the motherland for decades, and by racialist thinking for even longer. Australia has changed significantly since that hot summer's day in 1901. It is telling that just weeks before the great and good gathered in London to celebrate the success of the nation that had been calved, hundreds of thousands of quiet Australians had marched across bridges to signal their support for reconciliation with First Nations people. By the end of the year a million had joined these walks, and taken the first steps to the constitutional reform essential for a grown-up country. Their activism was diminished by conservative fearmongers, but they hold the key. Australians need to be less fearful, and to embody those changes in a revised document that is fit for the times. It might feel like a miracle, but it has happened before, and can again.

14

The More Things Change . . .

WHEN JARED DIAMOND, the renowned evolutionary biologist, arrived at the University of Queensland in 2008, he felt he had landed somewhere else. This was not the Australia, or the Queensland, that he had come to know in countless visits since 1964. To his American eyes, the old Australia had been a replica of England, a land more British than Britain, a place frozen in time, and overwhelmingly white. It was sun-drenched and laid-back, a monochromatic, unambitious place where luck and atrocious food prevailed. Any suggestion of distinctiveness was confined to the exotic fauna and flora—black swans, egg-laying marsupials, kangaroos, koalas, waratahs, banksias, gums and orchids—not found elsewhere. To his eye there was perplexingly little visible acknowledgement of Asia or the region that abutted the continent, as Donald Horne pointed out in his famous book that same year. The descendants of the people who had lived there for thousands of generations were invisible.[1]

Britain had always been the source of most Australian immigrants, and this was in full swing when the erudite American first arrived in 1964, after completing his graduate degree at Cambridge University.

His studies there had exposed him, like hundreds of thousands of other international students, to a country where the devastation of the war was still tangible. Bombsites cratered cities and neighbourhoods, the air was thick with pollution and the empire had crumbled. The lure of a new life in a sunny land was irresistible for many and by 1964 more than a million 'ten-pound Poms' had made their way south on assisted passages, their regional accents giving Aussie Strine new tones. At the same time, Britain remained a lure for Australians who had been brought up on Enid Blyton, Agatha Christie, royal tours and war films. But in the early 1960s that journey became a little harder. Britain restricted immigration from Commonwealth countries—revealing its racial intent with vouchers for whites from the former Dominions—while actively seeking to join the European Economic Community.

Australia was collateral damage. Her political leaders were dismayed and literally begged for reconsideration, but to no avail. The sense of abandonment was profound for a monarchist country; as Prime Minister Robert Menzies declared, 'We in Australia, of course, are British, if I may say so, to the boot heels.' The front-page editorial in the first edition of *The Australian* in July 1964 summed it up: 'The burning desire of Mother to leave us to our own affairs was a choice. It was a salutary shock. For it helped to make us understand that now, as never before in our short history, we stand alone.'[2]

It took almost a decade before Europe allowed Britain to join its economic zone, but the UK remained the biggest source of immigrants to Australia, as it would for the rest of the century. In the meantime, Australia found new trading partners, engaged with Asia, recognised the First Australians, ended the White Australia policy and detached her currency from sterling. Pounds became dollars—not *royals*, as Menzies had wanted. Although the queen took pride of place on the first dun-brown one-dollar notes, Francis Greenway, a convict forger who reinvented himself as an architect, and designed some of Sydney's finest colonial buildings, commanded the more valuable bright-blue tenner. Its design a powerful, very '60s, up-yours; the convict stain became ironic.

Seventy-one-year-old Jared Diamond saw that, by 2008, the Australia his son was about to experience in a semester studying abroad was almost unrecognisable. It was much more diverse, richer, and more self-confident, outward looking and Asia focused. He imagined that he could have been at his home campus in Los Angeles. He and his son walked across the University of Queensland's park-like grounds in the elbow of the ancient Brisbane River, through the jacaranda-dotted Great Court, under the sandstone-faced colonnades and through the bustling crowds of students from every corner of the globe. As they strolled, he reflected on the ways Australia had changed, what it meant and where it might lead.

That was when he decided to include Australia in his next book.

Jared Diamond has made a global reputation from explaining the big underlying drivers of change. In bestselling book after bestselling book, he has probed, not without criticism, the factors that have helped some societies flourish while others collapsed. Geography and environment are the frames he uses. The analyst of social transformation has documented the impact of climate, geography, environment, human ambition, biology, disease, competition, war and traditional knowledge. He has searched for patterns that make sense of the history of very different societies. He has distilled this complexity into long books with pithy titles, like *Guns, Germs and Steel* and *Collapse*; reached readers in scores of languages; and won some of the most prestigious literary prizes in the world. His scope is astonishing, but his critics have seen someone who ignores human agency and sanitises the ravages of colonial violence.[3] Big histories demand big brains, and his friends declare that his is one of the most capacious.[4]

The ability to collapse 13,000 years of human history into 480 pages is not a widely shared skill. Ever since Charles Darwin published *On the Origin of Species* in 1859—significantly also the year of Queensland's birth—any proponent of a major broad-brush biological theory has attracted critics and fans. Colonial Queenslanders embraced social Darwinism to mask their attempts at genocide, while Christian fundamentalists were outraged by Charles Darwin's thesis. Likewise, not everyone agreed with Jared Diamond's analysis.

His fans were legion, but books and ferocious reviews challenged his approach, identifying errors and blind spots.[5] The core critique amplified a drumbeat that was getting louder in the new century—that Diamond's approach buttressed the structures of global capitalism, and his focus on geographic accidents excused colonial and imperial powers from culpability.

It took a decade before the germ of an idea that had formed as he walked across the St Lucia campus became a book. In *Upheaval*, Diamond focused on a handful of countries he knew well, and broadened his frame to look back at the process of change. Rather than taking the perspective of an evolutionary biologist, he adopted a psychological crisis-management framework to explore the way nations have changed. Like the issues that we all deal with, a crisis besetting a nation can take many forms and express itself in different ways: it can erupt rapidly and unexpectedly (like a pandemic), build slowly to a flashpoint (like a war), or slowly and persistently unfold (like inequality, a collapsing empire or climate change).

The argument he advanced in *Upheaval* is that, like people, nations need to recognise the crisis, accept the urgency to do something about it, seek support, understand their history, develop shared values and be prepared to engage in honest self-appraisal. And then make real changes.

This prescription is hard enough for individuals, but for nations replete with jostling interest groups, pockets of entrenched wealth and grinding poverty, ways of doing things that have rusted on over time, and millions of people with their own histories and expectations, it is even harder. The modern political system has made an art form of smoothing out differences, or accentuating them when needed, to ensure the status quo remains substantially unchallenged. Distraction, obfuscation and other smothering processes are key tools in making real change feel impossible. But once a consensus about the urgency of its need is realised, the real work begins—and it can happen surprisingly quickly. It remains to be seen if the complex and multifaceted new reality being shaped by climate change, a lingering pandemic, continuing globalisation, weakening democracies, changing geopolitics, increasing inequality and digitisation will provide such an inflection point.

In Australia's case, Diamond argued, the crisis that provoked the change he saw around him in 2008 was separation from Britain. This predicament, he said, had been slowly unfolding for decades, 'so slowly that many Australians wouldn't even consider there to have been a crisis at all'.[6] But he attributed the transformation he observed over decades of visiting Australia to imperial detachment rather than something Australia sought. The end of the White Australia policy and deeper engagement with Asia followed. But still Diamond felt a fundamental question had not yet been satisfactorily or conclusively answered: *Who are we?* In his view, the honest self-appraisal essential to the resolution of the bigger question had yet to be undertaken by political leaders. It had been left instead to the slow graft of culture.

BRISBANE IN 2008 was a place where the promise of change drifted tantalisingly in the humid air. Even the Brisbane River, which had coursed its way for hundreds of millions of years—rising and falling with the tides, zigging and zagging through valleys and hills—was cleaner and more inviting than it had been for a century. It was no longer industry's drain, carrying fat and offal, dye and chemicals to the sea. Nor was it rapaciously dredged for sand and gravel, a process banned a decade earlier. It was being restored to its ancient role as the city's watery heart, a beautiful site for recreation and reinvigoration.

For the first time in living memory, it was possible to envision the mangrove-fringed river covered with blue waterlilies and jumping with fish. To contemplate why traditional owners regarded the river they called Maiwar as the source of life.

When Diamond brought his son to Brisbane, the city was bursting with pride. The chip on its shoulder, formed when some of the worst convicts were sent north to suffer under one of the most brutal penal regimes—reinforced by the suppressed knowledge of the extraordinarily brutal violence of settlement, and later the wounded pride of being considered more country town than capital—was mending. Many remember World Expo in 1988 as the beginning of the end, when those who lived in the hilly, subtropical city could hold their heads high. Twenty years later when the Diamonds arrived, it was no longer the butt of jokes, known for its venal politicians and angry, undereducated rednecks, notorious for its brutal treatment of First Nations people and contempt for civil liberties. Since it had thrown off the shackles of the corrupt, authoritarian Bjelke-Petersen government in the late 1980s, it had re-emerged as a vibrant city with a more diverse economy, an energetic arts scene and competing, life-affirming subcultures. Its long-ignored First Nations history was slowly becoming a source of pride, not shame.

During the increasingly imperious years, when Joh Bjelke-Petersen and his confrères held court from the top floor of 100 George Street, Brisbane was a place shaped by rumour, police surveillance and threat. Good people found a way to block out the angry noise, to ignore the worst excesses and get on with their lives, go to the beach and bush, in one of the most beautiful environments in the world. Others found it harder to reconcile the tensions, the control and the surveillance; many of the city's best and brightest left the state for bigger opportunities and the freedom of anonymity.

It took years of critical reporting and political agitation before the special commission into corruption, chaired by Tony Fitzgerald QC,

The More Things Change . . .

found the scope to identify the links that kept the edifice afloat. Police, politicians, property developers and more were brought to court. When Wayne Goss was elected as the first Labor premier for 32 years, reforms reached into the parliament, public service, business and culture. The cosy ties that had benefited some were broken. With the rule of law buttressed by new accountability mechanisms, ethical issues were no longer swept under the carpet, and the social and cultural dimensions of public life assumed new importance. Brisbane's South Bank riverside cultural precinct became the envy of the other capitals and, after it opened in 2006, the Gallery of Modern Art became the most visited gallery in the nation. The doors to the state were opened; it no longer reeked of the Deep North, which the *British Medical Journal* had once declared was unfit for human habitation by civilised people. For years, until the pandemic snapped it shut, more than 1000 people a week crossed the border to start a new life in sunnier climes. Many had past connections with the state, while others dreamed of endless summer holidays or the prospect of working for themselves in a more affordable city. Brisbane had changed for the better, retaining much of its authentic charm, its hilly suburbs dotted with timber Queenslanders on stilts, but with a distinctive gloss of homegrown sophistication, the smell of biscuits baking and beer brewing no longer heavy on the city air.

During the Second World War, 85,000 American soldiers were based in the city when it became the headquarters of the US command in the Pacific. For the second time in a century the riverside settlement was occupied by foreigners. American soldiers increased the city's population by a third—Blacks on the south, whites on the north of the serpentine river. Tensions were high; locals feared that a much-rumoured 'Brisbane Line' meant they would be abandoned by politicians down south should the Japanese invade.

Ever since, Brisbane and the Gold Coast have been the most American of Australia's cities, places of freeways, motels, drive-ins, fast food, neon lights and evangelical churches. When the grand sandstone

The Idea of Australia

Treasury building became a casino in the 1990s, a new name—*Brisvegas*—entered the lingo. It was not surprising, then, that the new arrivals who flocked to sunny south-east Queensland from the dreary recession-hit southern states during that decade were called Mexicans, nor that Jared Diamond and his son sensed a similarity with Los Angeles, thanks in part to the proliferation of Asian restaurants. When I was a student in Brisbane, the choice had been steak, steak, steak or barramundi; otherwise, there was a curry house, two French restaurants, and a few Chinese and Italian cafes in the Valley where corrupt police met their benefactors. The diversification of Australian cuisine had begun when international chefs brought to Melbourne for the 1956 Olympics decided to stay, but it took decades to reach Brisbane.[7]

In 2008, for the first time in Australian history since Sir Samuel Griffith had played a leading role in drafting the Constitution, the epicentre of national politics shifted to Brisbane. The governor-general, prime minister, treasurer and three other cabinet members were products of the state's brutal winner-takes-all public domain. Each had been involved in various ways in response to decades of vigorously contested politics and social relations. Each had, as a result, had a sip of the sweetness of power. In *Hidden Queensland*, a special 2008 edition of *Griffith Review* that marked this transition, I wrote:

> Australia's new leaders ... found themselves, by accident, birth or fate, living north of the twenty-seventh parallel with front-row seats, and the occasional bit part, in a brawl without precedent in this country that began in the 1960s and raged until 1989 and finally petered out a decade later. They learnt about caution and courage, compromise and opportunism ...
>
> Exposure to outrageous abuses of power, petty vindictiveness, wilful ignorance and self-serving denial is likely to fuel outrage and a heightened sense of justice and, if the punishments are not too high, a determination to change things.[8]

The More Things Change . . .

The experience of being involved in political change is instructive. It teaches the importance of courage, and makes you alert to the opportunists. Quentin Bryce, who became the first female governor-general in September 2008, opened doors for women throughout her career, first as a barrister and law lecturer at the University of Queensland, and later as director of the Queensland Human Rights and Equal Opportunity Commission, as federal sex discrimination commissioner and then as governor of Queensland. Despite her achievements, media profiles invariably focused on her five children, and perplexed male journalists felt obliged to note that she was an immaculately groomed and coiffed feminist, with matching accessories and carefully chosen lipstick.

Kevin Rudd, the prime minister who appointed her to the vice-regal role, became the first national leader not to make an oath of allegiance to the queen when he was sworn in. Rudd had made his mark in Queensland's Goss Labor government as the premier's ruthless right-hand man. He had observed that media support was crucial for political success, and prosecuted an unrelenting campaign to become prime minister, carefully cultivating influential people. This culminated in 2007, after years of intense activity, with not only a comfortable eight-seat majority, but the scalp of the former prime minister. John Howard became only the second prime minister in Australian political history to lose his seat at a federal election. It was only the third time since 1949 that Australians had voted to oust a conservative government.

CHANGE WAS IN the air and most of the population was excited and ready for it. Even the Murdoch flagship newspaper supported change and urged a vote for Labor. Chris Mitchell, then editor-in-chief of *The Australian*, had grown close to Kevin Rudd when they both lived in Brisbane, two bright, ambitious, socially awkward men whose fathers had died when they were boys. It was a relationship that benefited them both. As Mitchell later wrote, 'I was able to publish lots of good stories, and he was able to increase his profile.' At the time, the combative editor was convinced that 'voters wanted change'. To his 'later regret', Mitchell would 'persuade Rupert [Murdoch] to let *The Australian* back Rudd in the final election editorial of the 2007 campaign'.[9] He was correct to sense that Australians were ready for political change. Many felt the nation had been marking time for a decade while enjoying the riches of booming trade with China—minerals and primary produce out, whitegoods and students in.

The new prime minister immediately sought to put salve on chafing issues that had festered for years. On 3 December 2007, the day he was sworn in as Australia's 26th prime minister, Kevin Rudd ratified the Kyoto Protocol, then flew to Bali to meet with other world leaders the following week. He committed Australia to reduced carbon emissions; climate change was, he declared, the 'greatest moral challenge of our age'. With the speed that would blight his leadership, he revoked the Pacific Solution—the former prime minister's method of punishing and discouraging refugees arriving by boat—and started to bring back those who had been despatched to tent cities in Nauru. And he began planning the official apology to the stolen generations.

Even in the most pragmatic and prosaic of lands, politics is often symbolic. In February 2008, for the first time, the federal parliament commenced with an ancient smoking ceremony and welcome to country led by elders of the Ngunnawal people. The next day, 13 February, the symbolism became manifest.

Thousands of people had travelled to Canberra from around the country to hear the new prime minister deliver a long-awaited apology to the stolen generations, whose lives had been profoundly damaged by the deliberate policies of removing First Nations children from their families for much of the century. On the day of the long-awaited

The More Things Change . . .

apology, a group of elders lingered before entering Parliament House through the ceremonial entrance to the prime minister's courtyard. 'We just didn't think this was for real, or that it would really happen,' one recalled. They were then seated in the distinguished visitors' gallery with all the living former prime ministers, except John Howard.[10]

In an emotional and heartfelt speech, one carefully designed for television grabs, Prime Minister Rudd undid one of his predecessor's most provocative failures. In May 1997, the national inquiry into the removal of First Nations children from their families had reported on 60 years of the state and territory governments sanctioning the brutal policy and its traumatic, genocidal consequences. It made 54 recommendations, most crucially for reparations, guarantees against repetition, an archive of stories and a national Sorry Day. The simplest urged all the Australian parliaments to acknowledge their role and apologise. This had proved impossible for Prime Minister Howard. Even two years later, after withering public condemnation, he was only able to express 'deep and sincere regret that Indigenous Australians suffered injustices'.[11] By 1999, every state parliament had apologised, and within two decades embarking on truth-telling commissions and beginning to prepare treaties, finding a way to recognise the First Nations in their constitutions.

Prime Minister Howard persistently and repeatedly refused to do the same. He quibbled about the history, rejected the suggestion that destroying families and connection with culture amounted to genocide, and declared that one generation could not accept responsibility for the acts of another. His government argued that determining who was eligible for reparations, and how much, was virtually impossible. Something the Australian people would not countenance. His arguments would not have been out of place in the Federation parliament, when the prospect of enfranchisement for First Nations people was dismissed as a 'poor sort of justice'.[12] His arguments struck a chord with the angry people who felt they had been missing out—Pauline

Hanson had given them the freedom to again shout their darkest thoughts—but not with the hundreds of thousands who signed 'sorry books' and marched in support of reconciliation.

A cynic might say an apology was an easy win for a new leader. A sentimental moment replete with humble and humane words perfectly pitched for television—words that scratched the surface of what was needed, as the inequities in health, education, life expectancy, income and incarceration rates left huge gaps. There was no compensation, and thousands of First Nations children were still being taken from their families and put into state care. Shortly after the apology a weeping ten-year-old Vanessa Turnbull-Roberts was taken from her father's La Perouse home by a New South Wales Department of Community Services officer late one night, told to 'hug your dad one last time' and sent to the first of ten foster homes. Her parents appealed for her return. Twelve years later, when she was studying law and social work and dreaming of setting up a practice to protect children, more than 21,000 First Nations children—one in sixteen, ten times more than their non-Indigenous peers—were in the care of state welfare departments that still thought they knew best.[13] It took 24 years after the *Bringing Them Home* report for a prime minister to at last agree to pay reparations to still-living survivors. Scott Morrison struck a figure of $75,000—roughly the median salary for one year. The bureaucracy showed some signs of beginning to hear what First Nations community leaders were actually saying about the need for self-determination and family support, not removal and state care.

Prime Minister Rudd's speech that hot February afternoon was met with a tearful standing ovation. The elders in the gallery were optimistic that this might mark the beginning of a new era. All around the country, work stopped as people gathered in front of televisions in community halls, shopping centres and schools to absorb a transformative national moment. A new generation signalled it was prepared to own its country's past, even as the wheels of bureaucracy ground slowly and children were still being taken from their families in the name of protection.

The significance of these words being spoken by a politician from Queensland could not be underestimated. Ever since its formation as a separate colony in 1859, Queensland had been considered somehow different: hotter, rougher, more brutal, less educated, an embodiment of the Darwinian thesis of survival of the fittest. Or maybe, as the historian Henry Reynolds has argued, it was more authentically Australian—less a product of the Colonial Office and more its own creation. A vast land of promise where men could plunder, and the humidity guaranteed that women glowed. A polity that was conjured into being in the grand sandstone Customs House, neoclassical Government House, French Renaissance Revival Parliament House and imposing Treasury buildings on the riverbanks. It lured settlers by offering cheap land. They averted their eyes as tens of thousands of First Nations people were killed, their bodies burned, heads removed. Others turned into almost free labour, paid with opium dust, and rounded up and sent to distant missions in the name of protection. Decades later, the unspoken legacy of the violence of settlement hung heavily in air charged with fear, revenge, shame, bravado and pride.

The eighth year of the new century was to be a time for new ideas, for reconciling the past, and imagining and making a future rather than just letting it happen. Two weeks before his historic apology on behalf of the Australian people, Kevin Rudd had announced that a national summit would be held that April. Tens of thousands of people applied to attend, and over the following months meetings were held all over the country to formulate agendas and consider alternatives. As Jared Diamond had sensed as he wandered around his son's university campus, it was a time of change.

THREE DECADES BEFORE Jared Diamond's son enrolled at the University of Queensland, the student club at St Leo's, the Catholic boys' college at the university, decided to sponsor an annual lecture by a 'notable Australian'. One of the enduring legacies of the sectarianism that had put its stamp on Queensland was that lawyers and judges were most likely to be Catholic, and many spent their student days at St Leo's. The Catholic school system had long been the most extensive in a state that until the 1960s had only a handful of state high schools, along with the lowest rates of educational attainment on the mainland.

In 1979, the young men at St Leo's invited Professor Manning Clark to deliver the inaugural address. Clark had just been appointed Australian of the Year, the first and only historian to have received the honour; the year before, the fourth volume of his monumental *History of Australia* had been published, with the fifth due imminently. So, when Manning Clark was asked to explore 'the development of Australian culture', he took the opportunity to prosecute one of his enduring preoccupations: the quest for an Australian identity.[14]

The imposing professor delivered a speech with the passion and flair of a secular preacher. He wondered whether the inferiority complex, typical of colonial people, meant Australians had trouble identifying what they were and what they might become. The successes and failures of the previous decade weighed heavily. The momentum for change had never been greater, a spirit the former prime minister, Gough Whitlam, had captured with his successful 'It's Time' campaign in 1972. Over the following three years, no area of life had been untouched by Whitlam's reforms—business, education, defence, law, social welfare, arts, international relations. But when the Whitlam government was dismissed, the momentum was lost and a new libertarian, neoliberal orthodoxy began its ascendancy, an ideology that put markets, not nations, at the centre. 'We behave like a tango dancer,' Manning Clark told the young men in his audience. 'We rather boldly make one long glide forward and then slide two steps backwards.'[15]

The More Things Change . . .

When the Diamond *père et fils* arrived in 2008, it was a year that seemed to mark the beginning of what Clark had described as a glide forward, but the two sliding steps back were not far off. The sense of change that dangled so palpably in Brisbane that year was soon overwhelmed. The combination of deregulation, fraud and greed wreaked havoc on the global financial system, banks collapsed, the share market tumbled, jobs were lost. The global financial crisis was an undeniable crisis, one that tested the capacity of governments around the world. It soaked up almost all the energy in Canberra as the newly elected politicians, their advisers and public servants worked around the clock to ensure that the Australian economy and livelihoods would not be devastated.

The crisis shifted the focus from domestic reform and the 'greatest moral challenge of our age' to a disaster that was urgent and undeniable. This was a Labor government that was not inclined to follow the path towards austerity that was shattering European economies; Labor politicians had the lessons of conservative austerity during the Great Depression etched into their memory banks. Fortunately, the rapidly growing Chinese economy still needed iron ore and coal, but nonetheless the loss of jobs and security was tangible. Coalition opponents and the Murdoch press were scathing about the initiatives and magnified each misstep during a chaotic time.

Within two years, political ambition and personal flaws had destabilised and removed the prime minister. Two steps back: the vicious reality of party politics with the help of an unapologetically hostile press cemented the status quo, even as it installed the first female prime minister, who delivered a significant legislative agenda. As much as Australians enjoy the products of reform and celebrate leaders who are prepared to embrace change after they leave office, at the time those leaders are treated brutally, with incendiary claims, orchestrated campaigns and bruising personal attacks.

A spirit of cooperative and critical engagement is hard to come by. Rather than an active and responsive public debate using the new tools of deliberative engagement—community groups—the public space is still filled with those who prefer to stall, block, harangue and dismiss. The aim seems to be to undermine human instincts that are deeply rooted in fairness, compassion and integrity, to muddy, distract and foster fear. The game is most important, and standing still a perverse victory.

The process by which same-sex marriage became law is a telling example. Prime Minister John Howard explicitly changed legislation to prevent states and territories from legalising these unions, and a debate that belittled and dismissed the idea raged in some circles. But opinion polls had made it clear for years that most Australians would welcome the change. It could have been enacted by a simple vote in federal parliament, but instead the Coalition government opted for the brutal charade of a national plebiscite. This put tens of thousands of people under intense pressure, before revealing the same answer the surveys, and most members of parliament, had been predicting for years.

The capacity for an adult conversation about change has been diminished in a polarised public sphere. Instead, once-divisive issues are addressed by bureaucratic sleight of hand, such as changing one word in the national anthem—'we are young and free' to 'we are *one* and free'—or announcing reparations 24 years after a national inquiry has recommended them. Immediate problems are solved; big underlying issues are left unresolved.

I READ UPHEAVAL by chance. It was in a box of books a neighbour left on our suburban footpath with a big HELP YOURSELF sign. Shoshana Zuboff's *The Age of Surveillance Capitalism*, the most important book I had read in 2019, was on the top of the pile, so I thought it was worth seeing what else was on offer. The subtitle of *Upheaval* caught my eye: *How Nations Cope with Crisis and Change*. For years my friends and

The More Things Change...

I had discussed what it would take for Australia to boldly change, to acknowledge the sins of the past and plot a new way forward. We talked about how it might be possible to draw on our history rather than ignoring it, and to use it as a tool for imagining the future; to use the capital of a society still marked by strong institutions, relatively high levels of trust and less inequality than many other nations; to be ambitious, even slightly better than average, again.

We wondered if there were lessons for us in countries that had been transformed. How had Ireland managed to throw off the socially constraining legacy of the Catholic Church, its most powerful institution, to legalise abortion and gay marriage and remake itself? How had Germany turned its genocidal past, once a shameful history lesson, into a tool for an open and inquiring society that acknowledged the past and moved on? How had South Korea in a few decades grown from a divided and impoverished nation decimated by war to a thriving democracy and home to world-leading technology? And how had Taiwan embraced democracy and innovation under a fiercely watchful Chinese eye? What enabled New Zealand to revive the long-forgotten Treaty of Waitangi and integrate Māori language and traditions meaningfully into her contemporary life? All seemed to hold lessons and clues. Was it in response to crisis, the result of leadership, or the slow drip of debate and cultural and social expectations? There was one factor that seemed common: in country after country, there was a realisation that simply ignoring the past would not make it go away. Lessons and actions needed to be drawn from both the dark and the light.

Even though Jared Diamond chose countries that he thought he knew well for his book, Australia did not quite fit his framework. Most had endured wars and been forced by catastrophic loss to recalibrate. Australia accommodated the sort of change that happened when no one was paying attention or really wanted to talk about what it meant. There had been inquiries into heinous practices, but recommendations often languished. A cool-eyed assessment of real strengths and weaknesses that drew on international comparison and adapted the best international models, rather than ideas limited by the narrow agendas of powerful allies, seemed impossible. 'Myths help us live with contradictions, whereas histories help us analyse persistent contradictions so that we might avoid being lulled by the myths that we use to console and enable ourselves,' Ross Gibson writes in his haunting *Seven Versions of an Australian Badland*. This is why, he adds, 'we desire our myths and need our histories'.[16] A place where there is little appetite for facing the past is ill-equipped to create a bold future.

'Epic changes,' as the British historian Linda Colley has noted, 'are very occasionally rapid, but sometimes stretch over centuries. Most commonly, though, major changes become apparent within the canonical span of a human lifetime: three score years and ten.'[17] Her timeline applies to the changes Australia had made since Federation: from a nation defined by race to one that embraced cultural diversity; from one that expected its first peoples to die out to one where traditional welcome to country ceremonies precede every important event; from one where women could not vote to one where they were governors, premiers and prime ministers; from one tied to Europe to one that embraced Asia.

As I read *Upheaval*'s seventh chapter, 'Australia: Who Are We?', I could see why Jared Diamond thought the country had changed. But few Australians today would be able to identify the catalytic end-of-empire decisions that he—and many historians—consider central. For them it is the changing peacetime relationship with a foreign power, rather than decisions made at home, that changed the country.

The continuing relationship with Britain niggled at the heart of Diamond's analysis. To him, the decision to not become a republic was incomprehensible. He was perplexed about why Australia still had a British head of state and a flag with a Union Jack. Surely it would only be a matter of time, he speculated, before there was another—successful—referendum. Then the queen would be replaced as head of state, her image finally removed from the currency, and a new flag would fly. After all, Australians were taking a front seat in London, influencing politics, culture, academia and global business as their billions of dollars in superannuation funds sought an investment home. Yet within a couple of years of Jared Diamond's visit, for the first time since the 1920s, Australia elected two British-born prime ministers: Tony Abbott and Julia Gillard. Abbott reintroduced imperial honours, advising Queen Elizabeth II to create a handful of sirs and dames, until the public outrage killed this gesture of colonial genuflection. After they left office, they both took positions in London: Abbott as adviser on British trade, and Gillard joining Alexander Downer—the Anglophile former foreign minister and high commissioner—as a professor at King's College London, just across the Strand from Australia House.

When Scott Morrison turned up at 10 Downing Street in June 2021 for a final round of negotiations with the British prime minister over a free trade agreement, he brought a packet of Tim Tams, the chocolate-coated biscuit that had become an Australian staple, though its brand is owned by a US corporation. Boris Johnson traded a packet of Penguins, the British equivalent, owned by an international Turkish conglomerate. The age of empire had given way to the age of corporate capital. Morrison, who had reminded himself of his First Fleet origins earlier on the trip, signed the new agreement with Britain, by then just Australia's tenth-largest trading partner. Dan Tehan, his trade minister whose farming family had witnessed the dislocation caused by Britain opting for Europe six decades earlier, declared as he finalised the agreement that the deal 'rights a historic wrong'.[18] Few shared his view. If it was an historic wrong it was one that forced the nation to thrive. As Jared Diamond feared, it seemed there were still powerful forces who wanted to turn back the hands of time so Australia might again snuggle up to a once great and powerful 'mother' who would tell us who we are.

15

Personal Becomes Political

DURING MY LIFE Australia has changed a lot, but detachment from Britain rarely loomed large as the reason. By the time I started university in 1974, the global power of significance that was driving change came dressed in stars and stripes. It was America that Australia had turned to and depended on during the Second World War; it was America that had taken 60,000 Australians into the bitterly divisive Vietnam War, killing 521 and injuring 3000; it was America that had built a secret global surveillance base near Alice Springs; and it was America that most profoundly influenced popular culture, business and politics. But for some the tie to Britain—specifically England— was of almost spiritual importance.

When the referendum designed to begin the process of turning Australia into a republic failed to win the support of a majority of people in a majority of states in 1999, it seemed that the tie would never break; it would just become more attenuated and maybe less relevant. Even the most diehard monarchists suggested the relationship with Britain was largely symbolic, that Queen Elizabeth II operated only on the advice of the prime minister and only to appoint or dismiss the governor-general. But when Jenny Hocking eventually won access to the correspondence between Buckingham Palace and Government House that preceded the dismissal of Gough Whitlam's Labor government, it was a reminder that the increasingly frequent royal visits since 1975 were not just an entertainment. The influence was real; the queen remained the ultimate head of state.

The letters partly answered the question of who the needy John Kerr had turned to for advice, as everyone who knew him agreed he was unlikely to have acted alone. As former prime minister Malcolm Turnbull, who had led the republican referendum campaign, wrote in his foreword to *The Palace Letters*: 'This correspondence shows the governor-general as an anxious country manager reporting back to head office, seeking not just approbation for, but guidance on, his conduct in a worsening political crisis . . . it is a reminder of how absurd it is that an Australian governor-general reports to Buckingham Palace in a manner not much different from that of a colonial governor in the century before last.'[1]

Before this correspondence revealed the extent of the royal fingerprints on the dismissal of Prime Minister Whitlam, many had suspected that the Americans were somehow involved. The 1970s was the apotheosis of interventions driven by US intelligence, in Africa, Central America, Southeast Asia and Chile, before the agencies were subject to tighter controls by Congress. US disquiet with the Whitlam government was well documented, so those distressed by what they considered a coup focused their angry gaze on the leader of the free world. Complicated conspiracy theories of CIA duplicity were earnestly discussed.

For most, American popular culture prevailed. American politics, refracted through a local lens, drew thousands of protesters to the streets, concerned about how the global superpower exercised its might. This anxiety even reached the backblocks of rural Victoria. I remember a newspaper cartoon my mother pinned up in our country kitchen—Australia as a giant American aircraft carrier usefully located in the South Pacific—and the earnest discussions over card games in our isolated community about whether Australia was in danger of becoming America's 51st state.

We imbibed American television shows, dreaming of genies, talking horses, flying cars and the all-knowing FBI. We ate hamburgers on special occasions. We watched an American president, a presidential candidate and Black leaders die on television. We wished for blue jeans, not dresses homemade from Butterick patterns. It was America that showed how citizen movements could transform civil rights and race relations, oppose the military–industrial complex and elevate women. It was America that showed how journalism and access to information could make politics and those in public office more accountable. New York, not London, was the city I dreamed of going to when I grew up.

Britain was the past, conjured by black-and-white Ealing Studios war movies, rationing and absurd television comedy. My grandmother was awarded an Order of the British Empire for her community service and went to London to receive the honour from a queen who was not much older than her daughter. She returned with excited tales, but it sounded a bit stuffy to me, even though I had breathed in Enid Blyton tales of adventures and afternoon tea. Britain meant little more than the arcane images of fox-hunting men in red jackets, with horses and hounds, on my grandmother's best dinner-table placemats.

Britain was not, to my mind, our mother country, not that it was a subject much discussed. All my forebears started their journeys to Australia in Germanic middle Europe. At primary school in Gilgandra, I fleetingly wished that my surname were more Anglo, maybe Armstrong or Buchanan. In our Lutheran bubble in western Victoria, that soon became irrelevant. When I was nicknamed Sarge at high school—after Sergeant Schultz, the fat guard in *Hogan's Heroes* who *Saw nothing, knew nothing, heard nothing, did not even get up this morning*—I probably wished for a more anonymous, white-bread surname. But as a tall, skinny girl with an opinion on everything, I got the joke.

To my mind, Jared Diamond's description of a changed country missed the mark, lacked nuance and found the wrong source of crisis to drive change. Britain was the superpower of the past whose relevance had just withered. Trade and politics were important but national identity was cultural. The new nationalism that flowered as I was growing up was driven initially, and in large measure, by the same ambition that fuelled decolonisation debates around the world. It then took its own directions; decolonisation was less violent in Australia than in India, Malaysia or Rhodesia. When 'Mother' decided to 'leave us to our own affairs'—what *The Australian* described in its first editorial in 1964 as the 'salutary shock'—it simply forced long overdue decisions.

Southeast Asia and Japan became a new focus, rich with opportunities for trade, new perspectives and possibilities. My grandparents returned from trips to India, Indonesia, Singapore and Thailand with suitcases full of saris, batik, cheongsams, heavy silks, and beautiful wooden carved statues that today would be confiscated by diligent Border Force officials. These gifts were a tangible window on a more interesting world.

At high school in Hamilton, Victoria, in the year we watched Neil Armstrong land on the moon, a dozen of us began voluntary lunchtime lessons in Bahasa Indonesian. None of us could really imagine the holidays we would later enjoy on the exquisite and culturally rich islands. Even for us country kids, understanding the region seemed important—even then, even in that staid, self-satisfied, and isolated community. A different world was opening, but it was still charged with danger. Three years before, Indonesia had erupted in a proxy Cold War struggle, and the murderous battle between socialist (anti-American) and capitalist nationalists had left half a million people dead. The Vietnam War was already a bloody backdrop to our adolescence. It was clear that politics could put lives at risk.

The Idea of Australia

By the time we squeezed into the family car in 1971 and for the last time took the long drive north to Queensland, a sense of possibility and change was bubbling. Ours was a journey as old as the nation. It was the timeless dream of people drawn back to the place of their childhood, hoping to replicate the best of their memories and provide better opportunities for their kids.

On the Queen's birthday long weekend, I was dropped off at St Peters Lutheran College, not far from the heavily dredged river in Indooroopilly. I was to finish my last years of school as a weekly boarder at its leafy campus. It couldn't have been more different to Hamilton High. There were students from all over the state, sons and daughters of farmers and pastors, Aboriginal kids from Lutheran missions and the then-Australian colony of Papua New Guinea. My first night in Ross Roy, the former colonial mansion that housed the girls' dorm, made me wonder whether we had made the right decision. Overnight in June, without any heating, Brisbane was colder than the windswept Western District. The dorm's metal beds stood in two smart lines, their sheets tucked in with perfect hospital corners. It was as inviting as a recovery ward in a war movie.

A month later the city erupted. The all-white South African rugby team, the Springboks, was on a national tour, and Brisbane was the game's heartland in Australia. There had been protests in other cities, but the Brisbane demonstration was of a different order. Four hundred anti-apartheid activists, students, First Nations leaders and unionists battled five hundred out-of-town police who had removed their badges and been instructed to not hold back. It was a violent encounter, sanctioned by the government, that hospitalised many and radicalised a generation. At school we watched the angry rugby supporters castigating the protesters and discussed the underlying issues in class. One young English teacher, Roslyn Atkinson, had arrived at school wearing a Stop the Tours badge. She soon realised this was unwise. The next day the pastor's homily in chapel advised us that we must always obey the

Personal Becomes Political

government. Roslyn Atkinson tucked the protest badge inside her jacket and wondered about another career, maybe on the stage or in the law.

As our clandestine classroom discussions revealed, ideas could have lives of their own. Cultural change snuck through the crevices of a society that was slowly opening up. Revolutions were televised. The personal became political. In this environment, geopolitics and anti-authoritarian ideology formed the potent mix. It was there in the songs and books, the movies and art. We absorbed this while we were singing, dancing, reading, watching and protesting. Lives changed, opportunities emerged, and a different way to live and see the world became possible.

I FIRST HEARD Leonard Cohen during my orientation week at the University of Queensland. This was a couple of decades before he wrote 'Anthem', his hauntingly beautiful ode that describes how cracks and imperfection allow in the light that forces change. In 1974, even in the creepingly authoritarian state, cracks were opening; the air was thick with possibility. As I sat in the kitchen of a run-down student share house, the earnestness of Leonard Cohen's mournful, meditative declarations of love won and lost were a contrast to the loud, angry and impassioned music that was the more common rallying cry for a protesting generation. Cohen's haunting lyrics were more icepick than sledgehammer, but also subversive. It is almost impossible to remember now, when music is an inescapable, ever-present commodity, the threat it once embodied. Songs could be, and were, routinely banned in Queensland. Authoritarian politicians and conservative public figures railed against the devil's work. The generation gap became a gulf.

Culture is the real barometer of change. Politics often follows. Music, novels, plays, artworks, dance, film and television explore and test what is possible, find what strikes a chord. The sweep of visual, literary and performing arts flags and prefigures transformations. Pollsters play a constant game of catch-up with the prescient imaginings of creative artists and their uncanny ability to give voice to barely formed thoughts. Politicians are more inclined to put their fingers in the dyke than float on the rising sea. Legislation often lags social movements, as the same-sex marriage plebiscite so convincingly demonstrated decades later.

By the time I listened to Leonard Cohen sing about the 'half-crazy' Suzanne and his lost Marianne, women's lib had captivated the imagination and aspirations of my generation. Our mothers had been quietly nurturing the seed since we were little girls. The media scoffed and mocked those seeking equal treatment, branding us as dangerous bra-burning shrews. Casual, incidental sexism and sexual harassment were the corrosively demeaning norm; women were 'chicks' and 'birds'. Something as simple as choosing to drop the letters between the M and S of a title to obscure marital status could suck the oxygen out of a room. The fierce women slanderously depicted with 'hairy legs and wardrobes full of overalls', who met for consciousness raising, created space for everyone else—slowly, slowly—to assert themselves with more confidence.

Coming of age in this ferment gave a new meaning to growing up. Our lives would not simply replicate those of our mothers and grandmothers. Nothing was a given. We would have to fight, create and navigate a different social milieu. It was tricky terrain, even for the most privileged young women, themselves a minority of the small proportion of the population who made it to university. For many of those with power, we presented a dangerously incomprehensible challenge. Every issue became a struggle in a bigger battle, an opportunity to belittle and undermine. *What is it with girls like you? What was wrong with the old ways? Didn't we look after you?*

Personal Becomes Political

SEXUAL POLITICS IS difficult terrain for young people to navigate. Desire, threat and insecurity are a powerful combination in the most benign circumstances, even before teenagers were drenched in social media harassment and ubiquitous porn. Outside the privileged cloister where we tested the limits, my generation of assertive young women were surprised to realise we represented a visceral threat to those men who chose to remain unmoved by the new politics that took the personal seriously.

The chilling reality of this confronted me not long after I arrived in Cairns in 1975, on the first leg of my journey to interview the bush poets scribbling away in Far North Queensland. As I stood waiting for my brand-new suitcase to appear on the baggage trolley towed from the plane, I fell into easy banter with a cowboy from central casting. He didn't offer to carry my luggage but followed me to the hire-car desk. His insistent attention put me on alert. I brushed him off, then made my way to the car park and onto the highway to town. Phew.

The threat had felt real. I had absorbed the reports of the Bruce Highway horror stretch a little further south. Six unsolved murders in six years, and another two just months earlier. I locked all the doors of the little Mazda, wound the windows up tight, and kept an eye on the rear-vision mirror until I pulled into the motel, checked into my room and drew the curtains. Then the cowboy's harassment really started. First a phone call, then a knock on the door, angry pacing outside the room, another call and banging on the window. I rang reception to complain and was told to get over it. No one was sent up the stairs to tell him to get lost or that they would call the police.

The message was clear: women were fair game. It seemed like hours before he gave up. I was exhausted. In the morning, I gobbled the cardboard cereal and white toast pushed through the breakfast hatch, drank the pot of Robur tea, paid the bill and dashed to the car park. Then I locked myself in the car. I was a bundle of nervous energy. It scarcely dissipated on the hour-long journey through the stifling heat of the pre–wet season, down the palm-fringed tropical coast to Innisfail. I was too afraid to stop, though I desperately wanted to have a swim, even in crocodile- and stinger-infested waters. I worried that if I did, the angry cowboy—or some of his mates—might reappear. I had read enough newspaper reports to know that young women disappeared on remote country roads.

There was nothing exceptional about my experience. Everyone I knew had a similar story, or worse. The legacy of a violent frontier could not be wished away and did not just evaporate. It echoed through the generations, finding new targets. Modern Queensland was still pumped up with the testosterone-fuelled aggression that had marked its founding.

After I returned from my road trip, a friend told me she had seen brutal violence against women in some towns in Far North Queensland—assaults that were organised and condoned, the perpetrators beyond the reach of the law. It was, we would now say, structural. Not just a few bad eggs, but a system that treated young women as chattels. In her town, not far from my uncomfortable experience, gangs of men and boys routinely identified a female target at a public event and enticed her outside. They called the gang rape a 'train' and convinced themselves, and the police, that the woman was 'asking for it'. The traumatised victims were rarely believed, the legal system seemingly designed to humiliate, shame and silence them.[2]

When we helped journalists from the *National Times* with the research they needed to travel to the town and report what was going on, an ancient mechanism of control in new garb was fully revealed. Within no time at all, similar stories bubbled up out of other country towns. After the horror of these organised attacks was reported, the campaign to ensure that the victims of sexual assault were treated with respect in Queensland gained new momentum. One of the only two women in the state parliament made it an issue. Rosemary Kyburz was a Liberal MP who would do all she could to ensure these assaults did not go unpunished. Within a couple of years, the law changed a little. Inquiries, reports, submissions and debates followed, and changes continued to be made for decades as the legacy of embedded misogyny revealed itself over and over. Sexual abuse could no longer be dismissed with the mocking laugh that had once accompanied it.

Nevertheless, nearly 50 years on, the law still works against female victims. The suppressed anger that many women carry burst to the surface of public life when another generation of young women, led by Grace Tame, Brittany Higgins and Chanel Contos, declared *Enough is enough*. A few weeks after International Women's Day 2021, in cities and towns around Australia, women and men, many who hadn't marched for decades, took to the streets in response to the revelations of sexual abuse in Parliament House. The echo of past protests reverberated around the nation. It had not taken long for the 800,000 women who had been added to the electoral roll in 1903 to become a wellspring of conservative votes for decades, but the polls suggested they would be no longer.[3]

THE ANIMATING IDEA of the women's movement—that equality was a right, not a gift or a political deal—transformed interpersonal relations, and crept into workplaces and schools. Language changed, expectations were recalibrated, and before long behaviour followed. But it did not happen overnight and did not happen without a struggle. The ban on married women working in the public service had been lifted only two years before I started high school.[4] At that time, women were still the exception in the professions, paid one-third less than men and denied access to superannuation. In 1973, a few million dollars was made available by the federal government for the first time to support childcare and some support for women's refuges followed. It was tiny by today's standards but it transformed lives.

Four years later, the editor of the *Courier-Mail* drew my first serious job interview to a halt: *What it is with you girls, why do you all want to be journalists, what's wrong with teaching and nursing?* I didn't bother to turn up for the second interview after the editor of the *Gold Coast Bulletin*, which still featured women in bikinis on the front page, said, *If you're a pretty girl, come on down; if not, don't bother.* Soon the patter became more sophisticated. As Max Walsh, the editor at the *Australian Financial Review*, had told me at my job interview—in a pub—women would work twice as hard for half the money as men, and he thought they'd be more able to extract secrets from businessmen than male journalists. A few years later, in the early 1980s, when I was armed with a clipping-book full of front-page stories and some experience in television, the head of current affairs at ABC TV baited me for an hour before dismissing me, asking, *What makes you think you are pretty enough to be on television?* Belittling and shaming were still ready tools of choice to put women in their place.

The year before my experience at the ABC's Gore Hill headquarters, the High Court had ruled that Ansett Airlines could not discriminate against a woman who was otherwise qualified to be a pilot. I had reported on Deborah Wardley's case for years as her prospective employer invented one excuse after another to block her—women weren't strong enough; unions would object; menstrual cycles, pregnancy and childbirth would jeopardise safety and increase costs. The court ruled on technicalities, not on principle. When a group of older mentors urged me to make a complaint about my treatment at the ABC, the cost seemed higher than any possible reward. I kept my notes and moved on; revenge, as they say, is a dish best served cold.

It took until 1983 for Australia to sign the 1979 United Nations convention designed to eliminate all forms of discrimination against women. Legislation followed in 1984, but its principal proponent, the Labor senator Susan Ryan, was subjected to bitter personal and public attacks. At the big rallies in Canberra, anxious and angry Women Who Want to be Women pushed to the front to protest the changes. Some 80,000 people signed petitions opposing the relatively modest sex discrimination bill. Although key Liberal leaders supported it, the right wing of the party was bitterly opposed. It marked the beginning of a split that would dog the party for decades.[5]

Susan Ryan was a feisty campaigner, so the vicious onslaughts only increased her resolve. Women's rights were on the way to becoming human rights, talent was no longer sifted by sex, but the extent of the opposition stunned her. The Australian legislation passed with the support of some Liberal members of parliament who defied their party and crossed the floor to vote with the government. Women did not have a secure footing in the dominant political party, as deputy Liberal leader and foreign minister Julie Bishop and Liberal MP Julia Banks found in the internal party confrontation that ousted Malcolm Turnbull and replaced him with Scott Morrison. As Julia Banks declared in the House of Representatives, as she prepared to leave in 2018, 'Often when good women call out or are subjected to bad behaviours, the reprisals, backlash and commentary portrays them as the bad ones: the liar, the troublemaker, the emotionally unstable or weak, or someone who should be silenced.'[6]

'Tell us the story again about the newspaper job interview in the pub,' my teenaged daughter and her friends would say, at the turn of the century, each time we drove down Broadway past the old Fairfax building towards Sydney University. 'Can you believe it?' the girls would chuckle. Then they too entered the workforce and realised that the more subtle but deadening hand of sexual discrimination was still doing its evil work, now hidden behind laws and lofty rhetoric. Change rarely proceeds in a linear manner, but the trend was clear.

When Wayne Goss appointed Canadian-born Leneen Forde as Queensland's governor in 1992, she was only the second woman governor in Australian history. She had fallen in love with the son of former Australian prime minister Frank Forde and, like countless young brides, moved to Australia full of hope and expectation. She was shocked by what she discovered. Brisbane in the mid-1950s was a poor country town. The appliances she had taken for granted were considered luxury mod cons. A woman's place was in the home. But when her husband died eleven years later, this was no longer an option for her. With five young children to support, she began studying law and five years after her husband's death started work as a solicitor, eventually becoming the queen's representative in a state named for another.

Queensland, despite the gender of its name, was a place where men prevailed and women were meant to know their place. Matt Foley challenged this when, as the state's attorney-general, he decided that merit, not gender, would determine judicial appointments. My former English teacher, Roslyn Atkinson, by then a distinguished barrister who had been the inaugural president of the Queensland Anti-Discrimination Tribunal and deputy chair of the state's Law Reform Commission, despite outraged protests from the old guard, became one of Foley's first Supreme Court appointments in 1998.

Within a few years, despite bitter heckling from those who were still convinced that 'merit' meant 'men', seven of the state's 24 Supreme Court judges were women, and a woman was president of the Queensland Court of Appeal. Years later it was still driving the press mad. The *Courier-Mail* would roll out articles anonymously reporting lawyers who knew women *were just not up to it*. These eminently well-qualified women were derided as 'Matt's Girls'. In September 2015, Justice Catherine Holmes became the state's first female chief justice. This was a change that would not easily slide back.

The reaction to these newly assertive women was no less brutal in politics. When Labor's Anna Bligh became the first popularly elected female premier in Australia in 2009, the misogyny that later blighted Julia Gillard's prime ministership had an off-Broadway tryout in Brisbane. Anna Bligh's resolute leadership during the 2011 floods, like Julia Gillard's ability to navigate a hung parliament, counted for little. Her determination to privatise ports, roads, trains and coal terminals was not welcomed by traditional Labor voters. Union-sponsored billboards on major thoroughfares mocked her, the press despised her, and a vicious whispering campaign prevailed. The 2012 election was a disaster for Labor: the party went from holding 51 seats to seven. Electoral tides in Queensland are often more dramatic than normal swings on the carefully calibrated Australian electoral pendulum.

It was a relatively short-lived win for the blokes who had felt they were born to run the state. It lasted just one term. In 2020, the victorious Annastacia Palaszczuk became the first woman to be re-elected premier for a third time. Under her administration, women occupied an unprecedented number of positions of power in what was once the most macho state. It was a long way from the 1970s. In 2021, most of the ministers in her cabinet were women, as were the governor, chief justice, police commissioner, chief medical officer, head of the Department of Premier and Cabinet, and six of the state's seven university vice-chancellors.

Second-wave feminists had sometimes wondered, in the abstract, what would happen as occupations were dominated by women. Would that mean the profession had lost status? Was equality realised when mediocre women exercised as much achieved power as mediocre men had always done? But as Palaszczuk's legislation to introduce a Queensland bill of rights, legalise abortion, outlaw coercive control, enable voluntary euthanasia and better define consent laws showed in a few short years, a female perspective could change the agenda. And it could drive some men mad. This was a profound cultural and political change that had nothing to do with detachment from the 'mother country'.

RACE AND GENDER discrimination are inextricably linked and have long been defining Australian fault lines. Female convicts—'whores', in the view of some commanders and male prisoners—were outnumbered at least three to one and were shared among the men in what Anne Summers has described as 'imposed sexual slavery'.[7] But many were fiercely independent battlers who wanted a better life for themselves and their children and were prepared to challenge authority.[8] Similarly, the Cammeraygal woman Barangaroo, who became Bennelong's wife after her first husband died from smallpox, set the bar high. She was an independent woman, a fierce hunter and provider who saw little reason to compromise with the new arrivals. She once famously attended an official dinner at Government House in traditional garb, her naked body painted in white clay, a bone through her nose. She died in 1790, so was spared the distress of witnessing the brutal and demeaning treatment of her sisters and generations of others as the fight over the bodies of Aboriginal women became a recurring metaphor of settlement. Some formed loving relationships with settlers, others became leaders, but many were treated as chattels, emotionally destroyed as their children were taken away, their men emasculated.

Australia was and is a deeply male society. For those with enough determination and a strong sense of self-worth, frontier life encouraged a certain female fearlessness that is still evident. It is clear in the stars that shine abroad: writers and thinkers like Germaine Greer, Geraldine Brooks, Anne Summers and Kate Manne; scientists like the Nobel-winning Elizabeth Blackburn; actors like Cate Blanchett, Nicole Kidman, Rachel Griffiths and Margot Robbie, who luminously fill the world's screens; educators including Jill Ker Conway and Patricia Davidson; and anthropologists Genevieve Bell and Marcia Langton.

Ever since pastoralists recruited single men, not wanting to be encumbered by the additional expense of providing for families, the political economy of Australia has been built on the primacy of male labour, male power and male control. The native-born and immigrant populations grew in the nineteenth century, but it took the deaths of more than 60,000 men in the First World War for women to become the majority, although the generational loss reverberated for decades. Women remained, in Anne Summers' famous phrase, either 'damned whores or God's police'. Sexualised taunting was and still is the bedrock of abuse likely to rain down on Australian women who speak their mind, provide professional advice, demand more and expect R.E.S.P.E.C.T., as Aretha Franklin sang. Still, nothing fires up the angry Twitterati quite like women making otherwise unremarkable comments about their rights and expectations.

The intersection of these discriminations was on proud, unapologetic display when, in 1977, I flew three hours west of Brisbane to Cunnamulla. Peter Manning had commissioned me to report on a community that had been characterised as one of the most racist towns in the country for the independent *Nation Review* newspaper. As I had learned from my weeks on the road talking to bush poets, travelling alone on this assignment would have been foolhardy, so I accompanied two of my friends. Wayne Goss and Matt Foley were working for the Aboriginal Legal Service at the time, and they had a slate full of meetings and court hearings.

At the time, Cunnamulla was home to 1500 people (*about*, according to the signpost), seven pubs and seven draperies, and unemployment was officially running at 25 per cent. Eight of every ten Aboriginal people were without work. It was a town where grog ruled, dozens of children were malnourished, and the grief from scores of infant deaths each year was overwhelming. As the plane touched down, the local man sitting next to me asked where I was staying. The Club, I said. He spoke in the leering, patronising way I had come to expect in my travels through the state, setting the tone for the following week. As we left the plane he reassured me that I would be safe: 'They don't let the darkies into the Club Hotel.'[9]

Cunnamulla is one of a handful of outback Australian towns that has a grim, larger-than-life reputation. Wilcannia, in the far west of New South Wales, which briefly won national attention during the pandemic, is another. Both towns had had their reputations unfairly tarnished, as the requests of their leaders were persistently ignored and dismissed. It has long been easy to ignore those who live beyond the Great Dividing Range.

Not long after William Landsborough described the potential of the land he observed around what became Cunnamulla—as he crossed the continent from north to south in search of the ill-fated explorers Burke and Wills—the south-west of Queensland was rapidly divided into vast stations. Squatters soon claimed the mulga-clad countryside and murderous incursions became the norm. Native Police were stationed in the Cunnamulla township. Reports of the killings in the 1860s were so shocking that they provoked the Anglican bishop of Sydney to establish a mission. He had been outraged by a squatter's jape that if he had 'known how useful they might be he wouldn't have killed so many blackfellows'.

The unprepossessing settlement on the banks of the Warrego River about 800 kilometres due west of Brisbane is an unlikely entry in the compendium of noteworthy places. Its murderous history was conveniently forgotten and replaced with a pastoral fantasy. Maybe the mouth-pleasing ring of the name helped. Henry Lawson thought it suggested pumpkin pies. He immortalised the Cobb & Co. coach stop in his story 'The Hypnotised Township', but described the town as a place of 'troubled slumbers'. Years later the Aboriginal poet Herb Wharton, who was born near Cunnamulla, won international acclaim when he broke the hypnotic silence. He turned the settler stories on their heads and told the droving tales of Murri stockmen and women. He and his sister Hazel McKellar then recorded the tales of massacres, including the one their grandmother had survived. Still, the 'Cunnamulla Fella', who lived on damper and wallaby stew and was conjured by country singer Slim Dusty, is the figure who endures as a statue in the town. A selfie with the 'Fella' is a tick on the roaming grey-nomad bucket list.

Personal Becomes Political

Dark histories haunt places and often recur in other uncanny manifestations. Some may consider the Cunnamulla Fella a charming artefact of a bygone age, but there was nothing charming about 'Out of Sight, Out of Mind', the depiction of the town by ABC's *Four Corners* program in 1969. This film, broadcast just two years after the referendum that brought First Nations people into the mainstream, was one of those moments when current affairs television excelled. It brought the shameful reality of life in fringe camps into middle-class loungerooms. The pale, well-spoken journalist was doing a good job, but looked like a creature from another planet, dropped in to share his outrage. It was an excoriating portrayal of the wrongful conviction of an Aboriginal woman, and of the shocking conditions in the two town camps that were home to descendants of the Kunja people who had once been shot and poisoned by graziers.

Audiences around the country reacted with fury. 'I'm praying for [mayor] Jack Tonkin's soul in purgatory,' one wrote, 'but I don't like my chances.' ABC management prohibited the sale of the program to the BBC; the picture it painted was too ugly for international consumption.

The broadcast prompted an immediate political response: money suddenly became available to build 26 fibro houses scattered through the town. When I visited eight years later, the houses were built and only the remnants of the camps remained. The community links that had given life in the settlement its own coherence had dissipated; drunkenness had become the destructive norm. The angry racism that once fuelled the frontier wars still had full-throated voice. Like so many outback towns, Cunnamulla seemed to be dying. 'You have to blame it on something, what better than the boongs,' one angry newcomer told me.

Those I met on that short trip felt no need to hide their fury. The media had destroyed their town. 'We were doing the right thing by the blacks until *Four Corners* came along,' one self-appointed spokesman berated me when I attended a dinner organised by the Rotary Club. The anger in the room bubbled up as they listened to social worker Matt Foley's talk. When it came time for questions, the local solicitor chairing the meeting passed around handwritten notes: 'tone it down', 'no aggressive questions', 'calm down'. The back and forth continued until well after midnight. Then, like a storm that had passed, the tone changed. 'We're still friends, aren't we?' the man who had most aggressively blamed the media at the start of the evening asked as he wandered off to his car. He should not have been driving.

In the morning a taxi driver who had been part of the angry group the night before nearly ran me over and then demanded I get into his car for a tour of the camps and the new houses. He knew who to blame. As we drove along the uncurbed streets he pointed to one run-down house after another: 'Black house, white house, black house . . . I hope you are going to give those bastards heaps . . . I just want a fair go for the white fella.' In the previous six months there had been nearly 300 convictions for drunkenness: 163 Aboriginal men and 58 women; 55 white men and two women. 'You can't live here without drinking,' my not-so-friendly taxi driver declared.

Four of the women I met stood out and have remained with me ever since. One was the doctor's elderly receptionist. When I knocked, she answered the door to the surgery armed with a paper knife. 'You learn to expect anything, and prepare yourself,' she said as she put the blade in a drawer. Another was a tough, damaged woman who owned one of the three pubs that served Aboriginal people. She had installed a metal cage along the bar. 'I don't know why the blacks drink here. I like them, but I've lost control. I don't care how much I lose, I'm selling this place,' she told me. Outside her pub a young woman, who looked at least twenty years older than she was, grabbed my arm and repeated, over and over, 'I'm just a black mongrel bastard. I got no one, I got nowhere to go, I'm just a black mongrel bastard.'

Personal Becomes Political

The most outstanding person in the town was Hazel McKellar. She was the antithesis of what Bernard Smith would later describe as the 'tragic muse' of Australian arts, the 'old Aboriginal woman surviving precariously as a fringe dweller in some unknown country town'.[10] She was a handsome, intelligent woman who, since returning to Cunnamulla after working as a housemaid on stations, had devoted herself to holding her community together as external and internal forces conspired to pull it apart.

Even in progressive circles, the prevailing image of Aboriginal people in the late 1970s was as victims—people with little agency or authority, people who had been damaged or destroyed. Hazel McKellar did not fit this stereotype. She had big ideas and was prepared to pull whatever levers she could to realise them. She wanted a different school curriculum so children could learn about their culture, something the local school's principal thought 'might be helpful for slow learners'. Two-thirds of the 440 students at the primary school were Aboriginal, but the experience of their forebears was not evident in the curriculum. In Year 5 social studies, as the principal helpfully explained, 'We teach the kiddies about explorers and the opening up of Australia.'

Hazel McKellar's advocacy for including cultural knowledge was ahead of the zeitgeist. Within a few years she was writing books that captured this knowledge. Her brother Herb Wharton had put the old brigade on notice through his poetry, which they celebrated; they may not have liked what he said, but they understood his language. During those intense few days in 1977, Hazel and I talked about the immediate past, but not the longer past that had shaped it. Her focus was on the future. She campaigned relentlessly for improvements to health, housing and education, and for a cultural and community centre. 'It's the little things that niggle, like knowing there is only one white family in town whose kids will come to an Aboriginal kid's party,' she told me. 'I've just learnt to not go where I am not wanted. It used to make me angry, and I still resent it at times, but you have to accept it, I guess. But it's only us who are keeping this place going.'

By 2019, the map of south-west Queensland was closer to what it would have looked like about 170 years earlier, when Thomas Mitchell had swept through the region identifying land suitable for cattle. The aerial view of the region from the National Native Title Tribunal's map now shows a vast patchwork of native title lands, and many places of significant cultural heritage. To the west and south of Cunnamulla, 200,000 square kilometres of land has been returned to traditional owners.

When Hazel McKellar told me in 1977 that it was only her people who would keep the area going, neither of us could have anticipated this transformation. By 2021, the sign at the entrance declared Cunnamulla a 'Heritage Town', 'Settled in the Dreamtime'. The ancient stories of the land and its people, once a cause of such embarrassment and shame, had become a source of pride and inspiration. Anonymous trolls may rage on Twitter, but no one would say out loud the things that they had once said to me, notebook in hand, spell-checking names as I jotted down their comments.

Alexis Wright is a Waanyi woman who grew up in Cloncurry, more than 1000 kilometres north-west of Cunnamulla, at the other end of the Channel Country that regulates the cycles of life in the vast inland. It is the town where Scott Morrison tramped through the cemetery looking for his great-great-aunt Dame Mary Gilmore's graveyard. In 2007, Wright became the second First Nations writer to win the Miles Franklin Literary Award for her magisterial novel *Carpentaria*, then won the Queensland Premier's Literary Award for fiction—the first Aboriginal author to do so. It was recognition that would have been inconceivable 30 years earlier. The celebration of her remarkable book was, inevitably, tinged by politics. On the eve of her win in June 2007, the Howard government launched its Northern Territory Intervention, when troops and public servants were sent into remote First Nations communities. The softly spoken author was asked about the intervention and replied with passionate denunciation: there were real problems of abuse in some communities, but a unilateral intervention without consultation could not be the solution.

The gestation of *Carpentaria* had taken many years, as Wright had tried to bring to the page the stories and ways of being she had heard from the old people. Every major publisher rejected the opus before Ivor Indyk at Giramondo Press recognised the novel's unique brilliance. In an astonishingly original way, Wright tells hitherto invisible stories and captures the spirit of a different way of storytelling. Her stories wove back on themselves, rich with magic, symbolism, grit and determination; they turned time and place and the conventions of English literature inside out and made her a contender for the Nobel Prize for Literature. The profound change embodied in the accolades she continues to receive, and the insights she shares about the idea of Australia, have very little to do with anxiety about detachment from Britain. Her novels, like many others, better answer the question *Who are we?* than any politician has for decades. As has happened before and will happen again, by making the political personal and turning it into culture, Wright encourages a new, fit-for-purpose understanding to emerge.

In 1890, another Queensland novelist, Arthur Vogan, wrote *The Black Police* about the massacres in the state's Channel Country and his shocked reactions to the way they were applauded by settlers. It was a surprising popular success. Although local newspapers bristled with reports of deaths from incursions, it was a contentious subject, and one that made for a challenging novel. The critics were scathing, but it struck a nerve and was reprinted several times.

Arthur Vogan lost his job as a journalist, just as Carl Feilberg had done a decade before following his campaign against the Native Police in *The Queenslander*. Like Feilberg, Vogan also realised he was on a blacklist and had to leave. He moved as far away as he could—to Perth—and gave up writing for some time.[11]

He was one of many authors punished for writing an 'anti-Australian' novel. This was a smear that would be spread thickly for decades. In 1947, Ruth Park was subjected to an organised campaign of threats and vilification for the life she portrayed in Surry Hills in *The Harp in the South*, which had won a competition run by the *Sydney Morning Herald*. Subscription cancellations and letters poured into the editor, all asking different versions of the same question: 'Why should Australia, with all her beauty to choose from, have to go to the sewer for her literature?'[12] Ruth Park also retreated. She left the country amid a chorus of criticism and only returned years later. Now her novels are on school reading lists, Wikipedia lists the dozens of prizes she won, and in 2006 she was recognised in *The Bulletin*'s list of the hundred most influential Australians. Culture changes, and as it does, once unpalatable truths can be said out loud and challenge and correct ill-informed angry outbursts.

16

Soul Destroying

IT IS TELLING that the opening shots in the battle for the soul of the nation, that gathered momentum as the twentieth century drew to a close, were fired from an Ipswich branch of the Liberal Party. The city in south-east Queensland is the antithesis of a blue-ribbon conservative electorate. It is one of the industrial cities—there is at least one in every state—that for much of the last century did the dirty work for the nearby capital: home to coalmining, railways, agricultural processing, quarrying, manufacturing, ports, prisons and military bases. Out of sight and mind.

Ipswich is unlike most of the other industrial cities that generally had a provisional, prefab feel, at least until the demand for tourists drove waterfront developments and attempts to beautify ugly old buildings. The proud river city once—briefly, a long time ago—vied to be the state capital, and that legacy lives in pockets of its built environment. There are heritage buildings—distinctive Queenslanders practically elevated above the flood line, their verandas positioned to shade and catch the afternoon breeze—and well-established gardens and parklands.

In the days when settlers relied on a river-based trading system, its port on the banks of the Bremer River, a tributary of Maiwar, was essential. Ipswich became the distribution point for the wool grown by the squatters who had travelled north. Settlers, who ignored and then battled the Yagerra people to occupy the rich land they claimed, cleared and renamed Darling Downs.[1] Wool was central to these hard-won but ill-gotten rural fortunes, and the paddle steamers that moved it needed coal.

In Ipswich, or Limestone as it was then called, there was coal aplenty an easy wheelbarrow ride from the port. Before long it was known as a coal town. A pattern was established that would be repeated for generations throughout regional Queensland as men were recruited to do the dirty, back-breaking work of mining. The early arrivals, like Samuel Griffith's Welsh father, who arrived in 1854 as a missionary, were drawn from the 'living hell' of industrial centres in Germany, England, Ireland, Scotland and Wales. It was a hard life, but at least the air was clear and the sun shone. As steamers gave way to rail, the trajectory of the city was set—it was a tough town beset by more than its fair share of disasters, spectacular floods, devastating mining accidents and a rich seam of class conflict.

Like the people of Wollongong and Newcastle in New South Wales, Geelong in Victoria, Bunbury in Western Australia and Elizabeth in South Australia, the people of Ipswich were sitting ducks for the economic transformation that restructured industry all over Australia in the final decades of the twentieth century. Manufacturing moved offshore, mining above ground. Its electors suspected they had been ignored and taken for granted. Many grumbled that they had been punished for always voting Labor.

The city's blue-collar workers felt they had been left behind by the Labor governments in Brisbane and Canberra that had closed railway lines, restructured industry, deregulated the economy and floated the dollar. By 1996, they were prepared to hope against hope that maybe the party of business, led by an apparently plain-speaking suburban man, would deliver more opportunities. Old institutions and loyalties were crumbling. Even in Ipswich, one of the most diehard union towns, the number of unionists had halved over a decade to less than a third of the workforce and would keep falling. Class divides were being redrawn. Education, not income, was the new fault line and many Ipswich citizens slipped into the crack. The big enterprises, those that once employed hundreds of men who punched a card to clock on and kept a careful eye on their overtime, had shrunk. Many gave up on working for others and became sole traders, while women picked up low-paying jobs in shops and as carers. As a group they would later personify 'Howard's battlers'.

All of this was known by the officials at Liberal Party headquarters when, on 16 February 1996, they decided to disendorse one of their Queensland candidates in the upcoming federal election. Pauline Hanson was an Ipswich fish-and-chip shop owner who a year earlier had lost her seat on Ipswich City Council by just 130 votes. Disendorsing her was not a big deal for the party. She was standing in an unwinnable contest in the electorate of Oxley, the safest Labor seat in Queensland. The decision was provoked by a race-baiting letter she wrote to the editor of the local *Queensland Times*, in which she said things that some in the Coalition campaign thought but didn't want to say out loud. When the *Courier-Mail* turned the letter into a front page story, her subsequent disendorsement, and the reasons for it, briefly became national news.[2] It was just a fortnight before the election, too late to remove her from the ballot paper as the Liberal candidate.

This was just the opening shot in what would become the deliberately divisive world of populist new right campaigning within a couple of decades. At the time it was almost impossible to imagine that the shameless embrace of the oldest tactics of authoritarian leaders would become the new normal in democracies around the world.

From the seventh most economically disadvantaged electorate in the country,[3] Pauline Hanson looked down and blamed the lot of the people of Ipswich on those who were even worse off, just as the people in Cunnamulla had done so vociferously when I'd visited twenty years earlier. Aboriginal people got special assistance, she shrieked. Money going to them hurt her fair-skinned, sun-damaged mob. She channelled the grievances and resentments of those who had seen the old certainties disappear. When First Nations people in Queensland were finally free to leave the missions and reserves, many moved to Ipswich's working-class suburbs and began new lives on the western edge of what was known locally as the 'black belt'. This stretched to Eagleby and Inala, where the 'Brisbane Aboriginal underclass' was concentrated in 'mainly housing commission ghettos', as Melissa Lucashenko wrote when she later documented life in these hardscrabble suburbs. Everyone was poor; but these were places where, as one woman told her, 'you don't have to worry about snobs staring at you if you go to the shops in bare feet'.[4]

Industry was also changing. Coal was extracted from vast open-cut industrial complexes, not from the precarious underground tunnels that had taken so many lives; railways ceased to be the main mode of transport and no longer needed to be repaired and serviced; jobs in downstream industries evaporated; manufacturing moved to China, Vietnam, Bangladesh. Jobs in the rapidly expanding, privately owned prisons were one of the few areas of growth. Despite talk of tourism, service industries, tech, education and hospitality there was no clear pathway for people in Ipswich to a comfortable future.

At the time, two-thirds of Ipswich residents had no post-school qualifications. Most had only finished the legal minimum and left as soon as they turned fifteen. As a group they were significantly less prepared to cope with economic change than their neighbours in Brisbane or elsewhere in the south-east of the state. People in Ipswich, like their extended families in the other steel, coal and manufacturing cities on the doorstep of the major capitals, were not convinced there was a place for them in the new outward-looking, increasingly deregulated Australia, where services—not industry or agriculture—dominated the economy.

―――――

IT IS HARD to know who was most surprised when Pauline Hanson won a seat in the House of Representatives. Once secure Labor electorates were falling like dominos on 2 March 1996, especially in old working-class areas that had felt the hard bristles of industry restructuring and subsequent unemployment. Young people were staying at school longer, but their parents and grandparents had fewer choices and expressed their anger in the ballot box.

Traditional Labor voters shifted their allegiance and opted for the party of business, following a pattern US president Ronald Reagan had established a decade earlier when he converted southern Democrats into Republican voters. John Howard, armed with the insights from his campaign advisers and pollsters, was embarking on a similar transformation. As prime minister, he would claim the old myths, strip them of their collectivist ethos, contest uncomfortable history and turn red voters blue.

The scale of Pauline Hanson's victory was astonishing. An effective swing of nearly 20 per cent. Queensland voters can be fickle, poised like a king tide waiting for the right moon, ready to wash out those who have disappointed or angered them. Suddenly a sideshow—an internal battle starring a most unlikely Liberal-candidate-turned-independent—became a national cause célèbre. Reporters flocked to Ipswich to capture the views of the fish-and-chip lady who spoke it like she saw it. Lynton Crosby, the Liberal Party's campaign manager, reported that every time she opened her mouth her support increased.[5] In retrospect, Pauline Hanson's election looked like an out-of-town try-out for ideas that were beyond the pale of acceptable mainstream political rhetoric. It was so effective it was tempting to wonder if it had been planned—whether Pauline Hanson was a stool pigeon designed to draw fire and benefit the Liberal Party, while its leader appeared to wash his hands of her message.

Within a year of her unexpected victory, Pauline Hanson went from joke to celebrity. The times suited her. As an independent she was able to grow a political infrastructure to suit her ambition. One Nation, launched in 1997, adopted the name first used five years earlier by Paul Keating in a landmark economic policy. He had optimistically declared, 'We have learned that we can change our ways of doing things and change the way we think about things. We have proved that a more efficient economy can be combined with a fairer and more equitable society.'[6]

Hanson's supporters wanted one nation that looked and sounded like them. They were ready to lash out. Once Pauline Hanson had a platform, she warmed to her theme. She broadened her targets and declared the country was being 'swamped by Asians'. It was a fear she returned to when she was elected to the Senate twenty years later. By then she was convinced that the country was being 'swamped' by Muslims.

Pauline Hanson's claims were false, but many believed them. Polls showed they were in the minority, but they were ready to exercise their power. The electoral system gives power to the margins. John Howard, as the leader of the Liberal Party, had criticised Hanson from behind his campaign's white picket fence, and said that in the unlikely event she were elected, she would not be welcome in his government.[7] He was campaigning with the slogan 'For all of us'. *Us* did not necessarily mean everyone.

A 'them and us' divide was actively fostered over the coming decade. At the time, John Howard was 'anxious' that memories of his previous racially divisive and politically toxic comments—opposing multiculturalism and Asian migration, and describing the possibility of a treaty as 'repugnant' to his 1988 slogan 'One Australia'—would be revived.[8] Pauline Hanson picked up his message, and proudly championed it. She knew that many in her electorate shared this view and were more than usually susceptible to the charismatic appeal of a larger-than-life personality.[9]

Pauline Hanson's comments went to the heart of the unspoken agenda of the Liberal campaign. The noise, both for and against, underlined a core partisan message: that truth could not be spoken for fear of causing offence. Well-paid commentators declared that 'political correctness' was a near and present danger. David Marr, the erudite critic, saw in Howard a leader with a certain genius, someone who responded to Australians as they really were, not what they pretended to be.[10] Over the years Howard had perfected the art of doublespeak. With even more disdain than most men of his age and class, he had shown no interest in the First Australians—his instinct was to block and deny.

THE POLITICAL CONSENSUS that had shaped Aboriginal Affairs policy since the 1967 referendum broke in the 1980s under pressure from mining companies opposed to land rights.[11] John Howard made his position clear. In 1988, he had rejected a treaty and national land rights.[12] This was one of the all-too-frequent times when the politics of the powerful status quo prevailed, the reason Bob Hawke wept for his failure as he unveiled the Barunga Statement in Parliament House on his last day.

When in power, one of the first bills John Howard nudged through parliament used the 'race powers' of the Constitution to discriminate against Aboriginal people, and remove heritage protection for the Ngarrindjeri women of Hindmarsh Island.[13] In 2004, with the support of Labor, he abolished the Aboriginal and Torres Strait Islander Commission, again stopped the treaty process, and killed regional autonomy plans to enhance economic development. Three years later, without consultation, he suspended racial discrimination laws and, rather than working with communities, sent troops and public servants into remote Aboriginal communities in response to horrifying reports of abuse.

It would take until almost John Howard's last day in office in 2007 for him to promise a referendum on recognising First Nations people in the Constitution. He had been coached by the Cape York leader Noel Pearson, who was convinced that any victories for First Nations people in the conservative nation depended on the Coalition supporting the change. In a most unlikely speech, Howard told a Sydney Institute gathering that he would support a referendum. The small audience at the Wentworth, the Liberal Party's hotel of preference, was prepared to suspend judgement and accept that he may have seen the light on the road to Damascus of his impending defeat. To me it felt cynical. He must have known this was a promise he would never have to keep.

John Howard's anti-Asian comments twenty years earlier demonstrated that he had never moved far from the oldest trope in Australian political life—exclusion based on race, lubricated with money for those who were *us*. Even as he recalibrated his message, it was still potent, an insistent drumbeat that had shaped the society he grew up in and was again revived under his watch. This was a corner he was happy to defend. He echoed the protagonists of the White Australia policy in the Federation parliament when he declared, nearly 100 years later: 'I don't think it is wrong, racist, immoral or anything, for a country to say we will decide what the cultural identity and cultural destiny of this country will be and nobody else.'[14]

In her maiden speech, just days after John Howard had damned her with faint praise at a Liberal Party conference in September 1996, Pauline Hanson shifted the tone of national debate in a way that it has still not recovered from. She said the country was being swamped by Asians, that Aboriginal people got unfair advantages, and that migration and multiculturalism must stop. The parliament unanimously condemned her.

Those who had welcomed the new inclusiveness and outward-looking self-confidence of modern Australia didn't believe Pauline Hanson would last long. The country had been on a national education campaign for decades, learning more about the past, asserting independence, turning the economy outwards, embracing multiculturalism; even welcoming female equality, migrants, and refugees from Asia; and acknowledging the lie of terra nullius. All had been subjected to angry opposition that had then seemingly dissipated.

Astonishment that this throwback to an old Australia should find a large and supportive audience was not confined to one political party. Tony Abbott, before he became one of the most divisive prime ministers in the country's history, helped bring a civil case against One Nation for a breach of electoral rules that saw Hanson briefly jailed. Comics and satirists had a field day.

But jokes did not neutralise Pauline Hanson. The old men who had fallen in love with her chivalrously rose to defend her honour. Like Donald Trump twenty years later, her ignorance and certainty appealed to unexpectedly large numbers of people who felt they had missed out.[15] Every time she said 'Please explain' in response to a journalist's tricky question, her supporters—especially those who felt they had been left behind, bamboozled by clever words or simply didn't understand—rallied behind her. It was not their fault they had been left behind in the new meritocracy stewing in resentment; few were willing to engage deeply and offer a hand up to the new world.

Just as women and people of colour felt the wrath unleashed by President Trump's xenophobia, Pauline Hanson's ubiquitous profile meant the level of threat for those Australians who visibly embodied their heritage dramatically increased. First Nations students dropped out of university in record numbers; those of Asian heritage tried to become invisible; reports of racially motivated assaults skyrocketed; and governments in Asia expressed concern, even contemptuous outrage, that the country was poised to revert to its racially defined past. Before long Pauline Hanson became a celebrity draped in a flag, the go-to person for commercial media searching for new ways to connect with, prod and provoke their fickle and diminishing audiences.

Pauline Hanson had watered an old, neglected tree and to the astonishment of many it flourished. Years later John Howard still argued, contrary to the assessment of leading political commentators and many in his own cabinet, that he did not give her oxygen. It was not a slip of the tongue when he told the Liberal Party conference in 1996 that because of her presence in the parliament people felt 'able to speak a little more freely and a little more openly about what they feel . . . in a sense the pall of censorship on certain issues has been lifted . . . I think there has been a change and that is a very good thing.'[16]

The evidence is to the contrary. Being able to speak without regard for the hurt that might be done was not the mark of a respectful society, but of one that rushed to judgement without fear of consequences. The battle for the soul of the nation was on, waged in the gap that lies beneath the official call and response of political announcements and public policy.[17] An American term invented for a different purpose, *culture wars*, described the battleground; *dog whistling* was the preferred colloquialism for speaking in a code that was easily decipherable by its intended audience but missed by others. The divide opened between those who heard the subliminal messages with approval and those who were affronted by them. This played out in schools and universities, in workplaces, pubs and sportsgrounds and the media.

Those who had embraced a new language of respectful inclusion were dismissed as 'politically correct'. The Murdoch press and commercial shock-jock radio announcers tested their wings with a freedom and less fear of sanction than they had known before. They asserted the right to speak their minds, to say whatever they liked, to not give in.

Just how potent their rage had become was on full public display as the votes came in on the night of the 1998 Queensland state election. Pauline Hanson's ragtag One Nation party won eleven seats and more than 20 per cent of the vote, taking votes away from the Liberal National Party. Everyone in the tally room that night was in shock as the numbers clicked up on the vast screen. Those who felt their grievances magnified by her rhetoric gave her their votes. Those in the capital city affronted by her readiness to magnify disappointments that she could not resolve dropped their longstanding allegiance to the Liberal Party and voted in unprecedented numbers for Labor. Peter Beattie, who had had his first taste of political brutality when he was beaten up so badly that he needed to be hospitalised after the 1971 Springbok demonstration, formed a new government with the support of independents.

The media did its bit and boosted the dissemination of grievance, misinformation and outrage. As Pauline Hanson's notoriety grew, journalists were alternately blamed for amplifying her angry message and accused of misunderstanding the source of her appeal. Her willingness to say whatever came into her head made her a celebrity—perfect media fodder, outrage and consternation on tap, with a backstory as complicated as any television soap could conjure.

Throughout this period, journalists and editors struggled with the challenge of how to report a public figure who did not feel constrained by the truth. The obligation to be socially responsible, advocated by the *Courier-Mail*'s most distinguished editor, Ted Bray, in the 1960s, had been an aspiration for the press for decades, but was under lethal assault. Fact checking, and publishing the results, had not yet become a journalism routine. Instead the old *he said, she said*, competing views reported without judgement, prevailed. There was little appetite to provide context or to call out lies in the way that later became the norm under the Trump presidency, when newspapers ran daily tallies of the many mistruths he uttered. The long years of misinformation, criminality and threat under the Joh Bjelke-Petersen regime had both emboldened journalists around Australia to be more assertive, but also made them aware of their very real limits.

Newspapers thrive on conflict, especially accompanied by action and angry voices—an ever-reliable shortcut to news. This was long before the internet made it easy to enter a rabbit hole and meet thousands of like-minded people. Long before researchers discovered that anger could be as addictive as heroin. Much of the language was crude and brutal, echoing the hideous things that the aggrieved residents of Cunnamulla had been happy to say in front of a reporter with notebook in hand. There was no room for compassion, compromise or complexity.

In the days before the internet, it was harder to run deliberately divisive and dishonest campaigns that played to barely articulated anxieties. In the old days, political ads were crude and simple: a fistful of dollars, a wallet being pinched from a back pocket, 30 seconds of fear-invoking imagery. Emotionally charged words and images had been the stock in trade of party advertising since television became the principal medium of political communication. Campaigns could bend the truth, but it was regulated, and the Australian Electoral Commission was ready to pounce. The husband of one of John Howard's favourites, Jackie Kelly, the Liberal member for Lindsay in Sydney's far west, found this some years later when he was charged for distributing deliberately false and misleading election materials.[18]

Two decades on, this would be refined to devastating effect. Without easily detectable fingerprints, the free-for-all cauldron of social media with its canny, unconstrained ability to find and use slogans and images did the political heavy lifting. The subterranean world of emotion, fear and reaction that flashed across every available screen was almost impossible to monitor, regulate or control until after the damage had been done.

Soul Destroying

WELL BEFORE HE was elected prime minister, John Howard was determined to reset the way Australians thought about their history. He adopted the pejorative tag 'black armband', conjured by the feisty conservative historian Geoffrey Blainey, to dismiss those who explored deliberately forgotten aspects of the nation's story. Howard was a proud member of the *three cheers school*, preferring history that accentuated the positive. He was keen to draw the curtains on the critical engagement with the past that his predecessor had encouraged. Ever since a young Paul Keating had listened to tales of political derring-do at the feet of the ageing former NSW premier Jack Lang, he had been hungry to learn more about the past of the country he was to lead.

History had taken a long time to be established as an area of local inquiry and study. Now, under Howard, it was about to be weaponised. Before the Second World War there were only a handful of history professors in Australia. They accepted the prevailing viewpoint, pursued an 'objective account' of the past and prepared the best students to study abroad. Australian history was a poor cousin to British, imperial and European history. By the time John Howard graduated from the University of Sydney in 1961 there were still only 150 professional historians in the country, but he knew that history was the key to the soul of the nation.

Chris Mitchell, editor of the *Courier-Mail*, admired Howard and shared a fascination with history. He was a man who knew with every fibre of his being that news was what an editor said it was, and he was prepared to take risks. There was almost no bigger risk than publishing a story in August 1996 that claimed Manning Clark, Australia's most eminent historian, was a Soviet agent of influence. He was challenging a national treasure, a man admired by many, a man who had taught many who became leaders. His expansive writing had helped trigger a discussion about Australia's past.

When Manning Clark died in 1991, all the members of the House of Representatives respectfully stood to endorse Prime Minister

Bob Hawke's condolence motion and acknowledge the historian's contribution. Even those who quibbled that his grand histories were too pessimistic, too critical of British heritage and too preoccupied with fatal flaws and moral drama, conceded he had made a significant contribution. As a teacher at Geelong Grammar, he had had an enduring impact on his students, including Rupert Murdoch, who years later bought a Sidney Nolan painting of explorers in the desert that cryptically celebrated the historian's discoveries: 'Burke and Wills (after Manning Clark)'.

Like every creative person, Clark was sensitive to criticism, but he was courageous and ambitious. Yet no other Australian historian had endured 'greater public obloquy'.[19] Ever since he was condemned in the Victorian parliament in 1947 as one of the 'pink professors and puce pedagogues' subverting impressionable young minds, Clark had been watched, his comments carefully compiled by security agencies. As the Cold War developed momentum and the fear of communism shaped domestic politics, ASIO concluded that at worst the leftist professor may have been a 'communist sympathiser in the immediate post-war years'. Clark's book from his 1958 trip to the Soviet Union, *Making Soviet Man*, was condemned by both left and right. There was no middle ground. He was either, as Stuart Macintyre and Clark's granddaughter, historian Anna Clark, wrote, a 'fellow-traveller and apologist for communist tyranny or a timid capitulator to reactionary pressures'.[20]

Manning Clark wrote with a florid style that suited his persona of a towering man from another age. He believed that romantic stories of radical nationalism missed the mark and sought to confound these simple tales with the complexity of human nature and competition between competing forces. He was searching for explanations that went beyond the simple tales of racially inflected, gender-segregated nationalism that had become mythic. As his influence grew, so did his critics. Within months of becoming foreign minister in 1996, Alexander

Soul Destroying

Downer had decided that Clark's six-volume *History of Australia* was an inappropriate gift for him to present to Georgetown University in Washington, declaring 'history is a very, very powerful weapon'.[21]

There was plenty of critical material for Chris Mitchell to draw on, and plenty of envious colleagues with grievances and burnished memories. Manning Clark had lived a large life, much of it in the public eye. The newspaper's extraordinary eight-page syndicated attack, 'By Order of Lenin', asserted that the former Australian of the Year, recipient of a Companion of the Order of Australia, 'was indeed a communist . . . an undiscovered member of the communist world's elite'.

It was also untrue. Within days, key sources backed away from their claims, memories proved unreliable. Within a year the Australian Press Council had found there was insufficient evidence to support the newspaper's accusations. But Chris Mitchell stood by his claim.

When the Manning Clark story was published, the prime minister, who had been in the job for just five months, declined to offer an unqualified opinion. Instead, he welcomed it as 'part of the process', and said he had always had 'a less than rapturous view of the Manning Clark view of Australian history'.[22]

In the battle for the soul of the nation, the treatment of one man, his family and his legacy was important, but the consequences lingered more broadly. If one of the most eminent historians in the country could be subjected to such an attack after his death, the lesson to others could not have been clearer: engage in the public domain at your peril. Historians learned to keep their heads down, double check their footnotes and get on with their research.

Towards the end of his term as prime minister, after a decade of castigating critical historians for concentrating on the negative, John Howard convened a summit to devise a new curriculum for the study of Australian history, quibbling with his carefully selected group of advisers over nuance and interpretation.[23] It was a very different approach to that of the German president, who embraced his nation's grave legacy and said the memories needed to be kept alive so they were not repeated. Donald Trump was later more inclined to the Howard approach of a sanitised narrative history and also convened a summit in his final months as US president. Narendra Modi in India, Boris Johnson in Britain, authoritarian leaders in Poland and Hungary and many others have gathered selected historians who support their perspective. They are all acutely aware of George Orwell's enduring aphorism, 'Who controls the past controls the future.'

It was nonetheless surprising when, in 2021, the then Liberal education minister Alan Tudge, whose parents had migrated to Australia from the UK in the 1960s, became such a fierce defender of the 'three cheers' view of history. With loud cries of support from the backbench in parliament, he criticised the history curriculum for depicting a miserable country instead of celebrating the 'greatest, egalitarian, freest, wealthiest' country in the world. But the brilliant new histories that had been researched and written could not be ignored. The 'three cheers school' was no longer sufficient.

IN THE LATE 1990S, Queensland Newspapers was Rupert Murdoch's most profitable Australian pot of gold. Keith Murdoch had created its flagship in 1933 by merging *The Courier* with the *Daily Mail*, a paper owned by the notorious gambler and businessman John Wren (immortalised by Frank Hardy in his notorious novel *Power Without Glory*). Towards the end of the century the capital city daily was still a significant force in the state—every day about 700,000 people read the monopoly paper. The sprawling modernist plant, its linoleum floors polished to a high sheen every day, its canteen serving sandwiches on pre-sliced white bread, had space for more reporters than were needed. Newspapers were shrinking, monopolies were the new normal, one paper served the needs of a city that only a decade earlier had consumed three each day and two on Sundays.

This was where, during the ascendancy of Pauline Hanson, a young Lachlan Murdoch was sent to learn the family business, mixing with reporters, meeting with editors and managers. He was the very image of a cool young tycoon, a motorbike-riding, leathers-wearing scion with little reason to doubt his own good ideas. The heir apparent's comments were discussed in reverential tones in the canteen after each gathering. A handful of older editors and reporters who had not swallowed the Kool-Aid noted the grooming and got on with their jobs.

While newsroom reporters covered Hanson's every move, the section I edited welcomed other perspectives. We made room for writers who sought to make sense of her appeal, who looked at the underlying economic and social factors that drove her support. We provided opportunities for those who had been vilified by her supporters to tell their stories, alongside columns by those who encouraged and supported her.

Chris Mitchell was ambitious and wanted to show that, despite widespread public scepticism, it was possible to produce high-quality journalism not tainted by commerce or ideology. With his blessing, the page I edited welcomed dissent. He encouraged the range of opinions even though many were at odds with the usual output of a Murdoch newspaper. This was a small achievement that should have been unremarkable but was sufficiently unusual to be recognised in 1997 with an unlikely commendation from the Australian Human Rights and Equal Opportunity Commission at the Human Rights Awards.

At the time, Pauline Hanson's true believers were insisting that everyone shut up and listen to them. The High Court Wik ruling that pastoral leases did not extinguish native title had become another rock in the shoes of people who had never set foot on a remote property or had a conversation with a First Nations person. Many of these people were the newspaper's natural audience, even if they made up a minority of the population.

I was told I did not have to pander to them. The purpose of the opinion page was to make room for other points of view. I knew it would not last. But in the meantime, for a couple of years when the battle for the soul of the nation was gathering pace and Queensland was once again a battleground of national importance, it was worth a shot to try to inform and add nuance to an angry public debate. It should not have been too much to ask—to provide an oasis of pluralism to inform and enrich an increasingly angry public sphere, calm the febrile mood and allow civilised dissent. Even Rupert Murdoch had accepted this was an important role for newspapers, declaring in his 1972 A.N. Smith Memorial Lecture in Journalism that 'a complacent, lazy press . . . can only lead in short time to careless authoritarian government'.[24]

One day I left the office in Bowen Hills with the opinion page set for the next day. The paper I opened was different. On the front page a banner flagged a special feature on the opinion page, a long question-and-answer interview with the Member for Oxley. The editor had reached in and exercised his authority, driven by commercial considerations and reader pushback.

It was still the paper of record. This was a step towards becoming an inflammatory tabloid with lurid, accusatory, ideological front pages, stoking the addiction to anger that could turn lives inside out. The search for 'hot button' issues to draw and inflame readers was about to become a frenzy. Aggrieved commentators were given their heads; news more often filtered through an explicit point of view. Over the next decades, as newspapers became less profitable ('failing in the marketplace', as the media scholar Rod Tiffen put it), the established norms for even a monopoly press—objectivity, fairness and balance—broke down. Many of the best reporters and editors left or were pushed out. More than half a million Australians signed a petition calling for a royal commission into News Corp and its influence. They agreed with former prime minister Kevin Rudd, who had risen to prominence by courting the media and then collapsed without it, that the virtual monopoly of News Corp newspapers had 'impoverished Australian democracy'.[25]

Within one term, Pauline Hanson's power bloc also collapsed; she was jailed and later acquitted. Oxley voters returned to Labor, no longer feeling they were taken for granted. Two decades on they were among the best educated in the state, younger, more likely to have parents born overseas. They looked more like the rest of the country, not a disadvantaged outlier.

In the process, however, Pauline Hanson and the views she represented were normalised. They may have only been embraced at the margins, but like a virus infiltrated the nation. Her One Nation party was not robust but still it wounded the Coalition and almost fatally weakened its moderate wing. Those who used to be called small-l liberals were left wondering who to vote for, and eventually gave rise to new movements ready to advocate for traditional conservative values, respect, integrity, equality and environmental protection. Meanwhile, the choices on the far right and libertarian fringes proliferated; the National Party contorted itself; United Australia, Liberal Democrats, and the Shooters, Fishers and Farmers sprang up to nurture and capture the votes on those margins.

After carefully tending her profile on the hungry beast of reality television—dancing, cooking and surviving—in 2016 Hanson returned to the stage she had once made her own. Like the bogong moths that once descended on Canberra in huge numbers every year before drought so thickened the soils they could not burrow out, she again gravitated to the national capital. In the 2016 election, when Malcolm Turnbull struggled to hold government and preference whisperers exercised their magic to get more candidates from small parties elected than ever before, Hanson became a senator. With nearly 10 per cent of the Queensland vote, she won a guaranteed income for six years and a role on a platform she knew how to use.

Oxley had changed, but so had the times. The opprobrium Hanson once endured had almost evaporated. Populism was on the rise around the world, favouring apparently homespun politicians who spoke their minds and for whom causing offence was a badge of authenticity. Opposition briefly flared when Hanson entered the Senate dressed in a black burqa, demanding that the garment be banned, but she knew how to play the game. She was more often indulged than condemned. The world's media noticed when she introduced a motion to outlaw what she called 'white racism', with an explicitly white supremacist logic in 2018. It was another of her *look at me* moments, part of the theatre of parliament. Remarkably the motion nearly passed the Senate. The woman who had been unanimously condemned 22 years earlier only failed by three votes.

17

Remaking the Nation

PAUL KEATING COULD switch from grand visionary to patient teacher in a flash: explaining complex concepts one minute, berating his opponent with scarifying invective the next. Even those who disagreed with him admired his style, his ability to crystallise an idea in a few pithy words. He made a lie of the notion that Australians resist rhetoric, that as a quotidian people we don't like leaders who are also great speakers. They may have hated his arrogance, been mystified by his willingness to learn and change, but they thought he was inspiring.[1] So when he said in the dying days of the 1996 federal election campaign that *If you change the government, you change the country*, it seemed almost anodyne. Why would people who dislike change vote for it? Surely a vote for the Coalition would be just a return to some old normal.

The landslide swing against Keating's government on that Saturday in March 1996 made it clear that people had had enough. Over the past thirteen years, the country had been transformed. The economy had turned outwards to face the world, and a social compact had ensured that the excesses of neoliberal economics were curtailed by targeted income support, increased educational offerings, superannuation for all and more equal opportunities.

Paul Keating did not itemise a list of new policies in his 1996 election speech. Instead, he sketched a vision of a country that had matured and was better able to hold its place in a rapidly changing world:

> Our children will receive the inheritance we ourselves have been given, but they will employ it not as an enclave marooned on an abundant island but as a nation with a destiny flowing from the most generous benefaction of history; a continent of our own, a border with no one, a deep democracy, an egalitarian ethic. The challenge is to harness our confidence; to make ourselves stronger at home and more enterprising abroad.[2]

By contrast, John Howard's stump speech accentuated the negative. He had at last reached the end point of a campaign he had been waging for years, outlining his approach in a series of headland speeches. In one, he described the urgent need to fight back against the 'bureaucracy of the new class', which was 'a world apart from the myriad of spontaneous, community-based organisations which have been part and parcel of the Australian mainstream for decades'. In future, he declared, interest groups would be 'assessed against the national interest and sentiments of mainstream Australia'.[3] In his memoir he wrote that he wanted to 'rebalance the narrative' about the past. He saw 'no flaws' but wanted a vigorous debate about the need for change: 'I had a project, but was not so arrogant as to presume I should inflict on the Australian people a new vision for the nation. Successive generations had given her a good enough vision and sense of her identity.'[4]

In his 1996 campaign launch speech, rather than defining what this new vision might be, John Howard rolled off almost incomprehensibly

Remaking the Nation

big numbers. He described the threat of debt and the promise of privatisation. He promised dollops of cash for small business, farmers, families, mothers who wanted to stay at home and, unexpectedly, the CSIRO. Reducing the scale and scope of government was key. It was to be a spectacular success, one that would reverberate for decades. This became clear during the pandemic, when the weakened public sector was unable to cope, and billions was spent bringing in private consultants to help with basic strategy and services.[5]

The one measurable change John Howard said he wanted was for 'some restoration of the trust and confidence of the Australian people in the political process' by the end of the first term of a Coalition government. This was to be a fail. In 1996, just under half the population trusted government, according to the ANU's election survey, but by the end of Howard's first term it had fallen to less than one-third. During his eleven-year tenure it never recovered, and continued to fall. His cynically accurate view of the electorate reached new highs when even from this low base he campaigned against Labor's volatile leader Mark Latham in 2004 with a question, *Who do you trust?* Then in the early months of the pandemic as government took a more active lead, and splashed money like confetti, trust in institutions rose to new highs. But a new divide emerged, with those who would once have been categorised as Howard's battlers again losing faith. The inequality trust gap between them and those with more information and resources at their fingertips was the largest in the world.[6] A new group of battlers was poised to be exploited by demagogues promising freedom and encouraging distrust.

It did not take long to understand the brilliance of Paul Keating's truism about changing government and changing the country. The dramatic economic and geopolitical realignments of the previous decade were robust and continued to follow their own logic. Without a commitment to a social compact to soften the impact of neoliberalism's unbridled market, inequality increased, privatisations reached into what were once considered government services and the competition between the insiders and the rest gathered pace.

The change the incoming government was most interested in was the battle for the heart of the nation. John Howard didn't say it so explicitly but channelled Margaret Thatcher's famous remark: 'Economics are the method; the object is to change the heart and soul.'[7] Rather than Paul Keating's searing language and patient explanations, this battle was now conducted *sotto voce* by a prime minister who stressed the economic, valorised pragmatism, co-opted the myths and encouraged apathy. He had learned how to turn his childhood deafness into a way to hear the undercurrent, the structures of feeling that shaped the zeitgeist. He heard that people were 'tired of the endless seminar on national identity', but prosecuted it with unexpected ferocity under another guise.

The change was not just economic but involved a fundamental realignment of values. It did not take close observers long to realise that this was not going to be a quiet period to regroup, consolidate the changes of the '80s and early '90s and work through the complexity of what face to present to the world in a new century. Instead, the struggle between labour and capital, between the public good and individual advantage, between provincialism and cosmopolitanism that had played out since before Federation, was on again. This time shrouded in the dollars that flowed from China's hunger for Australian resources.

Even before he had been sworn in as prime minister, John Howard announced that the heads of six key departments—Immigration, Transport, Foreign Affairs, Health, Environment, and Employment, Education and Training—would be replaced. Senior public servants had been moved onto contracts before, but the speed and scale of the job losses, and the seniority of those who were replaced, were almost unprecedented. The National Party government had an out-of-town try-out in Brisbane the year before.[8] The ethos of a disinterested public service had been deeply ingrained; previous Coalition governments had retained senior public servants who had made their names working for Labor, and Labor ministers worked with public servants who argued against their preferred policies. Before the election Howard had promised there would be 'no slash and burn ... no punishment of people on the basis of ideology'. That was not what happened. His 'break with convention was stark', wrote political scientist James Murphy. 'For his idol, Robert Menzies, questioning the professionalism or loyalty of the civil service was strictly the preserve of conspiracists and radicals—not a matter for serious statesmen.'[9]

A lot had changed since the days when Robert Menzies governed with one eye on England and another on critics at home, and a firm hand on the tiller of state. Although critics liked to paint Howard as a man who wanted to retreat to the comfort of the 1950s, his was a more radical conservatism. His mild suburban exterior masked a different sensibility. The pro-market think tanks, particularly the Institute of Public Affairs and Centre for Independent Studies, had become more influential during the 1980s. John Howard was persuaded by their arguments. They did not just want to smooth the path for business and ensure that the market dominated; they wanted to win hearts and minds, to prevent more of the change that had realigned society over the previous decades. The quiet persuaders and enablers were in their sights: public servants, journalists, academics, historians, teachers, scientists, lawyers, judges, and First Nations people and their advocates. While dismissing talk about national identity, John Howard set about redefining it, with a harder heart.

Public enterprises had had a long history in Australia, a necessary product of the country's scale and remoteness. Their days were numbered.[10] The Hawke and Keating governments had used privatisation as a way of increasing competition and revenue, and between 1988 and 1995 sold fourteen organisations, including Qantas, the Commonwealth Serum Laboratories and the Commonwealth Bank.

Under John Howard, privatisation was less about competition and more about increasing opportunities for individuals, companies and bankers. Fifty-seven enterprises were sold in a decade—airports, telecommunications, land and railways. It was the 'biggest disposal of public enterprises in Australia's history'.[11] Public debt fell, investment bankers grew rich and global investors took notice and pounced. Outsourcing government services followed. Family dysfunction, unemployment and inequality became businesses; the companies that managed the distribution of public money had few incentives to see it end. The switch to user pays saw enrolments in private schools increase by nearly 25 per cent and the steady undermining of the public schools which had done so much to create a shared experience. The number of public servants plummeted, institutions were weakened, and regulators did their jobs with one hand tied behind their backs.

Most people enjoyed the material comfort that followed; some were distracted by the culture war fights. Changes to the tax system, reductions in government debt and the trade with China that swapped minerals for cheap consumer goods masked the scale of the project. It was a textbook adaptation of Margaret Thatcher's dictum: *use economics, change the heart and soul.*

THE COLLAPSE OF the Whitlam government had marked the beginning of the ascendancy of this new market-driven idea of Australia. When American economist Milton Friedman made his first barnstorming tour of the country in 1975, he planted the seeds of a more libertarian approach to Australian economic and political power. They germinated over the next decade. His was a world in which the market ruled and governments got out of the way. It was an ethos that had long enjoyed pockets of support, but was now on the ascendancy.

Remaking the Nation

The old Australian settlement, which shared resources and put a floor under the society, was to become a thing of the past. Some of the changes were overdue, but values were also under threat. With the old ideas went the system of centrally arbitrated wage determinations that had prevailed since 1907; the remaining tariffs that protected local industries and kept prices of imported goods artificially high; public-sector banking, telecommunications, media, pharmaceutical, air transport and infrastructure enterprises that had limited commercial oligopolies in the small market; highly regulated banking and insurance industries; very high union membership; immigration with an easy path to citizenship; a fixed exchange rate regime; and the short-lived public gift of free tertiary education.

The Keynesianism that had dominated economic thinking since the Second World War was challenged by this market-based ethos, and big structural changes soon followed. Marian Sawer is a political scientist who was watching closely. She saw the rise of this new politics in the early 1980s as a fundamental break with the old prevailing logic, and described the new ethos:

> The state's role is not to promote social change, but to hold the ring for a free market system. Goals such as equal opportunity for disadvantaged groups have entailed a growth of state interference in free market contracts, the pursuit of equality ... [they] go against nature and the natural workings of the market.[12]

It seemed a hard sell. Surely the dictum of self-interest would mean that people were alert to the threat? But, as ever, there were plenty of ready helpers with access to money and media to make the case. While they are still employed by major media companies, most journalists are reluctant to acknowledge how their reporting can have a political impact. Once they retire the scales sometimes fall from their eyes. David McNicoll was once the stylish doyen of Sydney journalism, a silver-haired fox who had worked for Australian Consolidated Press and the Packer family for five decades. In his retirement he acknowledged part of his role had been to persuade working-class people not to vote in their own interests. 'All those seats would have gone to Labor . . . without our right-wing influence . . . There's no doubt about that at all.'[13]

EVER SINCE THE Federation debates that pivoted on questions of intra-colony trade and protection, there have been active proponents of a market-led approach to the economy and the primacy of business.

In 1944 Sir Keith Murdoch was one of the Melbourne business leaders who established the Institute of Public Affairs (IPA). He was fearful that Australia was on a path 'towards centralised planning and socialism'. Its aim was to 'mobilise opinion to counter the threat to business autonomy reconstruction plans were seen to represent'.[14] And to advance the interests of the mining, manufacturing, agricultural, property and banking companies associated with the influential Collins House Group. In the post-war 23 years of Liberal–Country Party government there had been little need for the ginger group, but Whitlam's election again put wind into its sails.

When Milton Friedman arrived in the country the year before he won the Nobel Prize for Economics, he blew 'a breath of fresh air' into what these advocates considered moribund debates. He gathered acolytes in influential quarters. Decades later, these men—many of whom became leading bankers and industrialists and later buffed their public profiles chairing government inquiries and the boards of cultural organisations—recalled his visit with a lingering sparkle of excitement. It was a sophisticated argument that upended the prevailing economic orthodoxy around the world. It also made their fortunes.

Remaking the Nation

In Australia, the message was reduced to its extractive essence. It was distilled colloquially by the mining magnate Lang Hancock in the preface to the booklet that accompanied Friedman's tour. It still (perversely) resonates today. 'The emphasis must be placed at all times on making people understand that the basis of all civilisation is mining, because everything comes from the earth,' Hancock wrote. 'This is not understood by the media, bureaucracy and government, but it is understood by the communist controlled unions who realise that by destroying mining they are able to achieve their aim of destroying Australia.'[15]

As the IPA was revived, other free-market think tanks nudged in, and the pages of *The Australian* became their showcase. After the 1975 journalists' strike protesting editorial interference was lost and the government changed, the new regime at News Corporation's Holt Street headquarters accepted 'an evangelical role in the wider public debate'. The affirming nationalism of the *Australian*'s first editorial, of a young buck trying to make his way in the world after a rejection, was a thing of the past.

A new orthodoxy was emerging, and it was serious. Dominic Kelly documented the change of tone and content in *The Australian* for his doctoral thesis, which he published as a book with a title that unequivocally signalled his point of view: *Political Troglodytes and Economic Lunatics*. *The Australian*'s reporters covered the recommendations of the think tanks assiduously. Politics was reduced to a cynical competition over a fistful of dollars; self-interest was worshipped; there was little space for discussions of the harder to define public good. The articles in its pages helped set the scene for the fundamental reshaping of the economy that was to follow.[16] As the economy opened to international competition, tariffs were abolished, foreign investment rules loosened, the currency floated and state-owned businesses were privatised, many of the old verities were broken. Financialisation was the order of the day. Much of Australia prospered and some people got very, very rich.

The Idea of Australia

This structural transformation had begun under a Labor government with strong roots in the union movement. As a result, Australian neoliberalism in its first phase included more checks and balances than the United States or Britain. Fairness, social justice, human rights, decent wages and income support tempered the early stages of the transformation. But, as it developed, the nod to the public good became more cursory. The change was profound. Politicians became spruikers for the market and economics became the sole *lingua franca* of policy. The state was there to moderate and ensure the market flourished, rather than be the custodian of the public good.

THE AUSTRALIAN NATIONAL University was born in 1946 with close ties to the government departments on the south side of what later became Lake Burley Griffin. Department heads and ministers turned to the university for advice and research; in their retirement, many found sinecures—researching, teaching and feeding ideas back into political debates and public policy solutions.

By the end of the 1980s, the nation builders of the post-war generation were being challenged by this new market-driven orthodoxy.[17] Tension was thick in the air in the iconic and utterly confusing multisided Coombs Building, named for one of the university's first chancellors, Nugget Coombs. As the public servant charged with leading the post-war reconstruction, Coombs helped shape mid-century Australia. Under his administrative leadership, Keynesianism flourished, mass migration transformed society, local manufacturing grew, education and arts funding increased and arguments about the need for a treaty with First Nations people were put at the highest level. His was a nation-building agenda, one that suited and was supported by the times.

When the switch to neoliberalism became dominant in the late 1980s, the head of the ANU's Research School of Social Sciences was

Remaking the Nation

Geoffrey Brennan, an economist-philosopher with close ties to James Buchanan, a Nobel Prize–winning architect of American neoliberalism.[18] Geoffrey Brennan was keen to see similar ideas reflected here. His big project, *Reshaping Australian Institutions*, had a radical intent. Public choice theory was its technical term. In Australia it was called economic rationalism, often with a sneer. Not everyone believed that economics was rational, or that people would put self-interest first and make wise decisions based solely on money. In this theory, there was little room for the public interest; everything had a price, and human behaviour was one-dimensional. I well remember sitting in Geoffrey Brennan's office as he assured me that the economic impulse would prevail and rational decisions would be made, self-interest would win. No doubt my scepticism was infuriating for such a well-credentialed economist.

Nation builders and social democrats of the old school were not convinced either. They researched and wrote chapter after chapter for books arguing that despite some benefits in removing the rigidity of the old system, there was a fundamental problem with economic rationalism. Public goods—community services, arts, education, social cohesion—would be devalued, the rich would get richer, the state would struggle to effectively regulate.

The old guard—many of whom still had offices in the Coombs Building, and who had fought to abolish the White Australia policy, modernise and diversify the economy, pursue treaties with First Nations people, push Australia to have closer relations with China and take a more active role on the world stage—found it hard to jettison a lifetime of beliefs. They struggled for space in the press, but made their arguments in books, in journals and on radio, in tearooms and seminars where Chatham House rules applied. These veterans of depression and war knew in their ageing bones that an unfettered market-driven system would serve the needs of capital but be unlikely to meet the complex requirements of the society they had imagined and helped build. They advocated ways of finding a balance by asking tough questions. Did the market care about people for anything other than the contents of their wallets? What if people were not equipped to make rational choices? Wasn't being a citizen more than being a consumer? How could an independent, robust and knowledgeable public service continue in such an ideologically determined context? Why should international capital have any interest in Australian social or cultural priorities? Would government regulation be able to hold the powerful to account?

IT WAS NOT surprising, then, that the Australian Broadcasting Corporation became a target, again despite pre-election commitments to the contrary. Without any negotiation, the new Howard government removed $55 million from the ABC's 1997 budget and announced an inquiry to examine its ongoing role. It signalled a pattern of cuts and inquiry, criticism and undermining, that would be repeated for decades. At the time, the national broadcaster routinely topped the tables of the most trusted institution in the country. This was a problem for John Howard and his colleagues, who considered the broadcaster 'our enemy talking to our friends'.[19]

The ABC was a particularly infuriating enemy. At heart, its ethos was one embodied in the idea of the media holding power to account, and with an operational aim to educate, inform and entertain. It was an idea that had blossomed in an earlier form in the land of newspapers before Federation. It flourished a century later as journalists became more assertive, more self-consciously professional. Program makers were not embarrassed to think of themselves as educators.[20] When he was acquiring the first papers, and his future empire was almost unimaginable, it was a principle Rupert Murdoch also advocated and asked about the commercial media: 'What right have we to speak in the public interest when, too often, we are motivated by personal gain?'[21]

By the time one of the biggest media empires the world had ever known was under his control, the answer was clear. For Rupert Murdoch personal gain had won, just as the public choice theorists had predicted it would. The public broadcasters had a more complex master—their fellow citizens, a belief in independence and scrutiny, and faith in professionalism. Although the cuts prevailed and more were to follow, the inquiry into the ABC surprised those who commissioned it by tapping into an overwhelming groundswell of support. There was an unprecedented number of submissions from all over the country; thousands of people wrote to explain why the ABC mattered to them. This was to become the first shot in a Groundhog Day campaign that still continues. Conservative politicians reduced its budget, questioned its operational and editorial independence and authority, bombarded it with complaints, stacked the board, bad-mouthed its journalism and programming, and encouraged media competitors to keep it under relentless scrutiny.

The 1920s Italian communist leader Antonio Gramsci had once argued that political control came from winning public consent. It was a lesson that the other side of politics more seriously took to heart. The libertarian right in the US, unsettled by the civil rights movement, decided it needed to target institutions that produce cohesion and meaning, institutions that had once been considered the bulwark of conservatism. Irving Kristol, an American neoconservative, started the battle with his 1978 book *Two Cheers for Capitalism*. In it he damned, among others, 'scientists, teachers and educational administrators, journalists and others in communication industries, psychologists, social workers [and] those lawyers and doctors who make their careers in the expanding public sector'. In Australia, many of these people also worked in the public sector, and put the publicly funded cultural and education institutions in an invidious position.

Australians are good followers. A strong public sector has distinguished Australian administration since settlement, but it proved to be a surprisingly easy target. John Howard expanded those on the watchlist to include 'Indigenous activists, multiculturalists, feminists, republicans and black armband historians'.[22] Making life uncomfortable for these groups, whose jobs gave them a public platform, also sent a clear message about who was in control. The safeguards that had been so painstakingly won, allowing publicly funded organisations to operate accountably but with independence from the government of the day, were under assault.

This was mystifying to those of us who worked as journalists, lawyers, teachers and academics. How had our workplaces gone from being a part of the institutional fabric of the nation to its enemy? We were committed to broadening the conversation, encouraging education, helping people become more informed and less captive to sectional interests so that better decisions could be made. For most, this was not a matter of ideology. At heart it was a liberal lesson, one that could be traced back to the Enlightenment and conservative thinking about the value of life being more than economic.[23]

Instead, we were pilloried as elites, often by those who by virtue of birth, wealth or class were unequivocally elite. The University of Wollongong historian Greg Melleuish had little sympathy. 'From one perspective they are champions ... bringing into the public arena aspirations and ideals that previously had not been articulated, rather suppressed under the old politics. They represent a growing plurality,' he wrote in his treatise *The Packaging of Australia*. 'From another viewpoint they represent the values of a New Class seeking to establish themselves as the New Elite within the bureaucracy as a means of building and consolidating their power.'[24] By 2021 the IPA had 8000 members and the outgoing chief executive bemoaned his sense that they were on the losing side. 'We've now realised,' he told the *Australian Financial Review*, 'that politics is downstream of culture, and we have to engage in a debate about our community and values.'[25] It seemed unlikely that the interests of the real, quiet Australians would be defended by the richest and most powerful, who were more likely to think of them as 'proles' to be feared.[26]

VALUES SOON BECAME the preferred means of doing this winnowing of people into competing tribes. When the cabinet papers from the year 2000 were released, they showed just how central certain values were to John Howard's heart. That year he changed corporations law so the name of his hero Don Bradman could not be taken in vain. The cricketer's name was added to a small list of proscribed names—Anzac, Red Cross, Bank, United Nations. He also explored ways to ensure religious organisations could insist employees shared their beliefs, and to exclude same-sex couples from IVF treatment.[27]

Values can be political, but they are also a tool of commerce. The rise of global capitalism has underwritten the niche field identifying national values. Social scientists have been deployed to help transnational companies find a better, more profitable and more congenial foothold in the diverse places they operate. Gone were the days of colonial trade when an imperial mother could impose values and expect compliance. There are real dollars attached to understanding, and better exploiting, national difference—think a McDonald's McOz burger with tomato, beetroot and lettuce versus a Big Mac with pickled cucumber and two patties.

Australia routinely scores as one of the least distinctive in surveys that measure cultural similarities and differences. 'Australia is the second *least* distinctive culture of all, beaten to the gold medal by Brazil,' concluded Nick Haslam from the University of Melbourne, who analysed the results of an international values survey in 2017. 'It is hard to escape the conclusion that what is unique about Australian values is their averageness.'[28]

Australians are not uniquely tolerant, nor distinctively committed to respect, rule of law, equality or intellectual autonomy.

Few leaders are now willing to define values beyond the most general—respect, rule of law, freedom of speech. John Howard was once ready to dive in and put values at the heart of his vision of Australian social cohesion: *us and them*. He was skilled at using public events as useful props. Two days after Anzac Day 2006, a new citizenship test for migrants was announced. It took a little while to become policy, but before Howard lost his seat he had time to launch *Becoming an Australian Citizen*, a 46-page guide that was heavy on values, light on citizenship. It was better suited to preparing would-be citizens for a game of Trivial Pursuit. Readers were told the name of the national flower (wattle) and the national gemstone (opal), and that Sydney was home to the 'largest number of Rugby League clubs in Australia'. Seventy-five words expounded Donald Bradman's prowess half a century earlier—but did not mention that his batting average, 99.94, had a continuing life as the ABC's post office box number in every capital city.[29]

Vast sums of money have since been spent by government departments seeking to define the values that would-be Australian citizens must recognise before being permitted to fully participate in the life of the nation. The 2020 iteration, 94 pages and twenty multiple choice questions, is remarkable for its banality. Getting fifteen of the questions right flicks the switch to what has come to be regarded as the privilege (not the right) of citizenship. Many of the highly educated cohort of would-be citizens chortle as they complete the test, but the prize of citizenship and the gift of a native plant is incentive enough. At least the old Trivial Pursuit quiz questions have gone, replaced by questions that encourage would-be citizens who have lived in the country for at least four years to tick the boxes that demonstrate respect.

Remaking the Nation

VALUES WERE OFTEN mentioned during John Howard's prime ministership when talk turned to the culture wars, as they had become known. The phrase 'culture wars' conjures an arcane dispute between ideological opponents about matters of interpretation and understanding, but at heart there is an undeniable political economy. And in Australia, that comes from the four economic foundation stones: mining, agriculture, banking and their handmaiden, the media.

Pastoralists had been responsible for much of the settlement violence, and many enterprises grew rich with the help of underpaid First Nations workers and indentured slave labourers. But many of those who had farmed the land for generations worked hard and were deeply attached to it for more than the wealth it generated. As they battled floods, droughts and fickle markets, the best became increasingly alert to the need to be sustainable. When the High Court found, in its 1996 Wik judgment, that native title had not been extinguished by pastoral leases, the quest for a different form of sustainability gained new urgency. The National Farmers' Federation, under the leadership of former journalist Rick Farley, took the members of the federation on a transformative learning journey. Caring for the environment and finding a way to co-exist with traditional owners became the new priorities.

Mining companies were much more reluctant to embark on a similar journey. They were bigger, richer and more powerful. Ever since the goldmines had drawn thousands of prospectors to the colonies, mining had been central to the economy: gold, silver, coal, copper, lead, zinc, nickel, iron ore, oil, bauxite, uranium, gas, silica, lithium, rare earth metals. The country may have grown on the sheep's back, but mining made it, and many individuals and families, wealthy. No one knew this better than the legendary prospector Lang Hancock. He died bankrupt, but the legacy of his initiative in claiming vast iron ore–rich tenements in Western Australia made his daughter, Gina Rinehart, unimaginably rich.

The mining industry extracts and removes. It had less invested in finding a way to co-exist with First Nations people than farmers, who need to keep the land and its waters functioning to thrive. At the end of the twentieth century the enormous mining companies, by then listed on the London Stock Exchange, were unapologetically hostile to the growing land rights movement. They were ready to use their power to get their way. As became clear twenty years later with Rio Tinto's destruction of the Juukan Gorge sacred site in the Pilbara, destruction was in their DNA.

Mining is the ultimate zero-sum game. It was miners, and their supportive Western Australian premier, who scuttled national land rights and the treaty Bob Hawke promised when he signed the Barunga Statement. It was some of the richest mining companies in the world that suggested they were the successors of the rebels at the Eureka Stockade when they campaigned in 2010 to kill a tax on their super profits to finance national economic innovation. It was mining executives who talked themselves red in the face campaigning against the carbon tax designed to mitigate climate change.

In the 1990s, the industry's most assiduous leader, Western Mining's Hugh Morgan, sensed that the High Court's Mabo judgment could be an existential threat. During the case, the High Court had, for the first time, drawn on and referenced historical sources. That history had shaped its judgment was 'unprecedented'. Justice William Deane noted that the decision was informed not only by 'the material placed before us by the parties but by the researches of many scholars who have written in these areas'. [30]

This put historians in the firing line and opened a fresh opportunity for an historian, who had first made his mark writing about mining, to again step into the limelight. Geoffrey Blainey had been one of Manning Clark's students at the University of Melbourne, but when he graduated in 1954 there were few university jobs. Instead, the ambitious young man embarked on a writing life, taking commissions to record the history of companies and industries. His first book, *The Peaks of Lyell*, drew on his master's thesis and traced the brutal history of gold and copper mining in Queenstown, Tasmania. Over the decades he returned time and again to the stories of miners and their companies.

Within weeks of the Mabo judgment, Hugh Morgan 'embarked on a campaign to denounce the High Court and discredit the decision'. Morgan and his colleagues had already formed the Samuel Griffith Society, which they had said was inspired by their outrage at 'the chattering classes view that the Constitution was in need of reform'. So when the judgment was delivered, they were ready to attack: the court was naive; the High Court judges had 'no pride in their country'. Morgan suggested the judges had joined the 'Bolshevik left' to push for a 'separate Aboriginal state'. In speech after speech, he declared that the court was caught up in the 'guilt industry' and that the judges seemed to be ashamed to be Australian.[31]

In 1904, the first chief justice of the High Court, Sir Samuel Griffith, had stood his ground and demanded enough resources to ensure the independence of the High Court.[32] It was a lesson ingrained in his successors, even though they are appointed, without review, by politicians from the ruling party. Australian judges generally remain above the rough and tumble of public life, even in retirement. This attack was one they were no better prepared for than the historians. The convention that kept the High Court above politics almost broke under the weight of Morgan's orchestrated campaign.

After the Wik judgment in 1996, the most eminent judges in the land were further vilified. The deputy prime minister and National Party leader Tim Fischer was particularly strident in his denunciation. Judges were accused of being activists, with a sideswipe that they were elite—although surely that was an essential precondition for judges in the court of last appeal, charged with interpreting the Constitution.

As had previously happened in the United States, judicial activism became a new battleground. Geoffrey Blainey was ready to use his prestige and join the fray: 'What perturbs me, as an Australian', he wrote in 1995 in the *Law Institute Journal*, was that 'the highest court in the land, in its majority judgment [Mabo], denied the legitimacy of this country. That, I think is almost inexcusable ... The High Court has become too powerful.'[33] Attorneys-general failed to come to the defence of the court; public trust was eroded. Within a few years, judges had publicly distanced themselves again from the importance of the work of professional historians.

The High Court decisions then became a matter for politicians and the parliament to address. Public hysteria was fanned and inflammatory claims thrown on the fire. Those pastoralists willing to negotiate, who valued co-existence, were castigated as traitors. It was a heaven-sent opportunity for John Howard. He had always been uncomfortable with Paul Keating's Native Title Act, and this was an opportunity to water it down.

The spirit of the judgment was whittled away. New bureaucratic obstacles were put in the way of claimants, state governments could abolish native title in crown land, no claims could be made in the cities, strict time limits were imposed, and mining and pastoral leases were allowed to co-exist. It was not a Pyrrhic victory for traditional owners, but once again the onus of proof was on them. Traditional owners found themselves tied up in endless negotiations, legal cases and research to prove ownership. Cases took decades to resolve, and rights were limited.

Mining companies slowly realised that they had not lost. The oldest tactic of colonisation—divide and rule—was still available to them. They also realised that talking a big game and offering cooperation and jobs could make them look good, be productive and be lucrative.[34] As Chris Mitchell reflected in his 2016 memoir, 'It seems incredible today, given how little Aboriginal people actually gained from the two decisions, that there was such disquiet in the nation's rural heartland only twenty years ago about the emergence of native title.'[35]

EVENTS MAKE AND break leaders, and John Howard liked to boast that the times suited him. How leaders respond under pressure is the truest measure of character. In the final years of the century, decades of war in Afghanistan had broken the spirit of the people. More than four million had fled to refugee camps in neighbouring countries, and those who couldn't find a passage to a safe country did what they could to make a new life. The UN Refugee Convention had been adopted by a small number of countries, including Australia, in 1951. Forty-nine years later the Convention and its Protocol had been signed by 139 nations. They promised not to return those subjected to intolerable political persecution in their homelands. By the end of the century, 30 million refugees were on the road and in refugee camps trying to find new homes.

The 1990s had reminded many that the threat of political persecution and war was still alive, even in Europe. The world watched in shock as the Balkans exploded in murderous sectarian violence. Australia provided a temporary home to some of those fleeing Bosnia. Yugoslavia had been an important source of immigrants during the 1960s; there were strong family ties and political connections in Australia to smooth the passage. Those from other hotspots were not so fortunate, and the impulse to exclude was almost reflexive. In 1992 the Keating government legislated to allow mandatory detention, and the first remote centre at Port Headland for unauthorised arrivals seeking asylum was opened a couple of years later.

Refugees have always touched a political nerve in Australia. Jews fleeing pre-war Germany were sent to camps, as were Nazi sympathisers. There was much hand wringing about what to do with those fleeing Vietnam after that war, which had divided Australia as well.

The Idea of Australia

Despite Gough Whitlam's initial opposition, the Fraser government facilitated the arrival of 130,000 Indochinese refugees who arrived between 1976 and 1991. By the end of the century, most of those fleeing their homelands were from Afghanistan, Iraq and North Africa, places that were not traditional sources of Australian migrants.

On 26 August 2001, the Norwegian-flagged ship MV *Tampa*, en route from Fremantle to Singapore, responded to a request from the Australian Maritime Safety Authority to go to the aid of a boat that was breaking up in Indonesian waters, four hours south of Christmas Island. Over the previous six days, three boats carrying 1000 refugees had landed on the island, and the authorities suspected another 80 refugees were on the *Palapa 1*. The *Tampa* captain, Arne Rinnan, was advised by Canberra that under the International Convention for the Safety of Life at Sea it was up to him to decide what to do. He and his crew rescued 438 people—five Indonesian crew, the rest asylum seekers—from the unseaworthy vessel. They were brought aboard the open decks of a freighter that was equipped for just 42 people. The next day Rinnan was contacted by an Australian immigration official and told that if he took the people to Christmas Island he could be charged with people smuggling.

The political temperature was rising. With his ear ever cocked to talkback radio and his eyes on the tabloid front pages, John Howard announced that the *Tampa* would not be allowed to dock. Eventually a three-day stand-off broke when Arne Rinnan and his distressed and ill human cargo sailed into Flying Fish Cove on Christmas Island. In a high-stakes game that owed something to a war movie, John Howard directed the Special Air Service to take command of the ship. In a radio interview, he insisted that 'it is in Australia's national interest that we draw the line on what is increasingly becoming an uncontrollable number of illegal arrivals in this country'. This was two weeks before the terrorist attacks on the World Trade Center and the Pentagon, but the prime minister's political instincts were already primed. At the time it seemed like desperate politics from a leader who was behind in the polls; Paul Kelly called it 'inept crisis management' in *The Australian*. Over the next month, another twelve boats carrying more than 2000 passengers arrived; a thirteenth tragically sank en route with 353 lives lost; and another four were returned to Indonesia.[36] Fanciful stories that children were being thrown overboard were allowed to run without correction.

Before long, even though the media was denied access, it became clear that government ministers had lied, defence leaders had been put in an impossible position, and the laws of the sea and the Refugee Convention had been circumvented or ignored. Refugees were vilified; they were not like 'us'.

Australia was condemned in international forums for its failure to honour the long-established conventions. The government passed legislation to excise offshore islands from the nation and adopted a policy branded with the chilling title 'the Pacific Solution'. Asylum seekers were despatched to Nauru, its government larded with cash. Not for the first time Australian diplomats had to present an ugly a face to the world. As Sue Boyd, the senior diplomat in the Pacific, wrote in her book *Not Always Diplomatic*, it was 'opportunistic and racist'.[37]

John Howard went to the 2001 election prepared to snatch victory from the jaws of defeat. The brutal politics were driven from his prime ministerial office. In October, a week before the election, he received a standing ovation for an hour-long speech at the City Recital Hall in Sydney. David Marr was unsettled by the 'white prosperous audience baying for border protection', the ruthless political assessment and coy language as the prime minister played the race card, the joker in the Australian pack.[38] The night before the election, after he had been told there were no children thrown overboard, he still misspoke, and on election day there were full-page ads featuring the prime minister, fist clenched, declaring, 'We decide who comes to this country.'[39] It was a century after the governor-general had signed the bill passed by the Federation parliament that outlawed non-white, non–English-speaking immigrants. In the first year of a new century, another election had become a referendum on border control.

Australia was a product of immigration, immeasurably enriched by the arrival of refugees for decades. When polls showed that most people supported turning away those who arrived by boat, *over seas*, it was a sign that the soul of the nation, which had begun to heal when the White Australia policy was dismantled, had again been broken. What had seemed inconceivable before Pauline Hanson began her racist tirades four years earlier was now unremarkable. Racism was still at the heart of Australian politics and the very modern voters were as susceptible to its threat as their parents and grandparents had once been. It was a button both parties had pushed time and again, but by using all the tools of executive power this was a campaign of another order of magnitude. The brutal and cynical approach delivered victory for Howard with a narrow margin. Ironically, the scene was set for a period of unprecedented and diverse population growth.

18

People Like Us

ON THE EVE of the 2001 federal election, ten-year-old Yassmin Abdel-Magied was living in suburban Brisbane and decided it was time for her to dress like a woman. She knew this was an important decision, so she chose a date that would be recorded in history to help her remember it. When she got up on Saturday 10 November, she marched into breakfast and announced, 'I'm going to be Mahajabah from now on.'[1] Her mother, Faiza, had worn a hijab for as long as Yassmin could remember but they had never really talked about it. When she asked for a scarf Faiza told her to choose one from the dozens in her cupboard. There was nothing remarkable about the outspoken girl's decision; to her, it was an unexceptional expression of faith. Little white head coverings were part of her school uniform. As she later wrote in her memoir *Yassmin's Story*, she had been considering 'going full time' for some time, discussing it with her friends at the Islamic College of Brisbane. Some had already made the decision. Others tried; they were used to being stared at for being brown, but found that the extra attention the head covering brought made them even more uncomfortable. One friend acquiesced to her parents' fear that covering her hair would make her a target.

The Idea of Australia

Yassmin Abdel-Magied knew her own mind; she was a curious and brave child who had always tested the limits. There could scarcely have been a less auspicious day to make the decision to publicly declare her faith. The newspapers on that November election day were bristling with Liberal Party ads that implicitly targeted Muslims. You didn't need to be a semiotician to know that those who wore headscarves were unlikely to be high on the list of the people we would decide could come to this country so soon after fundamentalist Islamic terrorists had targeted the epicentre of global capitalism.

For much of the year, the polls had predicted the end of the Howard government. In March, the Liberal Party had lost a safe seat in Brisbane's leafy western suburbs. The well-educated, middle-class voters in Ryan, around the University of Queensland, had grown increasingly weary of the race-baiting belligerence that had become the norm ever since Pauline Hanson had been elected by voters further west.

The election in the year of the centenary of Federation should have been an opportunity to reset the national conversation, to finally jettison the racially defined politics of the previous century. Instead, many of the founding principles bubbled back with renewed urgency. It became a year defined by fear and threat, sorted by race. Yassmin Abdel-Magied's decision, made on a whim, to wear a hijab full time became 'one that would shape my future beyond anything I could have anticipated'.[2]

THE BRISBANE-BORN minister for immigration, Al Grassby, described Australia's future as multicultural in August 1973, and flagged a new beginning.[3] Before long and continuing under the Fraser government, English lessons were offered to new arrivals, a multicultural broadcaster was created, anti-racism laws were introduced, official information began to be translated and presented in multicoloured brochures, more translators were employed in the courts and hospitals. Names were slowly deanglicised—Lorries became Lorenzos, Annas became Annastacias. The appetite for tales from the suitcase grew; the sons and daughters of recent migrants who had once been called 'wogs' and derided for their 'smelly' sandwiches became the owners of the best restaurants, the most stylish boutiques and some of the most successful companies. Laws outlawing racial discrimination passed and restrictions on migrants' countries of origin eased. But still a caste system remained. Some struggled to have their international credentials recognised by local professional bodies. Many jobs were still sorted by ethnicity, as a proxy for class. Pacific Islanders picked fruit, Filipinas looked after old people, Indians and Chinese drove taxis, Vietnamese ran restaurants, and Brits and Americans took the corner offices in corporate towers. As had been the case since convict transportation ended, migrants were sought for the work the locally born couldn't or wouldn't do.

Population policies are older than the nation and have frequently changed. Multiculturalism replaced integration, which had replaced assimilation, which had replaced exclusion. In my office I have shelves of books exploring settler–Aboriginal relations, but those unpicking the detail of population policies fill just one shelf. Some experiences are well known; many are not. The architecture of silence made it easy to forget. Stories slid away, important only to those who lived them. The mass incarceration of foreign nationals during the wars and their subsequent deportation. The German place names, which briefly displaced ancient names, before they too were scrubbed out. The trials that prevented foreigners visiting or staying. The Black American soldiers who fell in love but were not allowed to remain in Australia. The Japanese war brides who were not welcome. Unless it was your family that was touched by the cruelty of the state or you were famous enough to feature on *Who Do You Think You Are?*, few knew.

Even when he was campaigning with an implicit racialist subtext, John Howard stressed how generous and welcoming Australians were. Some were, but it was not instinctive as the early government campaigns to encourage good neighbourliness demonstrated.

Cultural diversity was increasingly celebrated after multiculturalism became official policy in the 1970s, but it had been a hard sell. It was difficult to disagree that diversity made the place more interesting, the food better, the tales richer. Some stories became emblematic. One was that of Vietnamese refugee Hieu Van Le, who arrived in Darwin Harbour in 1977. After weeks at sea, he expected a gunboat to meet him. Instead a couple of blokes fishing in a tinnie, with 'zinc on their noses and a can of beer in their hands', greeted him and said, 'G'day mate. Welcome to Australia.' Hieu Van Le later became the governor of South Australia, his sons named after two famous Australian cricketers.[4] Another story was that of the weeping prime minister, Bob Hawke. He opened the door to Chinese students after the 1989 Tiananmen Square massacre. His tears eloquently declared that Australia, the country that had once fined, penalised, humiliated and punished Chinese people, was not what it once had been. The following year his government made it harder for other asylum seekers to find refuge and introduced mandatory detention; the treatment of refugees had not become a human rights issue.[5] It was always complicated.

John Howard acknowledged, but was reluctant to fully embrace, the transformation of the homogeneous country he had grown up in. His rashly expressed hostility to Asian migration destroyed his first bid to become prime minister. He later said he had moved on but the memory lingered. It gave Maxine McKew, his victorious opponent in Bennelong—an electorate that, in 2007, looked Asian—an edge.

Stereotyping came easily. Rather than leaders taking on the old fears and challenging the embedded racism, people were left to bump along as best they could, trying to blend in, not take offence, be grateful for tolerance. Unlike other countries transformed by immigration, Australia had only run a few public education campaigns in the early years. It had scarcely tackled the invisible structures that enabled racist sentiment to fester, and meant many new arrivals struggled. Not long after his election victory in 1996 John Howard disbanded the Bureau of Immigration, Multicultural and Population Research.[6] Other intractable behaviours had been routinely challenged: slothfulness ('Life. Be in it'), smoking ('You can quit'), drink driving ('Grow up') or seatbelts ('Towards zero'). But racism was too entrenched, too useful.

The ugly consequences of ignoring long-held fears did not evaporate. Even after the Howard years, as the population grew quickly and new arrivals from China and India recalibrated life in the biggest cities, few political leaders went beyond the platitudes of tolerance and multiculturalism. Some dipped their toes in the debates about a 'big Australia'. Population growth had become one of the drivers of economic growth—sometimes it seemed an end in itself. The new arrivals bought and furnished houses, purchased cars and white goods, sent their children to school and after-school activities, and established new lives. This churn took the pressure off thinking about the sort of economy that would best suit the comparative advantages of the nation that occupied the continent and no longer depended on foreign capital.

The idea of cosmopolitanism, of being at ease in the world, was dismissed as the preserve of elites, instead of being embraced as a statement about the benefits of inclusive diversity. Over time the ethos changed. Migration became less straightforward. By the 1990s a protracted, incremental approach to migration policy had been laden with unintended consequences. Immigration had become an increasingly complicated mess of expensive visa categories with different rights and prospects. Entrance was based on skills, work needs, compensating for an ageing population and low birthrate, with special pathways for those with money to invest.[7]

The *stop/go* sign was always within reach. Ever since the 1901 laws to remove enslaved Melanesian workers were passed, deportation had been a pillar in what Prime Minister Edmund Barton called the 'ring fence' around the nation. Despite human rights challenges, deportation was routinely used for decades. In 2001 Australia set the global record. More than 10,000 people were forcibly removed: visa overstayers, unapproved refugees and criminals born elsewhere. The immigration department boasted that it demonstrated 'world's best practice'.[8] The number of new arrivals was also at a record high and tolerance was the order of the day, but structural transformation that made acceptance real was slippery, schools became more segregated.

AFTER YASSMIN ABDEL-MAGIED eventually figured out how to arrange her mother's scarf, secured with a pin that a friend had given her for just this moment, she proudly walked back to the kitchen. The rest of the family were already eating their Saturday breakfast of traditional Sudanese *fool-u-bayd* (broad beans and eggs garnished with tomatoes) and flatbread. Her father, Midhat, pinched Yassmin's cheek and asked, with a mixture of pride and concern, if she had decided to wear a scarf. 'Are you sure?'

Midhat was right to be concerned. He could not have anticipated what was at stake. How his precious daughter—the child for whom he had fled the country of his birth, and given up his profession, his wealth, status and family influence—would become an inspiration to thousands, but be forced into exile, derided in the press as the 'most hated Muslim in Australia'. A few months earlier their mosque, which had served the small local Muslim community, had been burned down and abusive graffiti painted on its fence.[9] Over the next fifteen years the attacks would become more personal and vicious: death threats, pigs' heads dumped at the mosque, and enough online abuse to scramble an algorithm.

People Like Us

Australia had been Midhat and Faiza's country of choice. While studying for his doctorate in electrical engineering at Imperial College London, Midhat found he had more in common with the Australians he met than the proper, class-constrained English. He later told his daughter that he thought the Aussies were kind, and their country a place where faith and background were not the impediments that he knew they would be in England. The Sudanese experience of British colonialism was very different to the Australian, but there were points of similarity. Most Australians looked more like the English than either Arab or African Sudanese, but many still felt like exotic outsiders under London's grey skies.

The young Australians Midhat met were curious, open minded and proud that their country was asserting its own identity. The world was their oyster, their good fortune palpable. In the 1980s New York was nearly bankrupt and plagued by drugs and violence. De-industrialisation was devastating much of the United States. Britain was reeling under Thatcherism. Unemployment hit one peak after another. Up and down the British Isles, factories closed and industries shut down. The threat of the Cold War tainted Europe with fear. Terrorists from the Middle East and Ireland staged routine attacks. The Iron Curtain was still impenetrable. There were a few gaps in the Bamboo Curtain, but with much of Southeast Asia still recovering from war, only Japan was booming. The travelling Australians popped up everywhere, following, with more self-assurance, in the footsteps of generations of Aussie adventurers. They brought the sunshine with them, their dollars remarkably valuable; travel was cheap and visas negotiable. As Rupert Murdoch once quipped, they turned up on time and did the job, and that made them look like geniuses. They were in many ways the country's best advertisement, ready to party but interested, brave, respectful and conscientious.

And generous. It was during this time of optimistic possibility that Ken Morley, a Newcastle engineer and dedicated socialist, took his young family to visit the People's Republic of China, a destination not on the usual tourist trail. It was 1980, less than a decade after Australia had established diplomatic relations with the country whose people it had once been so determined to exclude. In Hangzhou they met Jack Ma, an enterprising teenager who was keen to learn English. A relationship developed, and after the Morleys left they continued to correspond. They helped Jack to complete his English degree and buy his first apartment. After his Australian visa application was rejected seven times, Jack was eventually permitted to visit—and realised the world was different to China. That experience planted the seed of an idea that became the e-commerce business Alibaba. For a time he was one of the richest men in the world, but then slid from view in 2020 when Chinese leader Xi Jinping considered he had overreached. It was, as Jack Ma often recalled in interviews, the generosity and openness of the Morleys and the values he learned in Australia that changed his life. He returned the favour with scholarships for students at the University of Newcastle in Ken Morley's home town.

Around the same time that Midhat was finding he enjoyed the company of the Australians he met in London, Faiza was in Sudan and responded to an ad for a pen pal. Ian Hamilton wanted his son to learn more about the world than was possible in suburban Brisbane in Joh Bjelke-Petersen's Queensland. It is hard to remember now, in a world so instantly and intimately connected in which even six degrees of separation is probably an overstatement. Only a few decades ago keeping in touch relied on slow mail, aerograms and almost impossibly costly phone calls. Answering a random request for a pen pal was like putting your hand into a lucky dip. Most came to nothing. At the time Faiza accepted the invitation to share her world and learn about Australia, she was studying architecture at the most prestigious university in Khartoum. She was the third of four daughters who would graduate into the best professions. That the Hamiltons were Jehovah's Witnesses and

Faiza was Muslim gave them more to share—different faiths to discuss and compare. It was not an impediment to their blossoming friendship.

When they married and settled in Khartoum, Faiza and Midhat had every reason to expect they would have a comfortable life together despite the growing political turbulence. She worked in one of the best architectural firms; he was the youngest lecturer in the university's engineering faculty. Sudan had been 'gifted' to Britain at the 1884 Berlin Conference that divided the continent between the fading European empires. By the 1980s, Sudan had been wracked by civil war for the best part of a decade and, like many countries in Africa, was struggling with the legacy of decolonisation.

Then, in the same month that the Chinese military attacked protesters in Tiananmen Square, Colonel Omar al-Bashir overthrew the democratically elected government in Sudan and introduced political Islam, draconian sharia law and authoritarian controls. Midhat was one of only three academics who objected to the Arabisation of the university curriculum. He feared that his brilliant engineering students would be marooned in an overwhelmingly English-speaking world. All three lost their careers. The new regime threated to send a heavily pregnant Faiza to an internal re-education camp after she defended another woman who was harassed by security forces.

Before Yassmin was born, the young couple realised that the life they had imagined they might have in Sudan was unlikely.[10] A couple of years later, without burdening their families with knowledge of their decision, they left for a weekend in Egypt. They took two suitcases, $2000 and their toddler. Within months, Faiza's pen pal Ian Hamilton had sponsored them as skilled migrants and the little family arrived in Brisbane. Their qualifications were not recognised, so they studied for local credentials. They were constantly 'reminded' of their uniqueness. Faiza cried every night for two years. Living in Brisbane, as Pauline Hanson's rhetoric began to poison the air, she realised that they were 'too different, too foreign' to really 'make it' in Australia. They decided to pick their battles to prevent exhaustion. Their decision to remain in Brisbane, as Faiza later explained to Yassmin, was not driven by fear but by trust. They were confident that they could deal with anything that came their way. Confident in the power of education and in their belief that if they worked hard, they would be accepted. Australians are open minded, Faiza assured her daughter. *They like people who are genuine.*

YASSMIN'S FAMILY VISITED the land of their birth every couple of years. This had become the new normal for millions of immigrant families. Saving the $10,000 dollars for family tickets was not easy, but going back was not the inconceivable luxury it had been for earlier generations of immigrants. By the turn of the century, flying halfway around the world for a few days or weeks for a holiday, wedding, family reunion or funeral was no longer exceptional. Travel had never been cheaper, distance less tyrannical.

Before the global pandemic turned airports into ghostly emporiums, they were excellent places to understand how Australia had changed in half a century. The former government-owned hangars and functional sheds had been transformed into slick sites of commerce, with malls in which to eat, drink, meet, shop and socialise, delivering healthy profits for their owners and shareholders. While a few decades earlier a handful of national carriers deposited international travellers into the nation just after dawn, by 2019 dozens of international airlines were flying into the country, carrying in more than eleven million short-term visitors and taking almost half the population away on twelve million journeys a year.

Airports were the showroom of multicultural Australia: women in hijabs and burqas and their children made way for men in turbans and kurtas and their wives in saris; buffed and tattooed men shepherded

People Like Us

large family groups through customs; young people rested against their huge backpacks in endless check-in lines; while the fearful jostled to get their suitcases shrink-wrapped in plastic. Australia was no longer so white; it looked much more like the rest of the world, and the overwhelming majority thought it was the best place on the globe to live.[11] The diversity of humanity was on display every day.

In 2007, the year John Howard lost his seat, more than a quarter of the population was born overseas, the highest proportion since 1898. In the decades since he was first elected prime minister, the population has increased by seven and a half million people who were born overseas, exceeding even the transformative post-war influx when two million people arrived over two decades. The largest number still came from Britain, but European-born immigrants had been overtaken by new arrivals from China, India, Vietnam, the Philippines and several African countries. The national complexion was changing, but with significant regional variations: Sydney was more Chinese, Melbourne more Indian; Queensland was the most Anglo; Perth still hummed with the voices of regional England, but now with the twang of accents from other former colonies: South Africa, Zimbabwe, Malaysia, India, Sri Lanka.

THIS VAST AND deliberate transformation was accompanied by complaints about overcrowding and inadequate infrastructure, and a half-hearted, economically driven debate about the need for a big Australia. Migration had become a tool of economic growth, smoothing the curves of age and skills, and, despite promises to the contrary, depressing wages. The parallel conversation of what sort of nation Australia wanted to become was only superficially broached. What might it be like to have twenty cities of a million people, rather than three giant conurbations? How could better access to education ensure everyone, regardless of country of origin, get an equal chance? How could we ensure that the virtual caste system was not even more entrenched? As the pandemic rolled on and the collapse of immigration became a reality, journalists began to show more interest. They reported with evident surprise that the rules around migration had changed so much. But still the big fundamental question remained unaddressed.

Refugees had been the focus of public attention for so long that the changes to the whole system had passed without the scrutiny they deserved. Immigration, like so much else, had become a market-driven commodity. Migration had ceased to be primarily about nation building, more a transaction importing human resources. It was up to each new arrival to make their own way, possibly with the support of their employer or community group. The pathways for skilled workers, and international students who graduated from Australian universities, were easier but far from certain as rules changed and loopholes kept people guessing. Without many really noticing, the whole basis of immigration policy changed on the day the Howard government implemented the Keating policy that made a temporary skilled 457 visa available to employers who wanted to sponsor workers. In the era of neoliberal economics, globalisation demanded a mobile workforce. Australia would no longer be a place of exile or a place from which return would be difficult. Instead, it became a place where tens of thousands of people landed with short-term rights to work and uncertain long-term prospects.[12]

Nor was it a place where immigrants could easily extend an arm to their homelands and bring the rest of the family. Immigration and possible citizenship became something to try before you buy—both for the new arrivals and the state.[13] This left some vulnerable to deportation, and others nervously detached for years as they jumped through one hoop after another.

The new processes of immigration—elaborate point scores and job categories for some, and a lack of sympathy for the complicated needs of real people's lives—were left to individuals to navigate. Everyone who encountered the system had a story to tell of an expensive, seemingly impenetrable bureaucracy. Within 25 years of Howard's introduction of the 457 visa, there would be more than two million people living in Australia on one of the 74 different, and costly, visas. For many there was no easy or obvious path to citizenship. Some paid taxes but also paid for their children to attend public schools and public hospitals. Some received benefits, but many were not entitled to the government support that Australian citizens took for granted. They were allowed to work, but an evolving hierarchy of belonging operated. The new caste system became painfully apparent when the rules for government support during the pandemic were released, leaving international students, certain visa holders and refugees on the pathway to permanency, without support.

The politicians who enacted the change of policy were inclined to ignore the transformative nature of the new rules. They were still inclined to pat themselves on the back for not presiding over 'a guest-worker society'. As became painfully clear for many during the pandemic, this was not true. Hundreds of thousands of people did not qualify for any public support—even if their employers had paid large sums for their visas, and even if they had been paying taxes for years. Prime Minister Scott Morrison even told international students to go home rather than expect to be looked after here.

The infrastructure of multiculturalism had crumbled. State health authorities did not have the data they needed to make informed decisions and translate pandemic management advice into the full range of languages people spoke. It took a long time before community leaders were drawn in to ensure the messages were appropriate. Instead, whole buildings of public housing tenants were locked down, airports were closed, Australians had to apply for special leave to depart, and hundreds of thousands of those living abroad found it almost impossible to return. Belonging had been privatised. Access was more likely to be determined by wealth than rights.

The Idea of Australia

It was clear that immigration policy was no longer primarily about settlement but about gatekeeping. It was no longer a matter of 'populate or perish' but 'populate to keep the economy ticking'. Visas had become a revenue line—just another contract ready to be outsourced to a private provider. As the newly appointed immigration department head Mike Pezzullo told his staff in an Australia Day address in 2015, their job was to look forwards. The mission of mass migration that had brought his family to Australia, he said, was a thing of the past. Now the challenge was gatekeeping: 'to act as the open conduits of Australia's engagement with the world . . . whether for the purposes of trade, travel or migration—for time-limited purposes or for tomorrow's settlers'.[14]

This marked a fundamental shift. For many working and studying in the country, the bureaucratic and financial barriers to becoming an Australian citizen had become too high. No wonder it confused would-be refugees and immigrants who had glimpsed the open Australia of the Sydney Olympics. No wonder the new approach angered the supporters of the refugees who were shipped off to remote islands or wrapped in the endless bureaucratic and legal red tape. No wonder it perplexed the descendants of earlier waves of refugees from Europe, Vietnam and the Middle East who had made good and generously reached out to help others like themselves managing the transition to a new land.

Just as the architecture of silence is visible in the built environment, the renaming of government departments is a guide to political priorities. The department responsible for immigration is a perfect case. After Tony Abbott became prime minister in 2010 the Department of Immigration and Citizenship was renamed Immigration and Border Protection, on its way to becoming Home Affairs with a fat finger in national security. Mike Pezzullo declared in his 2015 speech that the paradigm of immigration had changed, from what is 'fixed in collective memory'.[15] The new model, he noted, was very different to the one memorialised in black-and-white photos of people arriving on vast ships, their faces lit by expectation and promise. Those European migrants had been coming to fill the gaps in the labour force; the new model was even more transactional and devoid of sentiment.

Spouses of Australian citizens pay thousands of dollars and are told to expect to wait two years for a visa—and forget it if anyone in the family has a disability or chronic illness. This was not the racially based, linguistically and skin colour–coded selection process that had died an ignominious death in the early 1970s. Selection now took different criteria, and hid behind other tests that impacted every would-be settler and kept many in long-term limbo.

Asylum seekers were at the sharpest end, the flashpoint where the brutality of the decision-making process was, despite all the efforts to avert public attention, on clearest display. The political challenge paralysed politicians, who wept crocodile tears as they voted to close the borders to asylum seekers and send those who made it by sea to tropical islands. The same Labor prime minister who had released refugees from offshore detention in his first few days in office, Kevin Rudd, in the vicious realpolitik six years later declared that 'any asylum seeker who arrives in Australia by boat will have no chance of being settled in Australia as refugees'.[16]

The cruel and shameful experience was recorded with poetic force by the Kurdish refugee Behrouz Boochani in his profound, prize-winning memoir *No Friend But the Mountains*. Boochani arrived at Christmas Island in July 2013, one of more than 13,000 people who reached the remote island that year after a perilous journey from Indonesia. It was his great misfortune, and to Australia's enduring shame, that the gifted writer and poet arrived on the eve of the restoration of the policy that banned asylum seekers who travelled by sea from ever being accepted into Australia. Hundreds of people were sequestered in detainment camps for years. Boochani recorded their horrific plight with poetic insight in illegally written, painstakingly transcribed WhatsApp messages. 'We pride ourselves on decency, kindness, generosity and a fair go,' the Booker prize–winning novelist Richard Flanagan wrote. 'None of these qualities are evident in Boochani's account of hunger, squalor, beatings, suicide and murder . . . What has become of us when it is we who now commit such crimes?'[17]

IT WAS ALWAYS hard to get a taxi in Sydney around three in the afternoon. Traditionally that is the time when shifts change and cars are on their way to the depots, drivers racing to get back to base, switch over and go home. On a wintry July afternoon in 2017, I was lucky. I hadn't been waiting long before a cab pulled into the kerb, the wheelie bag at my feet signalling a lucrative airport run. I jumped in the back seat.

If one of the on-air demagogues are shouting their angry rants, I generally ask drivers to turn off the radio. This time I didn't. Chris Smith's 'Deplorables' on 2GB had just started, and I was intrigued by the way Smith was castigating Malcolm Turnbull for suggesting that the Liberal Party should occupy 'the sensible centre'. Surely that was self-evident, I thought—the political middle ground is the most contested. But the radio demagogues knew better. Such a suggestion was, they concurred, indulgent navel gazing by the prime minister. It was an approach that would destroy the party, betray conservative supporters and broaden the divide between us and them. More worryingly, Smith predicted, it would mean that there would be a landslide at the next election, and then it would take two terms for the Liberal–National Coalition to wrest control back from Labor.

Smith and his sidekick Prue MacSween were sure that Labor's Bill Shorten would be the one who benefited most from the prime minister advocating for a sensible centre. The talkback hosts knew better; if this continued, they fulminated, the country would be handed over to the socialists. The lack of logic was breathtaking. How could a conservative prime minister, the richest man ever to hold the office, send voters on a socialist frolic by advocating a middle-of-the-road liberal path? The driver and I were both perplexed.

Then the topic turned personal and triumphalist. The radio hosts breathed a sigh of relief as they announced that Yassmin Abdel-Magied, a 26-year-old drilling engineer, was leaving the country. 'We don't even give this flea a second thought anymore since she's slinked away from this country . . . If I'd seen her, I'd have been tempted to run her over,' MacSween crowed. Smith chuckled.[18]

My driver agreed. 'I'd run her over too if I could.'

'What? Why do you say that?' I asked, thinking I should have stuck to my normal rule and asked him to turn off the radio as I got in the cab. All of a sudden, the reasonable man I had been chatting with was furious, an (unlikely) defender of women's rights against the evils of political Islam. 'Good riddance to her. Hope she never comes back,' he declared.

'Whoa,' I said. 'Let me tell you a bit about her, and see if you still think that is a good idea. Imagine she was your granddaughter.'

I had known Yassmin for eight years. I liked her spirit, her energy and her curiosity; she could be very funny. She embodied the fearlessness that had marked generations of other brilliant Australian women. But in the previous few months she had become a household name, someone about whom it seemed everyone had an opinion. Someone my apparently mild-mannered, elderly taxi driver was now saying he would like to run over. In February that year, she had achieved notoriety when she stood her ground in an argument with Tasmanian senator Jacqui Lambie on the ABC program *Q&A*. The senator didn't know that Yassmin's family had left Sudan when a dictator with a taste for draconian sharia law took power. So when Lambie accused Yassmin of being an apologist for political Islam, her response was swift and angry. 'You are talking about stuff you don't know anything about,' she snapped. As the heated exchange raged, host Tony Jones urged them both to stop shouting.

The Idea of Australia

When I first met Yassmin, she was a student in the traditionally male-dominated engineering school at the University of Queensland. She was an impressive young woman who had been appointed to the state's Design Council, which I chaired. Her passion was motor racing; she wanted to design the best racing car in the world and had already made a mark. The legacy of her childhood had made her a natural activist; a few years earlier she had created the global youth support network Youth Without Borders and was appointed Young Australian Muslim of the Year, then was awarded Young Queenslander of the Year in 2010.

She thought the world was her oyster and she could make a difference. After she graduated with first-class honours, and as class valedictorian, she worked on mining sites in Queensland and on rigs offshore. We would periodically catch up. She had great stories: thriving in the hyper-male mining environment, she earned the respect of the men she worked with, winning one promotion after another.

At the time, women held some of the highest offices in the land, but the tide of officially condoned misogyny was swelling. Anna Bligh had lost the premiership in 2012, in a political campaign that drew on Queensland's deep-seated contempt for women, and prime minister Julia Gillard had been battered with a level of political invective that was unprecedented ('ditch the witch') because a woman had never before been prime minister. The year 2013 was one of those moments Manning Clark had described: Australia had taken one step forward, then slid two great steps back. Women were angry. This was about power. I commissioned writers for an edition of *Griffith Review* simply called *Women & Power*. I thought that Yassmin's optimistic voice, and her experiences as a hijab-wearing engineer on rigs and remote sites, might offset the disappointment and despair of some of the older writers.

Even then, Yassmin was a natural performer, keen to make her case, to celebrate openness and inclusion, to educate and inform. *Women & Power* generated enormous publicity, but Yassmin was the star of the edition. After each big public event I hosted, she was the person people queued to speak to afterwards. She made the first of many appearances on *Q&A*, which was then setting the national agenda. Publishers sniffed a memoir. TEDx producers sensed a talent who might draw millions. Her dream of designing racing cars receded. She conscientiously prepared for each public encounter, seeking counsel, listening and learning. She was brave and very young, the same age as my son.

I realised a backlash was building when a person seeking a reference for a prestigious position that she had applied for let his guard down over dinner. 'We worry she might really be a terrorist, or might become one,' he said. 'Can you guarantee she isn't?' It was an easy question to answer: 'Yes,' I said. Why would a young woman whose parents had left their homeland because of the excesses of political Islam side with the violent forces of reaction? People like her were more likely to be victims than perpetrators. As with the radio hosts who feared a more centrist Liberal Party would open the floodgates of socialism, the lack of logic was hard to fathom. This man, himself the son of Holocaust survivors, knew how discrimination worked, but he was not to be persuaded. Fear is hardy.

WATCHING THIS BRILLIANT young woman listening and learning was exhilarating—until it became a sport, with Yassmin as the bullseye. Early in 2017, the year that she became a national target, she had again written for *Griffith Review*, this time for an edition called *Millennials Strike Back*. In it she described the difference between her digital activism and the more direct political protest of her parents. She thought that their entreaties for her to just go offline missed the mark in the new world.

For the children of the waves of immigrants who had settled in Australia since the 1990s, the old stories of assimilation and quiet acceptance were, as Mike Pezzullo had said, of an old paradigm that no longer applied. He probably did not welcome the outspokenness of a new generation that was not waiting for permission to join public discussions. As Yassmin wrote, 'Those who lack a definitive "place" in society have little to lose by calling out injustices and structural inequalities, and much to gain by disrupting the status quo. For those with something to lose in that disruption, this can be a terrifying prospect. For everybody else, it is a reminder of the strength and conviction that is needed to fight for a more just world. On that, my parents and I agree.'[19]

On Anzac Day 2017, Yassmin had slept in and not made her usual journey to the Melbourne Shrine of Remembrance for the dawn service. About midday, she posted a comment on Facebook and forgot about it until a friend called an hour later and suggested she delete it for fear of misinterpretation. She had written: 'Lest We Forget (Manus Nauru Syria Palestine . . .)'. Within minutes it had gone viral; she apologised and withdrew the post.

Online, as in life, people say rash things, make mistakes and can seem tone deaf. When they are posted online, they live on as digital exhaust. The celebration of all things Anzac had become an unquestionable article of faith ever since 1990 when Bob Hawke took 75 veterans with him to Anzac Cove to commemorate the 75th anniversary of the ill-fated Gallipoli landing. As the remaining survivors died, the event became more venerated, the day more sacred. Digitised records were easily retrieved; lives could be reimagined. In 2015, Scott McIntyre, a sports journalist at SBS, lost his job after he tweeted on Anzac Day, 'Wonder if the poorly-read, largely white, nationalist drinkers and gamblers pause today to consider the horror that all mankind suffered.' Prime Minister Malcolm Turnbull described his posts as 'despicable'.[20]

Social media comments are a flurry of posting and deleting, but some tweets and posts have an unimaginable half-life. As the novelist Richard Flanagan remarked, Anzac Day had become a 'stalking horse for racism, misogyny and anti-Islamic sentiment'. In just

People Like Us

over a fortnight between 25 April and 11 May 2017, 64,160 angry, accusatory, abusive words were written about Yassmin and her deleted seven-word Facebook post. The overwhelming majority were published in News Corp papers, which increasingly had taken on the role of national bully-in-chief. Within a year, the number of abusive words written about her had reached 200,000—more words than in the New Testament.

For News Corp, this was personal. Anzac Day is particularly sacred for the company. It funded *Gallipoli*, the movie that brought the war to life for contemporary audiences. Corporate memory is deeply infused with pride that Keith Murdoch had written a letter that (sort of) sounded the warning bell about the ill-fated Gallipoli campaign, which cost 44,000 Allied soldiers, including 8000 Australians and 87,000 Turks, their lives.[21] As Rupert Murdoch told a British parliamentary inquiry in 2011, 'I remember what he did and what he was most proud of . . . which was expose the scandal in Gallipoli, which I remain very, very proud of.'[22] The dynasty had a vested interest in the national myth its founder had helped to create.

The loss was real and devastating, but Anzac Day is almost as unusual a national day as Australia Day. Both mark death and invasion rather than the victory, independence and success that most nations celebrate. When I was a child, Anzac Days were sad, desolate, windswept occasions when the surviving soldiers gathered quietly in the empty main street of Penshurst and spent the day in the pub drinking and playing two-up; after all, survival was a gamble and the odds were short. Every town had a war memorial, not all with as many names on them as Gilgandra's, but the lists told a poignant story. Until commemoration grew into an industry, the cultural products were dark and troubled—*The One Day of the Year*, *My Brother Jack*. Charles Bean, the great war historian, was himself damaged by the process and advocated a war memorial not to celebrate but to remind, so that the horrors would not be repeated.

The Idea of Australia

A few years before Yassmin made her ill-considered post, Richard Flanagan had won the Man Booker Prize for *The Narrow Road to the Deep North*, a harrowing re-creation of the experience and silences that dogged the lives of prisoners of war. 'The great disrespect to Anzac Day wasn't the original [comment],' he told the National Press Club in 2018, 'but the perverted attacks made on it, in, of all things, the name of the dead. Those who think they honour Anzac Day by forgetting contemporary victims of war only serve to make a tragic mockery of all that it should be.'

The headlines that accompanied the articles condemning Yassmin would have undermined the most self-confident and mature public figure. Instead of tar and feathers, she was targeted with words and images. She was tagged in thousands of vile social media posts full of abuse, death threats, rape threats and pictures of decapitated bodies. Pigs' heads were dumped at her home. Posters on telephone poles demanded her deportation.

At an event I hosted in June that year, she described how her life had turned upside down:

> I wake up every morning and the first thing I do is look at my phone, because that's what we all do. And I'm greeted with hundreds of, pretty much most days, hundreds of messages on my Facebook, my Twitter, my Instagram, my inbox. Of, you know, the fact that I'm a troubled person. I should die. I'm called everything under the sun. People send me screenshots of the guns they think I should be killed by, I get death threats sent to my post office box, my youth organisation's post office box. It's every day. And it's in every social space that I engage in.

Politicians demanded she be put in her place, giving angry speeches in parliament. Her employment contracts with the ABC and Department of Foreign Affairs (fortuitously, for her employers) had reached their expiration dates and were not renewed. The next step in her engineering career was pulled away by managers discomfited by her profile. She was mocked by male columnists in the business press. None of the institutions she had worked for asked the federal police to watch and provide her with protection. She was cut adrift and left to fend for herself. Her father's cautionary question on the 2001 election day, when she decided to wear a hijab and take the first step to becoming a public figure—*Are you sure?*— rattled in her head.

I assumed my Sydney taxi driver knew little of this, so I told him about the brave young woman I knew. She is tall and direct, with a great sense of style, a firm handshake and a twinkle in her eye—the embodiment of a can-do, fearless Queensland woman—and with a wardrobe of colourful hijabs. She was the antithesis of Pauline Hanson, another colourfully clad Queenslander whose election had helped set the scene for the abuse Yassmin endured.

As he dropped me off at the airport, my taxi driver conceded that maybe he had been too hasty in his judgement. He agreed that she sounded like an impressive young woman. One by one. I worried who would be the next target. It would take more than random exposure to outraged individuals to inoculate all the taxi drivers—and the nation.

THE BEAUTY OF the Australia that began to emerge in the years after multiculturalism was embraced in 1973 was that it was increasingly a place that was open and generous, prepared to engage rather than just tolerate. It was no longer a place where critical writers and artists would be forced into exile by a baying mob. It was a place where people in the regions formed groups like Rural Australians for Refugees, and Australians for Native Title and Reconciliation. It was a society more likely to work as 'a mechanism for the distribution of hope', an 'embracing society that generates hope among its citizens and induces them to care for it', as the Lebanese-born anthropologist Ghassan Hage wrote in *Against Paranoid Nationalism*, his definitive description of how racism flourishes. 'The defensive society ... suffers from a scarcity of hope and creates citizens who see threats everywhere.'[23]

In the 21st century, Australia was reverting from a society that generated hope to one that saw threats everywhere. Yassmin had taken the casual racism of suburban Brisbane in her stride; even when the community's mosque was desecrated and burned, she was inclined to believe the promise and rhetoric of multicultural Australia. After all, she had been appointed Young Queenslander of the Year twice, once under a Labor government, once under a Liberal National government. As she wrote in her diary a few weeks before I caught that cab and gave the driver some reasons to think again:

> I thought that if I worked hard enough, I could outperform my identity. I thought I could talk about statistics to do with discrimination, but I could outwork them. I would be the exception to the rule, I believed. I was smart, but I also played by their rules enough to pass. I was outperforming my identity. But really, I wasn't. I was just putting the inevitable on hold. They sold me the lie that I was accepted, that I could be one of them ... I got too fucken comfortable. I forgot my place.

'Knowing your place' is shorthand for the great Australian equaliser, something that again became clear during the pandemic, when recently arrived essential workers found themselves on the front lines. The citizens John Howard liked to call 'the mob' are always ready enforcers, their bullets shaped by demagogues, cowardly leaders and hotheads looking for a fight. Still, hundreds of thousands joined Black Lives Matter rallies, women's marches and other forums to demand equal opportunities.

People Like Us

The process of pulling people down, once called the tall poppy syndrome, is more practised than the process of celebrating heroes. Since 1960, an exceptional individual has been appointed Australian of the Year by a committee that works with some independence from the government of the day. In the early years public servants, diplomats and artists who had achieved international fame were the most likely recipients—a group that slowly gave way to soldiers, scientists, doctors, businessmen, sportsmen and singers. The national shame of failure to face the original sins has been half-heartedly atoned for by the appointment of eight outstanding Aboriginal leaders and one brilliant Chinese-born doctor.

As the awards evolved, the categories expanded to include a young Australian, an older Australian and a community leader, with nominees from each state and territory. Over the years they came to better represent the diversity of the country. In 2021 four women swept in: advocates for equality, and the importance of lifting the veil of silence and the blanket of forgetfulness. Despite the brilliance of the recipients, their recognition has also made them targets for the angry mob. This has little to do with the tall poppy syndrome, but is something darker and more primal, as 2015 recipient Rosie Batty, who while grieving for her son became the powerful public face of domestic violence, found. Sometimes the score settling happened after death, as Manning Clark's family found when he became the focus of destructive anger five years after his death. The brutality of this attack lowered the bar on what was to become acceptable public discourse.

Two years before Yassmin became the mob's preferred target, it was Adam Goodes, one of the most brilliant AFL footballers of his generation, who was reminded week in and week out of the racist heart beating in the national body—booed and heckled, forced off the field, vilified by commentators for his remarkable talent and assertion of First Nations identity. Thousands rallied to his side and turned up holding signs like *We Stand with Adam*, but no national politician, no senior football administrator and few public figures came to his public defence. It was shameful. Eventually, the mob turned, but not before Goodes had been forced to abandon the job he loved. A few years later, after enduring similar opprobrium, Yassmin felt she had no choice but to leave. In a population of less than 30 million, there is not enough talent and brilliance to waste, let alone destroy.

19

Power Players

THE SCENE OF an old man in a sparse room, a green-and-gold ribbon holding a medal around his neck, an unopened bottle of a Barossa Valley sponsor's cabernet by his side, accepting a lifetime achievement award for transforming the 'world's media landscape' was rich with irony. The man may have once owned a major movie studio, but there was no sign of make-up artistry on his craggy face, no money wasted on set design in the location. He may have had a personal wealth of $25 billion, but his black jacket and tie and white shirt gave no clue to his fortune.

The irony of the low-key performance at a virtual gala at Australia House in lockdown London had many layers. Rupert Murdoch accepted the 2021 special lifetime achievement award from the Australia Day Foundation UK, an organisation sponsored by mining companies and banks, to celebrate Anglo-Australian achievement and ties with the 'mother country'. He was the obvious recipient. The most powerful and influential Australian, not just in Britain but the world. Murdoch created his unprecedented empire from almost nothing, then spent decades shaping public opinion and influencing political outcomes in three countries. As he received the award, the 89-year-old mogul declared he was 'far from done', hinting, not for the first time, at immortality.

The man the Brits delighted in calling the Dirty Digger, as he acquired and reshaped one newspaper (and government) after another, had a complex relationship with this 'mother'. It was tinged with the stigma of colonial shame. Britain was where he learned the black arts of journalism from the legendary press baron Lord Beaverbrook, who he later surpassed in wealth and influence.[1] Britain was where his once-strident Aussie nationalism was burnished, and where he still delighted in ridiculing 'the toffs'.[2]

Australia Day that year was even more fraught than usual. The end-of-summer holiday had only been celebrated as a national public holiday since 1994. A newspaper survey indicated that most people enjoyed the holiday, but less than half knew what it celebrated.[3] After decades of agitation, First Nations communities were joined by local councils, companies and even Cricket Australia in acknowledging that the date was at best random (the date the First Fleet landed in Sydney Cove, but several days after Phillip's ship HMS *Sirius* arrived in Botany Bay, and ten days before ownership was proclaimed) and at worst offensive and a day of mourning (invasion).

To add to the confusion, news about Rupert Murdoch's special award in London was greeted with some mystification. The Australia Day Foundation UK looked like an official body. Its event was held in the imposing Art Deco High Commission building in London, a showcase of antipodean timber, marble and craftmanship from another era. But the organisation is a private trust, and the virtual event was sponsored by companies that could trace their roots to colonial commerce. As news of the award spread, it was accompanied by questions about the organisation's official standing. Within days, the Australian government's international trade promotion and investment attraction agency was no longer a listed partner.[4]

Power Players

MINING, BANKING, AGRICULTURE and media have always sat at the centre of power in Australia. More than most, these industries depend on close relationships with government. The list of sponsors of the Australia Day event was an abridged who's who of corporate power—BHP, National Australia Bank, Rio Tinto, Woodside, Westpac, Yalumba. Many started life in Australia but had London headquarters. Britain is no longer the hub of Australian commerce but the City of London, one of the epicentres of global capital, remains important, especially for the mining companies.

Gold lured tens of thousands to the colonies, but the discovery of lead, zinc and silver at Broken Hill in 1883 established a pattern that has been repeated ever since. The companies that ran the mines and smelters grew rich when Britain agreed, during the First World War, to buy all smelted lead and zinc concentrates they could produce, at a hefty premium, until 1930. Billy Hughes had promoted the Australian monopoly in London as a 'patriotic solution'. The owners of the companies who once despised the wiry Welshman became his biggest boosters. Although Adelaide is the closest capital to Broken Hill, and the mines were just inside the New South Wales border, the businesses aggregated under the Collins House Group were run from Melbourne. In the land of newspapers, Collins House was a player, closely aligned with The Herald and Weekly Times around the corner. Decades before the Adelaide *News* became the first building block in Rupert Murdoch's empire, the city's afternoon newspaper was created by the Collins House Group. Its purpose was to spread 'propaganda' and turn public opinion against union quests for better wages and working conditions.[5]

Mining has historically run second only to land as the most reliable source of wealth, power and influence.[6] It has generated enormous wealth, but also stalled First Nations' recognition, climate change mitigation and the development of a more diversified economy.[7] Its tentacles are long and strong. They reach into politics and media. Many of the most senior staff in Prime Minister Scott Morrison's office moved into politics after successful careers in the mining industry as executives and advocates.[8] His most senior media advisers built their careers on the Murdoch payroll. A similar pattern is repeated in premiers' offices—it's not limited to one side of politics.

The lessons learned by the Collins House grandees, who for decades controlled many of the most profitable companies in Australia, have been passed from one generation to another. Along the way these insights have been refined with the methodology of global management consultants, to maximise return for their clients' shareholders and the senior executives they advise. Close relationships with government sit at the core of these businesses, and underline why transparent and accountable processes are so important. It is governments that declared the gas and minerals that lie beneath are not the property of landowners. It is governments that open tenements for miners to explore, authorise exports, and regulate and tax the raw materials they produce. It is governments that manage the land title system, designating some property to the Crown and some for private sale or lease. It is governments that ensure Australia's banking system stands on the pillars of four banks that trace their origins to earliest settlement.

For all the talk about the market, good relations with ministers, senior public servants and regulators are central to commercial success. The crowded planes in and out of Canberra, before the pandemic interrupted, were proof. It is a powerful and necessary codependence. In Queensland, when it was at its most corrupt, the white shoe brigade of developers, miners and other entrepreneurs who needed a tick from the state to make their fortunes liked to brag that theirs was a *confluence* of influence, not a *conflict*. The Australian economy is more sophisticated and better regulated than it once was, but not as diverse or deep as it should be. Scholars note it still evokes the Florentine dynasty that dominated the Renaissance. In the so-called Medici Cycle, economic and political power reinforce each other in a feedback loop: economic clout is used to win political power and then more economic power.[9]

Power Players

Keith Murdoch was a skilled proponent of this model, providing one of many lessons for his son. Keith, the son of a Presbyterian minister, was born sixteen years before Federation and was determined to succeed. The stammering target of school bullies wanted to use journalism to 'make his voice heard' and 'train the public'. *Power* was the word he used most often in letters to his father, writing from London of his determination to 'become a power in Australia'. To this end he turned the press baron Lord Northcliffe into his mentor. As Sally Young documents in *Paper Emperors*, he wielded his youthful relationship with the world's second labour party prime minister Andrew Fisher to seek influence over wartime decisions. By doing this he established a pattern that was to be repeated. Next with Fisher's successor, Billy Hughes, for whom Keith Murdoch had been a 'confidential and largely unpaid agent'.[10] Murdoch revelled in the fruits of his proximity to power, and was ready to charm and seduce, inflate the reputation of those he favoured, enjoy their patronage and punish their opponents.

This approach became second nature to the newspaper proprietors in the small, clubby world of Australian media and politics. It reached a particular crescendo as the newspaper-owning Fairfax and Packer families, and The Herald and Weekly Times that Keith Murdoch had once headed, jostled for a share of the new television business in the late 1950s. They knew that these licences could guarantee profits—and their political influence—for the foreseeable future.

When Keith's scion returned to Australia after graduating from Oxford, he was initially as contemptuous of the country's leaders as he was of the business community in which he had grown up. The strident young nationalist 'loathed' Prime Minister Menzies 'in an almost visceral way'.[11] It did not take Rupert long to realise that if he wanted to settle his score with the establishment that thwarted him after his father's death, he would need an ally in government. Securing part of one of the first television licences on offer was not simply a matter of commerce. He needed political support, and enough bravado to upset established relationships. In the early 1960s he found that the Liberal leaders 'had all the editorial fulfilment they needed', so 'starting a liaison in the roomful of devoted couples' was a challenge.[12]

Rupert Murdoch had to fight for a place in the oligopoly. Eric Walsh, then a political journalist on the staff of Murdoch's recently acquired *Daily Mirror*, suggested his boss set his sights on the Country Party leader, 'Black' Jack McEwen, a 'horse-trader of tireless skill' who established a modus operandi that would be followed by his successors for generations. Before long, the deputy prime minister had become Murdoch's surrogate father and inducted him into the club 'where government is the business partner of deserving industries and firms'.[13] It was a lesson he never forgot. Power sat comfortably in a hand that held a newspaper (and television network).

———

IN THE MIDDLE AGES, English shepherds used castrated rams to help them keep tabs on their flocks. A bell around the wether's neck meant the shepherd could find the ewes, rams and lambs even if they wandered out of sight. The rich symbolism of *bellwether*'s origins enhances the contemporary definition. More recently, the word has come to mean those who create, influence or set trends. Rupert Murdoch trained to become the world's greatest bellwether at Oxford University. 'I think what drives me are ideas and what you can do with ideas,' he told his biographer William Shawcross in 1990. 'You can demonise me by using the word power. But that's the fun of it, isn't it? Having a little smidgen of power.'[14] This was power that was hard won, wrested from toffs and elites. Even as he reached extraordinary heights of commercial success and influence, he encouraged those he employed, as commentators and editors, to nurse a chip on their shoulders. Always alert to slights and threats, beckoning others to follow.

Power Players

The philosophy, politics and economics (PPE) degree began at Oxford in the 1920s. It was designed to equip its graduates for careers in public life, politics, journalism and the civil service. Scores of sons and some daughters of the English middle class, and of upper-class colonials—like Rupert Murdoch, former Treasury secretary John Stone and future Australian prime ministers Malcolm Fraser and Tony Abbott—enrolled in the program. Even its critics concede that if a student has any rhetorical aptitude, the Oxford PPE will maximise it.[15] Its graduates, more than any other group, have shaped Britain ever since. It may not have been the most intellectually rigorous degree, but writing two long essays each week, drawing on extensive readings and issues of the day, and backing them up with debate taught generations of politicians, journalists, editors and public servants how to make an argument. For almost anything.

This readiness to make a case, cherry-picking useful facts, distinguishes Murdoch's preferred style of journalism. 'We don't report the news,' one of his editors explained to his colleagues, 'we make it.'[16] Former prime minister Kevin Rudd, whose path in and out of power had been greased by News Corp, concluded after he had lost power this had become a cancer on democracy. In 2020, he garnered more than half a million signatures—a record 501,876—on a petition to the Australian Parliament calling for a royal commission into the operations of News Corp.[17] Murdoch's clarion call for freedom of speech, when receiving his lifetime achievement award, was not just ironic. It was, Rudd declared, 'rank hypocrisy'. 'He pretends to champion freedom of speech, but he's spent decades abusing his monopoly to bully Australians he doesn't like into silence. Murdoch invented "cancel culture" in Australia,' @Mr K Rudd tweeted on 27 January 2021.

The list of those who had been on the receiving end included people who had learned at their cost the consequences of not being fearful. Most were pre-emptively silent. Those in power or seeking it were careful to accommodate Murdoch. Those without power or past their prime were more likely to criticise. A key lesson in the manuals for trainee public servants considering recommending or implementing a new policy became 'Ask yourself the question: what would it look like on the front page of the *Daily Telegraph*, the *Courier-Mail*, *The Advertiser*, *Mercury* or *Herald-Sun*?' In this environment, there is little room for nuance, explanation or imaginative policies. Anything that could be demolished in an angrily capped, four-word, 128-point headline was unlikely to be proposed or even considered. A short-lived career awaited anyone responsible for such humiliation.

The straitjacket of sensibility was tightly fastened; threats could only be discussed in whispers. Rudd told the Senate committee set up in response to his petition: 'Everyone's frightened of Murdoch. They really are. There's a culture of fear across the country. The truth is as prime minister I was still fearful of the Murdoch media beast. It's not in your personal political interests ever to go after Rupert Murdoch or Lachlan Murdoch because they'll get you.'[18] This was power Australian-style, exercised behind the scenes with an ever-present threat of public exposure.

Murdoch got his first real taste of the political power at his fingertips as a media proprietor in the 1970s. At the time he was not unlike other men and women of his generation. He was keen to see a new Australia emerge, one less beholden to Britain, more independent, engaged with the world and open. He threw the support of *The Australian* behind the election of the Whitlam government and encouraged his editors in the nation-building venture. It was a short-lived alliance. As his disillusion with the government grew, journalists were in no doubt about what was expected. The owners of the other newspaper companies were no more enamoured of the Labor government, but in the febrile environment after Whitlam's dismissal they still urged journalists to exercise 'fairness, balance and professionalism'.[19]

Rather than lining up as the supporting troops of a warring proprietor, the traditional posture of Australian journalists in the tightly held oligopoly, *The Australian*'s reporters took industrial action. In the last week of the 1975 election campaign, they went on strike, protesting against 'the deliberate and careless slanting of headlines, seemingly blatant imbalance in news presentation, political censorship and, on occasion, distortion of copy from senior, specialist journalists, the political management of news and features, the stifling of dissident and even unpalatably impartial opinion in the paper's columns'.[20]

It was the first time Australian journalists had taken industrial action over a professional issue. 'We cannot be loyal to a propaganda sheet,' they declared.[21] A few years before, when Rupert Murdoch had given his flagship A.N. Smith Lecture in Journalism at the University of Melbourne, he had made it clear that he was not a disinterested proprietor: 'Yes, of course, I intervene. Running a newspaper organisation is not something one does by stealth . . . A publisher cannot abdicate his responsibilities as an editor.' Three years later, as his global empire grew with racy tabloids in both Britain and the United States, he looked wistfully at his homeland as he told a reporter for a US magazine, 'it would be a pity if I grew any bigger in Australia . . . If I were to grow bigger . . . that would be against the public interest . . . the fewer there are, the worse it is.'[22]

Rupert Murdoch jettisoned this view when he took advantage of a change in media ownership policy introduced by Treasurer Paul Keating in 1987. It was designed to break the old oligopoly. The family companies were invited to decide whether they wanted to be 'queens of screen or princes of print'. They didn't have to sell, but greed drove them, and most did. In the frenzy of buying and selling that followed, a fleetingly sentimental Rupert Murdoch acquired the company his father had once run.

With more than half the nation's newspapers under his control, the tipping point he warned about had been reached. In 1990, Murdoch's most sympathetic biographer, William Shawcross, asked the principal of Geelong Grammar, the school Murdoch had attended, what he thought of his former student. Sir James Darling replied by quoting from Martin Boyd's novel *Lucinda Brayford*: 'Sir, your newspapers for two decades have engaged in the degradation of the proper feelings of our people. What is vile they offer to gloating eyes, what is vindictive they applaud. You have done more harm to this country than any of its external enemies . . . I beg you will leave before my butler throws you down the steps.'[23]

AT TEN, AND despite the objections of his father, Rupert Murdoch was sent to the country's most prestigious boarding school, a windswept, spartan place designed to 'make rich boys humble'.[24] There they made their own beds, slept on verandas, took cold showers, served in the dining hall, did the dishes and grew their own vegetables. The ordinary little boy who didn't like 'pretendy things', and couldn't bear dissension at home, was sent to Geelong Grammar at the insistence of his mother. She wanted him to toughen up, 'learn to live with other people and be more unselfish', she told William Shawcross. Dame Elisabeth, as she became, had a well-developed Protestant sense of social responsibility. Rupert's sister Helen recalled the family 'trundling off to the poorer parts of Melbourne to open our eyes' to offset the strong consciousness 'if not shame about the comfort in which we lived'.[25]

The lessons the children learned on these trips were unlikely preparations for life in the most privileged school in Australia. There Rupert was bullied and considered a pest. The neo-Gothic buildings on the shore of Corio Bay were the heart of the school founded in 1855 to educate the sons of the Melbourne business elite, and of the squattocracy that had claimed the land in Victoria's Western District as their own, killed the people who were there already and filled it with sheep.[26] Their great-great-grandsons treated the young Rupert with disdain. They were the real establishment. Rupert's father—the most famous editor in the country, head of the most successful newspaper company, a man who dined with presidents, made and broke prime ministers and governments—was not. Despite his sophisticated artistic taste, in their eyes he was just a manager, a son of the manse, a 'parvenu who had become rich' since the war.

Rupert responded to the bullying dismissively, his charm a commodity he used sparingly. He was a loner, not popular, but curious and open minded, keen to debate ideas and politics. He warmed to teachers who had taken left-wing politics to heart after the war—including Stephen Murray-Smith and Manning Clark—and enjoyed the discussions they encouraged. But he told William Shawcross that he had 'hated' the school, and regarded the principal, the 'second strongman in his life', as someone he could defy. He learned a lesson he said he had applied ever since: 'not to have friendships which can compromise you'.[27]

The adolescent Rupert considered James Darling a poseur who talked about God and duty but lived it up at the Melbourne Club with the rich fathers of his students. The dislike was mutual. Darling considered his pupil hypocritical, manipulative and self-seeking. Out of deference to Keith Murdoch, who he knew was willing to use his power, and Elisabeth Murdoch, whom he liked, Darling helped Rupert secure a place at Worcester College, Oxford, in 1950.

There he took up residence in the grand room once occupied by Thomas De Quincey, the poet who earned enduring fame for inventing the addiction memoir with *Confessions of an English Opium-Eater*. Young Rupert was more interested in politics than opioids; he put a bust of Lenin on the mantelpiece for fun and to annoy his father. In 1950, Stalinism was at its most aggressive, terror was the new normal behind the Iron Curtain, and its refracted mirror image, McCarthyism, was ruining countless careers in the United States.

Not long after Murdoch moved into De Quincey's room and put Lenin on the mantelpiece, legislation to ban the Communist Party was passed in Australia. Although it was rejected as unconstitutional by the High Court and then rejected by a referendum, the Cold War was heating up at home. Murdoch's attachment to Lenin was, to put it mildly, an unusual adolescent fling for a rich boy from Down Under. Despite the best tutors, his results were poor. His disappointed father wanted to bring him home, but his mother prevailed. She shook her son to his bones when she warned that unless he applied himself he would 'lose her last shred of respect'.[28]

Rupert found little to like in dour, rationed Britain, still reeling five years after the war. He showed 'no sense of class nuances'; his British fellow students were dismissive and superior. As his Australian friend, the legal scholar George Masterman QC, later recalled, 'They never talked to us. Rupert was cocky, rich and communist. They hated that.'[29] Again, the feeling was mutual. He was, however, idealistic about Australia and regarded his countrymen who 'said they'd never go back' with contempt. He considered Britain complacent and uncompetitive; the ruling class 'left him bursting with spleen ever after'. In his final months at Oxford, he wrote that 'if it weren't for good friends I'd have shot myself in this bloody place long ago. Rain, wind, sleet, slush, shit, snow and starch.'[30]

In 1952, it took a gruelling three days to fly from London to Melbourne, so Rupert missed his father's funeral. Just days before he died on 4 October, Keith told his wife with some relief that he forgave his son for 'some of his misdeamours' and expressed confidence. 'I think he's got it.'[31]

Rather than a triumphant return to claim the family fortune Rupert found there was much less on offer than he had expected. The leaders of the Melbourne establishment were disinclined to make any exceptions for the former managing director's son. His father had tried to arrange his affairs to make it possible for his son to take over Queensland Newspapers and the Adelaide *News*, but once he returned to Oxford the Queensland shares were sold back to The Herald and Weekly Times.

Power Players

In Melbourne's network of interlocking power, the chairman of the company was also the chairman of his father's trustees. Rupert considered this a conflict of interest that enriched the company at his expense. For the first but not last time, Murdoch then cast himself as David battling Goliath. He urged his debt-averse mother to borrow the money to buy back the shares her husband had earmarked for the family. As the daughter of a man who had made her childhood precarious by betting on horses and cards, Elisabeth had a deep fear of debt and hatred of gambling. It was a caution she did not pass on to her son. If nothing else, he loved to gamble—the bigger the better. 'That's gambling,' he chided Chris Mitchell as they watched the Queensland state election coverage in 1995, 'when you risk everything and could lose your family's food for the week.'[32] Debt was, as he would show time and again, just a tool. He might have been a product of Melbourne's most elite institutions, but he had been excluded. He was an outsider with a chip on his shoulder, grudges to settle, points to prove and a lifetime before him. It was an ethos he inculcated in the empire he crafted.

When Murdoch returned to Australia, he found an economy controlled by a network of about 60 families that had grown rich from farming and mining, behind protective tariffs of manufacturing and the highly regulated banking and insurance industries. They belonged to the same clubs, went to the same schools, served on the boards of each other's companies, and encouraged their sons and daughters to marry within the tribe. Their parties and travels were recorded faithfully in the social pages of the *Australian Women's Weekly*, when the oversized magazine was still published every seven days. Their spiritual home was the wood-panelled Melbourne Club at the Paris end of Collins Street. It was easy to imagine why the disaffected former Geelong Grammar boy might have wanted to blow it up, expose the flaws of a complacent oligarchy, and make himself richer than they could ever imagine.

The Idea of Australia

BY THE TIME I moved to Melbourne to take up a job with the *Australian Financial Review* in 1977, a new breed of émigré businessmen had transformed manufacturing, retailing, hospitality and property development. The old establishment was struggling to find a way to work with the newcomers. The city still had its own stock exchange, was home to Australia's biggest companies, and had raised more prime ministers than any other city. The Collins House network was still powerful; BHP was the Big Australian, with a slogan that captured its self-importance: *what's good for the company is good for the country*. Two of the four big banks were based there. Mining might be done in faraway places, but the head offices were dotted along the spine of Melbourne's city grid; agricultural firms had morphed into manufacturers of food and beer and paper and building products.

The *Financial Review*'s Melbourne office was, at the time, a powerhouse of Australian journalism. It was also the training ground for a cluster of entrepreneurs—Trevor Kennedy, Christopher Skase, John Byrne, Greg Hywood, Alan Kohler—who would later apply the lessons they learned to make their own fortunes. It was rumoured that Rupert Murdoch called the paper *The Pigeon Fancier's Gazette*. We young journalists were encouraged to believe that, with careful reporting, we could get close to power. Day after day, fuelled by long boozy lunches with indiscreet sources, the small group of journalists broke stories that revealed more than the powers that be welcomed. The first hints that a citadel was under attack, with whispers of the takeovers that would reconfigure old companies, were invariably reported by Robert Gottliebsen, at the time the paper's eminent Chanticleer columnist.

When I joined the newspaper, the editor, Max Walsh, asked which industry I would like to cover: mining, banking, insurance and property were on offer. Each was as incomprehensible to me as the other. A year of university economics was no preparation for making sense of the imperatives and routines of business as it was done in stuffy Melbourne. My nominated mentor was little help. His key advice,

Power Players

delivered in a dimly lit, baroque bar in Queen Street, was how to appear to be drinking more than you were, excuse yourself to go to the bathroom and use toilet paper to take notes. It was scarcely promising but this man would often return from lunch, unscrunch his scribbled toilet-paper notes and turn them into front-page stories.

It did not take long for me to realise that at the city's business and political heart there was a network of interconnected companies, families and individuals who held sway. They also controlled the information flow. They determined who got the breaks and who was frozen out; who got the ear of the relevant government minister or departmental head. My first encounter came after writing some critical stories about one of the big paper-manufacturing firms that had turned hundreds of hectares of land into vast pine forests to create pulp for export. I was invited to meet the boss and on the way into his office was presented with a folio of the company's beautiful limited-edition Norman Lindsay etchings, including a voluptuous nude—a gift it seemed churlish to refuse, but which made me uncomfortable. I might have been the new girl in town, but the company's corporate affairs manager had done some homework and delighted in unsettling me, letting me know that my activist student life in Brisbane, and as a reporter for *Nation Review*, was no secret to them. In the days before Google, this took effort; it required personal contacts, and access to files and reports.

I was young and somewhat foolhardy. I failed to heed the lesson. I kept reporting. Within weeks I was invited to the regular lunch held by the men who ran public relations for the top companies. Not long into the lunch, the table crowded with bottles of wine and Crown Lager, they let me know that they knew more of my background, and chortled as they watched me squirm. If I played their game, they promised, I would be given a regular flow of exclusive stories.

As a reporter for *The Pigeon Fancier's Gazette*, it was a Faustian choice. It was a career-making offer—early access to information (when it suited them), and a path to the front-page stories that were the most prized currency in the newspaper business. But I knew, and no doubt they understood, that I would be an unreliable ally. The offer slipped away and with it a long-term future in business journalism.

It was the precursor of this club that the 22-year-old Rupert Murdoch had in his sights when he returned to Australia and began running the Adelaide *News* in 1953, with his father's protégé, Rohan Rivett, as editor. Murdoch disliked the club, and 'loathed' the prime minister who were their man. To his youthful mind, the longest-serving prime minister must have been cynical because of the way he 'belittled Australia', denying Australian nationalism and the physical growth of the country.[33] But his contempt for Menzies was nothing compared to his disdain for the wowserish Protestantism and gerrymandered politics that characterised the insular world of Adelaide at the time. He was ready to upset the old order.

It seems odd now, but there was a time when Murdoch was considered a quintessential Australian. Some would argue that he still is, but of a different sort of Australia. As a young man he was the embodiment of the raffish, nationalistic egalitarianism that had become the defining national characteristic both at home and abroad. He was a generation younger than Rivett, who had spent years as a prisoner of war, but shared his editor's ambition for an independent, self-sufficient Australia. They wanted her to be free of the shackles of empire and engaged with the Asia Rivett had come to know.

Rivett was not unique among the nation builders who had survived the war. This group had been enriched by a coterie of intellectuals, many of whom had fled Europe and by chance arrived in Australia. They included the brilliant young German and Austrian refugees who had been despatched from England on the *Dunera*, were interned during the war but fortunately stayed to reshape Australian intellectual life.[34] They imagined a new post-war order in which the four freedoms that President Roosevelt had defined as the core building blocks would flourish: freedom from want and fear, and freedom of speech and religion.

Rivett wanted the Adelaide *News* to be like the best newspapers in Britain, one that would educate its readers and break down fear and isolationism. The young proprietor shared the vision. It was tempered by his already strong tabloid instinct, which he tested when he added the Perth *Sunday Times* to his small stable. He pushed his journalists with gusto, exhausted them with questions and decisions. He was untroubled if he upset influential critics of his parents' generation.

The generation of ambitious nation builders first really noticed that Keith Murdoch's son was more than a chip off the old block when the *News* began to question the conviction of an Arrernte man, Rupert Maxwell (Max) Stuart, for the murder of a nine-year-old girl in Ceduna in 1959. The campaign against his death penalty gathered momentum as the newspaper reported evidence that had not previously been heard in court. It became Rupert Murdoch's first trial by newspaper. Stuart's death sentence was commuted, although not everyone was convinced he was innocent.

In the manner that marked his approach to newspapering, Murdoch himself rewrote the headline and poster to make them more sensational. Charges of contempt followed. The case triggered a royal commission, followed by defamation and sedition charges against Rivett and Murdoch. Although they were eventually vindicated, the close relationship between the two men broke. Murdoch thought his editor was showing 'socialist sentiments' and getting ahead of himself. By then his attention had shifted to his Sydney tabloid. He sacked Rivett by letter, without warning, not long after the decision was delivered.[35] He had learned that lesson at Geelong Grammar: *don't let a friendship get in your way.*

It's still a small country. Decades later, after years in and out of jail, Max Stuart became chairman of the Central Land Council and welcomed Queen Elizabeth II to Alice Springs during her pre-Olympics tour in 2000. Murdoch wrote to congratulate him.[36] Stuart's life story had become one of redemption, an Australian trope not often celebrated.

There are other men and women of his generation who still see Murdoch as the charming, ambitious, energetic boy-publisher. They don't regard him as a driven megalomaniac, but the superstar of a generation. To them he is a man who took his chances, made his luck and embodied such a distinctive Australianness that he became an American citizen. He touched and enriched many, even as his public profile grew darker and more menacing. As his first biographer George Munster wrote, this generosity and charm left a lasting impression that was hard to put aside: 'At a first meeting, he does not fit the contentious stereotypes that precede him. Wanting to make friends, he bubbles with eagerness, plunges into gossip, bestows fragments of information about his latest doings, shows no urge to pull rank.'[37]

Munster was one of those émigré European intellectuals who chummed up with the war veterans to develop an idea of Australia that built on the best of its egalitarian traditions and aimed to create a more open, sceptical and independent country. In some ways they were a throwback to the nineteenth-century republicans, socialists, intellectuals and feminists whose ambition informed, but was not instrumental in, the formation of the nation. Their ideas found expression in radical magazines like *The Nation, Meanjin, Overland* and later *Nation Review*, the more conservative *Observer* and CIA-backed *Quadrant*. The debate was vibrant, eclectic, and cosmopolitan; the ideas they developed on the page became essential building blocks for the new nationalism stripped of provincialism that flowered in the 1970s.[38] This was a vision that Rupert Murdoch initially shared. It was one he advanced with his vanity project, *The Australian*.

Not long into the Whitlam government's first term, Murdoch's support for the government, whose policies embodied some of the ideal Australia he had once championed, gave way to outright hostility. But as he built an empire abroad, at home his star burned brightly. George Munster recalled a weekend at Cavan, the Murdoch property near Canberra, in 1974. The recently widowed governor-general John Kerr dropped in looking for company and canvassed what he might have to do if the hostility engulfing the Whitlam government did not abate. It was the first hint of an action that would shock the nation a year later when Kerr dismissed Whitlam's government. At the time, Munster described Murdoch, the peripatetic powerbroker, as 'something of the home-town astronaut, who had soared in Britain and landed in America'.[39] He was about to soar again, renounce his Australian citizenship so his American empire could grow, casting his old distinctive identity off into the slipstream.[40]

By the late 1980s, Murdoch had become the bellwether of the new ideology that swept the world. 'I was more of an Australian nationalist when I was younger,' he told William Shawcross at the time. 'Today I would describe myself as totally internationalist, free market, believing that most people will benefit most and the world will be a better place from having free markets. In ideas as well as goods.'[41] A different sort of super-wealth emerged. Greed was good; international commercial success was most important. Money flowed and the social order reconfigured itself around principles of individualism. Sydney claimed the mantle of the national capital of business with investment banking at its core; Melbourne became the self-declared cultural capital. Bankers displaced industrialists at the top of the rich list, old Australian companies were sold and relocated their headquarters to London or New York, houses became assets first and homes second.

There was little room for old-fashioned nation building in this global capitalism. Now the country feels modern, sophisticated and affluent. Australia is undoubtedly one of the handful of rich countries. There are profits to be had and money to spend, but the economy remains one of the least complex and diversified in the world, ranking 87th after Uganda, according to the Harvard Atlas of Economic Complexity. The over-reliance on mining, decimation of manufacturing, and weak tech sector makes it less sophisticated than it should be.[42]

Global measures of gross domestic product have ranked Australia thirteenth for years. If wellbeing were measured by dividing the number of people into this massive number, all Australians would be wealthy. But such simple calculations are profoundly misleading. Inequality is real and punishing. Cartels have reasserted themselves, and monopolies are reappearing. In 2021 the outgoing chairman of the Australian Competition and Consumer Commission Rod Sims used his platform to argue that business was much too concentrated, and that this was a threat to the economy and the nation.[43]

On almost every international indicator, the country that liked to consider itself a model of fairness and opportunity has worsened in the 21st century. Wealth has become more concentrated, wages have failed to grow, gender equality has not kept pace with the educational attainments of women, business has become less productive and the economy less complex, housing and health care have become less affordable, corruption is more prevalent, household debt is second highest in the world, education achievements have dropped, and half the population have reported wanting more work.[44] Rather than taking a lead on the biggest issues of the day—climate change, human rights, security—Australian leaders have become content to dismiss international criticism as misguided, uninformed or self-interested. There are now winners and losers. Not so much *We're all in this together against the world*. Fairness is rarely invoked as more than a process aspiration. Egalitarianism is an embarrassing artifact of another age.

―――

ON THE WINTRY January night in London when he donned his lifetime achievement medal, Rupert's valedictory outrage focused on social media. His speech appeared to be cultural, targeting Facebook and Google—companies that had disrupted the business model on which his media fortune was built. Not only were they the new holders of the information keys as gatekeepers of news and viral thought, but they were the recipients of most advertising dollars. Their finely calibrated business models made the old idea of mass markets look like a crude sledgehammer. But, as always, a commercial heart sat at the core of his pronouncement.

At the beginning of 2021, News Corp was at a critical juncture in negotiations with Google and Facebook about the use of its journalism on their digital platforms. The Australian government provided a regulatory weapon to its trusted ally to claw back some of the losses. Governments in the other territories where News Corp thrived were also seeking ways to help maintain a media ecosystem that, to some degree, recognised the importance of public interest journalism to democracy.

The transfer of income from the old media companies to the new digital behemoths had been rapid and catastrophic. The media companies had grown fat and influential during the decades when profit margins of 30 per cent were the norm, and cross promotion delivered huge audiences and influence. Australian government agencies charged with assessing takeovers as the concentration of ownership got tighter and tighter tended to make judgements on the available advertising market. The marketplace of ideas and information was much harder to measure. That is a public good that does not sit comfortably in the metrics of the market. By the 2010s advertising revenue had plummeted. The internet—particularly Google and Facebook—had decimated the old media as a money-making, attention-generating machine. Gone was the mass audience, replaced instead with countless micro markets that could be measured, diced and sliced in a way the old media could only dream about. With it went the profits. Without the money, holding on to influence was much harder.

Over a decade, the number of working journalists halved. The media was more concentrated than ever: News Corp Australia owned all the newspapers in Queensland and South Australia and nearly three-quarters of the rest, even after closing 96 papers in 2020. In the year to February 2021 there had been 199 'contractions', closures, mergers or reduced services.[45]

The impact on public life was playing out in predictable ways, delivering more power to fewer companies. Many had close ties to government. A breathless news cycle meant there was little time for reflection or analysis. True to the methods of the Medici Cycle, the government came to the aid of some that lost from this seismic disruption, with special grants and allocations. Legislation designed to ensure the old companies could continue to flourish was introduced, dressed in the threadbare clothes of public-interest journalism. Early in 2021 the global CEO of News Corp, Robert Thomson, who had started his career as a cadet at the Herald and Weekly Times in Melbourne, announced from New York that a landmark agreement with Google to showcase its global journalism had been reached. Facebook soon followed. This was achieved, Thomson announced, thanks to the 'fervent, unstinting support of Rupert and Lachlan Murdoch' in their 'quixotic quest' to enhance journalism and society.[46] He particularly thanked Australian politicians and regulators who had 'stood firm'. Peter Cox, the eminent commercial media analyst, was more sceptical. He had watched the way media companies used their power for decades and told breakfast television: 'The situation has nothing to do with journalism . . . This is a group of bully boys, we've got the prime minister wanting to be on the international scene . . . You've got him trying to tie up News Corp and Fairfax for the next election. So he's trying to flow the money to those two organisations mostly. This is mostly about achieving political ends.'[47]

Power Players

THE ULTIMATE IRONY of the ceremony on the last weekend of January 2021 came from the old man's speech. The people he considered to be the new censors were in his crosshairs. Those who wanted to expand the scope of respectful conversation to include people and issues previously rendered invisible. Those interested in unpicking the way social, legal and commercial structural arrangements served to preserve the status quo and entrench disadvantage. This could not have been more different to the censorship his father had exercised when he was appointed as Australia's chief wartime censor. Keith Murdoch was despised by the other publishers in this role, not only for his excessive zeal in protecting the government, but because he used the position to advance his own commercial and political interests. He later became an ardent anti-censor, but rarely opposed the regimes that banned thousands of books, journals, films and other artworks, and kept the country in aspic.[48]

In the many Rupert Murdoch biographies, it is clear the filial relationship was supercharged: whatever Keith did, Rupert could do better. Now Rupert needed to take on the digital giants that had broken the lock on the information riches, advertising, attention, gossip and bile of the globe. He was no longer the master gatekeeper; other voices could be heard, and they were letting their displeasure with the old ways be known. The architecture of acceptable speech, of what was offensive and what was tolerable, was changing and moving beyond his control. He called it cancel culture.

For nearly 50 years his companies had been setting new benchmarks for how to use power. They had never hesitated to advocate political agendas, render critics silent, criticise institutions and advance commercial interests. With monopoly papers in most capital cities, and the biggest-selling papers in the others, his papers could set the tone of political conversation, establish the agenda for radio and television, provide fodder for social media and make public figures very nervous.

Australians had grown accustomed to the partisan hectoring; the data showed that the tabloids no longer tipped elections, but they remained a noisy irritant. When Fox News—the loudest voice in the US—became a presidential whisperer and loudspeaker for Donald Trump, this ability to shape politics moved to another level. Rupert Murdoch may not have liked the president, but he liked access and influence, and the tangible monetary reward they delivered. Fox News called the 2020 presidential election as a victory for Joe Biden on the night of the ballot. But it took two months, the day after the mob Trump incited to storm the Congress, before the jewel in Rupert's crown, the *Wall Street Journal*, finally urged the 45th US president to accept his defeat. Yet without the slightest sign of embarrassment, Rupert Murdoch declared in his speech accepting the award for his lifetime of achievement:

> For those of us in media there's a real challenge to confront: a wave of censorship that seeks to silence conversation, to stifle debate, and to ultimately stop individuals and societies from realising their potential. This rigidly enforced conformity, aided and abetted by so-called social media, is a straitjacket on sensibility. Too many people have fought too hard in too many places for freedom of speech to be suppressed by this awful woke orthodoxy.

Murdoch was not alone in declaring war on 'woke' culture. Conservative think tanks and political parties sensed that their power was at stake, and happily divided and castigated progressives for the nasty excesses of cancel culture. When in 2017 the *Oxford English Dictionary* defined the contemporary meaning of 'woke', it was a clear sign that the Black American slang had a meaning that went beyond being awake. It now meant being 'alert to racial or social discrimination and injustice'. Those who felt the sting of exclusion had become more forensic in identifying the origins and sources of the discrimination they faced and that limited their life choices. They had found their voice, and discovered they were not alone, on the internet. There they could express their opinions without navigating the stop/go signs held by the gatekeepers in the traditional media.[49] They wanted structures to change, not just rhetoric. Some wanted to ban and exclude, but most just wanted to be heard. Some companies looked to ways to incorporate and co-opt, surprisingly sensitive to critics they had once ignored.

This was only Murdoch's most recent cultural preoccupation. He had fostered similar campaigns for decades. Elites, postmodernism, human rights, 'political correctness', feminism, gay rights, critical theory and climate change had long been in his sights, prosecuted with quasi-intellectual zeal. Instincts for decency and empathy—key building blocks between cultural expectations and political realities—were derided. The world nurtured by his Australian outlets was a contemporary replay of penal times in which 'the cruel were rewarded and the merciful punished'.[50] Crude, inflammatory take-downs, devoid of human decency, were a flamboyant tabloid feature.[51] If anger was truly addictive as the neuroscientists were discovering, inflaming it had a dual purpose: profits and politics.

Like quicksilver, newspapers around the world echoed the siren call of the boss's Australia Day acceptance speech. The following Monday his *New York Post* screamed: 'Time to take a stand against the muzzling of America'.[52] Within days the *Daily Telegraph* had declared that the Australian National University was seeking to destroy the family by changing its child-care policies. A few weeks later, the Duke and Duchess of Sussex—Meghan Markle and Prince Harry—had described their experience of institutional racism and the exclusionary power of privilege in an interview with Oprah Winfrey. Greg Sheridan, one of the great man's most loyal acolytes, joined the fray. In *The Australian* he declared that support for the erstwhile royals sounded a potential death knell for Western civilisation—the woke cancel-culture brigade were poised for global success.[53]

There was no hint of irony that one of the biggest media groups the world has ever known should feel threatened by a bunch of activists who were seeking to extend rights and broaden the conversation to include them and address structural discrimination. As Yassmin Abdel-Magied noted, her vilification had been most poisonous and extensive in the old media.

In the Wild West of the digital age, the old gatekeepers had lost the absolute power to say *no*. Conversations, debates and information flowed without the old authorising control they had become accustomed to exercising. Angry, anonymous abuse became the silencing tool, but people who would once have never had a media platform found others who shared their views. Shaping debates in this environment required new techniques. Shouty, confected commentary tainted the atmosphere but was not so lucrative. Facebook and Google had learned that money could be made in the attention economy, that they needed to detach from regulatory frameworks, and that the power of outrage to fuel profit was leaving even the oldest and richest media empires in their dust. Rupert Murdoch, Australia's most successful talisman, must have sensed that the locus of power was switching.

20

From Little Things...

As the summer sun set over the bush capital on the evening of 25 January 2021, the contrast with Rupert Murdoch's dour virtual ceremony in London could not have been greater. The four women who had become the official Australians of the Year were a wonderfully unexpected embodiment of the contemporary nation. They took their places on the stage of the National Arboretum and looked directly at the cameras with pride, each unapologetic about the seriousness of her purpose. There was the Aboriginal elder from the Northern Territory, the Kenyan immigrant from Sydney, the young medical student and social entrepreneur from Adelaide, and the triumphant sexual abuse survivor from Hobart. Miriam-Rose Ungunmerr-Baumann, Rosemary Kariuki, Isobel Marshall and Grace Tame were these distinguished Australians, their elevation an unequivocal sign that the nation could both acknowledge the past and embrace the future.

By the evening's end, each of the colourfully dressed quartet held an elegant blue glass trophy, its facets catching the light to embody diversity, confidence and the exciting freshness of possibility under the ancient sky. They were proof that the oldest exclusions from the nation's story—of the First Australians, women and people of colour—could no longer be overlooked or patronised. They stood centrestage and spoke with clear voices about a different future, one they had glimpsed.

From the other side of the globe, the media mogul projected on the screen of the London gala launched his attack on the very cultural change that had made it possible for these four women to represent the nation. The sponsor's bottle of wine, the green-and-gold ribbon, the ordinary old man demeanour all spoke to a very different in-the-club idea of Australia. It had once dominated but was no longer sufficient. The old guard was poised to fight to hold on to a system that had served them exceptionally well, even if that meant just slowing things down.

Rupert Murdoch was literally and metaphorically an old white guy. He appeared to receive the award, for making an indelible mark on the globe, with world-weary expectation. Still, he wanted to prevail. His speech left no one in any doubt that he was angry about the threat from those who suggested equality might need far-reaching structural reform. At worst, this 'woke' agenda threatened to upend the world order that had made him so rich, so influential, so powerful. The danger was clear. One of his news outlets, with more than the usual number of old white guys in its employ, distilled the message: 'Go woke go broke.'[1]

Some of the people dearest to me could be described as old white guys. None fit this stereotype. They welcome the fact that, over their more than three score years and ten, new layers of meaning, inclusiveness and open mindedness have enriched lives. That the very idea of Australia had shifted to become more diverse, more informed, more critical. On this midsummer evening it was as if some future archaeologists, from the national university at the bottom of hill, had dusted the sand and ash and ochre to reveal how the nation in 2021 had evolved. The prime minister looked more than usually uncomfortable. He professionally elbow-bumped each woman as she came to the podium to accept her trophy and tell her story. After Grace Tame finished her excoriating speech, describing how her abuser had groomed and abused her, and how she had battled the legal system, Scott Morrison whispered, 'Well, gee, I bet it felt good to get that out.'[2]

Sitting in my living room watching, and being moved by, the unexpected ceremony and powerful speeches, I turned to my husband and said I was worried. I wondered: Is making a 26-year-old sexual assault survivor Australian of the Year an unreasonable burden? Will the agents of the old status quo who felt protected by the man receiving his lifetime achievement award in another hemisphere seek to destroy her?

They had form.

Australian of the Year is a job with a very high risk rating. The journey from nomination by other citizens through state selection processes means that only the most outstanding individuals are considered. The national awards committee has often demonstrated an admirable detachment from politics. At its best, this group of eminent people responds to the emerging groundswell of sentiment that has been distilled by the process and selects winners who reflect the mood of the nation—not its politics, or the preferences of the powerful. They are bellwethers of the zeitgeist rather than self-interest, often to the discomfort of the government of the day.

When the environmental scientist and climate change activist Tim Flannery was appointed Australian of the Year in the last year of the Howard government, the prime minister damned Flannery with faint praise: 'He has encouraged Australians into new ways of thinking about our environmental history and future ecological challenges.' Howard remained opposed to ratifying the Kyoto Protocol until the end of his term, but that year commissioned a high-powered taskforce to develop an emissions trading scheme.[3] It was an election year, and John Howard was a good earwigger; he sensed that the mood was changing.

Five months before the poll, after a decade of denial, he convinced the Liberal Party's federal council to adopt a climate change policy and an emissions trading scheme. Australia would not run ahead of the world. The plan was 'designed to last the whole of the 21st century if Australia is to meet our global responsibilities'.[4] Climate change mitigation has been a quagmire for prime ministers ever since. Despite public support, innovations by state governments and increasingly urgent pleas from business, fear has prevailed. None has been able to master the moral imagination and lead with enduring meaningful action.

Being named Australian of the Year is a complicated honour. The role of de facto national teacher-in-chief that comes with the title is not always easy, as Adam Goodes and others have found. Rosie Batty, whose son was murdered by her abusive partner, gave hundreds of speeches and changed countless lives, but was trolled within an inch of her life and stepped away, exhausted. Decades earlier, the young Galarrwuy Yunupingu had been recognised for fighting for his people, their land and culture and is still, three score years and three, fighting in old age; his co-winner, the late Alan Bond, is still on a plinth on Lake Burley Griffin's Australians of the Year Walk, despite having served time in jail for fraud.

MAYBE EXPERIENCE HAD made me more cautious, but I felt a tinge of fearfulness as I watched Grace Tame accept the award. I had seen how hard it can be to imagine change, achieve it and then make it stick. It is one thing to *Be Bold, be bold, be bold* as Rose Scott urged women to be more than a century before. But as she and many others have found, it can break your heart. I had seen how those with power fought to hold on to it, how meanness and brutality could overwhelm generosity and understanding. I had seen how idealists and people with imagination could be mocked and dismissed. I had seen the mediocre float to the top and then squander the privilege. But I had also seen people's lives transformed by the kindness of others, places become more interesting and welcoming by deliberate and thoughtful action, and education become an escalator to achievement, adding meaning and opportunity. I had seen how those who were prepared to make difficult and challenging arguments, to contest the comfortable status quo, in time eventually prevailed. Above all I had seen how an approach to life that encompassed constant learning could change opinions, enable new insights, enrich understanding, diminish fear and open new worlds.

A few days before the ceremony at the arboretum, another young woman—a self-described 'skinny black girl' raised by a single mother—recited a poem at the inauguration of the president of the world's most powerful nation. Amanda Gorman's 'The Hill We Climb' was unflinching in its critique of racism and inequality in the United States, but hopeful about her country's future under a new administration: 'We are striving to forge our union with purpose/To compose a country committed to all cultures, colors, characters and conditions of man.'[5] Within days Gorman had become a global star, dressed in designer garb and on her way to becoming a brand ambassador. But the racism she described meant that even a month later, after she had appeared on millions of screens, she was bailed up by a security guard at her apartment building who thought she looked 'suspicious'.[6]

Grace Tame similarly captured the moment. Her unflinchingly powerful words inspired others to utter the once unspeakable, describe their experiences of abuse and seek justice. Her speech to the National Press Club a month after receiving her Australian of the Year award drew an almost unprecedented standing ovation. Tearful journalists struggled to find ways to express their admiration for the transformative power of her words: to thank her for her courage and determination in speaking simple truths to power, for cutting through the spin that was obscuring the fact that little was being done to solve these problems.

Those nursing painful memories of sexual abuse and assault, those who had just accepted the slights along the way, were empowered to speak up. Brittany Higgins described her shocking experiences within Parliament House—an alleged sexual assault and a system that deliberately looked away and left her unprotected and vulnerable. The day after Grace Tame's Press Club speech, a tearful Christian Porter, the attorney-general, told the nation he had been wrongly accused by the ABC of an historical sexual assault and would step aside to clear his name.[7] The zeitgeist was undeniable.

Within weeks, more than 100,000 women and men had marched in rallies around the country to demand an end to sexual violence, and to demand that women be treated with respect and equality. They were old and young. Those who had been marching all their lives wanted meaningful equality, not another mealy-mouthed political deal like the one after Federation that gave women the vote via legislation instead of as a constitutional right. Theirs was not just a claim for economic and political equality, but for a time of reckoning. *Enough is enough* was the new slogan.

Sexual violence is inseparable from the Australian experience. It was there from the first days of the penal colony, through the years of colonial settlement and became embedded in the life of the nation. It was one of the issues that drove the women campaigning for suffrage and a different sort of Federation. Its legacy of shame, and shameless bravado, still stalks personal and institutional relations. This once-unspoken fact fuelled the rage that powered the marches that March, and the stories that were remembered and shared.

Enough was enough: for young and old, black and white, grandmothers and little girls. All women are vulnerable, but some are more vulnerable than others. Decades ago, Bernard Smith described this process by which Australian culture began to move to firmer ethical foundations. Culture led. As writers revealed and readers came to accept and atone for, the brutal truth that was 'at the heart of the

From Little Things . . .

Australian experience [is] a sexual tragedy of enormous historical dimension . . . performed across the bodies of Aboriginal women'.[8] Not all were victims, but too many women and girls were damaged and are still at risk. As has happened since the First Fleet arrived, exceptional First Nations women rose from the ashes of powerlessness and dysfunction to become some of the most inspirational leaders in the land—first in their own homes and communities, then touching others they had never even met.

As I feared, it did not take long for all this to prove too much for those associated with the old white man who had denounced the very social and cultural change that emboldened these women and their daughters, mothers, sons, brothers, husbands and friends, and open-minded old white guys. Good reporters, including Samantha Maiden at News Corp, gained Brittany Higgins' confidence and wrote of her alleged rape and the inadequate way it was treated. Maiden and her colleagues—particularly women—reported the passionate public and the inept political responses.

The gender fault line was impossible to miss and made many uncomfortable. Aaron Patrick wrote in the *Australian Financial Review* that the 'stories cleaved a schism through political journalism, exposing a shift in the centre of gravity from the male perspective to the female'.[9] His column provoked such a torrent of outrage that the editor felt the need to explain. The ground was shifting. The commentators who had guaranteed space on dedicated pages could not hide their discomfort. The prime minister stumbled from one misstep to another; his government's poll ratings plummeted as people, especially women, found it wanting. He was mocked by comics, taunted on social media, even jeered at on commercial television which, for all the political favours they had dispensed over the years, should have been a safe place.

Normal politesse would once have made it hard for powerful men to publicly humiliate young women. My son's elite school reminded the boys every day that *manners maketh the man*. Chanel Contos's survey showed that many had missed the message. Edmund Burke, father of the old style of conservatism that was coming into vogue as the First Fleet arrived, considered human society so complex that norms were needed to create a respectful society—'manners are of more importance than laws'.[10] It was a sentiment that had little room in the winner takes all world reshaped by forty years of neoliberal economics, and then overlaid by populist showmen dressed up as presidents and prime ministers. It had been shattered over the four years US president Donald Trump punched out his vitriol in 140 capped characters—until Twitter decided enough was enough and blocked him. The well-funded libertarian lobby groups that made culture their battleground appeared to target progressives. Their arrows were also aimed at the hearts of traditional conservatives, who had not bought the line that there was 'no such thing as society', as Margaret Thatcher had infamously pronounced.

In its own existential struggle much of the commercial media had lost the right to claim it was a fourth estate; it was unequivocally just another business scrambling to hold its customers. It amplified angry voices to provoke a response, and encourage addictive anger, in a debased public sphere. Social media gave the mob a new way to shout anonymously and without fear of consequences. Manners collapsed and laws struggled to catch up. It soon became clear that being young and female provided no chivalrous protection in public, by men who should know better. Instead, as Malala Yousafzai, Yassmin Abdel-Magied and Greta Thunberg found, it made you a very particular target.

As Greta Thunberg's voice resonated around the world after she first addressed the United Nations in 2018, commentators, many employed by News Corp, took the opportunity to publicly deride,

From Little Things . . .

belittle and condemn her. They were infuriated that the passionate sixteen-year-old Swedish climate change activist had not only galvanised a global movement of young people, but had spoken directly to the world's leaders. She might have been their daughter or granddaughter, but the abusive language of condemnation knew few bounds. The local mob had learned that anonymity meant restraint was unnecessary. They battered the country's first female prime minister—*Ditch the witch*— and the head of the Australian Human Rights Commission before they turned on Yassmin Abdel-Magied: *Run her down*.

Grace Tame was a more difficult target: young, beautiful, a very recognisable daughter of Australia's white middle-class suburbs, with a personal experience of evil that would make most crumble. Her candour was breathtaking. It didn't take long before the outlets owned by, and associated with, the old media mogul were deriding her, wondering why, just because she was an Australian of the Year, Grace Tame was entitled to an opinion.[11] Surely her position, more than any other in the country, was one that demanded opinions and the courage to express them? The furious opposition to what the old man called 'woke' culture suddenly had another target: a brave and brilliant young woman who had been brutalised by evil. And survived.

Who could have anticipated that by appointing a group of women as Australians of the Year they would use the platform to reignite a long-smouldering fire? It was infuriating for the keepers of the old idea of Australia: sexist, racist, meritocratic if you went to the right school or immigrated from the right sort of country. Their experiences would once have been considered suitable for private conversations, and as a side show on the national stage. When W.E.H. Stanner coined the iconic phrase 'the great Australian silence', he made it clear that this was not 'absent-mindedness' but a 'structural matter'. These women challenged the structure.

By early April, the pile-on had begun in earnest. 'Militant culture warriors make all men the bad guys,' the headline in *The Australian*'s opinion page declared. Nick Cater, executive director of the Menzies Research Centre, the Liberal Party's think tank, wrote for the section he once edited:

> Political correctness has hardened into a ground war headed by an activist vanguard enjoined by teachers, journalists, bureaucrats and other professionals who lack the courage to resist . . . The new radical feminism . . . has taken a harder form, turning men and women into class enemies . . . Woke, in other words, is no joke. It represents the biggest threat to liberalism, Australia's riding philosophy since European settlement, since the rise of totalitarian ideology a century ago.[12]

Six hundred and twenty-nine people, overwhelmingly men, fumed loudly, overwhelmingly in support in the comments section of the paper. The paper likes to comfort its core readers. But even using the old newspaper metric that one letter to the editor captures the views of a hundred others, these commenters were a minority of Australians. The outgoing head of the Institute of Public Affairs, John Roskam, worried out loud a few months later, saying, 'people feel that things have come apart very quickly'.[13] If they were, many who were not aligned with his think tank thought it was about time. The groundswell demanded something else: that women of all races, classes and ages be treated with respect and equality. Even the *Financial Review* editor turned somersaults on the page to defend the paper's suggestion that female journalists were on a 'crusade'.[14]

THE SURPRISE OF seeing those four women on the stage of the arboretum demonstrated the utility of what is rightly the most contested public holiday in the country. They demonstrated that traditions can be subverted and new layers of meaning added. Maybe this is the perverse Australian genius—just keep adding new layers. It's much more pragmatic than going back to first principles to test the robustness of the foundations, or the accuracy of the actual events commemorated. This failure lies at the heart of the troubled soul of the nation.

No other nation has a national day so problematically grounded in history, a day that celebrates an event so little understood, or a day that has provoked such an anguished reaction without a respectful response for so long. Australia Day falls on the anniversary of the day Arthur Phillip planted the Union Jack at Sydney Cove in a rushed, low-key imperial tussle with the captains of the French ships that had also made landfall. The somewhat desultory act occurred almost a week after the eleven ships and 1500 people of the First Fleet had all made it to Botany Bay. It was twelve days before the governor read King George III's annexation of all the land and islands on the Pacific east coast, and to the 135th meridian. Thirty years later, Governor Lachlan Macquarie made it a paid public holiday with an extra ration of meat and began a tradition now best marked by witty lamb advertisements by Meat & Livestock Australia and too much talk of barbecues. It had various iterations over the years. By the sesquicentenary in 1938, it was known as a Day of Mourning, and Xavier Herbert's *Capricornia*, with its devastating description of brutal racism, won a series of literary prizes that tainted the anniversary with shame.[15] Fifty years later, as the Coca-Cola–sponsored ships sailed into Sydney Harbour, no one who was watching could have failed to understand that white Australia had a black history, and this date was Invasion Day. It is one of only two national public holidays tied to the calendar—more than a moveable long weekend to mark the end of the holiday season.

The growing awareness of the problematic nature of the date should be an opportunity to re-examine, amend and consider the sort of nation Australia would like to become. Gough Whitlam used the day to announce the search for a new national anthem in 1973. For the previous two decades, a pattern of Australia Day seminars and summer schools had provided an opportunity to discuss big ideas and pressing problems, to bring together interest groups that might not otherwise meet. It is a tradition that could well be reprised in local communities around the nation to interrogate what it now means to be Australian, and what it might mean in the future.

Finding a day that really speaks to the foundation of Australia with more meaning than the arrival of men with orders to create a penitentiary is confronting. The confected nationalism that has been encouraged to flourish is enjoyed by many, but makes others uncomfortable. Countless suggestions have been made to change the date. It could be the day Queen Victoria signed the legislation creating a commonwealth, the day Federation began, the first sitting of the national parliament in Melbourne, the opening of Parliament House in Canberra, the passage of the Australia Act that formally cut most ties with Britain. Or it could stretch over three days as Wesley Enoch and Noel Pearson have suggested: begin with an overnight vigil and then celebrate the ancient heritage of First Nations, the British arrival and the creation of a unique Australian state.[16] In what was once called the land of the long weekend but where people now work longer hours than in comparable countries, a three-day celebration would have an undeniable appeal. Any of these would have a more accurate claim to the day's name, yet all would still leave the fundamental flaw of First Nations recognition structurally unaddressed.

Rather than engage with a civilised and informed debate, anyone who raised this self-evident flaw was hammered as unpatriotic and ungrateful. Prime Minister Malcolm Turnbull introduced legislation to strip councils critical of the date of the right to conduct citizenship ceremonies. His successor, Scott Morrison, used Twitter to take a cheap shot at the Byron Shire Council in New South Wales for moving its ceremony to the evening of the day 'the cultural decimation and denigration of the First Australians began'.[17] Until this

From Little Things . . .

flaw is structurally and meaningfully addressed, notwithstanding all her remarkable achievements and her brilliant and generous people, Australia will be a half-formed thing.

OVER THE 2008 Australia Day long weekend, Kevin Rudd and an old friend, the political scientist Glyn Davis, enjoyed the sunshine in the gardens of The Lodge, the dowdy prime ministerial residence in Canberra. They talked about how the new government might develop an innovative agenda for the nation. John Howard had governed with such deft control for so long that new ideas fell on fallow ground, and the habit of imagining—of the state leading rather than following the market—had almost been lost. In the age of neoliberal globalism the nation state at times seemed like an awkward artefact of another age.

The task of using economics to change the heart and soul of the nation had surprisingly achieved its purpose. It was about to take a step change. The libertarian values of the digital behemoths—everywhere and nowhere—were taking over. In 2008 the internet was still full of promise. Ideas about participatory and deliberative democracy were making their way from academic workshops to real-world trials. The free flow of information and the ability to connect communities of interest irrespective of where they resided was shifting social relations. The ability to manipulate, intimidate and harass was still a largely unrealised threat.

Thanks to China's seemingly insatiable appetite for Australian resources, the Treasury coffers were full. There were some early warning signs, but the financial system seemed robust and Australia in good shape. At the end of the weekend the prime minister emerged from The Lodge to announce his audacious 2020 Summit: 1000 people would be invited to the national capital for a weekend in April to share ideas and shape an agenda with a delivery date of 2020. It was an idea that suited the times and the internet's democratising promise.

There had been summits and conventions in Parliament House before, but most were designed for lobbyists and special interest groups. Instead this would range widely: from constitutional reform to creativity, productivity to foreign affairs, Indigenous recognition to education, tax to social welfare, agriculture to health. The public response was beyond the prime minister's wildest expectations. Even in the thin public soil, the seeds of ideas had been growing, waiting for a moment to blossom. Thousands of people applied to attend; others wrote to their local members of parliament with suggestions. Mini-summits sprang up almost spontaneously around the country. Those confused about why they weren't invited and mystified by the unlikely endeavour grumbled, certain it could never work.

It was an unprecedented experience for the 1002 delegates who swarmed around Parliament House that April weekend. Most had never before been beyond the building's official areas and into the generously proportioned and elegantly decorated party rooms, private offices and meeting rooms where the grunt work of government is done. It was exhilarating for bankers to sit down with artists, academics to swap notes with diplomats, welfare activists to talk to people from the top of the rich list, First Nations leaders to advocate constitutional law reform. The vision was grand—tax reform, national disability scheme, cultural policy, recognition of First Nations peoples. There were scores of ideas. Some were perfect for media announcements—2020 vision by 2020; others were less obvious or media friendly tweaks to systems of public administration.

It was as presumptuous as the critics feared. It was a brave experiment that hinted at the possible and foundered on the rocky shoals of public administration, vested interests and, as always, *events*. The global financial crisis, the collapse of the UN climate meeting in Copenhagen, lethal party politics, and resistant public servants scuppered the vision, belittled idealists and allowed the status quo to prevail.

The 2020 that arrived with a flash of fireworks in smoke-thickened skies and an invisible virus could not have been more different to that envisaged by the summit delegates. If the recommendation from the health and foreign affairs experts at the summit—to prepare for an inevitable pandemic—had been heeded, the nation may have been better prepared. In the meantime, the habit of disregarding expert advice became entrenched. Scores of specialist committees, royal commissions and other inquiries investigated problems requiring both urgent and long-term action. Most were ignored. Even those that attracted fleeting public attention could be made to disappear, tucked away in digital files for future investigators to use as sources for footnotes. Experts became jaundiced, the public cynical.

The pandemic provided an uninvited moment for reflection about the fragility of norms and the importance of expertise. The COVID X-ray revealed the flaws of an under-resourced public sector and increasing inequality. It highlighted the capacity of brilliant medical research, and of the strengths and weaknesses of the health system, manufacturing and the arts.

The limits of official imagining were revealed in who was asked for advice. The premiers were gathered into a makeshift national cabinet, but the opposition was excluded. They worked hard, and the death toll in Australia was a fraction of that in many other comparable countries, but it was uncharted, exhausting territory.

The experts gathered to provide formal and informal advice were drawn from a narrow stratum: epidemiologists went head to head with economists, industrialists with union leaders, medical researchers with regulators, mental health experts with bureaucrats. It was a very small subset of the range of expertise that was needed to really imagine the future in a climate-challenged world where pandemics would inevitably become more frequent. Unlike the reconstruction that began to be planned even as the Second World War raged, this time the range of expertise was shaped by demands of the moment. There were no historians or philosophers, few behavioural economists or technologists, but plenty of plutocrats. It highlighted how the political system had narrowed its vision, and the media had shrivelled. Still, human resourcefulness, resilience and adaptability shone through.

———

ALLITERATION IS A powerful marketing tool. Slogans that repeat the first letter are an acknowledged aide-mémoire to drive decisions and purchases. As the second year of the pandemic drew to a close, C was the letter of the problems—COVID, Climate, China, Corruption—and Community the solution. The excitement of conversations on-screen with remote friends and colleagues gave way to something more tangible. Millions of otherwise locked down people counted their steps and explored the hidden lanes and parks within their five-kilometre zone, noticing more of their *somewhere*. Streets they had once drove through looked different from the footpath; formerly nameless neighbours began to talk; locals chipped in to help charities deliver meals to those in need; stories about the past and dreams for the future were shared; acquaintances became friends on social media networks. Society was not a fiction. Yet cabinet ministers who were young and educated enough to know better still valorised the British prime minister who denied it, and damaged the social fabric everywhere her ethos prevailed.

In lockdown, as people juggled home schooling and isolation and struggled as their relationships and finances were put under unprecedented stress, community mattered more than Canberra. It was hardly surprising that the states became more important. The regional variations were perplexing and confusing, but the idea that Canberra should have more control was not widely shared. Politics looked more than ever like a remote game where different rules applied. One of the

From Little Things . . .

oldest contests in the Commonwealth's history—between the states and Canberra—was shamefully on display. Canberra was where behaviour that would not be tolerated in any other workforce was normal, where the reality of climate change could be smothered in empty words, where institutions could be eroded as corruption and incompetence were ignored, where a considered and thoughtful request for constitutional recognition could be sent to die in a committee room. It was little wonder that the readiness to trust government showed a gaping chasm between the winners—the people the prime minister called Team Australia—and the rest. The world shaped by what Rose Scott had once described as 'genius male politicians' was not one that many found comforting or reassuring.[18]

These were big challenges and demanded big brains and moral imagination and leaders willing to consult and compromise. There was not a lot on display in the routinised, cut-throat and detached world of professional politics.

The Black Summer fires that heralded the pandemic powerfully demonstrated that the climate crisis is not just technical but life threatening. The pandemic demonstrated that human ingenuity could, if the threat were taken seriously enough, prevail. The political parties were slow to join the dots and find an opportunity for reinvention. Just as vaccines had turned COVID-19 into an endemic disease, human ingenuity could mitigate the climate crisis and create a more liveable world.

Rose Scott and Vida Goldstein had argued for a different sort of local politics, unencumbered by party loyalty, to shape the newly federated nation, and a century on a new iteration of their ideas was taking form. Local communities in regional and urban electorates had shown they could successfully challenge the stranglehold of political parties and elect members whose primary responsibility was to them, not to the parties few belonged to. As the groundswell of dissatisfaction grew, community groups proliferated. Millions of dollars were raised in an organic campaign, would-be candidates put themselves forward and community groups formed to define the issues that mattered most to them. They shared a vision that paid homage to the best of the old values—fairness, imagination, resourcefulness, boldness, and faith in egalitarianism—that had been missing for many years as the desire the appease those on the margins swamped public life. It was a time to rebuild from the ground up, to revisit the old ideas of community and place-based civic engagement.

The habit and constitutional necessity of focusing on the national had been found wanting. Flaws in the big institutions had been revealed but scarcely acted on following royal commissions and other inquiries, the mass media was powered by outrage over hot-button issues rather than a disinterested desire to hold the powerful to account. Political party membership shrunk. Successful rebuilding is not a top-down exercise but something that needs to happen from the ground up, just as some had argued during the Federation debates. Local government is still not recognised in the Constitution, but now thanks to the internet new tools of local engagement are within reach. Lockdowns reminded us of the importance of the local, and social media was its powerful agent.

The best councils have grown in confidence to become more than proxies for property developers. They have listened to the changing priorities of their communities, endorsed the *Uluru Statement from the Heart*, and used citizen juries and other innovative and inclusive methods of deliberative democracy to learn and engage. Those that took the needless distress caused for some by Australia Day seriously and changed events were punished rather than rewarded for listening to their communities.[19] At a time when parliamentary reports are arguing that there is a need for more civics education to ensure greater understanding of Australian democracy, the decision to punish those who paid attention to history and its consequences sent a loud counter-message, in the time-honoured way. *Block your critics. Don't listen. Stay silent. Best we forget.*

From Little Things . . .

INSPIRATION FOR THIS journey towards a renovated idea of Australia, and indeed the model methodology of how we might embark upon it, comes from an unlikely source: the people who even three score years and ten ago were still routinely and unemotionally treated as vermin, described as a dying race. Despite extraordinary efforts to make this a self-fulfilling prophecy—massacres, incarceration, poisoning, family and cultural destruction, impoverishment—they have survived.

Theirs is arguably the greatest national achievement. The First Nations population now numbers more than 800,000 people, still less than it was when the proclamation was read at Sydney Cove on 7 February 1788. The attempt to 'breed out the black' spectacularly failed. First Nations people now draw on their ancient heritage and that of the Irish, German, Russian, English, Scottish, Chinese, Italian and others with whom their forebears formed relationships. Their interest is in an idea of Australia that respects them all. The *Uluru Statement from the Heart* described it as a fuller expression of Australia's nationhood.

Nationalism is a concept that has been rightly tarnished by misuse and abuse. As George Packer wrote in *Last Best Hope*, 'the most durable narratives are not the ones that stand up best to fact checking. They are the ones that address our deepest needs and desires.'[20] Nationalism is an idea that has often been distorted into sentiment that encourages people to define themselves by what they are not, not by what they might be. In the hands of self-interested populists who want to make their fiefdom great again, it can easily slip into what Fintan O'Toole, with a lifetime of experience of the worst excesses of Irish nationalism, calls 'a kind of nihilism where *us* is merely not *them*'.[21]

For the majority, the Australian experience of nationalism has been rather benign and a bit trite. This is probably why, in an age when the global dominates, it has fallen into disuse, appropriated by those with something to sell, or keen to distract. The stories of national formation are tarnished and unreconciled, making it harder to reimagine what a sense of national identity might productively mean in the 21st century. Ignoring it will not make it disappear. Australia is the *somewhere* that 25,931,300 people called home as the second year of the pandemic drew to a close. It is a place to belong and experience solidarity, with a shared inner life.

First Nations people have not had such a benign experience of Australian nationalism. More than any other group they have experienced and continue to experience the bristles of exclusion. This makes the offer from the delegates to the Uluru Constitutional Convention of a way to contribute to a fuller expression of Australian nationhood even more extraordinarily generous. The national renovation they propose is about culture and belonging, not race. It is structural and substantial. It provides an opportunity to aspire. To learn from the best of the past as well as atone for the worst. To remember the enlightened spirit that Arthur Phillip imagined might be possible. To remember the early encounters—most eloquently described in Kim Scott's *That Deadman Dance*—that suggested comity might be possible. To recall the transformation of the lives of transported felons. To remember the vision of the most literate nation in the world, of lives remade in a generous and fair land.

Truth telling is one of the cores of the *Uluru Statement from the Heart*. It is another gift that promises to keep giving. There are big national issues at stake, but as always it starts from little things. The stories of what happened, to whom, when and why are necessarily local, grounded in place. Learning from them demands listening. It was the survivors of the stolen generations who first started telling their stories, allowing the sunshine of exposure to begin to erase the paralysis of the shame they had been forced to feel. Others silenced by shame followed— unmarried mothers, those who had been sexually abused in once-trusted institutions, residents of aged care and disability centres. No one wants to dwell on trauma or be forced to retell the horrors over and over, which is why it must be accompanied by listening, structural change

From Little Things . . .

and reparations, not just platitudes. The 'morality gap' Bernard Smith described 'between our sympathies and our achievements' remains. My friend Melissa Lucashenko is a much-awarded author whose writing hums with the Goorie cultural knowledge she has devoted her adult life to learning. She once described the resulting 'torment of powerlessness' to me: 'Remember how frustrated you feel on your worst day, and imagine living like that all the time, with no money, fearful of authority, knowing you are disrespected and suspected and not considered an equal citizen. First Nations men who could be brilliant leaders are instead left destroyed by the demons of poverty, white supremacy and shame.' It is hardly surprising that this translates into extraordinarily high rates of incarceration, suicide, violence, family dysfunction and early death. Shame and rage are powerful mental clamps.

For Sir Samuel Griffith's great-grandson this provoked an uncomfortable reckoning. David Denborough has worked with First Nations people in South Australia for years, helping to reduce the burden of trauma from a history of abuse and dislocation. Time and again he heard the stories of their ancestors, bad stories and good of what happened when families, language and culture were put back together. Then he faced a personal challenge—could he bring his ancestors with him? What did *he* know? What uncomfortable truths in his family had been rendered silent?[22]

The journey was painful. Sir Samuel was a man of his time, and while he may have demonstrated humanitarian impulses from time to time he had also held high office during the worst of the frontier wars in Queensland. He opposed the slave traders who coerced Melanesians to work on their sugar plantations and he had made it possible for First Nations people to give evidence in court, but his record, even for the times, was far from unblemished. As Melissa Lucashenko put it, 'Slippery Sam: monster of the Maiwar.'

The process of putting together a critical family history that acknowledged the past and made way for a more honest future was challenging. But David Denborough found it was also liberating. Things unspoken could at last be said out loud and their consequences dealt with.[23] Like the bold women centrestage at the National Arboretum in Canberra on Australia Day 2021, the Uluru Generation has too much to teach us to be allowed to slide back into the shadows.

FOR CENTURIES, THREE score years and ten has been a rather poetic way of describing a good old age, long enough to have turned 'hours dreadful and things strange' into wisdom.[24] Even as average life expectancy stretches towards another score, 70 years remains a marker. As Linda Colley has noted, epic transformations can take centuries and are only very occasionally sudden; most take a lifetime.[25] Change does not happen by fiat, but by the accretion of debate and discussion; by a willingness to listen and learn; by a readiness to trial new ways of doing things and implement them if they work; by a robust dialogue, not abusive dismissal couched in economic and moral certainty. By a willingness to go to first principles in crafting solutions, rather than just picking the latest idea off the shelf. Like all fashions, many will seem quaint, odd or dangerous with hindsight. In retrospect the ideas that have shaped much of the world for the past 40 years have been found wanting, which makes the need to forge stronger bonds both harder and more urgent.

Sometimes change happens in response to catastrophe. Many believe that the early decades of the 21st century present a catastrophe that demands leaders who demonstrate they are willing to learn and change their minds, with the patience to explain and a clear eye on the public good rather than sectional interests. As the Harvard historian Jill Lepore wrote: 'What's needed is nothing less than a new social contract for public goods, environmental protection, sustainable agriculture, public health, community centres, public education, grants for small business, public funding for the arts. It won't be a new New Deal. Governments rest on a social contract, an agreement to live together. That contract needs renewing.'[26]

It is hard but starts with little steps. In Australia, climate change and the failure to recognise First Nations people are the talismans. Both can be addressed, powerfully and practically, locally and nationally, even though both will require a long overdue renovation of the idea of Australia and an updating of the social contract.

Ever since the First Fleet arrived, Australians have responded to international trends and movements. They have been active readers, writers and thinkers, prepared to engage with the big issues, learn from the experience of others, adopt and adapt. Some wrong decisions were made and continue to be made, but no one can claim ignorance. Many foundational flaws have been corrected, but there is still work to do.

The big global movements found their refracted vision in a state that could be protective and supportive, could challenge and provoke. The reconstruction after the end of the Second World War, and the human rights movement that accompanied it, eventually turned a defensive, inward-looking nation into one that was more confident and assertive. As deregulation and privatisation swept the Western world in the 1980s, it was adopted but leavened by social support and cultural adaptation. There was initial recognition in Australia that the market alone could not be trusted to put the best interests of most people first, before the full force of neoliberalism whittled away public goods and national confidence in autonomy and agency.

The pandemic and climate change demand unusual urgency. There is a need and an opportunity to develop a different industrial architecture with jobs that provide meaning and sustain lives and values that put respect and integrity first. The idea of a different sort of economics is emerging around the world that recognises that the state has a major and positive role to play beyond protecting mates and sectional interests. It will be resisted, but self-regulating democracies need to find a way to again value public goods that are not easily packaged and sold, but make life worth living. This will require more investment to develop capacity, bolster the institutions that provide democracy's skeleton and pay attention to the local.

During the pandemic, a plethora of books and seminars explored these possibilities. To embrace them would produce a very different idea of Australia, one that is prepared to face the past and make recompense, that looks beyond the land to people, institutions and culture to reinvigorate the economy and enrich the society. The ingredients are at our fingertips if we care to look.

It is striking to recall that one of the most important Aboriginal artists to have captivated the world came from a place called Utopia. For millennia before its brief life as cattle station, Emily Kame Kngwarreye's country was that of the Alyawarr people. It is a place as impoverished as any of the remote settlements in northern Australia that have been returned to their traditional owners with only grudging support of the state. But the semi-arid country is the source of Dreaming and a culture that speaks to the world when brought to life on canvas. Emily Kame Kngwarreye's paintings are displayed in galleries, palaces and private collections around the world. They are more than extraordinary works of art. In the words of the great Aboriginal scholar and advocate Marcia Langton, the paintings 'fulfil the primary historical function of Australian art by showing the settler Australian audience, caught ambiguously between old and new lands, a new way to belong in this place'. They do what Australian art always aspired to do.[27]

Creating a utopia, or at least an aspiration to do better, requires more imagination, boldness and courage than our current system of professional politics permits. It needs more art and better faith. Politics, like everything else, is now in thrall to corporate modes of organisation and communication. The emphasis is on the mission (to get elected) and KPIs (to deliver on promises). The headline of every corporate plan

From Little Things . . .

is the 'vision'. It is always the hardest thing to define. But without a vision, any plan is meaningless. Our utopia needs a new vision, one not tinged by shame. The old ones have not passed the test of time.

It is hard to escape the conclusion that until Australians are prepared to seriously consider the good and the bad of the past, to recognise and address the structural factors that, as a nation and as individuals, prevent us from realising our potential, we will be trapped forever on a treadmill, running but going nowhere. We need to pay attention.

After what the commentators agreed was one of the most poisonous and demeaning years for any political leader, Prime Minister Scott Morrison ended the year with a passionate speech to 'Team Australia' his most loyal supporters at a Sydney Institute dinner. It marked the unofficial beginning of his election campaign. He spoke in that sweet moment when state and international borders had opened, citizens were returning home, families reuniting for the first time in months, masks and QR codes were becoming optional—if you closed your eyes it seemed the good times might return. Meanwhile another COVID tsunami gathered force offshore, but the prime minister declared it was not a time to look in the rear vision mirror; it was time, he said, for government to get out of people's lives.[28] It seemed nothing had been learned. The permanent present, and a self-congratulatory strut, the Blatant Blatherskites prevailed.

John Hirst dedicated his book *The Sentimental Nation*, which traces the history of Federation, to 'the 422,788 Yes voters who have no other memorial'. These were the men, and a few women, who after a protracted process agreed to form a Commonwealth, one that was necessarily remote from most. Alfred Deakin called it a miracle, but Rose Scott said the model the men decided on 'broke her heart'. In a secular land, miracles have limited currency, but heartbreak has always been the companion of constitutional reform.

Those who supported this most bureaucratic foundation, of a land that had still not been fully 'explored', were given a commitment, much bolder than any that has been made since: 'Ours is not the federation of fear, but the wise, solemn, rational federation of a free people. Such a federation as ours has only become possible through the advance of intelligence and the development of a higher system of morality than the world ever saw before.'[29] Two years later 800,000 women were allowed to join the electoral roll, but the border barriers were high, First Nations people were largely confined to missions and reserves. Even as fear was fostered some hoped that this vision might be realised.

It was not. The promise was not kept. It didn't even have time to become a myth. When the First World War and Spanish flu devastated the new nation just two decades later, heartbreak displaced hope.

Yet, the aspirational ethos to belong, driven by people in communities all around the nation, could be revived, stripped of its foundational flaws. *Be bold, be bold, be bold. Reform is hard. But worth it.* Adopting this ambition and applying the values of respect and truthfulness, imagination, fairness and egalitarianism would be a start. Platitudes and myths are not enough. A fully formed nation—grounded in a civic, not ethnic, way of belonging—without fear is still possible. The soul of the nation has a rich inner life. It holds the dreams and stories of those who have always been here and those who have come in waves ever since.

My search for the soul of the nation tells me that despite the noise from the fringes, and Canberra's selective hearing, many, maybe even most, Australians are willing to be bold. Brave enough to make the nation in which they live more than 'slightly better than average, again'.

Acknowledgements

WHEN I FIRST PROPOSED this book I imagined it as a sort of meditation. I thought it would be short volume. One that floated lightly over the past to make sense of the present to distil a rich multilayered identity. As I began talking about it, researching and writing, it became clear that there was much to explain, context to provide, patterns to explore, reasons for pride, anger and disappointment, and it grew. Thank you for making this journey with me.

I am grateful to my enthusiastic and thoughtful agent Jane Novak and insightful and energetic publisher Jane Palfreyman for their unstinting support.

A lot of the background research that made the book possible came from the thousands of essays I commissioned and published in *Griffith Review* from 2003. Working with the authors and listening to audiences at public events was a great learning experience. I know many readers also heard what the literary critic Geordie Williamson recently described as 'the sound of Australian democracy and culture thinking out loud'.

I am grateful to everyone involved with *Griffith Review*: the many authors, supportive Griffith administrators and the small staff,

Acknowledgements

particularly Erica Sontheimer, Susan Hornbeck, Paul Thwaites, John Tague, Jane Hunterland and Ashley Hay.

Conversations with other colleagues at Griffith University were also formative, including particularly Anne Tiernan, Julian Meyrick, Pat Hoffie, Mark Finnane, Susan Forde, A.J. Brown and Brydie-Leigh Bartlett.

I am grateful that Kimberley Podger and the Griffith Centre for Social and Cultural Research made it possible for Clare McGregor to create a searchable database of the writing about the new nationalism of the 1970s, and that Kate Littlehales navigated the system to keep the books I ordered from the Griffith library flowing across the Queensland–New South Wales border during lockdown. Carol Ey provided valuable assistance navigating parliamentary and other Canberra records.

As the scope of the book grew I drew on the expertise of many friends and colleagues, including countless conversations too numerous to mention. I hope you remember them; I do. I am particularly grateful to those who read sections and chapters along the way, picking up mistakes, pushing for greater clarity and precision. Thank you: Yassmin Abdel-Magied, Roslyn Atkinson, Frank Bongiorno, Natasha Cica, Ann Curthoys, Trish Davidson, Darren Dale, Glyn Davis, Jill Eddington, Wesley Enoch, Raymond Evans, Tim Fairfax, Matt Foley, Tony Fitzgerald, Brendan Gleeson, Tom Griffiths, Anna Haebich, Jenny Hocking, Pat Hoffie, Herman van Eyken, Tony Koch, Melissa Lucashenko, Peter Mares, John Mitchell, Gavin Morris, Kerry O'Brien, Annmaree O'Keeffe, Tamson Pietsch, Noel Pearson, Isabelle Reinecke, Anne Tiernan, Rod Tiffen, Chris Wallace, Tone Wheeler and Clare Wright. Any mistakes remain my own.

Producing a book often feels like a solitary activity, but requires a dedicated and professional team. Jane Palfreyman has a well-deserved reputation as one of the very best, and busiest, publishers in Australia and I am honoured she took this on. The team at Allen & Unwin who

Acknowledgements

worked to produce the book have been exemplary: Tom Bailey-Smith, Rebecca Starford, Emma Driver, Garry Cousins, Jenn Thurgate, Isabelle O'Brien, Christa Moffitt, Lisa Macken, John Mahony, Richard Potter SC, Midland Typesetters, the printers and the sales and marketing team. The book business has been highly disrupted by the pandemic, but your professionalism remained exemplary.

As I retreated to my study, I am grateful to my husband Ian Reinecke for graciously tolerating my distraction, and for being my first reader. Knowing he is always in my corner with loving support and advice is a great gift of my life and made everything else possible. Isabelle and Carl Reinecke and their partners Lochie McQueen and Alex Grieve have been unstinting in their support under difficult pandemic circumstances. Even in old age my parents, Noel and Cynthia Schultz, remain remarkably attentive, engaged with the world, and skilful and thoughtful readers and editors. I am forever grateful for my good fortune of being their daughter, raised in their care with my sister Cindy and brother Andrew.

Two close friends deserve special thanks. Jane Camens, who has been reading my writing since we co-edited *Semper Floreat* in 1976, was meticulous and asked tough questions and didn't let me squib the answers. Anne Coombs read every word, reminded me to keep my sentences short, and provided invaluable input until the day she died—it was a selfless gift that I will always treasure.

Thank you, it takes a village to raise a book.

Notes

1. Terra Nullius of the Mind
1. Fiona Foley, *Biting the Clouds*, University of Queensland Press, 2021, p. 31.
2. Gavin Souter, *Sydney Observed*, Brio, 2017 (1965), pp. 31–34.
3. Souter, p. 40.
4. Stan Grant, *The Tears of Strangers*, HarperCollins, 2002, p. 5.
5. David Marr, *My Country*, Black Inc., 2018, pp. xi–xii.
6. In the Senate, Hanson said, 'People have a right to be proud of their cultural background, whether they are black, white or brindle. If we cannot agree on this, I think it's safe to say anti-white racism is well and truly rife in our society.' Australian Senate, *Debates*, no. 12, 2018, p. 7118.
7. *BBC News*, '"It's OK to be white" bill defeated in Australian Senate', 15 October 2018.
8. Matthew 16:26.
9. Ross Gibson, *Seven Versions of an Australian Badland*, University of Queensland Press, 2002, p. 171.
10. Department of Home Affairs, 'Australian Values Statement', DHA, 30 October 2020, immi.homeaffairs.gov.au/help-support/meeting-our-requirements/australian-values.
11. Joseph Brookes, '"Don't stop" at 2050 net zero: Andrew Liveris', *InnovationAus*, 15 October 2021, www.innovationaus.com/dont-stop-at-2050-net-zero-andrew-liveris/; Jack Detsch, 'Turnbull: AUKUS subs deal is an "own goal"', *Foreign Policy*, 6 October 2021, foreignpolicy.com/2021/10/06/aukus-us-uk-australia-biden-morrison-turnbull-submarines/.

2. Slightly Better Than Average, Again
1. Gavin Souter, *Sydney Observed*, Brio, 2017 (1965), p. 36.
2. David Llewellyn, 'Bentham and Australia', *Revue d'études benthamiennes*, no. 19, 30 January 2021, doi.org/10.4000/etudes-benthamiennes.8517.

Notes

3   Jeremy Bentham, *A Plea for the Constitution*, Maurnan & Hatchard, 1803, discovery.ucl.ac.uk/id/eprint/10055304/.
4   Grace Karskens, *The Colony*, Allen & Unwin, 2008; Thomas Keneally, *Australians*, Allen & Unwin, 2014; Grantlee Keiza, *Banks*, ABC Books, 2020.
5   Luke Beck, 'Federal Parliament just weakened political donations laws while you weren't watching', *The Conversation*, 4 November 2020.
6   Australian Trade and Investment Commission, 'Native title', ATIC, n.d., www.austrade.gov.au/land-tenure/native-title/native-title.
7   Ann Curthoys and Jessie Mitchell, *Taking Liberty*, Cambridge University Press, 2018, p. 14; Patrick Wolfe, 'Land, Labor and Difference', *The American Historical Review*, vol. 106, no. 3, 2005, pp. 4–12.
8   David Malouf, *Spirit of Play*, ABC Books, 1998, pp. 19–24; Ailsa McPherson, 'Theatre', *Dictionary of Sydney*, 2008, dictionaryofsydney.org/entry/theatre.
9   Richard Twopeny, *Town Life in Australia*, Elliot Stock, 1883, unpaginated, www.gutenberg.org/files/16664/16664-h/16664-h.htm.
10 Sally Young, *Paper Emperors*, NewSouth, 2019.
11 Twopeny, unpaginated.
12 Julianne Schultz, *Reviving the Fourth Estate*, Cambridge University Press, 1998.
13 Carl Reinecke, *Books That Made Us*, HarperCollins, 2021.
14 Rodney Tiffen, *Rupert Murdoch*, NewSouth, 2014, Sally Young, *Paper Emperors*.
15 Bridget Griffen-Foley, *Changing Stations*, UNSW Press, 2009, p. 23.
16 *Griffith Review*, no. 1, Spring 2003.
17 Raymond Evans, 'Strangers in the night', in Edwina Shaw (ed.), *Bjelke Blues*, AndAlso Books, 2019, p. 247.
18 Charles Darwin, *The Voyage of the Beagle*, Harvard Classics, 1997 (1839), unpaginated, www.gutenberg.org/cache/epub/944/pg944-images.html.
19 Conor Friedersdorf, 'Australia traded away too much liberty', *The Atlantic*, 2 September 2021.
20 'Rupert bare', editorial, *Saturday Paper*, 25 September 2019, p. 14.
21 Sean Kelly, 'Cowardice: What Morrison and Albanese have in common', *Sydney Morning Herald*, 19 September 2020.

3. From Somewhere

1   Sue Abbey, 'Noonuccal, Oodgeroo (1920–1993)', *Australian Dictionary of Biography*, National Centre of Biography, Australian National University, 2017, adb.anu.edu.au/biography/noonuccal-oodgeroo-18057/text29634.
2   Rosalind Kidd, *The Way We Civilise*, University of Queensland Press, 1997, p. 46.
3   Ross Wilson, *The Accidental Present*, forthcoming, AndAlso Books, 2022.
4   Megan Davis and George Williams, *Everything You Need to Know about the Uluru Statement from the Heart*, UNSW Press, 2021, p. 54.
5   Tim Rowse, 'A Liberal's case for the Voice to Parliament', *Inside Story*, 9 July 2021; AIATSIS, 'The 1967 referendum', n.d., aiatsis.gov.au/explore/1967-referendum.
6   Oodgeroo Noonuccal, 'Why Not Street', in *The Dawn is at Hand: Poems*, Jacaranda Press, 1966, www.poetrylibrary.edu.au/poets/noonuccal-oodgeroo/poems/why-not-street-0719013.

Notes

7. Gerhard Fischer, 'Immigration, integration, disintegration', *Griffith Review*, no. 48, 2015, Enduring Legacies, Text Melbourne, p. 37.
8. Fischer, p. 42.
9. Paul Daley, 'The room of the dead: How a museum became a halfway house for bones and spirits', *Guardian*, 5 July 2020.
10. W.E.H. Stanner, 'The Boyer Lectures: After the Dreaming', in Robert Manne (ed.), *The Dreaming and Other Essays*, Black Inc., 2009, pp. 189, 191.
11. Stanner, p. 224.
12. Stanner, p. 189.
13. Jim Davidson, *A Three-Cornered Life*, UNSW Press, 2010, p. 114.
14. Amy Mitchell-Whittington, 'Brisbane sculpture's hidden message about 94 massacres', *Brisbane Times*, 25 April 2017. See also Fiona Foley, 'The elephant in the room: Public art in Brisbane', *Artlink*, June 2012; Louise Martin-Chew, *Provocateur*, QUT Art Museum, 2021, p. 151.
15. Fiona Foley, *Biting the Clouds*, University of Queensland Press, 2021, pp. 38, 118–22.
16. Stuart Macintyre and Anna Clark, *The History Wars*, Melbourne University Press, 2003, p. 26; Raymond Evans, 'Blood Dries Quickly: Conflict Study and Australian Historiography', *Australian Journal of History and Politics*, vol. 41, 1995, pp. 80–102.
17. Malouf, p. 85.
18. Catherine Fisher, *Sound Citizens*, ANU Press, 2021.
19. Bernard Salt, 'This one's for you, Mum', *Weekend Australian Magazine*, 28–29 November 2020, p. 27.

4. Stories We Tell Ourselves

1. Marilyn Lake and Henry Reynolds, *Drawing the Global Colour Line*, Melbourne University Press, 2008, p. 4.
2. A.A. Phillips, 'The cultural cringe', *Meanjin*, vol. 9, no. 4, 1950.
3. Geoff Kitney, @4mambo, *Just marked a decade back in Australia . . .* , Twitter, 10 September 2021, twitter.com/4mambo/status/1436252374880833543.
4. Cameron Stewart, 'Fortress of fear', *Weekend Australian Magazine*, 26 June 2021.
5. Jane McAdam and Regina Jefferies, 'Why the latest travel caps look like an arbitrary restriction on Australians' right to come home', *The Conversation*, 7 July 2021.
6. Raymond Evans, '"Pigmentia": Racial fears and white Australia', in A. Dirk Moses (ed.), *Genocide in Settler Society*, Berghahn Books, 2004, pp. 103–24.
7. Julianne Schultz, 'Facing Foundational Flaws', *Griffith Review 73*; *Hey Utopia*, New South, 2021, p. 11.
8. Thomas Keneally, *Australians*, vol. 1, Allen & Unwin, 2009, p. 91.
9. Thomas Babington Macaulay, quoted in Charles Knife, letter to the editor, *Queenslander*, 26 June 1880, in Carl Adolf Feilberg, *The Way We Civilise*, G. & J. Black, 1880, p. 41.
10. Robert Hughes, *The Fatal Shore*, Alfred Knopf, 1987, p. 72.
11. Michael E. Miller, '"A search for villains": As Australia's outbreak grows, so does the covid shaming', *Washington Post*, 23 July 2021.
12. Isabel Wilkerson, *Caste*, Penguin, 2020, p. 99.
13. Michelle Arrow, *The Seventies*, NewSouth, 2019, pp. 2–4.

Notes

14 Fintan O'Toole, 'The state of us, part 1: Ireland's story doesn't make sense any more', *Irish Times*, 19 August 2017.

15 Tony Abbott, 'Now is a good time to assess what it means for us to be Australian', *The Australian*, 16 July 2020; Manning Clark, *The Quest for an Australian Identity*, University of Queensland Press, 1980, p. 4.

16 H.W. Arndt, 1981, quoted in James Curran and Stuart Ward, *The Unknown Nation*, Melbourne University Press, 2010, p. 89.

17 Jade Macmillan, 'Endeavour replica to sail around Australia to mark 250 years since Captain Cook's arrival', *ABC News*, 22 January 2019, www.abc.net.au/news/2019-01-22/endeavour-replica-to-sail-around-australia/10734998.

18 Katharine Murphy, 'Scott Morrison sorry for "no slavery in Australia claim" and acknowledges "hideous practices"', *The Guardian*, 12 June 2020.

19 Julianne Schultz, 'Stories We Tell Ourselves', *Griffith Review 58*, Storied Lives, Text, 2019, p. 9.

20 Nick Cater, 'Militant culture warriors make all men the bad guys', *The Australian*, 5 April 2021.

21 John Curtin, 'John Curtin's speech to America, 14 March 1942', John Curtin Prime Ministerial Library/ABC Radio Archives, 1942, john.curtin.edu.au/audio/00434.html.

22 Robert Manne, 'Bad News', *Quarterly Essay 43*, Black Inc, 2011.

23 John Daley, *Gridlock: Removing barriers to policy reform*, Grattan Institute, 2021, grattan.edu.au/wp-content/uploads/2021/07/Gridlock-Grattan-Report.pdf.

24 George Packer, *Last Best Hope*, Jonathan Cape, London, 2021, p. 81.

25 Ross Gibson, *Seven Versions of an Australian Badland*, University of Queensland Press, 2002, pp. 135–37.

26 George Orwell, *Politics and the English Language*, Penguin, 2013 (1946), gutenberg.net.au/ebooks02/0200151h.html.

5. Architecture of Silence

1 Robyn Ravlich, *Skywriting*, Brandl & Schlesinger, 2019, p. 77.

2 Bernard Smith, *The Spectre of Truganini*, ABC, 1980, p. 11.

3 Stuart Macintyre and Anna Clark, *The History Wars*, Melbourne University Publishing, 2003, p. 26.

4 Alan Tudge and Avani Dias, 'Triple J Hack—Interview with Avani Dias', Minister's Media Office, Department of Education, Skills and Employment, 7 September 2021, ministers.dese.gov.au/tudge/triple-j-hack-interview-avani-dias.

5 Brendan James Murray, 'Silence: The bleaching of history', *Griffith Review* [online], 17 September 2021, www.griffithreview.com/articles/silence/.

6 Smith, p. 24.

7 Raymond Evans and Robert Orsted-Jensen, '"Pale Death . . . Around Our Footprints Springs": Assessing Violent Mortality on the Queensland Frontier from State and Private Exterminatory Practices', in Mohamed Adhikari (ed.), *Civilian Driven Violence and the Genocide of Indigenous Peoples in Settler Colonies*, Cape Town, University of Cape Town Press, 2020, pp. 139–64.

8 Jonathan Richards, *The Secret War*, University of Queensland Press, p. 14.

9 Carl Adolf Feilberg, *The Way We Civilise*, G. & J. Black, 1880, p. 10.

Notes

10 Raymond Evans and Robert Ørsted-Jensen, '"I cannot say the numbers that were killed": Assessing violent mortality on the Queensland frontier', *Social Science Research Network*, no. 2467836, p. 4.
11 Barry Krosch, *The Queensland Police Special Branch 1948–1989*, MPhil thesis, Griffith University, 2013, p. 171.
12 Krosch, p. 150.
13 Mark Finnane, 'The National Archives matter for government as well', *Inside Story*, 2 July 2021.
14 Isaac Nowroozi, 'Celebrating Marion Mahony Griffin, the woman who helped shape Canberra', *ABC News*, 20 February 2021, www.abc.net.au/news/2021-02-20/design-canberra-marion-mahony-griffin-honoured-on-150th-birthday/13171164.
15 Jennifer Taylor, *Australian Architecture Since 1960*, Law Book Company, 1986, pp. 104–6.
16 Finnane, 2 July 2021.
17 Jenny Hocking, 'Secret history: The release of the Mountbatten archives and the fight for royal access', *The Conversation*, 3 August 2021.
18 Jenny Hocking, *Gough Whitlam: A moment in history*, Miegunyah Press, 2008; *Gough Whitlam: His time*, Miegunyah Press, 2012.
19 Jenny Hocking, *The Palace Letters*, Scribe, 2020, p. 5.
20 Tone Wheeler, 'Tone on Tuesday: The democratic spatial narrative of the Australian War Memorial', *Architecture & Design*, 3 March 2021, www.architectureanddesign.com.au/people/tone-on-tuesday-the-democratic-spatial-narrative.
21 Nicole Moore, *The Censor's Library*, University of Queensland Press, 2012.
22 Bernard Colleary, *Oil Under Troubled Water*, Melbourne University Publishing, 2020; Brian Toohey, *Secret: The making of Australia's security state*, Melbourne University Publishing, 2019.
23 Frank Bongiorno, 'The Dismissal Dossier: Everything you were never meant to know about November 1975 by Jenny Hocking', *Australian Book Review*, December 2017.
24 Moore, p. xii.
25 Malouf, *A Spirit of Play*, Boyer Lectures, November–December 1998, ABC Radio, www.abc.net.au/radionational/programs/boyerlectures/series/a-spirit-of-play-the-making-of-australian/3341006.
26 Stan Grant, 'Stan Grant', in Thomas Mayor (ed.), *Dear Son*, Hardie Grant Explore, 2021.
27 See Miriam Rose Foundation, www.miriamrosefoundation.org.au.
28 Judy Atkinson, *Trauma Trails, Recreating Song Lines*, Spinifex Press, 2002, p. 8.
29 Stan Grant, *The Tears of Strangers*, HarperCollins, 2002, p. 5.
30 See Dharug Dictionary, dharug.dalang.com.au/language/dictionary.
31 Atkinson, 2002, p. 8.
32 Judy Atkinson, 'The value of deep listening—The Aboriginal gift to the nation', TEDxSydney, 16 June 2017, tedxsydney.com/talk/the-value-of-deep-listening-the-aboriginal-gift-to-the-nation-judy-atkinson/.
33 Atkinson, 2002, p. 70.
34 Fergus Maguire and Michael Gordon, 'Elliott slur on "forgotten race"', *The Age*, 10 March 1999.
35 Smith, pp. 34, 52.
36 John Kampfner, *Why the Germans Do it Better*, Atlantic Books, 2020, p. 44.

Notes

6. Hidden in Plain Sight

1. National Archives of Australia, 'Fact Sheet 192: Japanese midget submarine attacks on Sydney, 1942', www.naa.gov.au/sites/default/files/2020-05/fs-192-japanese-midget-submarine-attacks-on-sydney-1942.pdf.
2. City of Sydney, 'Sydney Cove/Warrane', Sydney Barani, 2013, www.sydneybarani.com.au/sites/sydney-cove-warrane/.
3. By 1854, Double Bay had become a market garden. Lucy Turnbull, *Sydney: Biography of a City*, Random House, 1999, p. 386; Andrew Clark, 'The richest village divides', *Australian Financial Review*, 20 June 2009.
4. Grace Karskens, *The Colony*, Allen & Unwin, 2010, p. 133.
5. James Spigelman, *Australia Day Address 2008* [speech], Conservatorium of Music, Sydney, 22 January 2008, www.australiaday.com.au/whats-on/australia-day-address/australia-day-address-2008-by-the-hon-james-jacob-spigelman-ac/.
6. Turnbull, p. 387.
7. Paul Irish, *Hidden in Plain View*, NewSouth, 2017, p. 73.
8. Judy Atkinson, *Trauma Trails, Recreating Song Lines*, Spinifex Press, 2002, p. 59.
9. J.J. Curran, 'Seven Shilling Beach', *Sydney Morning Herald*, 25 August 1950. Seven Shillings Beach via trove.nla.gov.au/newspaper/article/27570125.
10. Account as told to Miss Dora Busby by her grandmother in *Some Houses and People of New South Wales*, G. Nesta Griffiths, Ure Smith, 1949, p. 142; 'Redleaf' Statement of Significance, New South Wales Heritage Database, Office of Environment and Heritage.
11. Woollahra Council records show that Elaine was built in 1863 and sold to Geoffrey Fairfax in 1891. Fairwater next door was built in 1881 and sold to Warwick Fairfax in 1910.
12. Seven shillings is an amount that has assumed almost mythic status in Australia. Seven shillings was the daily salary Justice Higgins decided was the minimum a man must be paid to provide for his family in 1907.
13. Grace Karskens, 'Appin massacre', *Dictionary of Sydney*, 2015, dictionaryofsydney.org/entry/appin_massacre.
14. Amy Fallon, 'The activist facing jail for Macquarie statue protest', *Saturday Paper*, 2 October 2021; Paul Gregoire, '"Defacing" the Governor Macquarie Statue: An Interview with Activist Stephen Langford', 17 July 2020, www.sydneycriminallawyers.com.au/blog/defacing-the-governor-macquarie-statue-an-interview-with-activist-stephen-langford/.
15. Spigelman, *Australia Day Address 2008*.
16. 'The AFR View: NSW can lead Australia out of gilded cage' [editorial], *Australian Financial Review*, 11 August 2021.
17. Natassia Chrysanthos, 'Hundreds of Sydney students claim they were sexually assaulted', *Sydney Morning Herald*, 19 February 2021; Lucy Clark, 'The trouble with boys: What lies behind the flood of stories about teenage sexual assault?', *The Guardian*, 28 February 2021.
18. Tim Winton, 'About the boys: Tim Winton on how toxic masculinity is shackling men to misogyny', *The Guardian*, 9 April 2018.

Notes

7. A Fair Go

1   Prime Minister of Australia, '$130 billion JobKeeper payment to keep Australians in a job', media release, 30 March 2020, www.pm.gov.au/media/130-billion-jobkeeper-payment-keep-australians-job; www.pm.gov.au/media/press-conference-australian-parliament-house-act-14 Transcript 30 March 2020.
2   Paul Kelly, *100 Years,* Allen & Unwin, 2001, pp. 117–18; David Potts, *The Myth of the Great Depression*, Scribe, 2006, p. 8.
3   Ruth Graham, 'The rise and fall of Carl Lentz, the celebrity pastor of Hillsong church', *New York Times*, 5 December 2020.
4   Mary Gilmore, *More Recollections*, Angus & Robertson, 1936, p. 246, cited in Caroline Graham, 'Of warriors, bad apples and blood lust', *Meanjin* (Winter 2021), meanjin.com.au/essays/of-warriors-bad-apples-and-blood-lust/.
5   Peter Cochrane, *Colonial Ambition*, Melbourne University Publishing, 2006, p. 174.
6   Commonwealth of Australia, *Parliamentary Debates: House of Representatives*, Hansard, no. 17, 29 November 2012, p. 14054.
7   Lyman Tower Sargent, 'Australian Utopian Literature', *Utopian Studies* N. Albinski, 'Visions of the 1890s', 1999, vol. 10, no. 2, 1999, pp. 138–73; *Journal of Australian Studies*, 1987, pp. 12–22.
8   'A "communal colony"', *The Mercury*, 16 August 1892, p. 3, quoted in Nick Dyrenfurth, *Mateship*, Scribe, 2015, p. 2.
9   AAP, 'Scott Morrison honours famous aunt', *SBS News*, 24 May 2019, www.sbs.com.au/news/scott-morrison-honours-famous-aunt/.
10 Donald Trump and Scott Morrison, 'Remarks by President Trump and Prime Minister Morrison of Australia at State Dinner', 24 September 2019, au.usembassy.gov/remarks-by-president-trump-and-prime-minister-morrison-of-australia-at-state-dinner/.
11 Donald Trump and Scott Morrison, 2019.
12 Tim Soutphommasane, 'Multiculturalism is a strength', in Tanya Plibersek (ed.), *Upturn*, NewSouth, 2020, p. 165.
13 Karen Michelmore, Rebecca Parish and Kendall O'Connor, 'Christmas Island locals surprised, split over quarantine of Australians from coronavirus epicentre', *ABC News*, 29 January 2020, www.abc.net.au/news/2020-01-29/christmas-island-locals-on-quarantine-for-coronavirus/11910326.
14 Bang Xiao, 'Australians in Wuhan conflicted over Christmas Island quarantine plan amid coronavirus outbreak', *ABC News*, 1 February 2020, www.abc.net.au/news/2020-01-30/wuhan-coronavirus-australian-families-christmas-island/11913304.
15 Soutphommasane, p. 170.
16 Commonwealth of Australia, *Parliamentary Debates: House of Representatives*, Hansard, 8 April 2020, p. 2909.
17 Toby Mann, 'Chinese Australians say questions from Senator Eric Abetz about their loyalties are not asked of other communities', *ABC News*, 16 October 2020, www.abc.net.au/news/2020-10-15/chinese-australians-questioned-about-loyalties/12770172.
18 Katharine Murphy, 'The meaning of Morrison's mantra about getting a fair go is clear. It's conditional', *The Guardian*, 17 April 2019.

Notes

19 Peter Hartcher, 'PM may lie, but real test is trust', *Sydney Morning Herald*, p. 30, News Review, 20–21 November 2021.
20 Marilyn Lake and Henry Reynolds, *Drawing the Global Colour Line*, Melbourne University Publishing, 2008, p. 156.
21 Gavin Souter, *Sydney Observed*, Brio, 2017 (1965), p. 96.
22 Kings Cross Community Aid and Information Service, *Memories, Kings Cross, 1936–1946*, 1981, p. 102.
23 Kings Cross Community Aid and Information Service, p. 7.
24 Luke Henriques-Gomes, 'Robodebt: Court approves $1.8bn settlement for victims of government's "shameful" failure', *The Guardian*, 11 June 2021.
25 Orietta Guerrera, 'Could you live on $40 a day? Readers respond to call for permanent increase in JobSeeker payment', *Sydney Morning Herald*, 20 November 2020.
26 Trust Barometer 2021 Australia, 19 February 2021, www.edelman.com.au/trust-barometer-2021-australia.

8. Lucky, Not So Smart

1 Carl Reinecke, *Luck's Hard Toil*, Honours thesis, Australian National University, 2015, pp. 46–8.
2 Jan Davis, 'More than 25 years after "the clever country" little has changed', *The Mercury*, 2 July 2014, www.themercury.com.au/news/opinion/more-than-25-years-after-the-clever-country-little-has-changed/news-story/53c45ed466e2b4c6840f4271d1952cad.
3 Graham Freudenberg, 'No child in poverty', *Pearls and Irritations*, 30 May 2019.
4 Richard Twopeny, *Town Life in Australia*, Elliot Stock, 1883, unpaginated, www.gutenberg.org/files/16664/16664-h/16664-h.htm.
5 Gough Whitlam, *The Whitlam Government 1972–1975*, Viking, 1985, p. 291; Richard Twopeny, *Town Life in Australia*, gutenberg.org/files/16664/16664-h/16664-h.html
6 Stuart Macintyre, *Australia's Boldest Experiment*, NewSouth, 2015, p. 213, quoting C.E.W. Bean, *War Aims of a Plain Australian*, Angus & Robertson, Sydney, 1943, p. 93.
7 Commonwealth of Australia, *Parliamentary Debates: House of Representatives*, Hansard, no. 49, 2 December 1953, p. 837.
8 Whitlam, pp. 315, 328.
9 Jackie Huggins, Foreword, in Raymond Evans, *Fighting Words*, University of Queensland Press, 1999, p. xii.
10 Colin Tatz, *Human Rights & Human Wrongs*, Monash University Publishing, 2015, pp. 131–51.
11 'Aboriginal Girl Matriculates', *Canberra Times*, 11 January 1957, trove.nla.gov.au/newspaper/article/91231699.
12 'Education and Work, Australia: Survey data over time on current or recent study, educational attainment, and employment', Australian Bureau of Statistics, reference period May 2021, 9 November 2021, www.abs.gov.au/statistics/people/education/education-and-work-australia/latest-release.

Notes

13 Barry Jones, 'How the Knowledge Nation diagram evolved', *Sydney Morning Herald*, 6 July 2001; Alan Ramsay, 'Spaghetti and meatballs lands Kim in soup', *Sydney Morning Herald*, 4 July 2001, p. 15.
14 George Megalogenis, *Exit Strategy: Politics after the Pandemic*, Quarterly Essay 82, Black Inc., June 2021, p. 55.
15 Julia Horne, 'How universities came to rely on international students', *The Conversation*, 22 May 2020.
16 Australian Education Network, 'International student university enrolment numbers', University Rankings, n.d., www.universityrankings.com.au/international-student-numbers/.
17 Commonwealth of Australia, *Parliamentary Debates: Senate*, Hansard, 7 October 2020, pp. 5175–6.

9. Utopian Dreaming

1 'Australian fatalities at Gallipoli', Australian War Memorial, www.awm.gov.au/articles/encyclopedia/gallipoli/fatalities.
2 Peter Cochrane, *Best We Forget*, Text, 2018, p. 207.
3 Ann Curthoys, *Freedom Ride*, Allen & Unwin, 2002, pp. 60, 77, 127.
4 Curthoys, p. 60.
5 Paul Barclay, 'Where have all the utopian thinkers gone?', *ABC Radio National*, 24 April 2017, www.abc.net.au/news/2017-04-24/where-have-all-the-utopian-thinkers-gone/8460352.
6 Ken Gelder and Rachel Weaver, *The Colonial Kangaroo Hunt*, Miegunyah Press, 2020, p. 195.
7 Stephen Yarrow, 'The Ancient Greeks', The Discovery and Exploration of Australia, n.d., pocketoz.com.au/encounters/maritime-greeks.html.
8 'Secret Instructions to Lieutenant Cook 30 July 1768 (UK)', Museum of Australian Democracy, www.foundingdocs.gov.au/item-did-34.html.
9 Sir Walter Scott: Ireland at the time, 'a state of society well calculated to inspire the worst opinions of human nature . . . a faction of petty tyrants and a nation of trampled slaves, the penal laws, not less remarkable for their absurdity than their iniquity seemed as if the party of the ascendency regarded persecution as a toy, or plaything, and made human suffering and unhuman sport'. *Memoirs of Jonathan Swift*, vol. 2, 1829, p. 198.
10 James Curran and Stuart Ward, *The Unknown Nation*, Melbourne University Publishing, 2010, p. 90.
11 Matthew Flinders, *Terra Australis*, Text Classics, 2000 (1814), p. 51.
12 Flinders, p. 34.
13 Flinders, p. 58.
14 Henry Reynolds, *Truth-telling*, NewSouth, 2021, p. 14; Hugo Grotius, *The Rights of War and Peace*, vol. 2, trans. Jean Barbeyrac, 1738, p. 550.
15 James Cook, *Journal of HMS Endeavour*, 23 August 1770, southseas.nla.gov.au/journals/cook_remarks/092.html.
16 Megan Davis and George Williams, *Everything You Need to Know about the Uluru Statement from the Heart*, UNSW Press, 2021, p. 60; Tim Rowse, *Indigenous and Other Australians since 1901*, UNSW Press, 2017, p. 294.
17 Tim Rowse, 'Mabo and moral anxiety', *Meanjin*, vol. 52, no. 2, 1993, pp. 229–52.

Notes

18 Alan Atkinson, *The Europeans in Australia*, vol. 3, *Nation*, UNSW Press, 2014, p. x.
19 Laura McBride, 'Always was, always will be, Aboriginal land', Australian Museum, 9 July 2021, australian.museum/learn/first-nations/always-will-be-aboriginal-land/; Monica Tan, '"We've got to tell them all our secrets"—how the Barkandji won a landmark battle for Indigenous Australians', *The Guardian*, 23 June 2015.
20 Emma Christopher, *A Merciless Place*, Allen & Unwin, 2010, p. 35.
21 Alan Frost, 'Matra, James Mario (Maria) (1746–1806)', *Australian Dictionary of Biography*, National Centre of Biography, Australian National University, 2005, adb.anu.edu.au/biography/matra-james-mario-maria-13084.
22 Manning Clark, *The Quest for an Australian Identity*, University of Queensland Press, 1980, pp. 4–5.
23 Bevan Shields, 'Scott Morrison's secret G7 side trip to explore his family history', *Sydney Morning Herald*, 21 June 2021.

10. Gliding Forward

1 Paul Keating, 'The centenary of Federation: Beyond the celebrations', in *After Words*, Allen & Unwin, 2011, p. 114.
2 Clive James, 'The art of sport', in Sydney Organising Committee for the Olympic Games (SOCOG), *Olympic Opening Ceremony: Sydney 2000*, 2000, p. 10.
3 Keating, p. 115.
4 Gavin Souter, *Sydney Observed*, Brio, 2017 (1965), p. 56.
5 Keating, p. 115.
6 Stuart Macintyre and Anna Clark, *The History Wars*, Melbourne University Press, 2003, pp. 98–101.
7 Macintyre and Clark, p. 94.
8 Eric Hobsbawm, *The Age of Extremes*, Vintage, 1994, p. 3.
9 Macintyre and Clark, pp. 98–100.
10 Robert Drewe, 'The new nationalism', *The Australian*, 9–12 April 1973, quoted in James Curran and Stuart Ward, *The Unknown Nation*, Melbourne University Publishing, 2010, pp. 59–61.
11 Vance Palmer, 'Battle', *Meanjin Papers*, vol. 1, no. 8, March 1942, pp. 5–6, meanjin.com.au/essays/battle/.
12 International Council Report on Monuments and Sites to the UNESCO World Heritage Committee, 2007.
13 Souter, p. 83.
14 Paul Kelly, *100 Years*, Allen & Unwin, 2001, p. 32.
15 Kelly, p. 198.
16 Malcolm J. Turnbull, *Safe Haven*, National Archives of Australia, 2000, pp. 18, 41.
17 Anna Haebich, *Spinning the Dream*, Fremantle Press, 2008, p. 119.
18 Raymond Evans, 'Wading into the Deep End', in Annemarie McLaren (ed.), NewSouth Publishing (forthcoming); John Norwood, *The Australia Book for English Boys and Girls (and Their Parents)*, Dorothy Crisp and Co., c. 1947.
19 National Archives of Australia (NAA), 'Directions for applying the dictation test from the Home and Territories Department' [4 March 1927]', 2010, www.naa.gov.au/learn/learning-resources/learning-resource-themes/society-and-culture/migration-and-multiculturalism/directions-applying-dictation-test-home-and-territories-department.

Notes

20. Gwenda Tavan, *The Long, Slow Death of White Australia*, Scribe, 2005, p. 62.
21. Haebich, pp. 160–1.
22. Raymond Evans, 'Picking over the bones', *Zertschrift für Australien-Studien*, 331/4, 2019/2022.
23. Nick Richardson, *1956: The Year Australia Welcomed the World*, Scribe, 2019, pp. 144, 183.
24. Carl Reinecke, *Books That Made Us*, HarperCollins, 2021.
25. National Museum of Australia (NMA), 'Defining moments: Patrick White wins Nobel Prize', 2021, www.nma.gov.au/defining-moments/resources/patrick-white-wins-nobel-prize; 'Interview of 1973 Nobel laureate Patrick White (1912–1990)', Italia Film, YouTube, 2010, www.youtube.com/watch?v=j02E06UFOcg.

11. The Incurable Flaw

1. Geoffrey Wharton, *The Day They Burned Mapoon*, Honours thesis, University of Queensland, 1996; Stephen Armbruster, 'Forced Aboriginal removal "forgiven, not forgotten"', *SBS News*, 15 November 2013, www.sbs.com.au/news/forced-aboriginal-removal-forgiven-not-forgotten.
2. Noel Pearson, *Mission*, Black Inc, 2021, pp. 8–12.
3. Museum of Australian Democracy, 'Yirrkala bark petitions 1963', Magna Carta and Modern Australia, n.d., magnacarta.moadoph.gov.au/story/bark-petitions/.
4. Galarrwuy Yunupingu, 'Tradition, truth & tomorrow', *The Monthly*, December 2008–January 2009.
5. Giordano Nanni and Andrea James, *Coranderrk*, Aboriginal Studies Press, 2013, pp. 8–9.
6. Megan Davis and George Williams, *Everything You Need to Know about the Uluru Statement from the Heart*, UNSW Press, 2021, pp. 8–9.
7. Yunupingu, unpaginated.
8. Tim Rowse, *Indigenous and Other Australians since 1901*, UNSW Press, 2017, p. 3.
9. Davis and Williams, p. 1; The Uluru Statement from the Heart, 2017, ulurustatement.org/the-statement.
10. Jeremy Bentham, *A Plea for the Constitution*, Maurnan & Hatchard, 1803, discovery.ucl.ac.uk/id/eprint/10055304/.
11. Davis and Williams, p. 136.
12. Daniel McKay, *Uluru Statement: A Quick Guide*, Parliamentary Library, Parliament of Australia, 19 June 2017, www.aph.gov.au/About_Parliament/Parliamentary_Departments/Parliamentary_Library/pubs/rp/rp1617/Quick_Guides/UluruStatement.
13. Megan Davis, 'The long road to Uluru: Walking together—truth before justice', *Griffith Review 60: First Things First*, Text, 2018, pp. 13–22.
14. Davis, p. 14; The Uluru Statement from the Heart, 2017.
15. Referendum Council, www.referendumcouncil.org.au.
16. Dean Parkin, 'The Uluru Statement from the Heart—an idea whose time has come', TEDxCanberra, September 2018, quoted in Stephen Fitzpatrick, 'A fresh canvas for Indigenous politics', *The Monthly*, May 2019.
17. Ron Levy and Ian McAllister, 'Our research shows public support for a First Nations Voice is not only high, it's deeply entrenched', *The Conversation*, 9 December 2021.

Notes

18 Fitzpatrick, unpaginated.
19 Malcolm Turnbull, *A Bigger Picture*, Hardie Grant, 2020, pp. 571, 574.
20 Government of Canada, 'Treaties and agreements', 2020, www.rcaanc-cirnac.gc.ca/eng/1100100028574/1529354437231.
21 Henry Reynolds, *Truth-telling*, NewSouth, 2021, p. 29.
22 Boyd H. Hunter and John Carmody, 'Estimating the Aboriginal population in early colonial Australia: The role of chickenpox reconsidered', *Australian Economic History Review*, vol. 55, no. 2, 2015, pp. 112–38; Liz Allen, *The Future of Australia*, NewSouth, 2020, p. 29.
23 David Andrew Roberts, 'The denial of Aboriginal rights', in David Andrew Roberts and Martin Crotty (eds), *Great Mistakes of Australian History*, UNSW Press, 2006, pp. 15, 19, 30.
24 Yunupingu, unpaginated.
25 K.S. Inglis, *The Stuart Case*, Black Inc., 2002; Penny Debelle, 'Max Stuart reflects, finds peace', *The Age*, 19 August 2002.
26 Caroline Davies, 'Australian papers reveal Queen's thoughts on Charles as governor-general', *The Guardian*, 15 July 2020.
27 Lucy Marks and Georgia Hitch, 'Prince Charles tours Nhulunbuy for sixth visit to the Northern Territory', *ABC News*, 9 April 2018, www.abc.net.au/news/2018-04-09/charles-visit-nhulunbuy-royals-northern-territory/9632620.

12. Making the Nation

1 Harry Evans, 'Bad King John and the Australian Constitution: Commemorating the 700th Anniversary of the 1297 Issue of Magna Carta', Papers on Parliament, no. 31, June 1998, www.aph.gov.au/About_Parliament/Senate/Powers_practice_n_procedures/pops/pop31/c04.
2 Zachary Gorman, *Summoning Magna Carta*, Institute of Public Affairs, 2021, p. 1.
3 Linda Colley, *The Gun, the Ship, and the Pen*, Profile Books, 2021, p. 96.
4 Colley, p. 101.
5 James Dunk, *Bedlam at Botany Bay*, NewSouth, 2019, p. 17.
6 National Capital Authority (NCA), 'Magna Carta Place', n.d., www.nca.gov.au/attractions-and-memorials/magna-carta-place.
7 Judith Brett, *The Enigmatic Mr Deakin*, Text, 2017, p. 3.
8 John Williams, 'Andrew Inglis Clark: The republican of Tasmania', in David Headon and John Williams (eds), *Makers of Miracles*, Melbourne University Publishing, 2000, p. 49.
9 Williams, p. 54; Geoffrey Bolton, 'Lucinda Oration', Supreme Court of Queensland, 30 March 2001, in Michael White and Aladin Rahemtula (eds), *Sir Samuel Griffith*, Lawbook Co., 2002, p. 8.
10 John Playford, 'Kingston, Charles Cameron (1850–1908)', *Australian Dictionary of Biography*, National Centre of Biography, Australian National University, 1983, adb.anu.edu.au/biography/kingston-charles-cameron-6966/text12099; John Hirst, *The Sentimental Nation*, Oxford University Press, 2000, p. 84.
11 Marilyn Lake, '"In the interests of the home": Rose Scott's feminist opposition to Federation', in Headon and Williams, pp. 125–31; Judith A. Allen, *Rose Scott,*

Notes

Oxford University Press, pp. 94–170; Clare Wright, *You Daughters of Freedom*, Text, Melbourne, pp. 60–76.
12 Bolton, p. viii.
13 'Honouring the states: Mr Hughes proposes toast', *Sydney Morning Herald*, 13 March 1913, p. 10; Raymond Evans, '"Pigmentia": Racial fears and white Australia', in A. Dirk Moses (ed.), *Genocide in Settler Society*, Berghahn Books, 2004, pp. 103–24; Peter Cochrane, *Best We Forget*, Text, 2018.
14 Gavin Souter, *The Lion and the Kangaroo*, William Collins, 1976; Brio, 2017.
15 Vance Palmer, *The Legend of the Nineties*, Melbourne University Publishing, 1954, p. 133.
16 David Walker, *Anxious Nation*, UQP, 1999, p. 150. Evans, pp. 103–26.
17 Evans, pp. 103–26.
18 Hirst, p. 297.
19 Clive Moore, 'States of mind: Federation and the problematic constitution', in David Andrew Roberts and Martin Crotty (eds), *Great Mistakes of Australian History*, UNSW Press, 2006, p. 170.
20 Palmer, pp. 133, 135.
21 Bolton, p. 4.
22 Palmer, p. 132.
23 Palmer, p. 142.
24 Palmer, p. 152.
25 Brett, p. 202.
26 Bolton, p. 8.
27 Williams, p. 44.
28 Brett, pp. 227–8.
29 Moore, pp. 171, 176.
30 Palmer, p. 142.
31 Helen Irving, *To Constitute a Nation*, Cambridge University Press, 1997, pp. 21, 24.
32 Irving, pp. 22, 215.
33 Ross Gibson, *Seven Versions of an Australian Badland*, University of Queensland Press, 2002, p. 92.
34 Irving, p. 172; Clare Wright, *You Daughters of Freedom*, Text, 2019, ch. 10.
35 Colley, p. 253.
36 Hirst, p. 314.
37 Donald Wallace, *The Web of Empire*, London, 1903, p. 45.
38 Souter, p. 391.
39 Botanic Gardens & Centennial Parklands, 'Federation Pavilion', Centennial Parklands, 2021, www.centennialparklands.com.au/visit/history-and-heritage/heritage-buildings-and-structures/federation-pavilion.
40 Botanic Gardens & Centennial Parklands, unpaginated.
41 Hirst, p. 332.

13. Small Brown Bird

1 Patrick Keane, 'The People and the Constitution' [speech], Lucinda lecture, Monash University, Melbourne, 11 August 2016, www.hcourt.gov.au/publications/speeches/current/speeches-by-justice-keane.

Notes

2. 'Noisy miner', Wikipedia, 2021, en.wikipedia.org/wiki/Noisy_miner.
3. Courtney Melton et al., 'Should we cull noisy miners? After decades of research, these aggressive honeyeaters are still outsmarting us', *The Conversation*, 13 October 2021.
4. Megan Davis and George Williams, *Everything You Need to Know about the Uluru Statement from the Heart*, UNSW Press, 2021, p. 78.
5. Davis and Williams, p. 82.
6. Souter, p. 398.
7. Thomas Ginsberg, Zachary Elkins and James Melton, 'The Lifespan of Written Constitutions', University of Chicago Law School, 15 October 2009, p. 1; Linda Colley, *The Gun, the Ship, and the Pen*, Profile Books, 2021.
8. Vance Palmer, *The Legend of the Nineties*, Melbourne University Publishing, 1954, p. 144.
9. Colley, p. 284.
10. Colley, pp. 161, 127.
11. Palmer, p. 145.
12. Patrick Keane, 'In Celebration of the Constitution' [speech], Banco Court, Brisbane, 12 June 2008, www.austlii.edu.au/au/journals/QldJSchol/2008/64.pdf.
13. Centre for the Study of the Legacies of British Slavery, University College London, www.ucl.ac.uk/lbs/.
14. 'Council asked to consider Moreland name change', moreland.vic.gov.au; 'Queensland mayor issues historic apology over blackbirding slavery of Pacific Islanders', *ABC News*, 30 July 2021, www.abc.net.au/news/2021-07-30/queensland-mayor-sorry-blackbirding-south-seas-slavery/100333302; 'Renaming of Ben Boyd National Park', NSW Department of Planning, Industry and Environment, 14 November 2021, www.environment.nsw.gov.au/topics/parks-reserves-and-protected-areas/park-management/community-engagement/ben-boyd-national-park-renaming.
15. Marilyn Lake and Henry Reynolds, *Drawing the Global Colour Line*, Melbourne University Publishing, 2008, p. 49.
16. Lake and Reynolds, p. 11.
17. Lake and Reynolds, pp. 137–8.
18. Isaiah Berlin, *The Crooked Timber of Humanity*, Pimlico, London, 1990, p. 20.
19. Raymond Evans and Robert Orsted-Jensen, '"Pale Death . . . Around Our Footprints Springs": Assessing Violent Mortality on the Queensland Frontier from State and Private Exterminatory Practices', in Mohamed Adhikari (ed.), *Civilian Driven Violence and the Genocide of Indigenous Peoples in Settler Colonies*, University of Cape Town Press, 2020, pp. 139–64.
20. Paul Kelly, *100 Years*, Allen & Unwin, 2001, p. 160.
21. Kelly, p. 160.
22. Myra Willard, *History of the White Australia Policy to 1920*, Melbourne University Press, 1923, pp. 119, 189.
23. Willard, pp. 77, 211.
24. Samia Khatun, *Australianama*, University of Queensland Press, 2018, pp. 45–6.
25. Isabel Wilkerson, *Caste*, Penguin, 2020.
26. Wilkerson, p. 159.
27. Lake and Reynolds, p. 149.

Notes

28 Judith Brett, *The Enigmatic Mr Deakin*, Text, 2017; Lake and Reynolds, p. 49.
29 Paul Keating, 'The centenary of Federation: Beyond the celebrations', in *After Words*, Allen & Unwin, 2011, p. 113; Mark McKenna, 'The stunted country', *The Monthly*, December 2021–January 2022.
30 Souter, p. 384.

14. The More Things Change . . .

1 Jared Diamond, *Upheaval*, Allen Lane, 2019, p. 256.
2 James Curran and Stuart Ward, *The Unknown Nation*, Melbourne University Publishing, 2010, p. 39; 'Facing the challenge of adulthood' [editorial], *The Australian*, 15 July 1964.
3 David Correia, 'F**k Jared Diamond', *Capitalism Nature Socialism*, vol. 24, no. 4, 2013, pp. 1–6.
4 Sue Lin, 'Jared Diamond: Evolutionary biologist', *The Harvard Crimson*, 1 June 2008, www.thecrimson.com/article/2008/6/1/jared-diamond-author-jared-m-diamond/.
5 Anand Giridharadas, 'What to do when you're a country in crisis', *New York Times*, 17 May 2019.
6 Diamond, p. 258.
7 Nick Richardson, *1956: The Year Australia Welcomed the World*, Scribe, 2019, p. 100.
8 Julianne Schultz, 'Disruptive influences', *Griffith Review 21: Hidden Queensland*, ABC Books, 2008, p. 10.
9 Chris Mitchell, *Making Headlines*, Melbourne University Publishing, 2016, pp. 33, 43.
10 Kevin Rudd, *The PM Years*, Pan Macmillan, 2018, pp. 24–37.
11 Megan Davis and George Williams, *Everything You Need to Know about the Uluru Statement from the Heart*, UNSW Press, 2021, p. 74.
12 Paul Kelly, *100 Years*, Allen & Unwin, 2001, p. 161.
13 Family Matters, *The Family Matters Report 2021*, www.familymatters.org.au/the-family-matters-report-2021/; Ella Archibald-Binge, 'Power Generation', *Sydney Morning Herald*, Good Weekend, 27 November 2020, pp. 28–32.
14 Manning Clark, *The Quest for an Australian Identity*, University of Queensland Press, 1980.
15 Clark, p. 4.
16 Ross Gibson, *Seven Versions of an Australian Badland*, University of Queensland Press, 2002, p. 171.
17 Linda Colley, 'Can history help? The problem with winning', *London Review of Books*, 22 March 2018.
18 Andrew Tillett, 'UK trade deal "rights a historic wrong"', *Australian Financial Review*, 16 June 2021.

15. Personal Becomes Political

1 Malcolm Turnbull, 'Foreword', in Jenny Hocking, *The Palace Letters*, Scribe, 2020, pp. xiii–xvi.
2 Julianne Schultz, 'The Ingram Case', in *The Other Side of Rape*, Paul R. Wilson, University of Queensland Press, 1978, pp. 112–25.

Notes

3   Clare Wright, 'A wave of female candidates powered by historic swell', *Meanjin*, 13 December 2021, meanjin.com.au/blog/a-wave-of-female-candidates-powered-by-historic-swell/

4   Marian Sawer, 'The long, slow demise of the "marriage bar"', *Inside Story*, 8 December 2016.

5   Margaret Thornton and Trish Luker, 'The *Sex Discrimination Act* and its rocky rite of passage', in Margaret Thornton (ed.), *Sex Discrimination in Uncertain Times*, ANU Press, 2010, p. 28.

6   Julia Banks, *Power Play*, Hardie Grant, 2021, p. 1.

7   Julie McCrossin, 'Sex on the fatal shore is no laughing matter', *Australian Financial Review*, 3 December 1999; Anne Summers, *Damned Whores and God's Police*, NewSouth, 2016 (1975); Grace Karskens, *The Colony*, Allen & Unwin, 2010; Russel Ward, *The Australian Legend*, Oxford University Press, 1958.

8   Babette Smith, *Defiant Voices*, National Library of Australia, 2021.

9   Julianne Schultz, 'Cunnamulla revisited', *Nation Review*, 21 July 1977, pp. 13–15.

10   Bernard Smith, *The Spectre of Truganini*, ABC, 1980, p. 16.

11   Raymond Evans, *Fighting Words*, University of Queensland Press, 1999, pp. 181–2.

12   Carl Reinecke, *Books That Made Us*, HarperCollins, 2021, p. 126.

16. Soul Destroying

1   Libby Connors, *Warrior*, Allen & Unwin, 2015, p. 20.

2   Chris Mitchell, *Making Headlines*, Melbourne University Publishing, 2016, p. 15; Scott Balson, *Inside One Nation*, Interactive Presentations, 2000, p. 8.

3   Gerard Newman and Andrew Kopras, 'Socio-economic indexes for electoral divisions', *Current Issues Brief*, Parliament of Australia, no. 4, 1998–99, www.aph.gov.au/About_Parliament/Parliamentary_Departments/Parliamentary_Library/Publications_Archive/CIB/cib9899/99CIB04.

4   Melissa Lucashenko, 'Sinking below sight', *Griffith Review 41: Now We Are Ten*, Text, 2013.

5   Paul Kelly, *The March of Patriots*, Melbourne University Publishing, 2009.

6   Paul Keating, *One Nation*, AGPS, 1992, p. 4, parlinfo.aph.gov.au/parlInfo/search/display/display.w3p;query=Id%3A%22media%2Fpressrel%2F5051390%22.

7   Mitchell, p. 115.

8   Pamela Williams, *The Victory*, Allen & Unwin, 1997, p. 102.

9   Another big Ipswich character, Paul Pisasale, the city's mayor for thirteen years from 2004, was later jailed for fraud, official corruption, perjury, unlawful drug possession, sexual assault and extortion.

10   David Marr, 'Baying for border protection', 2001, in *My Country*, Black Inc., 2018, pp. 245–246.

11   Stuart Macintyre and Anna Clark, *The History Wars*, Melbourne University Publishing, 2003, p. 143.

12   Tanya Josev, *The Campaign against the Courts*, Federation Press, 2017, p. 127.

13   Megan Davis and George Williams, *Everything You Need to Know about the Uluru Statement from the Heart*, UNSW Press, 2021, p. 74.

14   Richard Ackland, 'When talk of racism is just not cricket', *Sydney Morning Herald*, 16 February 2005, p. 17.

Notes

15. Michael Stahl, 'Pauline Hanson is the Donald Trump of Australia', *Narratively*, 13 October 2016, narratively.com/pauline-hanson-is-the-donald-trump-of-australia-and-she-just-won/.
16. Kelly, p. 368.
17. Raymond Williams, 'Culture is Ordinary', in John Higgins (ed.), the *Raymond Williams Reader*, Blackwell Publishing, 2001, pp. 10–24.
18. Erik Jensen, 'Jackie Kelly's husband fined $1100 for election leaflets', *Sydney Morning Herald*, 19 May 2009.
19. Macintyre and Clark, p. 64.
20. Macintyre and Clark, p. 54.
21. Macintyre and Clark, p. 68.
22. Macintyre and Clark, p. 51.
23. John Hirst, 'How best to write? Narrative or theme', in *Looking for Australia*, Black Inc., 2010, pp. 15–27.
24. Rupert Murdoch, 'Publishing Newspapers in the Seventies', Arthur Norman Smith Memorial Lecture in Journalism, University of Melbourne, 1972; Sally Young, *Paper Emperors*, UNSW Press, 2019.
25. Rodney Tiffen, 'Rudd has become Murdoch's accuser, but once he was his cheerleader', *Sydney Morning Herald*, 13 October 2020; see also Rodney Tiffen, *Rupert Murdoch: A Reassessment*, NewSouth, 2014.

17. Remaking the Nation

1. Sarah Cameron and Ian McAllister, *Trends in Australian Political Opinion: Results from the Australian Election Study 1987–2019*, Australian National University, December 2019, australianelectionstudy.org/wp-content/uploads/Trends-in-Australian-Political-Opinion-1987-2019.pdf.
2. Paul Keating, election speech, Melbourne, 14 February 1996, electionspeeches. moadoph.gov.au/speeches/1996-paul-keating.
3. Tanya Josev, *The Campaign Against the Courts*, Federation Press, 2017, p. 154.
4. John Howard, *Lazarus Rising*, HarperCollins, 2010, p. 232.
5. Rick Morton, 'How private management consultants took over the public service', *Saturday Paper*, 9 October 2021.
6. Sarah Cameron and Ian McAllister, Edelman Trust Barometer, 19 February 2021, www.edelman.com.au/trust-barometer-2021-australia.
7. Ronald Butt, Margaret Thatcher interview, *Sunday Times*, 3 May 1981, www.margaretthatcher.org/document/104475.
8. Rose Verspaandonk, Ian Holland and Nicholas Horne, *Chronology of Changes in the Australian Public Service 1975–2010*, Parliamentary Library, Parliament of Australia, 11 October 2010, www.aph.gov.au/About_Parliament/Parliamentary_Departments/Parliamentary_Library/pubs/BN/1011/APSChanges.
9. James Murphy, 'Long knives, short memories', *Inside Story*, 9 December 2019. In his memoir, Howard wrote of this decision: 'controversially I decided not to reappoint six secretaries who had served Labor'. Howard, p. 238.
10. Chris Aulich and Janine O'Flynn, 'John Howard: The great privatiser?', *Australian Journal of Political Science*, vol. 42, no. 2, 2007, pp. 365–81.

Notes

11 Aulich and O'Flynn, p. 365.
12 Marian Sawer, *Australia and the New Right*, Allen & Unwin, 1982, p. x.
13 Sally Young, *Paper Emperors*, NSW Press, 2019, p. 121.
14 Dominic Kelly, *Political Troglodytes and Economic Lunatics*, La Trobe University Press, 2019, p. 18.
15 Sawer, p. 17.
16 Kelly, p. 213.
17 Michael Pusey, *Economic Rationalism in Canberra*, Cambridge University Press, 1989.
18 Nancy MacLean, *Democracy in Chains*, Scribe, 2018; James M. Buchanan, *The Collected Works of James M. Buchanan*, 20 vols, Liberty Fund, 1999–2002, with forewords by Geoffrey Brennan, Hartmut Kliemt and Robert D. Tollison.
19 Denis Muller, 'Australian governments have a long history of trying to manipulate the ABC—and it's unlikely to stop now', *The Conversation*, 13 February 2019; Richard Ferguson, 'Cabinet papers 1996–97: Bigger cuts to ABC avoided', *The Australian*, 31 December 2018.
20 Julianne Schultz, *Reviving the Fourth Estate*, Cambridge University Press, 1998.
21 Henry Mayer, *The Press in Australia*, Lansdowne, 1964, p. 51.
22 Carol Johnson, 'Anti-elitest discourse in Australia: International influences and comparisons', in Marian Sawer and Barry Hindess (eds), *Us and Them*, API Network, 2004, p. 117.
23 David Brooks, 'What happened to American Conservatism?', *The Atlantic*, January–February 2022.
24 Gregory Melleuish, *The Packaging of Australia*, UNSW Press, 1998, p. 66.
25 Patrick Durkin, 'John Roskam exits IPA amid losing cultural battle', *Australian Financial Review*, 17 November 2021.
26 Pru Goward, 'Why you shouldn't underestimate the underclass', *Australian Financial Review*, 19 October 2021.
27 Anne Davies, 'Cabinet papers 2000: John Howard sought to restrict IVF treatment—and protect Don Bradman's name', *The Guardian*, 1 January 2021.
28 Nick Haslam, 'Australian values are hardly unique when compared to other cultures', *The Conversation*, 1 May 2017.
29 Kerry Ryan, 'Aussie Aussie Aussie: Is the Australian citizenship test fair?', *The Conversation*, 15 November 2011.
30 Josev, p. 125.
31 Josev, pp. 129–33.
32 Ian Callinan, 'Griffith as the Chief Justice of the High Court of Australia', in M.W.D. White and Aladin Rahemtula (eds), *Sir Samuel Griffith*, Lawbook Co., 2002, p. 13.
33 Richard Evans, 'The Blainey view: Geoffrey Blainey ponders Mabo, the High Court and democracy', *Law Institute Journal*, vol. 69, no. 3, 1995, p. 203; Josev, p. 132.
34 Paul Cleary, *Title Fight*, Black Inc., 2021.
35 Chris Mitchell, *Making Headlines*, Melbourne University Publishing, 2016, pp. 15, 142.
36 Peter Mares, 'A line in the water', *Inside Story*, 28 August 2021.
37 Sue Boyd, *Not Always Diplomatic*, UWA Press, 2021.

Notes

38 David Marr, 'Baying for border protection', in *My Country*, Black Inc., pp. 245–6.
39 Stuart Macintyre and Anna Clark, *The History Wars*, Melbourne University Publishing, 2003, p. 301.

18. People Like Us

1   Yassmin Abdel-Magied, *Yassmin's Story*, Vintage, 2016, p. 78.
2   Abdel-Magied, p. 76.
3   Elsa Koleth, *Multiculturalism: A Review of Australian Policy Statements and Recent Debates in Australia and Overseas*, Parliament of Australia, Research Paper no. 6 (2010–11), 8 October 2010, www.aph.gov.au/About_Parliament/Parliamentary_Departments/Parliamentary_Library/pubs/rp/rp1011/11rp06.
4   Gary Rivett and Simon Royal, '"G'day mate": Unexpected greeting for the Vietnam refugee who will now be next SA Governor', 27 June 2014, *ABC News*, www.abc.net.au/news/2014-06-26/gday-mate-greeting-for-vietnam-refugee-who-rose-to-sa-governor/5552828.
5   Frank Bongiorno, 'From little things Australia's asylum seeker policy grew', *The Conversation*, 1 January 2016, theconversation.com/cabinet-papers-1990-91-from-little-things-australias-asylum-seeker-policy-grew-51988.
6   Andrew Jakubowicz, 'Don't mention it: What the Australian government wants to hear and why about multicultural Australia', in Charles Husband (ed.), *Research, Good Intentions and Ambiguous Outcomes*, Policy Press, 2014.
7   Peter Mares, *Not Quite Australian*, Text, 2016, pp. 34–5.
8   Glenn Nicholls, *Deported*, UNSW Press, 2007, p. 145.
9   Frank Robson, 'Garden City burning', *SBS*, 3 August 2016, www.sbs.com.au/topics/life/feature/garden-city-burning-who-set-mosque-fire.
10 Melissa Fyfe, 'Yassmin Abdel-Magied on becoming "Australia's most publicly hated Muslim"', *Sydney Morning Herald*, 18 August 2017.
11 ABC, Australia Talks National Survey, 2019, www.abc.net.au/news/2020-12-10/australia-talks-data-explorer-2019/12946988#/.
12 Mares, p. 21.
13 Mares, p. 21.
14 Mares, p. 39.
15 Mares, p. 33.
16 Joint press conference, Kevin Rudd and PNG prime minister Peter O'Neil, Regional Resettlement Agreement, 19 July 2013, parlinfo.aph.gov.au/parlInfo/search/display/display.w3p;query=Id:%22media/pressrel/2611766%22.
17 Richard Flanagan, 'Foreword', in Behrouz Boochani, *No Friend But the Mountains*, Picador, 2018, p. ix.
18 2GB, 'Smithy's Deplorables: Prue MacSween' [radio segment], 12 July 2017, www.2gb.com/podcast/smithys-deplorables-prue-macsween-22/.
19 Yassmin Abdel-Magied, 'A little too close to the sun', *Griffith Review 56: Millennials Strike Back*, Text, 2017.
20 Helen Davidson, 'Former SBS reporter Scott McIntyre repeats Anzac Day accusations on Twitter', *The Guardian*, 25 April 2016.
21 MZ Ministry for Culture and Heritage, 'The Gallipoli campaign', New Zealand History, 2017, nzhistory.govt.nz/war/the-gallipoli-campaign/gallipoli-in-brief.

Notes

22 Maureen Dowd, 'From Gallipoli to Singapore', *New York Times*, 19 July 2011.
23 Ghassan Hage, *Against Paranoid Nationalism*, Pluto Press, 2003, p. 3.

19. Power Players

1   William Shawcross, *Rupert Murdoch: Ringmaster of the Information Circus*, Chatto & Windus, 1992, p. 80.
2   Rodney Tiffen, *Rupert Murdoch: A Reassessment*, NewSouth, 2014, p. 96.
3   Henry Reynolds, *Truth-telling*, NewSouth, 2021, p. 131.
4   Amanda Meade, 'Rupert Murdoch denounces "woke orthodoxy" as Rudd rages against Australia Day award', *The Guardian*, 29 January 2021.
5   Sally Young, *Paper Emperors*, NewSouth, 2019, pp. 209–13.
6   *Australian Financial Review*, Rich List, 20 March 2021.
7   Judith Brett, *The Coal Curse*, Quarterly Essay 78, Black Inc., June 2020.
8   Michael West, *Dirty Power: Big Coal's Network of Influence over the Coalition Government*, Greenpeace, May 2019, act.greenpeace.org.au/dirtypower; Tom McIlroy, 'Australia's 10 most covertly powerful people in 2021' *Australian Financial Review*, 1 October, 2021.
9   Lindy Edwards, *Corporate Power in Australia*, Monash University Publishing, 2020, p. xi.
10 George Munster, *A Paper Prince*, Penguin, 1985, p. 15.
11 Shawcross, p. 87.
12 Bruce Page and Elaine Potter, *The Murdoch Archipelago*, Simon & Schuster, 2003, p. 112.
13 Page and Potter, p. 112.
14 Shawcross, p. 550.
15 Page and Potter, p. 78.
16 Bruce Guthrie, *Man Bites Murdoch*, Melbourne University Publishing, 2011, p. 89.
17 Kevin Rudd, *Petition EN1938—Royal Commission to Ensure a Strong, Diverse Australian News Media*, House of Representatives Petition, Parliament of Australia, 2020, www.aph.gov.au/e-petitions/petition/EN1938.
18 Daniel Hurst, 'Kevin Rudd says Australian politicians "frightened" of "Murdoch media beast" in Senate inquiry', *The Guardian*, 19 February 2021.
19 Tony Wright, 'On the wrong side of Rupert', *Sydney Morning Herald*, 13 October 1995.
20 *News Limited and The Australian Journalists Association* [1976], Commonwealth Arbitration Reports, no. 1788, p. 23 (C 3528 of 1976, 9 August 1976), www.austlii.edu.au/au/cases/cth/CthArbRp/1976/1788.pdf; Denis Cryle, *Murdoch's Flagship*, Melbourne University Publishing, 2008.
21 Tiffen, p. 115.
22 Tiffen, p. 9.
23 Shawcross, p. 62.
24 Shawcross, pp. 55–62.
25 Shawcross, p. 61.
26 Shawcross, p. 57.
27 Shawcross, p. 61.
28 Shawcross, p. 63.
29 Shawcross, p. 67.

Notes

30 Shawcross, p. 78.
31 Shawcross, p. 75.
32 Chris Mitchell, *Making Headlines*, Melbourne University Publishing, 2016, p. 95.
33 Munster, p. 47.
34 Ken Inglis, Bill Gammage et al., *Dunera Lives,* Monash University Publishing, 2020.
35 Page and Porter, pp. 102–3.
36 Penny Debelle, 'Max Stuart reflects, finds peace', *The Age*, 19 August 2002.
37 Munster, p. 4.
38 Dominic Kelly, *Political Troglodytes and Economic Lunatics*, La Trobe University Press, 2019, p. 27.
39 Munster, p. 106.
40 John Lanchester, 'Bravo l'artiste: What is Murdoch after?', *London Review of Books*, 5 February 2004.
41 Harvard Growth Lab, The Atlas of Economic Complexity, 2018, cited in Julian Hill, *Australia's Global Performance: Falling Behind*, February 2021, p. 11, www.julianhillmp.com/FBR.pdf.
42 Rod Sims, 'Concentration in Australia Faces Big Challenges', speech, University of SA and ACCC Economics Workshop, 15 October 2021, www.accc.gov.au/speech/competition-in-australia-faces-big-challenges.
43 Hill, p. 2.
44 Gary Dickson, *Australian Newsroom Mapping Project*, Public Interest Journalism Initiative, February 2021.
45 AFP, 'Mogul vs Mogul', *Bangkok Post*, 22 February 2021.
46 Peter Cox, 'Social Media Showdown', *Sunrise*, 19 February 2021.
47 Nicole Moore, *The Censor's Library*, University of Queensland Press, 2012.
48 Nicholas Birns, 'Receptacle or reversal? Globalization down under in Marcus Clarke's "His Natural Life"', *College Literature*, vol. 32, no. 2, 2005, p. 135.
49 Tiffen, p. 314.
50 Katie Robertson, 'Rupert Murdoch, accepting award, condemns "awful woke orthodoxy"', *New York Times*, 25 January 2021.
51 Greg Sheridan, 'Royal "celebs" Harry and Meghan add to toxic assault on the West', *The Australian*; 11 March 2021.

20. From Little Things . . .

1 Sky News, '"Go woke go broke": ABC's *Q+A* program ratings suffer major blow', *Sky News*, 11 April 2021, www.skynews.com.au/opinion/outsiders/go-woke-go-broke-abcs-qa-program-ratings-suffer-major-blow/video/52bc9b187a8d9aa9b3f0ab55fccad46b.
2 Paul Karp and Katharine Murphy, 'Grace Tame says Scott Morrison told her "I bet it felt good to get that out" after powerful speech', *The Guardian*, 24 May 2021.
3 John Howard, *Lazarus Rising*, HarperCollins, 2010, pp. 551–5.
4 Anita Talberg, Simeon Hui and Kate Loynes, *Australian Climate Change Policy to November 2013: A Chronology*, Parliamentary Library, Parliament of Australia, 4 August 2021, www.aph.gov.au/About_Parliament/Parliamentary_Departments/Parliamentary_Library/pubs/rp/rp1516/ClimateChron; Nick Feik, 'Zero Ambition: The charade of Coalition climate emissions plans', *The Monthly*, November 2021, pp. 12–14; Howard, p. 552.

Notes

5. Amanda Gorman, 'The Hill We Climb: The Amanda Gorman poem that stole the inauguration show', *The Guardian*, 21 January 2021.
6. Michael Levenson, 'Amanda Gorman says security guard confronted her, saying she looked "suspicious"', *New York Times*, 5 March 2021.
7. *ABC News*, 'Read the full press conference transcript, Christian Porter denies historical rape allegation', *ABC News*, 3 March 2021, www.abc.net.au/news/2021-03-03/christian-porter-press-conference-transcript/13212054.
8. Bernard Smith, *The Spectre of Truganini*, ABC, 1980, p. 31.
9. Aaron Patrick, 'PM caught in crusade of women journos', *Australian Financial Review*, 31 March 2021.
10. David Brooks, 'What Happened to American Conservatism?', *The Atlantic*, January–February 2022.
11. Kyle Lang, 'Petty Snipe at PM does Grace Tame no favours', *Courier-Mail*, 3 April 2021.
12. Nick Cater, 'Militant culture warriors make all men the bad guys', *The Australian*, 5 April 2021.
13. Patrick Durkin, 'John Roskam exits IPA amid losing cultural battle', *Australian Financial Review*, 17 November 2021.
14. Michael Stutchbury, 'Financial Review responds to criticism' [editorial], *Australian Financial Review*, 6 April 2021.
15. Carl Reinecke, *Books That Made Us*, HarperCollins, 2021, pp. 94–5.
16. Jane Albert, 'If Australia Day Makes You Uncomfortable', *Broadsheet*, 22 January 2019.
17. Adam Gartrell, 'Senate to challenge Turnbull's council citizenship ceremony bans', *Sydney Morning Herald*, 15 October 2017.
18. Alan Atkinson, 'Did Federation compromise our democracy?', *The Monthly*, December 2021–January 2022.
19. Geoff Chambers, 'Councils warned over Australia Day ceremony snubs', *The Australian*, 22 January 2020.
20. George Packer, *Last Best Hope*, Allen Lane, 2021, p. 65.
21. Matt Seaton interview with Fintan O'Toole, *New York Review of Books*, 10 June 2021.
22. David Denborough, *Unsettling Australian Histories*, Dulwich Centre, 2021.
23. Denborough, *Unsettling Australian Histories*.
24. William Shakespeare, *Macbeth*, Act II, Scene IV.
25. Linda Colley, 'Can history help? The problem with winning', *London Review of Books*, 22 March 2018.
26. Jill Lepore, 'Is society coming apart?', *The Guardian*, 25 November 2021.
27. Ian McLean, *How Aborigines Invented the Idea of Contemporary Art*, Power Publications, 2011, p. 63.
28. Scott Morrison, 'Remarks, Sydney Institute Dinner', 13 December 2021, www.pm.gov.au/media/remarks-sydney-institute-dinner.
29. John Hirst, *The Sentimental Nation*, Oxford University Press, 2000, p. 297; Julian Meyrick (ed.), *Australia in 50 Plays*, Currency Press, 2022; Clare Wright, 'A Wave of Female Candidates Powered by Historic Swell', *Meanjin*, 13 December 2021.

Index

2GB 354
7 Stages of Grieving (Mailman and Enoch) 177
457 visas 350–1
2020 Summit, Parliament House, Canberra (2008) 44, 69, 195–7, 403–4

Abbott, Tony 63, 271, 303, 352, 371
ABC 21, 25, 29, 42, 71, 127, 212, 282, 289, 326–7, 396
Abdel-Magied, Faiza 339, 344, 346–8
Abdel-Magied, Midhat 344–8
Abdel-Magied, Yassmin 339–40, 344, 348, 354–62, 390, 398–9
Abetz, Eric 129
Aboriginal and Torres Strait Islander Commission 301
Aboriginals Protection and Restriction of Opium Act 1897 (Qld) 35
Aborigines *see* Indigenous Australians
academics *see* universities
Adelaide 380
Administrative Appeals Tribunal 82
Afghan War 49, 335
African-Americans 242, 341
African immigrants 349
Against Paranoid Nationalism (Hage) 362
The Age of Surveillance Capitalism (Zuboff) 268

agriculture 38, 193, 331, 367, 377
air travel 348–9
al-Bashir, Omar 347
Albanese, Anthony 57–8
Alfred, Duke of Edinburgh 211
Alibaba 346
Alice Springs 211
aliens, internment of 39–40, 48, 341
Alyawarr people 414
America, as a penal colony 169–70
American Civil War 242, 244–5
American immigrants 341
American War of Independence 169–70
America's Cup 200–1
Ampe Akelyernemane Meke Mekarle: Little Children Are Sacred (Anderson) 203
A.N. Smith Memorial Lecture in Journalism 312, 373
Anderson, Pat 203
Ansett Airlines 282
anti-apartheid protests 276
Anzac Day 73, 357–9
apologies 48–9, 90
Appin 103
arbitration 321
archives 76–9
Aristotle 161
Armstrong, David 178
Armstrong, Neil 275

442

Index

Arndt, Heinz 165
Arnhem Land 167, 199
art, and truth 177
the arts 194
Asia 254
Asians, in Australia 125–6, 302–4, 342
ASIO 308
assimilation 66, 88, 185–6, 189, 341
asylum seekers *see* refugees
Atkinson, Alan 168
Atkinson, Judy 88–90
Atkinson, Roslyn 276–7, 284
The Atlantic 28
Aurukun Mission 200
Australia (Hancock) 46
The Australia Book for English Boys and Girls 184
Australia Council 192
Australia Day 359, 366, 400–3, 408
Australia Day Foundation UK 365–6
Australia House, London 365–6
Australia II (yacht) 200–1
Australia Post 64
Australia Talks surveys 6, 29
The Australian 19, 77–8, 180, 254, 261, 275, 323, 336, 372–3, 382, 389, 399–400
Australian Bicentennial Authority 176, 178
Australian Border Force 54
Australian Broadcasting Corporation 21, 25, 29, 42, 71, 127, 212, 282, 289, 326–7, 396
Australian Competition and Consumer Commission 384
Australian Consolidated Press 321–2
Australian Constitution 80, 128, 204, 213–14, 218, 222, 225–6, 233–5, 237–9, 302
Australian Democrats 83
Australian Electoral Commission 306
Australian Financial Review 108, 112, 282, 328, 378, 397, 400
Australian House of Representatives 227, 248, 283
Australian Human Rights Commission 399
Australian Institute of Aboriginal and Torres Strait Islander Studies 44
Australian Labor Party 66, 157, 284–5, 296
 see also specific governments, e.g. Hawke government
Australian literature 192–3
Australian Media Hall of Fame 74
Australian Medical Association 127

Australian National University 324–5, 389
Australian Press Council 60, 309
Australian Senate 5–6, 227
Australian Values Statement 9–10
Australian War Memorial, Canberra 80
Australian Women's Weekly 377
Australians for Native Title and Reconciliation 361
Australians of the Year 87, 109, 198, 266, 363, 391, 393–4

baby boomers 13
Balfour, Lord 242
Balkans 335
banking 107, 367, 377
Banks, Joseph 15, 170–1, 210
Banks, Julia 283
Barambah, Maroochy 177
Barangaroo 286
Barkandji people 168
Barton, Edmund 128, 222, 228, 245, 343
Bartone, Tony 127
Barunga Statement 201, 207, 332
bastards 71–2
Bateman, John 210
Bathurst 249
Batty, Rosie 363, 394
bauxite 199
Bean, Charles (C.E.W.) 142, 359
Beattie, Peter 305
Beaverbrook, Lord 366
Beazley, Kim 148
Becoming an Australian Citizen 330
Bedford, Randolph 223–4
Bediagal people 14, 59
Bell, Genevieve 286
Bennelong 201, 286
Bentham, Jeremy 15, 179, 204
Berejiklian, Gladys 108
Berlin Conference 347
Berlin, Isaiah 243
Best We Forget (Cochrane) 158
Betty Blockbuster's Follies 176
BHP 367, 378
bicentennial 176, 178–80
Biden, Joe 388
The Biggest Estate on Earth (Gammage) 41
Bijou Theatre, Balmain 176
bill of rights 214
Biloela 61
Bishop, Julie 283
Bjelke-Petersen, Joh 75, 258, 306

443

Index

'black armband' view of history 307, 328
Black Lives Matter movement 10, 103
The Black Police (Vogan) 293
Black River (Schultz) 177
Black Summer 407
blackbirding 240–1
Blackburn Cove 97–9
Blackburn, David 97
Blackburn, Elizabeth 286
Blackstone, William 214
Blainey, Geoffrey 307, 332–4
Blanchett, Cate 286
Blaxland, Gregory 155
Bligh, Anna 284–5, 356
Bligh, William 106
Blue Mountains 155
Bond, Alan 198, 200, 394
Boochani, Behrouz 353
book publishing 19
border control 337–8
Botany Bay 366, 401
Bounty (ship) 230
Box the Pony (Purcell) 106
The Boy Adeodatus (Smith) 91
Boyd, Ben 241
Boyd, Martin 374
Boyd, Sue 337
Boyer Lectures 42–3, 71–2, 83–4
Braddon, Edward 244
Bradley, William 98
Bradman, Don 329
Bragg, William Henry 140
Bragg, William Lawrence 140
Bray, Ted 305
Brennan, Geoffrey 324–5
Brett, Judith 220
Brexit 211
Bringing Them Home report 86–7, 264
Brisbane 230–1, 257–60, 265, 276, 283–4, 347
Brisbane Magistrates Court 47
Britain *see* United Kingdom
British Empire 3
British immigrants 253–4, 341, 349
British Museum 214–15
Broken Circles (Haebich) 186
Broken Hill 122, 367
Brooks, Geraldine 286
Bryce, Quentin 261
bubonic plague (1900) 126, 230
Buchanan, James 325
Budj Bim Cultural Landscape 41, 182

The Bulletin 191, 193, 230, 294
The Bulwark of our Liberties (exhibition) 214
Bunbury 296
Bundaberg 241
Bungaree 64, 102, 165
Bureau of Immigration, Multicultural and Population Research 343
bureaucracy 73–4, 343, 352
Burke, Brian 201
Burke, Edmund 398
Busby, Dora 100–1
Busby, William 100–1
bush poetry 193–4, 279
bushfires 26, 29, 407
business 105–6, 131, 147, 329
Byrne, John 378
Byron Bay Council 402

Caesar Godeffroy (ship) 188
Cairns 279
Calwell, Arthur 185
Canada 209
Canberra 79–80, 223, 227, 407
cancel culture 387–9
Capitol riot 2021 (US) 28
Capricornia (Herbert) 401
Carroll, Lewis 161
Carpentaria (Wright) 292–3
Carrington, Lord 224
Carroll, Lewis 91
cartels 384
Castlereagh River 156–7, 159
catastrophe, and change 412
Cater, Nick 400
Catholic Church 65, 269
Catholics 40, 112, 157, 266
The Censor's Library (Moore) 83
censorship 18, 26, 49, 81, 83–4, 145, 387–8
Centennial Park, Sydney 229, 231
Central Land Council 381
Central West, New South Wales 155–7
Centre for Independent Studies 319
Centrelink 116, 118, 135–6
change 28–9, 268–70, 277–8, 412–13
  see also climate change
Chapman, Norma 134
Charles, Prince of Wales 211–12
Chifley, Ben 202
childcare 281
children, in poverty 140
'children overboard' incident 69, 336–7
China 125–6, 129, 150–1, 345–6

444

Index

Chinese immigrants 9, 125–6, 128–9, 221, 224–5, 246, 341, 343, 349
Chinese students, in Australia 150–2
Chipp, Don 83
Christmas Island 61, 126–9, 336, 353
CIA 273
citizenship 352
citizenship ceremonies 402
citizenship tests 330
Clark, Andrew Inglis 220, 225–6
Clark, Anna 308
Clark, Manning 48, 170, 232, 266, 307–9, 332, 356, 363, 375
Clark, Ralph 98
class 108, 111, 114
Clays Bookshop 134
the clever country 139–40, 147
climate change 12–13, 394, 413
Cloncurry 292
coal industry 296, 298
Coalition *see* Liberal–National Coalition
Cobb & Co. 288
Coca-Cola 401
Cochrane, Peter 158
Cockatoo Island 127
Cohen, Leonard 277–8
Cold War 75, 129, 308, 345, 375–6
Collapse (Diamond) 255
Colley, Linda 6, 270, 412
Collins House Group 122, 322, 367–8, 378
Colonia Nueva Australia, Paraguay 122, 124
Colonial Office (UK) 210, 227
colonialism 103, 180
Comalco 199
commerce *see* business
Commonwealth Bank 319
Commonwealth Department of Home Affairs 352
Commonwealth Games 211
Commonwealth Literary Fund 84
Commonwealth of Australia 219, 224
Commonwealth Serum Laboratories 319
communism 75, 375–6
Communist Party of Australia 375–6
community groups 407–8
Confessions of an Opium-Eater (De Quincey) 375
conscience 7
conscription 158
consent 110
conservatism 5, 7, 29, 53, 83, 327–8, 388
constitutional citizenship conferences 189

Constitutional Conventions
   1891 237
   1996 249–50
   1998 235–6
Contos, Chanel 110–12, 114, 281, 398
convicts 18, 24, 59, 141, 169–71, 240
Conway, Jill Ker 286
Coo-ee March 156–7
Cook, James 35, 59, 64, 98, 103, 166, 169–70, 229
Coombs, H.C. 'Nugget' 141, 324
Cooper, William 201
COP 26 summit, Glasgow 11–12
corruption 258–9, 384
Counting and Cracking (Shakthidharan) 177
Courier-Mail 46, 281, 284, 297, 305, 307, 310–13
COVID-19 pandemic
   Australians evacuated from Wuhan 126–9
   Australia's early success 137–8
   border closures 150–1, 227, 243
   coping with 51–2
   corporations given $20 billion 131–2
   dobbing of neighbours during 59
   failure to secure vaccines 56–8
   financial stress during 131
   first appearances of 125–6
   first reactions to 11
   government response to 404–5
   income support during 116, 118–19, 130–1, 135–6
   isolationism during 53–5
   migration stops as a result of 130
   Morrison creates national cabinet 82
   Morrison's first response to 129
   problems revealed by 9–10, 12, 136
   property market during 106
   public shaming during 59–60
   quarantine during 57–8, 126–9
   restrictions during 60
   social impact of 6, 26–8, 52–3, 406
   state governments during 227–8
   travel policy during 351
   universities excluded from support during 150, 152
Cox, Peter 386
Croissant D'Or 134
Cronulla riot (2005) 68, 195
Crosby, Lynton 299
culture
   as a barometer of change 277–8
   censorship of 83–4

Index

corporatisation of 84
culture wars 8, 304, 320, 330–1
  in Australia 329
Cunnamulla 287–92
Curtin, John 66, 141, 248

dadirri 87, 89, 163
Daily Mirror 370
Daily Telegraph 389
Dampier, William 164
Dark Emu (Pascoe) 41, 43
Darling Downs 296
Darling, Sir James 374–5
Darling, Ralph 35
Darwin 12, 124, 181
Darwin, Charles 24, 219, 255–6
Davidson, Trish 286
Davidson, Sir Walter 158
Davis, Glyn 21, 403
Davis, Megan 203, 205–7
The Dawn is at Hand (Noonuccal) 36
de Foigny, Gabriel 160
De Quincey, Thomas 375
Deakin, Alfred 219–21, 224, 226, 232, 245–6, 248, 415
Deane, William 332
Deben, Lord 11
decimal currency 254–5
Declaration of Independence (US) 218, 233, 238
decolonisation 275
Defoe, Daniel 163
Delaware Indians 209
Denborough, David 411–12
Dennis, C.J. 36
deportations 343–4, 350
deregulation 107, 320–1, 323–4, 413
Dharawal language 88
Dharawal people 103
Dharug language 86, 88
Diamond, Jared 253, 255–7, 260, 269–70, 275
dictation test 53, 246
Dietrich, Amalie 188
The Dismissal 78, 192, 273
dog whistling 304
Domain, Sydney 228
Dot and the Kangaroo (Pedley) 161
Double Bay, Sydney 98, 101
Downer, Alexander 271, 308–9
Drewe, Robert 180
The Drum (television program) 25

Du Bois, W.E.B. 242
Dunera (ship) 380
Dusty, Slim 288
Dutton, Peter 127

earwigging 121
economic rationalism 323–5
ecosystems 32
Edelman Trust Barometer 136
education 46, 49–50, 67, 73, 94, 140–53, 297, 320
Edward VII, King 230
egalitarian myth 66–7, 120, 132, 384
Elaine (house) 101
elites 328
Elizabeth Bay 134
Elizabeth, South Australia 296
Elizabeth II, Queen 78–9, 202, 209, 211, 216, 271–3, 382
Emigrant (ship) 34
emotional baggage 109
employers 132
Endeavour (ship) 59, 64, 169–70, 229
The Enigmatic Mr Deakin (Brett) 220
Enoch, Wesley 177, 402
Eora people 16, 100, 169
ethnicity 341
Eureka Stockade 67
European Economic Community 254
Europeans in Australia (Atkinson) 168
Evans, Harry 213–14
Evans, Raymond 144, 184, 223, 244
exclusion 53–4, 69, 341
exploration 162, 164–6

Facebook 385–6, 390
'fair go' 120
Fairfax family 20, 105, 369
Fairfax, Tim 101–2
fairness 119–21, 125, 130–2, 136, 384
Farley, Rick 331
federal elections
  1975 192–3
  1996 69
  2001 337–8
  2007 65–6, 68
  2016 313
  2019 121
Federation 219–32, 249, 415–16
Federation Centenary 67–8, 216, 247, 250, 340
Federation Pavilion 231–2

Index

Federation Stone 228, 231
Feilberg, Carl 74, 293
feminism 112, 221, 285
Filipino immigrants 341, 349
finance, deregulation of 107
First Fleet 2, 59, 170–1, 184, 366, 401
First Nations *see* Indigenous Australians
First Nations National Constitutional Convention (2017) 204–5, 410
First World War 12, 39, 73, 80, 142, 156–8, 286
Fischer, Tim 333
Fisher, Andrew 369
Fitzgerald, Tony 75, 258–9
Flanagan, Richard 354, 358, 360
Flannery, Tim 393
Flinders Island 127, 201
Flinders, Matthew 35, 64, 102–3, 165
Foley, Fiona 46–7, 86
Foley, Matt 284, 290
Forde, Frank 283
Forde, Leneen 283
fortress mentality 174, 182, 196
Four Corners (television program) 289
the fourth estate 19, 398
Fox News 388
Foxtel 25
Framlingham 41
Franklin, Aretha 287
Fraser government 117, 336
Fraser Island 46
Fraser, Malcolm 133, 136, 176, 183, 371
free markets 383
free trade agreements 271
freedom of information laws 75, 81
freedom of speech 80–1
Freedom Ride (1961) 48
Freedom Ride (1965) 159–60
Freeman, Cathy 197
Friedman, Milton 84, 320, 322
frontier wars 16, 47, 59, 80, 155, 158, 188, 219, 411

Gadigal people 14, 98, 100
Gallery of Modern Art, Brisbane 259
Gallipoli 156, 358
Gallipoli (film) 359
The Game (Kelly) 11
Gammage, Bill 41
Gandangara people 103
Gardening Australia (television program) 86
Gariwerd people 41

Garton-Ash, Timothy vi
gas pipeline 11
gays 5
Geelong 296
Geelong Grammar 373–5
gender 285–7
 see also women
gender equality 384
generational change 195–6
Geographia (Ptolemy) 162
George V, King 201, 230
German immigrants 39–40, 48, 188, 194, 274
Germany 92, 269, 310
Gibson, Ross 270
Gilgandra 156, 158–60, 274, 359
Gillard, Julia 230, 267, 271, 284, 356, 399
Gilmore, Mary (née Cameron) 36, 119–25, 132–3, 292
Gilmore, William 124
Giramondo Press 293
Glasgow climate summit 11–12
global capitalism 197, 383–4
global financial crisis (2008) 267
global indicators, Australia's place in 383–4
Goenpul people 35
Gold Coast 259
Gold Coast Bulletin 282
Goldstein, Vida 221, 407
Goodes, Adam 363–4, 394
Google 385–6, 390
Gorman, Amanda 395
Goss, Wayne 46, 259, 261, 283
Gottliebsen, Robert 378
government
 openness in 79–83
 outsourcing of services by 320
 public trust in 136, 317, 407
 relationship with industry 368, 370
 role of 413–14
Gramsci, Antonio 327
Grand Synagogue, Sydney 184
Grant, Stan Jnr 85, 87
Grant, Stan Snr 86–7
Grassby, Al 340
Great Depression 12, 102, 117, 141
Great South Land 2
Greek immigrants 189
Greenway, Francis 254
Greer, Germaine 286
Grey, Sir George 237–8, 250
Griffin, Marion Mahony 76

447

Index

Griffin, Walter Burley 76–7
Griffith Review 21–3, 260, 356–7
Griffith, Sir Samuel 22, 222, 226–7, 260, 333, 411
Griffith University 21, 186
Griffiths, Glynda Nesta 100
Griffiths, Rachel 286
Grotius, Hugo 166
The Guardian 12
Gulargambone 160
Gulliver's Travels (Swift) 163–5
Gunditjmara people 39, 41
Guns, Germs and Steel (Diamond) 255
Gurrah (Gadigal man) 100–2
Gweagal people 14, 59, 168

Haebich, Anna 185–6
Haebich, Bert 186–7
Hage, Ghassan 362
Hall, Joseph 61, 126
Hamilton (musical) 218–9
Hamilton, Ian 346–7
Hamilton, Victoria 37–8, 50
Hancock, Gina 208
Hancock, Keith 46
Hancock, Lang 322–3, 331
Hanson, Pauline 5–6, 68, 125, 263–4, 297–305, 311, 313, 338, 340, 347
Hardy, Frank 310
Hare-Clark electoral system 220
The Harp in the South (Park) 294
Harry, Prince 389
Hartcher, Peter 131
Harvey, Gerry 131–2
Haslam, Nick 329
Hasluck, Paul 76, 144–5
Hawke, Bob
  allows Chinese students to stay 342
  concedes a treaty not possible 177
  declares a national holiday 200
  increases education funding 140
  offers condolences after Clark's death 308
  on the clever country 139, 147
  opens Federation Pavilion 232
  promises treaty 332
  signs Barunga Statement 201
  unveils Barunga Statement in Parliament House 200–1, 301
  visits Anzac Cove 358
Hawke government
  changes media policy 20
  fails to get referendums through 235
  modifies Bicentennial plans 178
  privatisation under 319
  recession under 117
Hawkesbury River 225–6
Henry IV Part One (Shakespeare) 18
The Herald and Weekly Times 20, 367, 369, 376
Herbert, Xavier 401
Hermannsburg Mission 41
hermit democracy 52, 246
Hidden Queensland 260
Hieu Van Le 342
Higgins, Brittany 109, 281, 396
High Court of Australia 79–80, 132, 282, 331–4
higher education *see* universities
hijabs 339–40
Hirst, John 224, 415
history
  'black armband' view of 307, 328
  teaching of 73, 307
  'three cheers' view of 307, 310
  writing of 46, 48, 72, 307–8, 332–3
A History of Australia (Clark) 48, 266, 309
Hobsbawm, Eric 177–8
Hocking, Jenny 78–9, 273
Hogan's Heroes (television program) 274
Holmes, Catherine 284
Holocaust Memorial, Berlin 47
homeless people 135
homosexuality 176
Hopetoun, Lord 228, 245
Hopevale Mission 203
Horne, Donald 137–9, 193, 253
household debt 384
Housewives' Association 186
housing 384
Houston, Brian 119, 124
Howard government
  attitude to same-sex marriage 268
  cuts funding to ABC 326
  education funding under 149
  gives free reign to market economy 66
  migration policy 69–70, 337–8, 350–1
  Northern Territory Intervention 203, 293
  refugee policy 335–8
Howard, Janette 217
Howard, John
  at Olympic opening ceremony 175
  attitude towards Asians 300, 302, 342
  co-writes preamble to Constitution 236
  constitutional conventions under 249–50

Index

controls political agenda 403
disbands immigration research bureau 343
elected prime minister 249
expands his watchlist 328
in 1996 election campaign 299–301, 316–17
loses seat in 2007 election 68, 261
makes policy to reflect values 329–30
on Pauline Hanson 304
on Tim Flannery 393
opposes multiculturalism 300
outplays Turnbull in republic referendum 208
policy towards Indigenous Australians 301–2
proposes emissions trading scheme 393–4
purges public service 318–19
radical conservatism of 319
refuses to apologise to stolen generations 175, 179, 263
reinvents myths of the Australian legend 66–7
rhetoric on migration policy 69
ten-point plan for native title 168
view of history 307, 309–10
wins 1996 election 318
wins 2001 election 337–8
Howard Springs quarantine centre 129
Hoxton, David 44
Huggins, Jackie 144
Hughes, Billy 39, 157–8, 223, 367, 369
Hunt, Greg 55
Hyatt Hotel, Canberra 216
Hyde Park, Sydney 103
Hywood, Greg 378

the idea, of Australia 1–2, 4, 161–2
  see also national identity
idealists 122–3
immigrants *see* migration
Immigration Restriction Act 1901 244–6
indentured labour 64, 219, 240, 245, 411
Independent Voices campaign 221
Indian immigrants 9, 55–6, 341, 343, 349
Indigenous Australians
  1967 referendum 36
  absent at Federation ceremony 231
  as survivors 409
  categorisation of 242
  Cook on 166
  counted in 1971 census 53
  decimation of 243

destruction of records of massacres 74–6
education of 141, 143–6
excluded from minimum wage 132
failure to come to legal agreement with 15, 179, 210, 228–9
forced to take part in re-enactment 229
Freedom Ride (1965) 48, 159–60
frontier wars 16, 47, 59, 80, 155, 158, 188, 219, 411
Hanson on 298
Hawke proposes treaty 201
Hawke provides extra funding for education 141
Howard refuses to apologise to 175, 179, 263
Howard's policy towards 301–2
  impact of colonisation on 14–16
  in Cunnamulla 287–92
  in Gilgandra 159–60
  in Ipswich 298
  in Queensland 47, 74–6, 188, 265
  in Sydney Harbour area 100–1
  in Western Victoria 41, 44
  incarceration of 8
Indigenous artists 414
land rights 17, 167–8, 194, 200, 292, 331–4
languages of 65, 85–8, 185
Mabo judgment 166–8, 332
Macquarie's declaration regarding 103
map of First Nations 44
March for Freedom, Justice and Hope 179
negotiations with government 201–2
new generation of leaders 203–4
Northern Territory Intervention 203, 293, 302
on missions and reserves 35, 145, 200, 203, 416
on Stradbroke Island 35
origins 162–3
placenames 3, 65, 86
policy of assimilation 88, 144, 185–6, 189
population 210, 409
Prince Charles visits Mount Nhulun 212
protest at Bicentennial 232
removal of children from families of 35, 48, 86–7, 186, 262–4
removal of families from Mapoon 199–200
removal of to islands 127
reparations to stolen generations 179, 264
right to vote 210, 244

449

Index

Rudd says sorry to 262–4
silence on Indigenous issues 43–5, 47
Smith's Boyer Lecture series 71–2
Stanner's Boyer Lecture series 42–3
treated as indentured labour 241
Uluru Statement from the Heart 72, 146, 203–8, 218, 408, 410
under colonial administration 229
violence towards 5, 59, 74–6, 120, 122, 188, 200, 240, 288, 293
Wik judgment 167–8, 311, 331, 333
Indigenous Voice to Parliament 204
Indochinese refugees 336
Indonesia 275
industry policy 147
Indyk, Ivor 293
inequality gap 136, 384, 405
Institute of Public Affairs 208, 214, 319, 322–3, 328, 400
institutional abuse 48, 65
insularity 12, 189
integration 341
intergenerational knowledge 112
international students 149–53
International Women's Day 281
internet 21, 25, 306
see also social media
Investigator (ship) 165
Ipswich 295–9
Ireland 65, 164, 269
Irish immigrants 112, 120, 158
Isaacs, Sir Isaac 184, 214
Islamic College of Brisbane 339
isolationism 53–5, 60, 138, 174

Jacaranda Press 36
Jackson, Sir George 98
Jakubowicz, Andrew 189
James Clive 173
Japan 138–9, 181–2, 246
Jefferson, Thomas 237
Jewish immigrants 184, 335
JobKeeper allowance 131, 152
John, King 213, 216
Johnson, Boris 271, 310
Jones, Barry 149
Jones, Tony 355
journalism 148, 282–3, 305–6, 311–12, 326–7, 371–3, 378–80, 386
Joyce, James 49, 83
judiciary, attacks on 333–4
Juukan Gorge caves 17–18

Kama Sutra 83
Kamilaroi people 159
Kariuki, Rosemary 391
Karskens, Grace 99
Keane, Patrick 233, 239
Keating government
introduces mandatory detention for refugees 335
privatisation by 319
system of temporary skilled visas 350
Keating, Paul
at 1996 Constitutional Convention 249
changes media ownership policy 373
delivers speech on republic 247–8
in 1996 election campaign 315–16
introduces Native Title Act 333
mentored by Jack Lang 307
on change of government 317
on the Olympic Games 174–5, 197
One Nation economic policy 300
Redfern Address 167
stays home for Federation Centenary 247
Kelly, Dominic 323
Kelly, Jackie 306
Kelly, Ned 219–20
Kelly, Paul 336
Kelly, Sean 11
Kemp, David 149
Kennedy, Trevor 378
Kerr, Sir John 78, 273, 383
Keynesian economics 141, 321, 324
K'gari country 46, 86
Kidman, Nicole 286
King, Philip Gidley 18, 85, 128
King's College, London 271
Kings Cross, Sydney 132–4
Kingston, Charles 220–1, 248
Kitney, Geoff 52–3
Kngwarreye, Emily Kame 414
Knowledge Nation 148–9
Kohler, Alan 378
Korea 139
Kristol, Irving 327
Kulin people 201, 210
Kunja people 289
Kyburz, Rosemary 280
Kyoto Protocol 262, 393

Lake Condah 41
Lambie, Jacqui 153, 355
land 15–17, 38, 99, 106–8
land grants 98–9

Index

land rights 17, 167–8, 194, 200, 292, 331–4
Landsborough, William 288
Lane, William 123–4
Lang, Jack 307
Lang, John Dunmore 238, 240
Langford, Stephen 103
Langton, Marcia 286, 414
Langton, Stephen 216
language 85–8
Last Best Hope (Packer) 68, 409
Latham, John 248
Latham, Mark 317
Laurence, Janet 47
Lavarch, Michael 86
Law Institute Journal 333
Lawrence, D.H. 13
Lawson, Henry 288
Lawson, Louisa 221
Lawson, William 155
lead mining 367
Lebanese immigrants 114
The Legend of the Nineties (Palmer) 191
Lepore, Jill 412–13
lesbians 5
Lewis, Peter 12
Liberal–Country Party Coalition 322
liberal democracy 28
Liberal Democrats 313
Liberal–National Coalition 5–6, 235, 267, 305
 see also specific governments, e.g. Howard government
Liberal Party 54, 83, 283, 295, 297, 299–301, 340, 394
liberalism 313
Lincoln, Abraham 240
Lindsay, Norman 379
Lion & Kangaroo (Souter) 248
listening 87–9, 112, 114, 121, 410
literacy 19, 191
literature 191–3, 292–4
Livermore, Reg 176
local government 408
lockdowns 27, 29, 59–60, 107, 406, 408
Logan, Patrick 35
London 367
Lovell, Henry 61
Lucashenko, Melissa 87, 298, 411
Lucinda (ship) 222, 225–6, 239
Lucinda Brayford (Boyd) 374
luck 137–40
The Lucky Country (Horne) 137–9

Luganville, Vanuatu 241
Luther, Martin 40
Lutherans 154, 187
Lyons, Joseph 141

Ma, Jack 346
Mabo judgment 166–8, 332
Macintyre, Stuart 308
Macquarie Bank 104
Macquarie, Lachlan 103–4, 141, 401
MacSween, Prue 354–5
Magabala Books 43
Magna Carta 81, 213–18
Magna Carta Place 80, 216
Maiden, Samantha 397
Mailman, Deborah 177
Makarrata 72, 205, 207
Making Soviet Man (Clark) 308
male dominance, in Australian society 286–7
Malouf, David 49, 236
Malysiak, Jane 57
Man Booker Prize 360
Mandela, Nelson 145
Manne, Kate 286
manners 398
manufacturing 11, 113, 147, 193, 296–8, 322, 324, 384, 405
Māori 269
Mapoon 199–200
Maria Island 127
market-driven economics 320–1, 325
Markle, Meghan 389
Marr, David 4, 6, 24, 301, 337
marriage ban 281
Marshall, Isobel 391
Marx, Karl 124
masculinity 111
Masterman, George 376
Mat-te-wan-ye 61, 126
mateship 197
Matra, James 170–1
Mazzini, Giuseppe 220
McCarthy, Joseph 129
McCarthyism 375
McEwen, 'Black' Jack 370
McIntyre, Scott 358
McKellar, Hazel 288, 291
McKew, Maxine 342
McNicoll, David 321–2
Meanjin 382
Meat & Livestock Australia 401
media 19–21, 25

451

Index

media companies 385
media ownership 373, 385
Medici Cycle 368–9, 386
Megalogenis, George 148
Melanesians 47, 69, 219, 240–1, 245, 343, 411
Melbourne 189–90, 230, 260, 349
Melbourne Club 375, 377
Melbourne University Press 245
Melleuish, Greg 328
Menzies government 20, 199
Menzies, Pattie 217
Menzies Research Centre 400
Menzies, Sir Robert 142, 216, 254, 319, 369, 380
Mercury 220
Midnight Oil (band) 174–5
migration
  after the Second World War 182–5
  as an economic lynchpin 130
  as gatekeeping 54, 352
  constitutional citizenship conferences 189
  dictation test for migrants 53, 246
  diversity of migrants 349
  employment of migrants 341
  Immigration Restriction Act 1901 244–6
  impact of on social fabric 191
  in the 1960s 3
  market-driven nature of 350
  migration policy 69–70, 337–8, 343–4, 349–54
  multiculturalism 190, 340–1
  new model of 352–3
  percentage of migrants in population 349
  policy of assimilation 185, 189
  populist attacks on migrants 5
  silence about migrant trauma 47
  stops as a result of pandemic 130
  Whitlam abolishes White Australia policy 183
  see also refugees; *specific nationalities, e.g.* German immigrants
Miles Franklin Literary Award 292
Millennials 357–8
Millennials Strike Back 357
minimum wage 132
mining industry 67, 122, 167, 199–201, 296, 301, 331–4, 367–8, 377–8, 384
Minjerribah 31–5
Miranda, Lin-Manuel 218–19
Mitchell, Chris 261–2, 307, 309, 311, 334, 377
Mitchell, Elyne 15–16
Mitchell, Thomas 292
Modern Manufacturing Strategy 11
Modi, Narendra 310
the monarchy 208–11, 235, 272–3
Monash, John 184
monopolies 384
moon landing 275
Moore, Nicole 83
morality gap 91, 411
Moreland 241
Moreton Bay 32, 225
Moreton Island 187–8
Morgan, Hugh 332–3
Morley, Ken 345–6
Morris, Stanley 96
Morris, Valda 96–7
Morrison government 130–2, 150, 153
Morrison, John 121
Morrison, Scott
  addresses Sydney Institute 415
  announces reparations to stolen generations 179, 264
  as Mary Gilmore's great-great nephew 119
  at the Glasgow summit 11–12
  attends state dinner with Trump 124–5
  awards Australians of the Year 393
  becomes prime minister 283
  closes border to travellers from China 151
  creates national cabinet 82, 405
  derides Byron Bay Council 402
  employs ex-mining executives on senior staff 367–8
  evacuates Australians in Wuhan 126
  gives $20 billion to corporations 131
  in the 2019 election 121
  meets British PM 271
  on Australia 54
  on Cook's 'circumnavigation' 64
  on fairness 119–20, 130
  promises museum of Aboriginal Australia 79
  response to COVID pandemic 57–8, 116, 118–19, 129–31, 405
  response to sexual abuse of women 397
  tells international students to go home 351
  visits Cornish cemetery 171
  visits Gilmore's grave 124, 292
Mulgumpin 187–8
multiculturalism 66, 190, 303, 340–2, 351, 361
Munster, George 382–3
Murdoch, Dame Elisabeth 374–5, 377

Index

Murdoch, Helen 374
Murdoch, Sir Keith 20, 158, 310, 322, 359, 369, 375–6, 387
Murdoch, Lachlan 311, 372, 386
Murdoch, Rupert
  at Geelong Grammar 373–5
  at Oxford University 375–6
  campaigns to have death sentence overturned 211
  cultural preoccupations 389
  earns profit from Queensland Newspapers 310
  learns history from Manning Clark 308
  mentored by McEwen 370
  on Australian travellers 345
  on free markets 383
  on his father's exposure of Gallipoli scandal 359
  on public interest and personal gain 326–7
  on running a newspaper 373
  on social media 385, 387–8
  on the role of the press 312
  personality of 382
  power of 20, 370–3, 387–8, 390
  receives lifetime achievement award 365–6, 388, 392
  returns to Australia from Oxford 369–70, 376–7
  runs the Adelaide *News* 211, 380–1
  style of journalism 371
  supports a republic 236
  supports Institute of Public Affairs 208
  supports Rudd's election 261–2
  uses *The Australian* to advance nationalism 382
  visited by Kerr 383
  withdraws support for Whitlam 382–3
  see also News Corp
Murphy, James 319
Murray, Sir Keith 141–2
Murray, Les 235–6
Murray River 225
Murray-Smith, Stephen 375
Murugappan family 61–3
Museum of Australian Democracy 217–18
Museum of Sydney 47
Muslims 5, 339–40, 344, 355–6, 358
My Brother Jack (Johnston) 359
My Country (Marr) 4
MyGov 116
Myora mission school 35
myths 270

Namatjira, Albert 42
The Narrow Road to the Deep North (Flanagan) 360
The Nation 382
Nation Review 379, 382
national anthem 178–9, 401
National Archives of Australia 76–9, 83, 215, 218
National Archives (US) 218
National Australia Bank 367
national cabinet 82
National Capital Authority 217–18
National Congress of Australia's First Peoples 144
National Farmers' Federation 331
national identity 63–6, 69, 137, 165, 180–1, 191, 250–1, 266, 270–1, 275, 409–10
National Library of Australia 77, 83, 215
National Life and Character (Pearson) 243
National Museum, Canberra 80
National Native Title Tribunal 292
National Party 313, 318, 333
  see also Liberal–National Coalition
National Portrait Gallery, Canberra 80
National Press Club 395
national pride 180
National Times 280
nationalism 66, 120, 409–10
Nationalist Party 157
Native Americans 209
native title 17, 167–8, 292, 331
Nauru 262, 337
neoliberalism 13, 66, 68, 197, 320–5, 398, 413
Network 10 25
New Australia movement 122
New Australians 3, 183
New South Wales, as a penal colony 170
New South Wales Mounted Police 155
New York 345
New York Post 389
New Zealand 118, 209, 230, 237, 269
Newcastle 296
News 211, 367, 376, 380–1
News Corp 28, 60, 67, 78, 214, 236, 261–2, 267, 304, 311–13, 323, 359, 371, 385–8, 397–8
  see also specific newspapers, e.g. The Australian
newspapers 19–21, 50, 310–13, 367, 382, 386
Ngangikurungkurr people 87
Ngarigo country 15

Index

Ngarrindjeri people 201, 301
Ngugi people 35
Ngunnawal people 262
Nicholls, Doug 202
No Friend But the Mountains (Boochani) 353
Nobel Prize 140–1, 196
noisy miner birds 234
Nolan, Sidney 308
Noongar language 86
Noongar people 186
Noonuccal, Oodgeroo 33–6
Norfolk Island 61, 126–7
North Stradbroke Island 31–5
Northcliffe, Lord 369
Northern Territory Intervention 203, 293, 302
Not Always Diplomatic (Boyd) 337
Nunukul people 35

Observer 382
O'Connor, Richard 244
O'Dowd, Bernard 232
Old Australia 5
Olympic Games
  Melbourne (1956) 189–90, 260
  Sydney (2000) 172–4, 196–7
On the Origin of Species (Darwin) 24, 255
The One Day of the Year (Seymour) 359
One Nation 300, 303, 305, 313
openness, in government 79–83
Orwell, George 70
O'Toole, Fintan 63, 65, 409
Otter (ship) 36
outsourcing, of government services 320
Overland 382
Oxford English Dictionary 388
Oxford University 370–1, 375–6
Oxley, John 35

Pacific Islands, immigrants from 341
Pacific Solution 262, 337
The Packaging of Australia (Melleuish) 328
Packer family 20, 321, 369
Packer, George 68, 409
The Palace Letters (Hocking) 273
Palaszczuk, Annastacia 285
Palawa people 201, 226
Palm Island 127
Palmer, Nettie 190, 195
Palmer, Vance 181, 190–1, 195, 225, 227, 237, 239
pandemic *see* COVID-19 pandemic
Paper Emperors (Young) 369

Paris Peace Conference 158, 242
Park, Ruth 294
Parkes, Henry 121, 221–2, 224
Parkin, Dean 207
Parliament House, Canberra 215–16
Parliamentary Budget Office 131
parochialism 227
Pascoe, Bruce 41, 43
the past 177–8, 181
pastoralists *see* agriculture
Paterson, Banjo 172
Paterson, James 150
Patrick, Aaron 397
Patrick, Rex 82
The Peaks of Lyell (Blainey) 332
Pearson, Charles 128, 242–3, 245
Pearson, Noel 200, 203–4, 302, 402
Pedley, Ethel 160–1
Pemulwuy 16
pen pals 346
penal colonies 169–70
Perkins, Charles 48, 146, 160, 203
Perkins, Rachel 44, 203–4
Perlez, Jane 83
Perth 349
Pezzullo, Mike 352, 357
Phillip, Arthur 14, 58–9, 97–8, 126, 166–7, 201, 209–10, 215, 401
Pinchgut 61
Pine Gap 272
Pinikura people 17
Piper, John 104
Pitcairn Island 230
place, sense of 31–2, 34–5
placenames 3, 65, 86, 97–8
plebiscites 179, 268, 278
poetry 36, 193–4, 279
Point Lookout 35
Point Macleay mission 201
Point Piper, Sydney 104
political correctness 301, 389, 400
political parties 408
Political Troglodytes and Economic Lunatics (Kelly) 323
politics 24–6, 29
Pompidou, Georges 177
popular culture 273–4, 277
population 130, 210, 343, 349, 352
populism 5–6, 297–8, 300, 303–5, 313–14, 409
Port Headland 335
Porter, Christian 396

454

Index

Possession Island 166
Potts Point 134
poverty 8, 135–6, 140
power 367, 369–70, 372
Power Without Glory (Hardy) 310
Pringle, J.D. 174
private schools 110–11, 320
privatisation 319–20, 413
Privy Council 179, 200, 221, 248
The Project (television program) 25
property developers 106–7
property ownership 16–17, 99–100, 106–8, 167
Protestants 157
Ptolemy 162
public choice theory 325, 327
public consent 327
public enterprises 319–20
public good 68
public records, destruction of 74–6
public service 76, 281, 318–20
public shaming 60
Purcell, Leah 106
Puutu Kunti Kurrama people 17
Pythagoras 161

Q&A (television program) 355, 357
Qantas 319
Quadrant 382
Quandamooka people 32
quarantine 57–8, 126–9
Quarantine Beach 59
Queensland
  1975 federal election 192
  1998 state election 305
  2012 state election 284–5, 356
  as different from the rest of Australia 265
  childhood trips to 45–6
  destruction of public records 74–6
  hosts Commonwealth Games 211
  immigrants 188, 238, 349
  Melanesian 'indentured labour' 240–1, 245
  mining industry 368
  Native Police 74–6
  native title lands 292
  Palaszczuk elected for third time 285
  school textbooks 46
  sexual abuse 279–81
  Supreme Court 222–3, 284
  treatment of Indigenous Australians 35, 47, 74–6, 188, 200, 265, 411
  votes for federation 227

Queensland Newspapers 310, 376
Queensland Police Special Branch 75
Queensland Premier's Literary Award 292–3
Queensland Times 297
The Queenslander 74, 293
Questacon 77, 80

race, and gender 285–6
racism
  against Chinese Australians 129
  at the Paris Peace Conference 242
  Coalition supports Hanson's bill 5–6
  Cronulla riot (2005) 68
  equation of race with civilization 243
  fostered by Pauline Hanson 5–6, 300, 302–4, 314, 338
  Hage on 362
  Hughes opposes racial equality clause in treaty 158
  in Cunnamulla 289
  in football 363–4
  in Gilgandra 160
  in textbooks 46
  in the United States 242, 395
  Parkes rails against Chinese 221
  proposed racism in the Constitution 239
  public education campaigns 342–3
  race as a criterion of exclusion 132, 341
  racial discrimination laws passed 341
  Wuhan evacuees sent to Christmas Island 127
  see also White Australia policy
radio 20–1, 49
railways 230–1
Ramsay, Alan 149
rape 280
Reagan, Ronald 299
real estate 106–8
Reconciliation Australia 144
reconstruction, after Second World War 324, 413
record-keeping 76, 131
Redfern Address 167
Redleaf (house) 99–101
referendums 36, 208, 236–7, 248, 272–3
refugees 5, 10, 49, 61–3, 69–70, 127, 184, 262, 335–8, 342, 353
Reid, George 222
Rein, Therese 127
republic referendum 208, 248, 272–3
republicanism 220, 235–7, 248, 272
research 153

455

Index

Reshaping Australian Institutions (Brennan) 325
Returned Sailors', Soldiers' and Airmen's Imperial League 184
Reynolds, Henry 42, 166, 265
Richards, Jonathan 75
Rinehart, Gina 331
Rinnan, Arne 336
Rio Tinto 17–18, 367
Rivett, Rohan 380–1
R.M. Williams (company) 67
Robbie, Margot 286
Roberts, William 171
Robinson Crusoe (Defoe) 163, 165
Robodebt 48, 135–6
Roosevelt, Teddy 246, 381
Rorty, Richard vi, 63
Roskam, John 400
Rottnest Island 127
Rowse, Tim 167, 202
Royal Commission into Human Relationships 61, 86
Rudd, Kevin
  apologises to stolen generations 262–4
  bars refugees from settling in Australia 61, 353
  becomes prime minister 261
  discusses political agenda with Davis 403
  friendship with Chris Mitchell 261–2
  holds 2020 Summit 265, 403–4
  initiatives during financial crisis (2008) 267
  on the Murdoch press 313, 371–2
  on the Yirrkala bark petition 213
  revokes Pacific Solution 262
Rum Rebellion 99
Rural Australians for Refugees 361
Ruska family 33
Ruska, Lucy 35
Ruska, Ted 35
Ryan, Susan 282–3

Salt, Bernard 49
same-sex marriage plebiscite 268, 278
Samuel Griffith Society 333
Samuels, Gordon 249
Sarah Island 127
Sawer, Marian 321
scholarships 142
Schultz, Noel 37, 50, 154, 156, 186–7
Scott, Kim 86, 410
Scott, Rose vi, 221, 394, 407, 415

sea voyages 154–5
Second World War 12, 40, 95, 124, 141, 181–2, 184, 259, 272
secrecy, in official circles 79–81, 90
The Secret War (Richards) 75
sectarianism 40, 157, 266
segregation 160, 185
self-interest 121, 321–2, 325–7
Selkirk, Alexander 163
The Sentimental Nation (Hirst) 224, 415
Sesquicentenary (1938) 401
Seven Shillings Beach 96–7, 100–2, 107
Seven Versions of an Australian Badland (Gibson) 270
Sex Discrimination Act 1984 54
sexism 278–9
sexual abuse 109–11, 280–1, 393, 396
sexual discrimination 54, 282–3
sexual harassment 278–81
sexual politics 279
Sharpeville massacre 144
Shaw, George Bernard 133
Shawcross, William 373–5, 383
shearers' strike 225
Sheridan, Greg 389
Shooters, Fishers and Farmers Party 313
Shorten, Bill 354
Sidaway, Robert 18
silence
  destruction of public records 74–6
  Hasluck censors Tatz's findings 145
  keeping records private 78–9
  on Indigenous issues 43–5, 47
  responses to breaking 90–1
  secrecy in official circles 79–81, 90
  silencing by refusing to discuss 73
  Stanner's great Australian silence 399
  use of fear to silence 82
Sims, Rod 384
Singapore 139, 248
Sirius (ship) 97, 366
Skase, Christopher 378
Sky News 25
slavery 169–70, 219, 240–2, 245
smallpox vaccines 128
Smith, Adam 124
Smith, Bernard 71–3, 83–4, 91, 291, 396–7, 411
Smith, Chris 354–5
Snowy Mountains 15
social Darwinism 256
social hierarchy 105–6

456

Index

social media 306, 358–60, 385, 387–8, 390, 398
socialism 124
soldier settlers 38
Sotheby's 215
Souter, Gavin 3, 132–3, 174, 248
South Africa 144, 237, 246, 276
South Australia 229, 237
South Australian Museum 42, 44
South Korea 269
Southeast Asia 275
Spanish flu (1918–19) 10
species extinction 16
The Spectre of Truganini (lecture series) 71–2
Spence, Catherine Helen 220, 222, 229
Spence, Michael 152
Spigelman, Jim 99, 160
Spinning the Dream (Haebich) 186
Springboks 276, 305
squatters 288
St Ambrose Church, Gilgandra 158–9
St Helena 127
St Leo's College, University of Queensland 266
St Peters Lutheran College, Brisbane 276–7
Stalinism 375
Stanner, W.E.H. 42–3, 45, 48, 399
Stanthorpe 200
State Library of New South Wales 103
the states 227–8
statues, from the colonial period 103
Statute of Westminster 1931 248
Steel City Blues (Schultz) 113–14
steel industry 113–14, 117, 185
Stoker, Amanda 77
Stone, John 371
stories 63, 90, 114–15, 176
Stradbroke Dreamtime (Noonuccal) 33
Stradbroke Island 31–5
Stephen, Sir Ninian 232
Stuart, Rupert Mawell (Max) 211, 381–2
submarines 11
Sudan 345–7
Summers, Anne 286–7
Sunday Times 381
Swift, Jonathan 163–4
Sydney 3, 60, 93–108, 132–4, 349
Sydney Cove 98, 366, 401
Sydney Gazette 19
Sydney Harbour 93–5, 98, 154–5, 179, 181
Sydney Institute 415

Sydney Morning Herald 57, 100–2, 131, 149, 174, 294
Sydney Opera House 182
Sydney Town Hall 230

tall poppy syndrome 363–4
Tall Ships (1988) 401
Tame, Grace 109, 281, 391, 393–5, 399
Tampa (ship) 336–7
tariffs 321
Tasmania 220
Tatz, Colin 144–5
Tatz, Sandra 145
Tehan, Dan 271
television 20–1, 49
temporary skilled visas 350
Tent Embassy 217
terra nullius 166, 185, 210
terrorism 345
tertiary education 94, 141–53, 193
textbooks 46
That Deadman Dance (Scott) 410
Thatcher, Margaret 318, 320, 398
theatre 18, 85
think tanks 322–3
Thomson, Gordon 127
Thomson, Robert 386
Thunberg, Greta 398–9
Tiananmen Square massacre 342, 347
Tiffen, Rod 312
Tillers, Imants 232
Tonkin, Jack 289
Toowoomba 187
trade 138–9
transportation 19, 170–1, 215, 240
Trauma Trails (Atkinson) 90
treaties, with First Nations 209
Treaty of Waitangi 209, 269
Trump, Donald 124, 303, 310, 388, 398
Tudge, Alan 73, 310
Turnbull government 207–8, 268
Turnbull, Malcolm 207–8, 273, 283, 313, 354, 358, 402
Turnbull-Roberts, Vanessa 264
Twitter 398
Two Cheers for Capitalism (Kristol) 327
Tzannes, Alec 231

Uluru Statement from the Heart 72, 146, 203–8, 218, 408, 410
Ulysses (Joyce) 49, 83
Unaipon, David 145–6, 201

Index

Unaipon, James 145
unAustralianness 63
unemployment 152–3
unemployment benefits 131, 135
UNESCO World Heritage List 41
Ungunmerr-Baumann, Miriam-Rose 87–90, 391
unions 67, 122, 284–5, 297
United Australia Party 313
United Kingdom
  abolishes slavery 242
  Australian ties to 248, 270–1
  British immigrants 253–4, 341, 349
  displacement of by the US 274
  in the 1980s 345
  joins European Economic Community 138, 254, 271
United Nations COP 26 summit, Glasgow 11
United Nations Permanent Indigenous Forum 203
United Nations Refugee Convention 335, 337
United States
  abolishes slavery 242
  as an ally of Australia 66, 272
  Civil War 242, 244–5
  in the 1980s 345
  influence on Australia 239–40, 273–4
  treaties with Native Americans 209
  War of Independence 169–70
United States Constitution 226
Uniting Church 200
Universal Declaration of Human Rights 13
universal suffrage 230
universities 94, 141–53, 193
Universities Commission 142
University Grants Committee (UK) 142
University of Melbourne 142, 146
University of Queensland 94, 144, 146, 148, 266
University of Sydney 146, 152, 307
University of Technology, Sydney 148
Upheaval (Diamond) 256, 268, 270
USS *Chicago* (ship) 95, 124, 181
utopianism 244

vaccines 56–8, 128
Valadian, Margaret 146
values 7, 197, 328–30
Van Diemen's Land 127
Victoria, Queen 160, 201, 218, 227–8, 230, 239

Victoria Street, King Cross 134
Victoria, Western District 37–8, 124, 182, 374
Vietnam War 193, 272, 275
Vietnamese immigrants 336, 341–2, 349
visas 350–2
Vogan, Arthur 293–4
von Weizsäcker, Richard 92
vote, for women 229–30, 416
voting rights 244
A Voyage to Terra Australis (Flinders) 165
Vuitton, Louis 67

wage determination 321
wage stagnation 384
Wailwan people 159
Walgal country 15
Walker, Kath *see* Noonuccal, Oodgeroo
Walker, William 100–1
Wall Street Journal 388
Walsh, Eric 370
Walsh, Max 112, 282, 378
Wanganella (ship) 154–5
The War Aims of a Plain Australian (Bean) 142
Wardley, Deborah 282
Warrane 98
We Are Going (Noonuccal) 36
wealth, concentration of 384
Weil, Simone vi
Weipa 200
welfare recipients 135–6
Wentworth, William Charles 19, 155
West Africa 170
Western Australia 227, 240
Western District, Victoria 37–8, 124, 182, 374
Western Mining 332
Westminster Abbey 247
Westpac 367
Wharton, Herb 288, 291
whistleblowers 81–2
White Australia policy
  abolition of 53, 183, 247
  Barton on 245
  campaign to revoke 182–3
  Deakin on 245
  fear of Chinese immigration 128
  Hanson's bill revives memories of 6
  Howard's rhetoric evokes 69
  Hughes on 157
  impact on families 114
  legislation of 244–6
  Parkes as the father of 221

Index

proposal to enshrine in Constitution 239
provokes name of hermit democracy 52
supported by Calwell 185
The White Australia Policy to 1920 (Willard) 245
White, Patrick 196
white supremacism 314
Whitlam, Gough
  abolishes university fees 143
  abolishes White Australia policy 183
  dismissed as prime minister 78, 192, 273, 383
  initial opposition to Vietnamese refugees 336
  'It's Time' election campaign (1972) 266
  Murdoch supports election of 372
  Murdoch withdraws support for 382–3
  program of reform 78, 266
  replaces national anthem 401
  supports federal funding of universities 142
  wins 1972 election 322
Wik judgment 167–8, 311, 331, 333
Wilcannia 287–8
Willard, Myra 245
Williams, Margaret 146
Winch, Tara June 86
Winfrey, Oprah 389
Winton, Tim 111
Wiradjuri language 86
Wiradjuri people 155, 159
Witnessing to Silence (Foley) 47
'woke' culture 388–9, 392, 400
Wolfe, Patrick 17
Wollongong 113–14, 117, 185–6, 296
women 5, 10, 54, 229–30, 261, 278–87, 356, 396–400, 416

Women & Power 356
Women Who Want to be Women 282
women's refuges 281
Woodside 367
wool industry 37, 296
Woollahra Council 99
The Worker 124
World Expo (1988) 258
Wren, John 310
Wright, Alexis 292–3
Wright, Judith 36
Wuhan, China 118, 125–6, 150

X-ray crystallography 140
Xi Jinping 346

Yagerra people 296
Yalumba 367
Yassmin's Story (Abdel-Magied) 339
The Yield (Winch) 86
Yirrkala 167
Yirrkala bark petition 199–201, 207, 212–13
Yolngu people 167, 199, 209, 212
Yothu Yindi 176
Young, Sally 369
Yousafzai, Malala 398
Youth Without Borders 356
Yugoslav immigrants 335
Yugoslavia 335
Yunupingu, Galarrwuy 198–202, 209–11, 394
Yunupingu, Mungurrawuy 199

zinc mining 367
Zuboff, Shoshana 268

Julianne Schultz AM FAHA has for decades fostered conversations about the idea of Australia, what it is and what it might be. As a writer, editor and academic she has published widely, been an active participant in public and media debates and on boards including *The Conversation*, the ABC and Australian Film Television and Radio School. The founding editor of *Griffith Review*, and now emeritus professor of Media and Culture at Griffith University, she has a particular interest in the transformative power of culture to lead politics. Julianne is the author of *Reviving the Fourth Estate*, *Steel City Blues*, *Not Just Another Business* (ed.), *The Phone Book* (with Ian Reinecke), librettos to the award-winning operas *Black River* and *Going into Shadows*, numerous chapters, articles and speeches, and edited 62 volumes of *Griffith Review*. She lives in northern New South Wales on Bundjalung Country, between a river named for a German princess and a beach named after an English town.